한번 보면 절대
잊혀지지 않는

영어 회화 암기노트

MENTORS

한번 보면 절대 잊혀지지 않는

영어회화 암기노트

2025년 8월 20일 인쇄
2025년 8월 27일 발행

지은이	Chris Suh
발행인	Chris Suh
발행처	**MENTORS**

경기도 성남시 분당구 황새울로 335번길 10 598
TEL 031-604-0025 FAX 031-696-5221

mentors.co.kr
blog.naver.com/mentorsbook

*Play 스토어 및 App 스토어에서 '멘토스북' 검색해 어플다운받기!

등록일자	2005년 7월 27일
등록번호	제 2022-000130호
ISBN	979-11-94467-89-2
가 격	29,600원(MP3 무료다운로드)

잘못 인쇄된 책은 교환해 드립니다.
이 책에 게재된 내용의 일부 또는 전체를 무단으로 복제 및 발췌하는 것을 금합니다

"네이티브는 절대 어려운 말로 영어를 하지 않는다!"

"네이티브는 절대 어려운 말로 영어를 하지 않는다!"라는 사실을 모르는 사람이 있을까?
"네이티브는 어떻게 그렇게 쉬운 말로 영어를 잘할까?"하고 얄미운 생각이 들어본 적이 없는 사람이 있을까?

우리나라의 영어실력은 언제나 상위권에 들지 못한다. 영어를 못한다는 이유로 항상 단골메뉴인 '실수를 두려워하는 습성,' '완벽한 영어를 지향하려는 갸륵한 시도' 등을 감안한다 하더라도 10년 넘게 영어교재를 학습하고, 영어강의를 듣거나 영어학원을 다니면서도 여전히 네이티브 앞에 서면 꿀먹은 벙어리가 되는 것은 왜일까? 혹 실수를 하려고 해도 표현들이 머릿 속에 없어서 그런 것은 아닐까?

"SMART한 영어학습법"

영어의 가치를 강조하는 건 이젠 입이 아프다. 듣는 사람도 지겨울 것이다. 스마트폰의 통역기능 그리고 AI의 발달이 이루어진다해도 기본적으로 자신의 머리속에 영어회화표현들을 어느 정도 저장해놓지 않고서는 제대로 신기술을 활용할 수 없을 것이다. 따라서 어떻게든 영어표현을 빨리 배워서 사용할 수 있는 방법을 깨우치는 게 급선무다. 방법은 딱 한가지이다. 네이티브들이 즐겨 사용하는 쉬운 표현들을 머릿속에 아주 많이 'save'해놓는 것이다. 이것이 스마트한 시대에 가장 잘 어울리는 현명한 영어학습법이다. 이 목적을 달성하기 위해 각 표현마다 사진을 넣었으며 사진 이미지를 보고 의미를 연상해보는 훈련을 많이 해보면 많은 표현들이 머리에 저장되는 것을 알게 될 것이다.

한번 보면 잊혀지지 않는 <영어회화 암기노트>

족집게로 집어내듯이 네이티브들이 즐겨 사용하는 쉬운 표현들만 모아서 영어회화를 학습하는 분들에게 가장 효율적으로 전달하는 방법을 연구하였다. 미국 현지에 있는 네이티브들의 도움으로 그들 머릿속 구석구석을 탐사하면서 활용빈출도가 매우 높은 표현들을 세심하게 골라 빨리 이해하고 오래 기억될 수 있도록 상황별로 약 1,000여개의 표현들을 집중해서 정리하였다. 이 표현들을 눈으로만 보는 게 아니라 큰소리로 따라 읽고 조금은 많지만 입에 착 달라붙게 달달 암기하여 머릿속에 저장해야 한다. 그래서 필요할 때마다 마음대로 꺼내 사용할 수 있는 경지(?)에 올라 영어 말하기가 무서움이 아닌 즐거움이 되어야 한다.

"영어회화 학습교재의 종결서"

물론 어려운 표현도 알아두면 좋겠지만 이는 듣기용이면 족하다. 스피킹용으로는 절대적으로 쉬운 표현만 알아도 영어로 끝내주게 말할 수 있다는 점을 명심해야 한다. 이책 <한번 보면 잊혀지지 않는 영어회화 암기노트>는 영어회화 학습교재의 종결서로, 완전히 달달달 암기하여 단단히 저장해 두면 태산같아 보이던 영어회화의 산을 정복하는 그 날이 성큼 다가올 것이라고 확신한다.

<영어회화 암기노트>의 특징

"네이티브들이 일상생활에서 반드시 쓰게 되는 기본표현을 난이도 단계별로 사진을 보고 이미지 연상을 하여 머리속에 잊혀지지 않도록 꾸며져 있다"

1. 네이티브들이 안 쓰고는 못배기는 기본표현을 한자리에 모았다.
2. 난이도별로 구분하였으며 어렵지 않게 단계별로 영어학습을 나아갈 수 있다.
3. 각 표현에는 사진이 있어, 이를 보고 표현을 연상하여 암기하도록 꾸며졌다.
4. 각각의 표현에는 해설이 간략하게 1줄로 컴팩트하게 되어 있어 지루하지 않다.
5. 미국 현지에서 날아온 생생한 다이얼로그와 예문을 통해 영어 표현을 완전히 내 것으로 만든다.

<영어회화 암기노트>의 특징

Section 01, 02, 03의 난이도별로 1,000여개 넘는 표현들이 정리되어 있다.

Section 01 001-374
영어회화 기본표현
이정도는 기본으로 알아야
영어로 말문이 트이는 표현들

Section 02 001-341
영어회화 핵심표현
제대로 된 영어회화문장을 만들려면
꼭 알아두어야 하는 핵심표현들

Section 03 001-362
영어회화 응용표현
네이티브와 1분이라도 프리토킹을
가능하게 하는 영어말하기 표현들

MP3 파일 듣기!
모든 표현은 생생한 네이티브의 녹음이 되어 있기 때문에 따라만 읽어도
어느새 자신도 모르게 입에서 네이티브들이 쓰는 표현들이 나오게 되는
자신을 발견하게 될 것이다.

<영어회화 암기노트> 한 눈에 보기

넘버링
섹션별로 넘버링을 하였으며 대표 문장과 우리말 해석을 넣었다.

009

I'm tired from working all day
난 하루종일 일해서 피곤해

be tired는 '피곤하다,' '지치다' 그리고 '지겹다'라는 의미로 쓰인다. 뒤에 전치사는 of가 자주 쓰인다.

우리말 설명
우리말 해석 밑에 한줄로 표현을 설명하여 빠르게 그리고 정확하게 의미를 파악할 수 있다.

Example

- I'm tired of hanging around this boring town.
  이 따분한 동네에 죽치고 있는게 지겨워.
- It seems that you are really tired because of this homework.
  숙제하느라 너 완전히 지친 것 같아.

Example
미국 현지에서 전문적인 Writers' Group이 심혈을 기울여 쓴 살아 있는 영어문장을 접할 수 있다.

Dialog
A: I don't understand why my wife is so tired all the time.
B: Put yourself in her shoes and you'll see why.
A: 아내가 왜 항상 피곤해하는지 모르겠어.
B: 아내 입장이 돼봐 그러면 이유를 알게 될거야.

Dialog
대표표현을 이용하여 실제 미국현지에서 사용되는 영어회화 대화문을 제시하여 표현이 실제로 어떻게 쓰이는지 알 수 있다.

Guess What?
기본표현 외에 곳곳에 미국영어의 관용표현으로 역시 사진과 함께 수록하여 잠깐 쉬면서도 영어표현을 이해하고 머릿속에 저장할 수가 있다.

Guess What?

Think outside the box
창의적으로 생각해

고정관념에서 벗어나 창의적으로 생각하다. 뭔가 돌파구를 찾을 때 일반적으로 하는 방식이 아니라 비전통적이며 남다른 방식으로 뭔가 하는 방법을 고려(consider different ways to do something in a nontraditional or unusual way)하는 것을 말한다.

007p

Section 01 001-374
영어회화 기본표현

이정도는 기본으로 알아야
영어로 말문이 트이는 표현들

001 I'm just doing my job부터
⋮
374 As for me, I like to watch TV까지

201p

Section 02 001-341
영어회화 핵심표현

제대로 된 영어회화문장을 만들려면
꼭 알아두어야 하는 핵심표현들

001 I'm on it부터
⋮
341 Let's say you're right about that까지

377p

Section 03 001-362
영어회화 응용표현

네이티브와 1분이라도 프리토킹을
가능하게 하는 영어말하기 표현들

001 I've been swamped at my job부터
⋮
362 The store closed without notice까지

Section 01
영어회화 기본표현

"이정도는 기본으로 알아야
영어로 말문이 트이는 표현들"

I'm just doing my job
난 그냥 내 일을 할 것뿐이야
여기서 job은 '직업'이 아니라 '맡은 일'을 뜻한다.

💡 **Example**

- Don't mention it. I'm just doing my job.
  무슨 말씀을. 그냥 내 일을 할 뿐인데.

- Please get out of my way so I can do my job.
  좀 비키세요 내 일 좀 하게.

A: I have to do my job at night.
B: Does it work for you?

  A: 밤에 일을 해야 돼.
  B: 괜찮겠어?

I'm working on it
지금 그 일 하고 있어
work on sb는 '…에 대해 공을 들여 설득하다'란 뜻. 음식을 아직 먹고 있다고 할 때도 쓴다.

💡 **Example**

- I'm going to work on this stuff at home tonight.
  오늘 밤 집에서 이 일을 할거야.

- Did you hand in the report you were working on?
  네가 작업하던 리포트를 제출했니?

A: I'm so stressed out these days.
B: Oh? Do you have to work on a big project?

  A: 요즘 스트레스를 많이 받고 있어.
  B: 그래? 큰 프로젝트를 맡아서 해야 되는 거야?

003

You have to work hard
너 열심히 일해야 돼
hard는 부사로 '열심히'라는 의미. '야근하다'는 work late, '밤새일하다'는 work all night.

💡 **Example**
- We work hard and we deserve to relax.
  우린 열심히 일했기 때문에 휴식을 취할만해.
- My boss said I need to work harder.
  보스는 내가 좀 더 열심히 일을 할 필요가 있대.

 Dialog

A: You have to work hard. Don't let me down.
B: I'll do my best, boss. Believe me.

　A: 열심히 일 해야 돼. 날 실망시키지 마.
　B: 사장님, 최선을 다할게요. 믿으세요.

004

It started to rain suddenly
갑자기 비가 오기 시작했다
start to+V는 begin to+V라 해도 되며, 진행형 be starting to~는 시작하는 행동을 강조.

💡 **Example**
- Many people have started to save money.
  많은 사람들이 저축하기 시작했어.
- We need to start with netiquette education for children.
  우린 애들을 위해 네티켓 교육부터 시작할 필요가 있어.

 Dialog

A: Are you working out these days?
B: Yeah, I started to go to the gym every day after work.

　A: 요즘 운동하니?
　B: 응, 퇴근 후 매일 헬스에 가기 시작했어.

You can try again!
다시 한번 해봐!
try again은 좌절하지 않고 다시 해본다는 의미로 조언이나 격려할 때 사용하면 된다.

💡 **Example**
- Even though Carrie failed, she'll try again.
  캐리가 실패했더라도 걘 다시 해볼 거야.
- Exactly! Get out there and try again.
  바로 그거야! 가서 다시 한번 해봐.

 Dialog

A: I don't know what I'm going to do.
B: Don't worry. You can try again.
　A: 뭘 해야 할지 모르겠어.
　B: 걱정마. 다시 한번 해봐.

I'm trying to learn English
난 영어를 배우려고 노력하고 있어
try to+V는 '노력하다,' '시도하다'라는 뜻이고, 반면 try ~ing는 '시험삼아 …을 보다'라는 의미.

💡 **Example**
- I'll try to get back as soon as I can.
  가능한 빨리 돌아오도록 할게.
- Why are you trying to get away from me?
  왜 내게서 멀어지려는 거야?

 Dialog

A: I'm serious. She's in a really bad mood.
B: I'll try to avoid her.
　A: 정말이야, 걔 기분이 패나 안 좋은 것 같아.
　B: 피해 다녀야지.

007

It has been a very busy day
아주 바쁜 날이었어

반대로 약간 바쁠 땐 kind[sort] of busy, 바쁜 이유는 be busy with+N, be busy (with) ~ing.

💡 **Example**

- They were busy traveling this weekend.
  걔네들은 이번 주말에 여행하느라 바빴어.
- I'm busy with a client at the moment.
  지금은 손님 때문에 바빠요.

A: It has been a very busy day.
B: That's for sure. I haven't had a break.

A: 아주 바쁜 날이었어.
B: 확실하지. 나는 쉴 시간이 없었어.

008

I'm in a hurry to get home
난 서둘러 집에 가려고 해

hurry 대신에 rush라는 단어를 사용해도 된다.

💡 **Example**

- Pam and Tina are in a hurry to finish their homework.
  팜과 티나는 숙제를 마치느라 서두르고 있어.
- I am in a hurry to get to my house.
  난 집에 도착하려고 서두르고 있어.

A: Why is everyone rushing around?
B: They are in a hurry to clean up the place.

A: 왜 모두가 서두르고 있니?
B: 걔들은 그곳을 청소하느라 서두르고 있어.

I'm tired from working all day

난 하루종일 일해서 피곤해

be tired는 '피곤하다,' '지치다' 그리고 '지겹다'라는 의미로 쓰인다. 뒤에 전치사는 of가 자주 쓰인다.

Example

- I'm tired of hanging around this boring town.
  이 따분한 동네에 죽치고 있는게 지겨워.

- It seems that you are really tired because of this homework.
  숙제하느라 너 완전히 지친 것 같아.

Dialog

A: I don't understand why my wife is so tired all the time.
B: Put yourself in her shoes and you'll see why.

A: 아내가 왜 항상 피곤해하는지 모르겠어.
B: 아내 입장이 돼봐 그러면 이유를 알게 될거야.

We hope you'll be able to join us

우린 네가 우리와 함께 할 수 있기를 바래

be able to는 능력을 의미하며 be capable of와 같은 의미. can의 미래형으로 유명하다.

Example

- She will be able to do better next time.
  걘 다음 번에 더 잘 할 수 있을 거야.

- We hope you'll be able to join us.
  우리랑 함께 할 수 있으면 좋겠는데.

Dialog

A: How soon will you be able to get here?
B: That depends on the traffic conditions.

A: 언제쯤 여기에 도착할 수 있죠?
B: 그거야 교통상황에 달렸죠.

011

He's better than me at cooking

걘 나보다 요리를 더 잘해

가장 기본적인 비교급을 써서 비교대상보다 우위에 있다고 말할 때. 반대는 be worse than~.

💡 **Example**
- Your apartment is better than mine.
  네 아파트는 내 것보다 좋아.
- Joe's car is better than his neighbor's.
  조의 차는 이웃의 차보다 좋지.

 Dialog

A: This ice cream is better than the other one.
B: Yeah, this ice cream is delicious.
   A: 이 아이스크림은 다른 것보다 나아.
   B: 그래, 이 아이스크림은 맛있어.

012

Your son is good at sports.

네 아들은 스포츠에 능해.

be great at도 같은 의미. at 다음에 명사나 ~ing를 붙인다. 반대는 be poor[terrible] at.

💡 **Example**
- Actually, I'm not good at using smart phones.
  실은 스마트폰에 능숙하지 않아.
- My boss says I'm good at discussing things with clients.
  보스가 말하길 난 고객들과 상담에 능하대.

 Dialog

A: Your son is good at sports.
B: He's the best athlete in the family.
   A: 네 아들은 스포츠에 능해.
   B: 걘 우리 집안에서 제일 뛰어난 운동선수야.

013

It's over between us
우리 사이는 끝났어
be 앞에 오는 주어가 끝나다라는 뜻. be over sb하면 '…을 완전히 끝내다,' '잊다'라는 의미.

💡 Example
- The time for our coffee break is over.
  커피 휴식시간이 끝났어.
- The dinner was over and people went home.
  저녁식사가 끝나 사람들이 집에 갔어.

 Dialog

A: Am I in time to see the soccer match?
B: No, it's over. You missed it.

  A: 내가 축구경기에 맞춰서 왔니?
  B: 아니, 이미 끝났어. 넌 놓친 거야.

014

I'll check if he's finished working.
걔가 일을 끝냈는지 알아볼게
finish 다음에는 명사[명사상당어구]인 명사[~ing]가 온다. be finished with[~ing]도 같은 의미.

💡 Example
- I'll check if he's finished working.
  걔가 일을 끝냈는지 알아볼게
- Have you finished the project you started?
  시작한 프로젝트 끝냈어?

 Dialog

A: What time do you think you will show up?
B: I'll come after I finish working.

  A: 몇 시에 올 수 있을 것 같아?
  B: 일 마치고 갈게.

She didn't meet the deadline

걘 마감일을 맞추지 못했어

여기서 meet은 '…을 충족시켜주다'라는 뜻. meet the needs of~도 함께 알아둔다.

💡 **Example**

- If you hurry, you'll meet the deadline.
  서두르면 마감시간을 맞출 거야.
- All new soldiers must meet the requirements of their training.
  모든 신참병은 훈련이 요구되는 것을 맞춰야 한다.

A: This has to be ready by tomorrow morning.
B: We're never going to meet the deadline.

A: 이건 내일 아침까지 준비되어야 해.
B: 우린 결코 마감시간을 맞추지 못할 거야.

It was all my fault

그건 다 내 잘못였어

'…한 것은 …의 잘못이다'라고 하려면 be one's fault for ~ing 혹은 be one's fault that S+V.

💡 **Example**

- I kind of feel like it's my fault.
  조금은 내 잘못인 것 같기도 해.
- It's not my fault I'm late. The train broke down.
  지각은 내 잘못아냐. 기차가 고장났었어.

A: You don't have to say you're sorry.
B: Sure I do. It was all my fault.

A: 미안하단 말은 할 필요 없어요.
B: 어떻게 그래요. 이게 다 제 잘못인데.

What's wrong with you?

무슨 일이야?, 왜 그래?

~ with는 …이하가 잘못된 것, ~about하면 잘못 알고 있다, 그리고 go wrong은 진행중 문제가 발생.

💡 Example

- There's something wrong with my wife.
  아내한테 문제가 있는 것 같아
- Sorry, I was dead wrong.
  미안해, 내가 완전히 틀렸어.

A: What's wrong with your throat?
B: I'm not sure. I just can't stop coughing.

A: 목이 뭐 잘못되었어?
B: 잘 모르겠어. 기침이 멈추질 않아.

He failed to get a good job

걘 좋은 직장을 구하지 못했어

fail to+V는 '실패하다'라는 의미외 단순히 '…하지 못하다'라는 의미. failure는 '실패한 사람이나 일.'

💡 Example

- Leo failed to get a good job.
  레오는 좋은 직업을 구하는데 실패했어.
- He has failed to close many deals.
  걘 많은 계약을 맺는데 실패했어.

A: Why did Eli get in trouble?
B: He failed to pay for the item he took.

A: 일라이는 왜 어려움에 처한 거야?
B: 걘 집어 든 상품에 대해 지불을 하지 못했어.

I made a mistake
내가 실수했어

make a mistake는 '실수하다,' 그리고 큰 실수라면 awful, terrible 혹은 huge란 형용사를 mistake 앞에 넣는다.

💡 **Example**

- I made a mistake. It's my fault.
  내가 실수했어. 내 잘못이야.

- I'm sorry. I dialed your number by mistake.
  미안. 다이얼을 잘못 돌렸어.

 Dialog

A: You shouldn't have hit your brother.
B: Right. I made a mistake.

A: 형을 때리지 말았어야지.
B: 맞아. 내가 실수했어.

I have a job interview today
난 오늘 취업면접이 있어

have a job interview는 회사에 가서 면접 보는 것으로 회사를 언급하려면 at+회사를 덧붙이다.

💡 **Example**

- I've got a job interview next Monday. Wish me luck.
  다음 주 월요일에 취업면접이 있어. 운을 빌어줘.

- A good cover letter will help you get an interview.
  커버레터를 잘 쓰면 면접받는데 도움이 될거야.

 Dialog

A: You seem to be worried about something.
B: I have a job interview this afternoon.

A: 너 뭐 걱정하는게 있는 것처럼 보여.
B: 오늘 오후에 취직 면접이 있어.

She was hired as a school teacher

걘 학교 선생님으로 고용됐어

be hired as~는 '…로 고용되다.' as 다음에는 직종, 즉 teacher, secretary 등을 붙인다.

💡 **Example**

- Cindy was hired as a school teacher.
  신디는 학교 선생으로 고용되었어.
- I'm going to be hired as an editor.
  난 편집인으로 고용될거야.

 Dialog

A: What kind of work do you do?
B: I was hired as a lawyer.

A: 무슨 종류의 일을 하고 있니?
B: 난 변호사로 고용되었어.

You should get a job

넌 일자리를 구해야 돼

get a job은 돈을 받고 하는 '일자리를 얻다.' get 대신 find를 써도 된다.

💡 **Example**

- It is getting so hard to find a job right now.
  이제 구직은 갈수록 어려워져.
- You should get a job and make some money.
  너도 취직해서 돈을 벌어야해.

 Dialog

A: I'm sure I will get a job with a high salary.
B: Maybe not. Nothing is as easy as it seems.

A: 난 고임금 일자리를 얻을 걸 확신해.
B: 아마도 아닐 걸. 어느 것도 보이는 것처럼 쉽지 않거든.

I decided to take a job in Seoul
난 서울에서 일자리를 맡기로 결정했어
take a job은 제안받은 '일자리를 수락하다'라는 뉘앙스. '해외취직'은 take a job overseas.

💡 **Example**
- Paula took a job at the factory.
  폴라는 공장에 취업했어.
- Will you take a job with our company?
  우리 회사에 취직할래요?

 Dialog

A: Brian is living in England now.
B: He took a job as a university instructor.
   A: 브라이언은 이제 영국에서 살고 있어.
   B: 걘 대학 강사로 취직했어.

She has a job in Japan
걘 일본에서 직장다니고 있어
have a job은 get[take] a job을 해서 현재 직장을 다니고 있다는 의미.

💡 **Example**
- They have a job in Japan.
  걔들은 일본에서 직장을 다니고 있어.
- Each person has a job at the company.
  각 개인은 이 회사에서 업무를 보고 있어.

 Dialog

A: Neil seems very happy with his work.
B: He has a job working with children.
   A: 닐은 자기 일에 매우 행복해하는 것 같아.
   B: 걘 애들하고 일하는 직장을 다녀.

025

I'll be on duty all night

밤새 근무할거야

be on duty는 '현재 근무중이다,' 반대로 be off duty는 '휴무중이다'라는 의미.

💡 **Example**

- The cop was on duty near my house.
  그 경찰이 내 집 근처에서 근무했어.
- Kevin will be off duty until 10 pm.
  케빈은 밤 10시까지 휴무할거야.

 Dialog

A: Will you have to work a long shift?
B: Oh yes. I'll be on duty all night.

　A: 일하는 교대 시간이 길어?
　B: 그럼. 밤새 근무할거야.

026

After breakfast, I went to work

아침식사후 난 출근했어

go to work는 '출근하다,' '일을 시작하다,' get to work는 '직장에 도착해 일을 시작하다.'

💡 **Example**

- Howard's father goes to work on the subway.
  하워드 아버지는 지하철타고 출근하셔.
- She went to work at the clothing store.
  걘 옷 가게로 일하러 갔어.

 Dialog

A: Wake up! You have to go to work.
B: Just let me sleep a few more minutes.

　A: 일어나! 출근해야지.
　B: 단지 몇 분 만 더 자게 해주라.

027

He lost his job at Google
갠 구글에서 실직했어

lost one's job은 '직장을 잃다'로 be out of a job 혹은 between jobs라고도 한다.

 Example

- My dad lost his job at Samsung.
  아빠가 삼성에서 실직했어.
- Farah may lose her job next week.
  파라는 다음 주 실직하게 될 가능성이 있어.

 Dialog

A: Cheer up! You look so sad.
B: I just lost my job and my wife has threatened to leave me!

A: 힘 좀 내봐! 너 정말 슬퍼 보여.
B: 방금 직장을 잃었어. 게다가 아내는 내게서 떠나겠다고 하고!

028

Please make a copy of your ID
신분증을 복사하세요

make a copy of~는 '종이[디지털 파일]를 …을 복사하다'라는 의미. 여러 장이면 make copies of.

 Example

- Make some copies of your passport.
  네 여권을 몇 부 복사해.
- Jen made copies of her study sheets.
  젠은 학습지를 복사했어.

Dialog

A: What are those papers you're carrying?
B: I have to make copies of some files.

A: 들고 있는 서류가 뭐니?
B: 파일 몇 개를 복사해야만 해.

029

She's in a meeting right now
갠 지금 회의중이야
be in a meeting은 '회의중이다,' be busy with meetings는 '여러 회의로 바쁘다.'

💡 **Example**

- He's in a meeting right now.
  갠 지금 회의 중이야.

- I'm in a meeting all morning, but I'm free after two o'clock.
  오전 내내 회의가 있지만 오후 2시 이후에는 시간이 있어요.

 Dialog

A: Is Louis in the office today?
B: He is, but he is in a meeting right now.

A: 오늘 루이스가 사무실에 있나요?
B: 예, 그런데 지금은 회의에 들어가 있어요.

030

You've got a meeting at three
3시에 회의 있어
have a meeting은 '회의가 있다,' have 대신에 hold를 사용해도 같은 의미가 된다.

💡 **Example**

- I have an important meeting in ten minutes. I've got to run.
  10분후에 중요한 회의가 있어. 빨리 가야 돼.

- You've got a meeting at three.
  3시에 회의 있어.

 Dialog

A: Why are you taking me to the board room?
B: There is a meeting there for all directors.

A: 왜 날 중역실로 데려가려는 거니?
B: 전체 이사회가 있어.

The computers are on sale
컴퓨터가 세일 중이야
be on sale은 '할인판매중이다,' be for sale는 그냥 '판매중.' a rip-off는 '바가지 요금.'

💡 **Example**
- The digital TVs are on sale.
  디지털 TV들이 세일 중이야.
- Many items are on sale before Christmas.
  많은 품목들이 크리스마스 전에 세일 중이야.

A: We can't afford a new washing machine.
B: They're going on sale next week.

A: 우린 새로운 세탁기를 살 여유가 없어.
B: 걔들은 다음 주에 세일을 할 거야.

He invested in our company
걘 우리 회사에 투자했어
invest in~은 '…에 투자하다.' make one's money in~이라고도 한다.

💡 **Example**
- Many people don't want to invest in stocks.
  많은 사람들이 주식에 투자하기를 원하지 않아.
- I decided to invest in real estate.
  난 부동산에 투자하기로 결정했어.

A: I'm not sure what to do with my money.
B: You should invest in our company.

A: 내 돈을 어떻게 해야 할 지 모르겠어.
B: 우리 회사에 투자해야 해.

033

I'm trying to save money
난 돈을 절약하려고 하고 있어
save money는 '돈을 절약하다,' 비용[노력]을 절약할 때는 spare를 쓰면 된다.

💡 **Example**
- I stopped smoking to save money!
  난 돈을 아끼려고 담배를 끊었어!
- The duty-free shop is a good place to save money.
  면세점에 가면 돈을 많이 아낀다.

 Dialog

A: Are you traveling to Hawaii?
B: No, we're trying to save money.

  A: 하와이로 여행할 거니?
  B: 아니, 우린 돈을 절약할 거야.

034

My father has a lot of money
아버지는 돈이 많다
have a lot of money는 '돈이 많다.' have enough money to+V는 '…하는데 충분한 돈이 있다.'

💡 **Example**
- My new boyfriend has a lot of money.
  내 새로운 남친은 돈이 무지 많아.
- People in this apartment building have a lot of money.
  이 아파트 빌딩에 사는 이들은 돈이 많은 사람들이야.

 Dialog

A: Your uncle always has nice cars.
B: That's because he has a lot of money.

  A: 네 삼촌은 항상 좋은 차들을 가지고 있어.
  B: 돈이 많기 때문이지.

I want to **make more money**

난 돈을 더 벌고 싶어

make money는 '돈을 벌다'로 money 앞에 관사를 쓰지 않는다. '많은 돈을 벌다'는 make a fortune.

Example
- Some people make money easily.
  일부 사람들은 돈을 쉽게 벌어.
- How can we make some money?
  어떻게 하면 돈을 벌 수 있을까?

A: I want to **make money** and be comfortable.
B: You need to work hard to become rich.

A: 난 돈을 벌어 좀더 편안해지고 싶어.
B: 넌 부자가 되려면 일을 열심히 해야 돼.

I **am totally broke**

돈 한푼 없어

be broke는 '빈털터리가 되다,' be out of[low on] money도 함께 알아둔다.

Example
- The older couple is always broke.
  저 노인 커플은 항상 빈털터리야.
- Helen was broke after she paid the doctor.
  헬렌은 의사에게 지불후 돈이 바닥났다.

A: Come on, let's go out tonight.
B: I can't go anywhere. I **am broke**.

A: 이봐, 오늘 밤 외출하자.
B: 난 어디도 갈 수가 없어. 빈털터리거든.

I'd like to pay the bill
계산을 좀 할려구요
pay the bill은 '청구된 돈을 지불하다,' pay one's rent는 '집세를 내다.'

💡 **Example**
- I'd like to pay the bill, please.
  계산을 좀 할려구요.
- I can't afford to pay my rent this month.
  이번 달 월세를 낼 돈이 없어.

A: How would you like to pay the bill?
B: I'd like to put it on my credit card.
  A: 대금지불은 어떻게 하시겠습니까?
  B: 신용카드로 하고 싶은데요.

I can lend her some money
난 걔에게 돈을 좀 빌려줄 수 있어
lend sb money는 '돈을 빌려주다,' loan을 써도 된다. 또한 '빌리다'는 borrow sb money.

💡 **Example**
- Abby lent her brother money for his bills.
  애비는 남동생이 청구서들을 지불하도록 돈을 빌려주었어.
- Can you lend me some money until payday?
  급여 날까지 돈 좀 빌려줄 수 있어?

A: Larry is broke this week.
B: I can lend him some money.
  A: 래리는 이번 주 돈이 다 떨어졌어.
  B: 내가 좀 돈을 빌려줄 수 있는데.

I went to college in New York

난 뉴욕에 있는 대학에 입학했어

go to college는 '대학에 진학하다,' '법대에 입학하다'는 go to law school.

 **Example**

- I went to college in California.
  난 캘리포니아에 있는 대학에 입학했어.
- Where does he plan to go to college?
  걔는 어느 대학갈거래?

Dialog

A: What are your plans for the future?
B: I'll go to college for the next four years.

A: 넌 미래 계획이 뭐니?
B: 향후 4년간 대학에 입학해서 공부할거야.

Guess What?

Think outside the box
창의적으로 생각해

고정관념에서 벗어나 창의적으로 생각하다. 뭔가 돌파구를 찾을 때 일반적으로 하는 방식이 아니라 비전통적이며 남다른 방식으로 뭔가 하는 방법을 고려(consider different ways to do something in a nontraditional or unusual way)하는 것을 말한다.

You must study harder

넌 더 열심히 공부해야 돼

study hard는 '열심히 공부하다,' '밤새공부하다'는 study all night.

💡 Example

- Everyone studied hard for the final exam.
  모두가 기말시험 때문에 열심히 공부했어.
- You need to study hard to get good grades.
  좋은 학점을 받으려면 열심히 공부해야 해.

A: I'm aware of John's poor grades.
B: Should we help him to study harder?

A: 존의 성적이 안 좋다는 거 알고 있어.
B: 공부 더 열심히 하도록 도와줘야 할까?

Was she absent from school?

걔 결석했어?

be absent from school은 '결석하다,' = play hooky = play the truant from.

💡 Example

- Some people were absent from church today.
  일부 사람들이 오늘 교회에 빠졌어.
- I was absent from class because I was sick.
  난 아파서 결석했어.

A: Was Wendy absent from school?
B: No, she came to classes today.

A: 웬디가 결석했니?
B: 아니, 걘 오늘 수업에 왔어.

I forgot to do my homework!

내 숙제 하는 걸 잊었어!

do one's homework는 '숙제하다,' finish one's homework는 '숙제를 마치다.'

💡 Example

- I forgot to do my homework!
  내 숙제하는 걸 잊었어!

- The teacher was happy we did our homework.
  우리가 숙제를 하니 선생님이 기뻐했어.

A: I did my homework on the subway.
B: Me too. Now it is all finished.

A: 난 지하철에서 숙제를 했어.
B: 나도 그래. 이제 다 끝냈지.

How often do you go online?

넌 얼마나 자주 인터넷을 사용하니?

go online은 '인터넷에 연결되다,' 그래서 go online to Google하면 '구글에 연결되다.'

💡 Example

- Jim went online to research the book.
  짐은 그 책을 연구하기 위해 인터넷을 했어.

- I go online when I need to email people.
  사람들과 이메일할 필요가 있을 때 인터넷 사용해.

A: How often do you go online?
B: Usually I'm on the Internet a few times a day.

A: 넌 얼마나 자주 인터넷을 사용하니?
B: 보통 하루에 몇 번 정도 사용하지.

Do you have access to the shared folder?

너 그 공유 폴더에 접근할 수 있어

have access to는 '이용하다,' '접근할 수 있다.' 이용가능하다고 할 때는 accessible.

Example

- I must have access to a new computer.
  난 새 컴퓨터를 이용해야만 해.
- John had access to his e-mail account.
  존은 자신의 이메일계정을 이용할 수 있었어.

A: Many people use computers in the library.
B: That's because they have access to the Internet there.

A: 많은 사람들은 도서관에 있는 컴퓨터를 사용한다.
B: 거기서 인터넷 접속이 되기 때문이지.

You have to log in right there

바로 거기에 로그인을 해야 돼

log in[on to]는 '로그인하다,' 반대는 log out.

Example

- Use the box on the screen to log in.
  화면에 있는 박스를 이용해서 로그인을 해라.
- You must log in to use a library computer.
  도서관컴을 이용하려면 먼저 로그인 해야 돼.

A: How do I use this e-mail account?
B: You have to log in right there.

A: 이 이메일 계정을 어떻게 사용하니?
B: 바로 거기에 로그인을 해야 돼.

I played computer games all night

난 밤새 컴퓨터 게임을 했어

play computer games는 '컴겜을 하다,' play some online games는 '온라인 게임을 하다.'

💡 Example

- I'm not interested in playing computer games.
  컴퓨터 게임하는데 관심없어.
- I forgot how much fun it is to play computer games.
  컴퓨터 게임을 하는게 얼마나 재미있는지 잊었어.

A: What did you do last night?
B: I played computer games all night.

A: 어제 밤에 무엇 했니?
B: 난 밤새 컴퓨터 게임을 했지.

They met online

걔네들은 온라인에서 만났어

meet online은 '온라인에서 만나다,' '인터넷에서 만나다'는 meet sb on the internet.

💡 Example

- You can't trust people you meet on the Internet.
  인터넷에서 만난 사람들 믿지마.
- I went on a date with the guy I met online.
  온라인에서 만난 남자와 데이트했어.

A: Gina and her boyfriend met online.
B: I think he's a really nice guy.

A: 지나와 걔 남친은 온라인에서 만났어.
B: 걘 아주 괜찮은 친구로 생각돼.

Do you have an e-mail account?

이메일 계정이 있니?

have an e-mail account는 '이멜계정이 있다,' have a Gmail account라고 쓴다.

💡 **Example**

- I have had an e-mail account for 10 years.
  난 10년 동안 이메일 계정 하나로 썼어.

- Steve has a secret e-mail account.
  스티브는 이메일 비밀 계정을 가지고 있어.

 **Dialog**

A: Do you have an e-mail account?
B: Yes, let me give you the address.

   A: 이메일 계정을 가지고 있니?
   B: 그럼, 이메일 주소를 줄게.

Let me check my e-mail first

내 이메일부터 먼저 확인할게

check one's email은 이멜이 왔는지 확인하다.

💡 **Example**

- I'd like to know how I can access my e-mail.
  메일 접속방법을 알고 싶은데요.

- I check my e-mail about as regularly as I brush my teeth.
  난 양치질하는 만큼 정기적으로 이메일을 확인해.

 **Dialog**

A: Hurry up, we're going to be late.
B: Let me check my e-mail first.

   A: 서둘러, 우리 늦겠다.
   B: 내 이메일부터 먼저 확인할게.

I got email from Jim today

난 오늘 짐으로부터 이메일을 받았어

get (an) email from sb는 '…로부터 이메일을 받다.' 발신자는 from sb.

 Example

- I got an e-mail from him early this afternoon.
  난 걔로부터 오늘 오후 이메일을 받았어.
- I got an e-mail from a friend in the US.
  난 미국에 있는 친구로부터 이메일을 받았어.

Dialog

A: **I got an e-mail from Julie today.**
B: **How are her classes at school?**

A: 난 오늘 줄리로부터 이메일을 받았어.
B: 학교에서 걔 수업은 어떻대?

I sent it to your Naver e-mail

난 그걸 네 네이버메일로 보냈어

send sth to one's Naver email은 받는 상대 이메일 계정까지 언급할 때.

 Example

- Hank sent the file to Bart's Naver e-mail.
  행크는 바트의 네이버 이메일로 파일을 보냈어.
- Don't send anything to my Yahoo e-mail account.
  내 야후이메일에 아무것도 보내지마.

Dialog

A: **I sent an attachment to your Naver e-mail.**
B: **Really? I didn't receive anything.**

A: 난 네 네이버 이메일에 첨부파일을 보냈어.
B: 정말? 난 아무 것도 받지 못했는데.

Don't forget to drop me a line
잊지 말고 꼭 연락해
drop a line은 종이 및 디지털로 연락하는 것을 말한다.

💡 **Example**

- Drop me a line when you get the chance.
  기회되면 편지해.

- Drop me a line to let me know how you're doing.
  어떻게 지내는지 편지나 좀 써.

A: Don't forget to drop me a line.
B: I'll make sure that I keep in touch.

A: 잊지 말고 꼭 편지해.
B: 내가 꼭 연락할게.

I'll call back later in the afternoon
오후에 다시 전화할게
call back은 못받은 전화에 '답신 전화하다'라는 의미. call again과 구분없이 쓰기도 한다.

💡 **Example**

- That's okay. I'll call back later in the afternoon.
  괜찮아. 오후에 다시 전화할게.

- Hi Jason, it's Nick. I'm returning your call.
  안녕, 제이슨. 닉이야. 전화했다고 해서.

A: Could you tell her to call back after lunch?
B: I'll tell her right now.

A: 점심식사 후에 전화해 달라고 그 사람한테 전해주겠니?
B: 지금 바로 하지 뭐.

Call the hotel and book a room

호텔에 전화해서 방을 예약해라

call sb[sth]은 목적어로 사람 혹은 911, security 혹은 the police처럼 기관이 올 수도 있다.

🔆 **Example**

- Call the hotel and book a room.
  호텔에 전화해서 방을 예약해라.
- Call the store and see when they open.
  가게에 전화해서 언제 여는지 알아봐라.

 Dialog

A: **The bank is being robbed!**
B: **I'll call 911 and get the police!**

A: 은행이 털리고 있어.
B: 911을 호출해서 경찰을 부를게.

Give me a call

전화해

give sb a call에서 call 대신 벨소리를 뜻하는 ring이나 buzz를 써도 된다.

🔆 **Example**

- Feel free to give me a call if you have any questions.
  궁금한 점이 있으면 조금도 주저하지 마시고 전화주세요.
- Why didn't you give me a ring yesterday?
  왜 어제 내게 전화 안한거야?

 Dialog

A: **Let's have dinner sometime.**
B: **OK. Give me a call.**

A: 언제 한 번 저녁 먹자.
B: 알았어. 전화해.

056

She's not in right now
지금 안계세요
be not in은 사무실 안에 없어서 전화를 바꿔줄 수 없다고 말할 때.

💡 **Example**

- Susan stepped out of the office and can't take your call.
  수잔은 방금 사무실을 나가서 전화를 받을 수 없어요.

- My boss is not in, but maybe I can help you.
  사장님 안계신데 제가 도와드릴까요?

A: Hello, could I speak to Jason Lane?
B: Sorry, but he's not in right now.

A: 여보세요, 제이슨 레인있나요?
B: 죄송하지만 지금 없는데요.

057

He's on the phone
통화중이야
be on the phone은 '통화중이다,' 통화중 사람은 ~to sb라 하면 된다.

💡 **Example**

- Linda was on the phone for hours.
  린다는 여러 시간 동안 전화통화 중이야.

- Quiet! I'm on the phone right now.
  조용히 해! 나 지금 통화 중이잖아.

A: Is Jimmy at home right now?
B: Sorry, but he's on the phone.

A: 지미가 지금 집에 있니?
B: 미안해 걔가 지금 통화 중이야.

Can I leave a message?

메모 남길 수 있을까요?

leave a message (for sb)는 '메시지를 남기다,' '메시지를 받다'는 take a message.

💡 **Example**

- Could I take a message?
  메시지를 전해 드릴까요?
- She didn't answer her phone. I left a message.
  걘 전화를 받지 않아 메시지를 남겼어.

Dialog

A: I'm sorry he's out on business.
B: Can I leave a message for him?

A: 미안한데 걘 일로 밖에 나가 있어.
B: 걔한테 메시지 좀 남길 수 있을 까요?

He's not answering his cell phone

걘 핸드폰을 받지 않아

answer one's cell phone은 '…가 거는 핸드폰을 받다.'

💡 **Example**

- He's not answering his cell phone.
  걘 핸드폰을 받지 않아.
- Your cell phone's ringing.
  네 핸드폰 전화온다.

Dialog

A: Why didn't you answer your cell phone?
B: I forgot it at home today.

A: 왜 네 핸드폰 안 받았어?
B: 오늘 집에 두고 왔어.

She is on a cell phone

걘 핸드폰으로 통화중이야

be on a cell phone은 '핸드폰으로 통화중이다' = talk on a cell phone.

🔆 Example

- Let Gary **talk on your cell phone**.
  게리에게 네 핸드폰으로 전화하라고해.
- She **is on a cell phone**, talking to Mom.
  걘 핸드폰으로 엄마에게 전화 중이야.

A: My roommate is driving me crazy.
B: Yeah, she **talks** all night **on her cell phone**.

A: 내 룸메이트가 날 미치게 해.
B: 그래, 걘 밤새 핸드폰으로 전화해.

Did you send a text message to her?

너 걔에게 문자보냈어?

send a text message (to sb)는 '…에게 문자메시지 보내다' = text sb.

🔆 Example

- Did you see that I **sent you a text message**?
  내가 보낸 문자 메시지 봤어?
- I can't remember, but I'll **send** it to you **in a text message** later.
  기억이 안 나지만 나중에 문자로 알려줄게.

A: Are you ready to leave yet?
B: Wait, I need to **send Ted a text message**.

A: 너 떠날 준비가 되었니?
B: 기다려, 테드에게 문자메시지를 보내야 해.

I was video chatting with her

난 걔와 화상통화를 했어

video chat = video call. video chat에는 have를, video call에는 동사 make를 쓴다.

Example

- It's easy to video chat with people around the world.
  전세계 사람들과 화상통화를 하는 것은 쉬워.
- Just make a video call to Tommy.
  토미에게 화상전화를 걸어봐.

Dialog

A: What were you doing last night?
B: I was video chatting with my boyfriend.

A: 지난밤에 뭐했어?
B: 남친과 화상통화를 했어

I was late because of a traffic jam

차가 막혀서 늦었어

be a big traffic jam은 '차량이 많이 막히다.' be stuck in traffic은 '차가 막히다.'

Example

- I decided to walk and avoid driving in the rush-hour traffic.
  난 러시아워에 운전하는 것을 피하기 위해 걷기로 결정했지.
- There was a big traffic jam on the highway.
  고속도로에 교통이 크게 막혔어.

Dialog

A: How come she didn't show up?
B: She's probably just late because of a traffic jam.

A: 어떻게 걔가 나오지 않았어?
B: 차가 막혀서 좀 늦을거야.

I had a car accident in the morning
아침에 교통사고가 났어
have a(n) (car) accident는 '교통사고가 나다,' 가벼운 접촉사고는 have a fender-bender.

💡 **Example**
- Sam, have you ever had a car accident before?
  샘, 이전에 자동차 사고 나본 적 있어?
- I had a fender-bender on the way here.
  여기 오는 길에 가벼운 접촉 사고가 났어.

 Dialog

A: I had a small accident when I was driving your car, dad.
B: I'll never let you drive my car again.
  A: 아빠, 아빠 차를 몰다가 조그만 사고를 냈어.
  B: 다시는 내 차를 운전하지 못하게 할거야.

I got on the bus at the station
정류장에서 버스를 탔어
get in[out]은 자동차, get on[off]은 높이가 좀 있는 버스나 기차일 때 쓴다.

💡 **Example**
- Is this where we get on the train to New York?
  뉴욕 행 기차 여기서 타나요?
- Take the subway for two stops and get off at Paddington Station.
  지하철로 두 정거장 가셔서 패딩턴 역에서 내리세요.

 Dialog

A: Please let me know where to get off to get to Bloomingdale's.
B: You can just get off at the next stop.
  A: 블루밍데일 백화점에 가려면 어디서 내려야하나요.
  B: 그냥 담 정류장에서 내리면 돼요.

Can you get me a taxi, please?

택시 좀 불러줄래요?

take[get, catch] a taxi[cab]은 '택시를 타다,' hail a cab은 '손짓으로 택시잡다.'

 **Example**

- We'll grab a taxi to the hotel and get some rest.
  호텔까지 택시타고 가서 쉴거야.
- Why don't you take a taxi with me and stay overnight at my place?
  나랑 택시로 가서 내 집에 가서 하룻밤 지새면 어때?

Dialog

A: Can you get me a taxi, please?
B: I'd be glad to.

A: 택시 좀 불러줄래요?
B: 그럼요.

I ride a bicycle to work

난 자전거타고 출근해

ride a bicycle[bike]는 '자전거를 타다.'

 **Example**

- Is it hard to learn how to ride a bike?
  자건거 타는 법을 배우기가 어렵니?
- I started to ride the bus to work this week.
  난 이번주 버스로 출근하기 시작했어.

Dialog

A: You know how to ride a bike, don't you?
B: Of course!

A: 너 자전거 탈 줄 알지, 그렇지 않아?
B: 그렇고 말고!

Is it all right to park my car here?

차 여기다 주차해도 돼요?

park one's car (on the street)는 '(노상에) 주차를 하다.'

💡 Example

- Is it all right to park my car here?
  차 여기다 주차해도 돼?
- I don't think it's very nice of you to park here.
  여기 주차하는 건 좋지 않은 것 같아.

 Dialog

A: How much does it cost to park here?
B: The parking charge is $4.50 per hour.

　A: 여기에 주차하는데 얼마예요?
　B: 주차요금은 시간당 4달러 50센트입니다.

Get off at the third stop

3번째 정거장에서 내리세요

get off at~는 (버스나 전철을 타고 가다가) '…에서 내리다.'

💡 Example

- Take Line Number 2 and get off at Seolleung Station.
  2호선을 타서 선릉역에서 내려요.
- Take bus number 9000 and get off at the third stop.
  9000번 타고 3번째 정거장에서 내려요.

 Dialog

A: What's the fastest way to get to Kwangwhamoon?
B: Take the Line Number 3 and get off at Gyeongbokgung Station.

　A: 광화문 가는 가장 빠른 방법이 뭔가요?
　B: 3호선을 타고 경복궁역에서 내리세요.

070

Can I get there by bus?

버스로 갈 수 있나요?

go (to+N) by bus는 '버스로 (…에) 가다'라는 의미. 'by+차량'은 이동수단으로 무관사.

 Example

- Can I get there by bus?
  버스로 갈 수 있나요?
- Why don't you go by train?
  기차를 타고 가렴.

 Dialog

A: Have you got any plans for the break?
B: I'm going to my hometown by bus.

A: 휴가때 무슨 계획을 가지고 있니?
B: 난 버스로 고향에 갈거야.

071

I caught the flight to Boston

난 보스톤으로 가는 항공편을 탔어

catch the flight은 '비행기를 타다.' take를 써도 된다.

 Example

- I caught the flight to New York City.
  난 뉴욕시로 가는 항공편을 탔어.
- We need to make sure we catch the flight.
  비행기 타는 거 확실히 해야지.

Dialog

A: We need to catch the flight to Miami.
B: OK, let's go buy our tickets.

A: 우린 마이애미로 가는 비행기를 타야 해.
B: 그래, 항공권을 사러 가자.

043

072

The store is next to the station

그 가게는 역 옆에 있어

be next to~는 '…가 …의 옆에 있다'는 위치를 말하는 표현.

💡 **Example**

- The store is just next to your building.
  그 가게 네 빌딩 바로 옆에 있어.
- The store is across the street, next to the station.
  가게가 길건너 역 바로 옆에 있어.

A: **My car is next to the post office.**
B: **Let's walk there and go for a drive.**

A: 내 차는 우체국 옆에 있어.
B: 거기까지 걸어가서 드라이브하러 가자.

073

I have no time to go there

거기 갈 시간이 없어

have no time to+V는 '…할 시간이 없다,' have (the) time to+V는 '…할 시간이 있다.'

💡 **Example**

- I have no time to waste. Please give me a break.
  시간이 없어요. 한번만 봐주세요.
- I have no time to go there.
  거기 갈 시간이 없어.

A: **You should come out with us.**
B: **I have no time to hang out these days.**

A: 넌 우리랑 함께 나가야 해.
B: 난 요즘 같이 어울릴 시간이 없어.

074

We spent time drinking coffee

우리는 커피마시며 시간을 보냈어

spend time (on) ~ing은 '…하면서 시간을 보내다.' time 대신 시간명사가 와도 된다.

Example

- I'm planning to spend a lot of time on the beach.
  해변에서 실컷 있으려고 해.
- We spend too much time commuting back and forth to work.
  출퇴근에 너무 많은 시간이 걸리는 것 같아.

A: What did you do with your friends?
B: We spent time talking and drinking coffee.

　A: 친구들과 뭐했어?
　B: 얘기하고 커피마시며 시간보냈어.

075

Don't waste my time

내 시간을 뺏지마

waste one's time (on) ~ing는 '…하면서 시간을 낭비하다.'

Example

- The traffic jams in Seoul waste everyone's time.
  서울은 교통체증으로 모든 사람들의 시간을 낭비하고 있어.
- Using the Internet all day long wastes your time.
  하루종일 인터넷을 하면 네 시간을 낭비하는거야.

A: I have something you really should buy.
B: I don't want it. Don't waste my time.

　A: 네가 진짜 살 만한 걸 내가 가지고 있어요.
　B: 원하지 않아요. 제 시간을 뺏지 마세요.

It takes time to go there

거기 가는데 시간이 걸려

take time to+V이나 take time ~ing는 '…하는데 시간이 걸린다'라는 의미.

💡 Example

- It'll take time to repair that computer.
  컴퓨터 수리하는데 시간이 좀 걸릴 것 같아요.

- It will take time for him to drive here.
  걔가 여기로 운전해오는데 시간이 걸릴거야.

 Dialog

A: It's easy to fall down on the snow and ice.
B: It will take time getting to the subway station.

A: 눈과 빙판에서 넘어지기가 쉬워.
B: 지하철 역까지 가는데 시간이 걸릴거야.

We can't eat until she arrives

걔가 도착할 때까지 우린 먹을 수 없어

not A until B는 'B에 이르러서야 비로소 A하다.' until 다음에는 S+V를 써준다.

💡 Example

- You can not go out until you finish working.
  넌 일을 마무리할 때까지 외출할 수 없어.

- He did not smile until he saw Bonnie.
  걘 보니를 볼 때까지 웃지 않았어.

 Dialog

A: I'm getting really hungry now.
B: We can't eat until Katie arrives.

A: 난 이제 무지 배고파지네.
B: 케이티가 도착할 때까지 우린 먹을 수 없어.

078

I have other plans

난 다른 계획이 있어

have a plan for sth[to+V]은 '…할 계획이 있다.' '다른 계획이 있다'는 have other plans.

 Example

- We have a plan to retire early.
  우린 조기 은퇴 계획이 있어.
- I've got other plans for this evening.
  오늘 저녁 다른 계획을 가지고 있어.

Dialog

A: You should go out with us on Friday night.
B: I'd like to, but I have other plans.

A: 금요일 밤엔 우리랑 같이 나가자.
B: 그러고는 싶지만 다른 계획이 있어.

 079

You plan to quit your job?

직장을 그만 둘거야?

plan to+V[plan on ~ing]는 '…할 계획이 있다,' '…할거다'라는 의미.

 Example

- What do you plan to do this weekend?
  이번 주말에 뭘 하실 계획이에요?
- She's planning on getting married this year.
  걘 금년도 결혼할 계획을 세우고 있어.

Dialog

A: I heard that you plan to quit your job.
B: All I need is a better job.

A: 직장 그만 둘 거라며.
B: 내가 필요한 건 더 나은 직장이야.

It left the stop ahead of schedule
그건 예정보다 빨리 정류장을 떠났어

ahead of schedule은 '예정보다 빨리,' '늦게'는 behind schedule, 그리고 '예정대로'는 on schedule.

💡 **Example**
- The building was finished ahead of schedule.
  그 빌딩은 예정보다 빨리 완공되었어.
- Our train arrived ahead of schedule.
  우리 기차는 예정보다 빨리 도착했어.

A: Where did my school bus go?
B: It left the stop ahead of schedule.

A: 내 통학버스는 어디로 갔나요?
B: 그 버스는 예정보다 빨리 정류장을 떠났어요.

He is expected to get home early
걘 집에 일찍 올거라 생각돼

be expected to+V는 '…할거라 기대되다'라는 의미.

💡 **Example**
- Everyone is expected to bring a present.
  누구나 선물을 가져와야 돼요.
- Brian is expected to enter Harvard University.
  브라이언은 하버드 대학에 입학할 것으로 예상돼요.

A: How much was your new dress?
B: It was three times what I had expected to pay.

A: 새로 산 옷은 얼마줬어?
B: 예상보다 3배나 더 나갔어.

It's going to rain tomorrow

내일 비가 올거야

be going to+V는 '…할 것이다'(의도)와 '…일 것이다.' 더 가까운 시점은 be about to+V.

 Example

- I wonder how it's going to turn out?
  난 일이 어떻게 될 지 궁금해.
- I'm going to work on this stuff at home tonight.
  오늘 밤 집에서 이 일을 할 거야.

Dialog

A: Aren't you afraid he's going to be angry?
B: Who cares what he thinks?

A: 걔가 화낼 거라는 건 걱정 안하니?
B: 걔가 무슨 생각을 하든 누가 신경이나 쓴대?

The train is scheduled to arrive at 3:30

기차는 3시 30분에 도착할 예정입니다

be scheduled to+V는 공식적인 일이나 계획 등을 말할 때 쓰는 좀 격식있는 표현.

 Example

- The bus is not scheduled to leave for another 45 minutes.
  버스는 45분간 더 정차할거야.
- When is he scheduled to arrive at the airport?
  그 사람이 공항에 언제 도착할 예정이니?

Dialog

A: When is your flight scheduled for?
B: At 6 a.m. I've got to wake up early.

A: 비행기가 언제 뜨기로 되어 있지?
B: 오전 6시에. 일찍 일어나야 돼.

I guess it's getting late
늦을 것 같아
be getting[running] late는 '늦어지고 있다,' '늦어지다.'

💡 **Example**
- It is getting late in the day.
  너무 늦었어.
- I'd love to, but it's really getting late.
  그러고 싶지만 정말 늦었어.

 Dialog

A: It has been dark for a few hours.
B: I guess it is getting late.
  A: 어두워진지 몇시간이 되었어.
  B: 늦어질 것으로 생각해.

I was late again for work
나 또 회사에 지각했어
be late to+V[for+N]는 '…에 늦다,' 늦은 시간은 be+시간+late for~라고 한다.

💡 **Example**
- He was 15 minutes late for class.
  걘 수업시간에 15분 늦었어.
- We were an hour late for the movie.
  우린 영화시간에 1시간 늦었어.

 Dialog

A: Do you care if we're late?
B: I don't care if we are a little late for the party.
  A: 늦을 까봐서 걱정되니?
  B: 파티에 조금 늦는다고 해도 신경안써.

Why don't we get together tonight?
오늘 저녁에 만나자

get together는 사교적으로 '만나다'로 목적은 for sth, 만나서 할 행동은 and do로 말한다.

Example
- I wonder if we could get together on the 15th?
  15일에 만날 수 있을까?
- Why don't we get together on Saturday?
  토요일에 좀 만나죠?

Dialog

A: Why don't we get together on Saturday?
B: Sure. Call me in the morning.

A: 토요일에 좀 만나죠.
B: 그래요. 아침에 전화해요.

Guess What?

I need to sleep on it
깊이 생각해봐야겠어

곰곰이 생각하다. 뭔가 결정을 해야 하지만 아직 마음을 결정하지 못했을 때 쓰는 표현이다. 최종 결정을 하기 앞서서 시간을 더 갖고서 신중하게 생각하다(take some time to think carefully about it before making a final decision)라는 의미이다.

Come over to my place tonight

오늘 저녁 우리 집에 와

come over (to one's place)는 '…집에 놀러가다,' '들르다.' Come over here는 "이리로 와."

💡 **Example**

- Feel free to come over to my place.
  어려워말고 집에 들러.
- Why don't you come over here and talk to me for a second?
  이리 와 나랑 잠시 얘기하자.

 Dialog

A: When can I come over to see you?
B: Whenever you like. Just don't forget to bring some food.

　A: 언제 보러 가면 돼?
　B: 너 좋을 때 아무때나. 음식 가져오는 것만 잊지마.

Please stay for a while longer

좀 더 있다 가

stay for+시간명사는 '…동안 머물다.' say for+식사는 '식사하기 위해 남다.'

💡 **Example**

- I'm planning to stay for three weeks.
  3주간 머물거야.
- That's too bad. I was hoping you'd stay for dinner.
  그렇군요. 남아서 식사하시기를 바랬는데요.

 Dialog

A: It's late and I should go home.
B: Please stay for a while longer.

　A: 늦었어, 난 집에 가야해.
　B: 좀 더 머물러 주세요.

She stopped by to say hi

걘 인사하려고 잠깐 들렀어

stop[drop] by to+V(…하려고 잠시 들르다), stop by+장소(…에 잠시 들르다).

Example

- We're going to stop by a nightclub.
  우린 나이트클럽을 잠시 들를거야.

- I'll stop by your house on my way home.
  집에 가는 길에 네게 들를게.

A: I'm going to stop by the store on the way to work.
B: Can you pick me up some snacks?

A: 난 출근 길에 그 가게에 잠시 들를 거야.
B: 내게 스낵 좀 사다줄래?

Can you hold on a second?

잠시 기다려줄래?

hold[hang] on은 '기다리다'는 말로 전화상(hold the line) 혹은 일상에서 많이 쓰인다.

Example

- Hold on, there's a stain on your shirt.
  가만 있어봐, 네 셔츠에 얼룩이 있어.

- Just hold on for a second and I'll find it.
  잠깐만 기다리시면 찾아 드리겠습니다.

A: The key's stuck in the lock.
B: I can fix it. Hold on.

A: 키가 자물쇠에 박혔어.
B: 내가 고칠 수 있어. 기다려.

I'm waiting for the train

난 열차를 기다리고 있어

wait for+sb나 wait for+시간명사로 '…을 기다리다.' wait until S+V는 '…때까지 기다리다.'

 Example

- Can you wait for me in my room?
  내 방에서 잠시 기다려 줄래요?

- We have to wait for the bride and groom to cut the cake.
  신랑, 신부가 케이크를 짜르기를 기다려야 해.

 Dialog

A: I need to do my hair before we go.
B: I'll be waiting for you in the living room.

A: 가기 전에 머리를 해야 되는데.
B: 거실에서 기다려줄게.

Say hello to your parents for me

부모님께 내 안부 전해줘

say hi[hello] to sb는 '…에게 안부를 전해주다.' '작별인사하다'는 say goodbye to~.

 Example

- Say hi to your mom and dad.
  네 부모님에게 안부 좀 전해줘.

- Say hello to your parents for me.
  부모님께 내 안부 전해줘.

Dialog

A: By the way, Jim said to say hello to you.
B: Where did you see him?

A: 그런데 짐이 너한테 안부 전하래.
B: 넌 짐을 어디서 본거니?

Can I **make reservations**?

예약을 할 수 있을까요?

make a reservation을 한단어로 하자면 reserve(예약을 하다).

💡 Example

- I want to reconfirm my reservation.
  예약을 재확인하려구요.
- I didn't have time to make a hotel reservation before leaving.
  출발전에 시간이 없어 호텔 예약을 못했어.

 Dialog

A: Can I **make reservations**?
B: No, it's on a first come, first serve basis.

A: 예약을 할 수 있을까요?
B: 죄송하지만, 저희는 선착순이라서요.

He doesn't **say much about** it

걘 그것에 대해 말을 많이 하지 않아

say something to sb는 '…에게 할 얘기가 있다.' 많으면 say much about~.

💡 Example

- I have to say something to all of you.
  난 여러분 모두에게 꼭 할 말이 있어요.
- He doesn't say much about it.
  걘 그것에 대해 말을 많이 하지 않아.

 Dialog

A: Have you asked about the price of this vase?
B: No, I'll **say something to** the clerk before we go.

A: 이 꽃병 가격에 대해 물었니?
B: 아니요, 우리가 가기전에 점원에게 할말이 있어요.

We need to talk about that
우린 그 문제를 얘기해야 돼
talk about~는 '…에 대해 얘기하다,' talk to sb는 '…에게 말하다.'

💡 **Example**
- Are you ready to **talk about** it?
  그거에 대해 얘기할 준비 됐니?
- I don't know what you're **talking about**.
  어째서 그런 소리를 하는거야?

A: What do you think about my proposal?
B: We need to **talk about** that.

A: 내 제안에 대해 어떻게 생각해?
B: 그것에 대해 얘기 좀 해야 되겠어.

Tell me about your girlfriend
여친에 대해 말해줘
tell me about~는 '내게 …에 관해 말해줘,' tell A B라고 말해도 된다.

💡 **Example**
- Can you **tell me about** it over the phone?
  그거 전화로 얘기해줘.
- Can you **tell me** your address?
  네 주소 좀 알려줘.

A: Can you **tell me about** the pyramids in Egypt?
B: Sure. I visited them a few years ago.

A: 이집트 피라미드에 대해 내게 말해줄 수 있니?
B: 그럼. 전 몇 년전에 그곳을 방문했어요.

I'd like to go abroad for a few years

난 몇 년간 해외로 가고 싶어

go abroad는 '해외로 가다' = go overseas. study[travel] abroad 등을 알아둔다.

💡 Example

- I'd like to go abroad for a few years.
  난 몇 년간 해외로 가고 싶어.
- Have you traveled overseas?
  해외 여행해본 적 있어?

Dialog

A: I heard a lot of students are going abroad these days.
B: True. It's because we aren't satisfied with our education.

A: 요새 유학가는 학생들이 많다더라.
B: 맞아. 우리나라에서 받는 교육이 만족스럽지 못해서 그래.

I'm going to leave for New York

뉴욕으로 떠날거야

leave A for B는 'A를 떠나 B로 향하다.'

💡 Example

- Brad and Andrea leave for their vacation tonight.
  브래드와 앤드리아는 오늘 밤 휴가를 떠날거야.
- I'm going to leave for Canada.
  캐나다로 떠날거야.

Dialog

A: Why are you packing your clothes?
B: I leave for Mexico in the morning.

A: 왜 네 옷을 꾸리고 있니?
B: 난 아침에 멕시코로 떠날 거야.

I came here to see you
난 너를 만나러 여기 왔어
come here to+V는 '…하러 여기에 오다' = be here to+V.

💡 **Example**
- Do you need me to come to your house?
  내가 네 집에 가야할 필요가 있니?
- I came here to see if I could get a job.
  난 취업을 할까해서 여기에 왔어.

 Dialog

A: When did your dad come to the States?
B: When he was in his thirties.
　A: 아버님이 언제 미국에 오셨니?
　B: 30대에.

I'm going hiking on Sunday
일요일에 하이킹갈거야
go ~ing는 '…하러 가다.' go shopping, go camping 등을 알아둔다.

💡 **Example**
- I'm going jogging tomorrow morning.
  내일 아침에 조깅하러 갈거야.
- Are you ready to go shopping?
  쇼핑 갈 준비 다 됐어?

 Dialog

A: What are your plans for this weekend?
B: I'm going hiking on Sunday.
　A: 이번 주말에 뭐 하려고 해?
　B: 일요일에 하이킹갈거야.

Would you like to go for a drive?

드라이브 갈래?

go for+N의 형태로 for 다음에 명사를 넣어서 '…로 가는 목적'을 말한다.

💡 **Example**

- Would you like to go for a drive?
  드라이브 갈래요?
- Let's do that now and then go for a coffee.
  지금 하고 나서 커피 마시러 가자.

A: Did you have any plans on Sunday?
B: I'd like to go for a hike in the country.

A: 일요일에 무슨 계획이 있었니?
B: 지방에 하이킹하러 가고 싶어요.

I arrived on time for the meeting

난 회의시간에 맞춰 도착했어

arrive on time은 '정시에 도착하다.' in time은 '간신히 시간에 맞춰'라는 뜻.

💡 **Example**

- I hope the bus will arrive on time.
  버스가 정시에 도착하기를 바래.
- Make sure that you arrive on time tomorrow.
  내일 정시에 꼭 도착하도록 해.

A: When is he scheduled to arrive at the airport?
B: He's supposed to arrive tomorrow after lunch.

A: 그 사람이 공항에 언제 도착할 예정이니?
B: 내일 점심 후에 도착하게 되어 있어.

I'll be there as soon as I can

될 수 있는 한 빨리 갈게

be there = go, be here = come.

 Example

- We'll be there in a few minutes.
  우리 몇 분후에 도착할게.
- I'll be there as soon as I can.
  될 수 있는 한 빨리 갈게.

 Dialog

A: Make sure that you arrive on time tomorrow.
B: Don't worry. I'll be there early.

A: 내일 정시에 도착할 수 있도록 확실히 해.
B: 걱정하지마. 일찍 갈테니까.

It takes hard work to get there

성공하려면 일을 열심히 해야 돼

get there 1. (거기에) 도착하다 2. 성공하다, 목표를 달성하다

 Example

- They tried to finish, but they didn't get there.
  걔들은 끝내려고 노력했으나 달성하지 못했어.
- I hope we all get there after we graduate.
  우린 졸업 후 모두 목표를 달성하기를 희망해.

Dialog

A: How do I become a rich person?
B: It takes a lot of hard work to get there.

A: 난 어떻게 부자가 될 수 있나요?
B: 목표를 달성하려면 일을 열심히 해야 돼.

How will you get to the airport?

공항까지 어떻게 갈거야?

get to+장소명사는 '…에 도착하다.'

💡 **Example**

- How will you get to the airport?
  공항까지 어떻게 갈 거야?
- I cannot wait to get to New York.
  어서 뉴욕에 가고 싶어.

🧠 **Dialog**

A: Could you tell me how I get to the subway?
B: Go straight ahead until you see the sign.

A: 지하철로 가려면 어떻게 가야 하나요?
B: 지하철 표지판이 나올 때까지 앞으로 쭈욱 가세요.

Don't go over there. It's dangerous

저쪽으로 가지마. 위험해

go over there는 '저쪽으로 가다,' come over here '이쪽으로 오다.'

💡 **Example**

- Go over there and buy me some coffee.
  거기 가서 커피 좀 사와라.
- Would you come over here please?
  좀 이리로 와볼래요?

🧠 **Dialog**

A: I need you to come over here at 5 p.m. tomorrow.
B: I'm sorry, I can't. I have another appointment.

A: 내일 오후 5시에 여기로 와주셨으면 해요.
B: 죄송하지만 안돼요. 선약이 있어서요.

I wish I could go with you
나도 같이 갈 수 있으면 좋으련만

go with sb는 '…와 함께 가다,' '선택하다', '연애하다'라는 의미로 쓰임.

💡 **Example**

- Do you need me to go with you?
  함께 가줄까?
- I decided I'm going to go with her.
  걔랑 연애하기로 결정했어.

 Dialog

A: I'm going to visit Beijing this summer.
B: I wish I could go with you.

A: 올 여름에 베이징에 갈 거야.
B: 나도 같이 갈 수 있으면 좋으련만.

I'll be back in ten minutes
10분 후에 돌아올게

be back in+시간명사는 '…후에 돌아오다.'

💡 **Example**

- I have a feeling that we will be back here soon.
  곧 여기 다시 올 것같은 예감이 들어.
- What time do you think she will be back?
  걔가 몇 시에 돌아올 것 같니?

 Dialog

A: Are you going to be long?
B: No, I'll be back in ten minutes.

A: 오래 걸리나요?
B: 아뇨, 10분 후에 돌아올거에요.

Do you have to go back to work?

일하러 돌아가야 돼?

go back to+장소명사[to+V]는 '…로 돌아가다,' '…하러 돌아가다.'

💡 Example

- Do you have to go back to work?
  일하러 돌아가야 돼?
- I'd rather die than go back.
  돌아가느니 죽는 게 낫겠어.

Dialog

A: What are your plans for next year?
B: I'm going to go back to live in LA.

A: 내년도 네 계획은 어떠니?
B: 돌아가서 LA에서 살려고.

I was too tired to drive home

난 너무 피곤해서 운전해서 집에 가지 못했어

drive home은 '운전해서 집에 가다,' 다른 사람을 태운 경우 drive sb home.

💡 Example

- Bart didn't drive home when it was snowing.
  바트는 눈올 때 차로 귀가하지 않았어.
- Rachel plans to drive home tomorrow morning.
  라헬은 낼 아침 차로 집에 갈거야.

Dialog

A: Thanks for your time.
B: It was nothing. Have a safe drive home.

A: 시간 내줘서 고마워.
B: 별거 아냐. 운전 조심해서 가.

063

I have to go home early tonight

오늘 저녁 일찍 집에 가야 돼

go home은 '집에 가다.' 집으로 '출발'하는 초점, 반면 get home은 '도착'에 초점이 있다.

💡 Example

- I'd love to, but I have to go home early tonight.
  그러고 싶지만 오늘 저녁 집에 일찍 가야 돼.

- I wanted to let you know that Sam went home.
  샘이 집에 간 것을 알려주고 싶었어.

A: Just say when and we can go home.
B: I'll let you know when I want to go.

A: 시간만 말해, 집에 갈 수 있으니까.
B: 언제 가고 싶은지 알려줄게.

She wants to move to Chicago

걘 시카고로 이사하고 싶어해

move to+장소명사는 '…로 이사하다.' move in(이사오다), move out(이사가다).

💡 Example

- Sal wants to move to Brooklyn.
  샐은 브루클린으로 이사가길 원해.

- I may have to move to New York for my job.
  일 땜에 뉴욕으로 이사가야 할지 몰라.

A: I've decided to move to Japan this year.
B: Really? Are you sure about that?

A: 올해 일본으로 이사가기로 했어.
B: 정말? 확실한 거야?

We'll stay at my uncle's house

우린 내 삼촌 집에 머물거야

stay at+장소명사는 '…에 머물다,' '…에서 지내다.'

💡 Example

- We'll stay at my uncle's house.
  우린 내 삼촌 집에 머물거에요.
- They didn't stay at the university.
  걔들은 대학에서 묵지 않았어요.

 Dialog

A: Where did Tim stay in Chicago?
B: He stayed at an expensive hotel.

A: 팀은 시카고 어디에서 묵나요?
B: 걘 비싼 호텔에 있어요.

This snack is called a Twinkie

이 스낵은 트윈키라고 불려져

be called A는 '…로 불리다.' call A B는 'A를 B라고 부르다.'

💡 Example

- This snack is called a Twinkie.
  이 스낵은 트윈키라고 불려져.
- Our New Year's celebration is called Sul-nal.
  우린 새해 명절을 설날이라고 부르지.

 Dialog

A: Does Michael have a nickname?
B: He is called Micky by his friends.

A: 마이클은 별명이 있니?
B: 걘 친구들이 미키라고 불러.

115

Will you go out with me tonight?
오늘 나하고 데이트할래?

go out with는 '데이트하다,' '단순히 외출하다.' go out, go with 역시 같은 의미.

Example
- She doesn't want to go out with you.
  갠 너하고 데이트하는 것 원하지 않아.
- It's hard to get women to go out with me.
  난 여자한테 작업하는 게 어려워.

 Dialog

A: Will you go out with me tonight?
B: I'd rather stay home and watch TV.

A: 오늘 나하고 데이트할래?
B: 그냥 집에서 TV나 볼래.

116

I've got a date with Jill this evening
오늘 저녁 질과 데이트가 있어

have[get] a date with sb는 '…와 데이트가 있다.'

Example
- I've got a date with Lilly this evening.
  오늘 저녁 릴리와 데이트가 있어.
- Can you believe she had a date with the teacher?
  걔가 선생님이랑 데이트했다는게 믿겨져?

 Dialog

A: What are your plans for tonight?
B: I have a date. We're going out for dinner.

A: 오늘밤 뭐해?
B: 데이트가 있어. 나가서 저녁 먹을 거야.

I have feelings for her

난 걔를 좋아해

have feelings for sb는 '…을 좋아하다.'

Example

- He had feelings for his co-worker.
  걘 자신의 동료를 좋아했어.
- Sandy had feelings for my boyfriend.
  샌디는 내 남친을 좋아했어.

Dialog

A: Are you in love with my sister?
B: Yes, I have feelings for her.

A: 내 여동생을 사랑하고 있니?
B: 그럼, 좋아하고 있어.

Guess What?

A little bird told me

누구한테서 들었어, 얘기 들었어

지나가는 작은 새가 말해줬다는 것으로 뭔가 소문형태로 들은 소식을 얘기해 줄(someone heard some news, usually in the form of gossip) 때 사용하는 표현이다. 특히 누구한테서 소식을 들었는지 말하지 않을 때 사용하기 좋은 표현이다. 소문의 내용까지 함께 말하려면 A little bird told me that S+V의 형태로 쓰면 된다.

I like you better than her

난 걔보다 너를 더 좋아해

like sb better than~는 '…보다 …을 더 좋아하다.' like ~ing better than ~ing도 쓰임.

💡 **Example**

- I like her better than any other girl.
  난 다른 여자 애보다 걔가 더 좋아.
- He likes Matt better than his other friends.
  걘 다른 친구들 보다 매트를 더 좋아해.

 Dialog

A: How is your new math teacher?
B: I like her better than my history teacher.

A: 새 수학 선생님은 어때?
B: 역사 선생님 보다 더 좋아.

She got married to Chris

걘 크리스와 결혼했어

get married to~는 결혼하는 '행위'(marry sb), be married to~는 결혼한 '상태.'

💡 **Example**

- The point is that you're married to Jane.
  요는 네가 제인과 결혼했다는 거지.
- Why did you choose to get married to your wife?
  왜 네 아내와 결혼한거야?

 Dialog

A: Is that woman your girlfriend?
B: No, I'm married to her.

A: 저 여자가 네 여자친구지?
B: 아니, 내 아내야.

Alicia gave birth to twins

알리샤는 쌍둥이를 낳았어

give birth to~는 'to 이하를 낳았다.' give birth to a baby boy는 '사내아이를 낳다.'

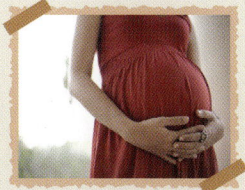

💡 Example

- Do you remember when I was giving birth to the twins?
  내가 쌍둥이를 낳았을 때 기억하니?
- My wife recently gave birth to a beautiful baby daughter.
  내 아내가 최근 예쁜 딸을 낳았어.

 Dialog

A: Alicia gave birth to twins.
B: Let's go visit her in the hospital.

A: 알리샤는 쌍둥이를 낳았어.
B: 걔 병문안 가자.

Chris is related to the boss

크리스는 사장과 친척관계야

be related to~는 '…와 관계가 있다.'

💡 Example

- Are you related to Emily Thompson?
  에밀리 톰슨과 관계가 있니?
- Chris is related to the boss.
  크리스는 사장과 친척관계야.

 Dialog

A: You're not related to Kirk Smith, are you?
B: Actually, he's my father

A: 커크 스미스씨와 친척 정도 됩니까?
B: 사실은 제 부친되시는데요.

Do you mind if I sit here for a sec?

여기 잠시 앉아도 돼?

mind ~ing[if~]는 '…을 상관하다,' '꺼려하다.' mind는 부정적 의미를 갖는 동사임.

Example

- Do you mind picking me up tomorrow?
  내일 나 좀 태워 줄 수 있겠니?
- Do you mind if I sit here for a sec?
  여기 잠시 앉아도 돼?

A: Would you mind if I take a look around here?
B: Not at all, be my guest.

A: 내가 여기 좀 둘러봐도 괜찮겠니?
B: 그럼, 물론이지.

I'll take part in the school festival

난 학교축제에 참가할거야

take part in~은 '…에 참여하다.' 어떤 일이나 경기, 행사 등에 관심이 있어 참가하는 것.

Example

- Did you take part in the game show?
  넌 그 게임쇼에 참가했니?
- Come and take part in our celebration.
  이리 와서 우리 기념행사에 참석해라.

A: You have been running a lot lately.
B: I want to take part in a marathon.

A: 넌 요즘 상당히 뛰고 있네.
B: 난 마라톤에 참가하고 싶어.

I want in when you start

네가 시작하면 나도 참석할게

want in~은 '어떤 일에 끼고 싶어하다' = count[be] in = count[be] out = want out.

💡 Example

- Things have changed since then. I want in.
  그 이래 상황이 바꿨어. 난 참가할거야.
- I know what's going on, and I want in.
  난 돌아가는 상황을 알아. 난 참가할거야.

A: We're setting up a game of cards.
B: Great. I want in when you start.

A: 우린 카드놀이를 준비할 거야.
B: 좋아. 네가 시작하면 나도 참석할게.

I need to go to bed now

난 이제 자야 할 시간이야

go to bed는 '잠자리에 들다,' '자다' = go to sleep. sleep tight는 '푹자다.'

💡 Example

- I go to bed really late last night.
  난 지난 밤 정말로 늦게 잠자리에 들었어.
- I'm getting ready to go to sleep.
  난 자러 갈 준비됐어.

A: I just called to talk to you.
B: It's 2:00 in the morning. Go to sleep.

A: 너하고 얘기하려고 전화했어.
B: 새벽 2시야. 좀 자라.

I get up at 9 a.m. every day

난 매일 아침 9시에 일어나

get up은 잠자리에서 '몸을 일으켜 일어나다,' wake up은 '잠에서 깨 눈을 뜨다.'

Example
- Do you need to get up early tomorrow morning?
  내일 아침 일찍 일어나야 돼?
- Why do you get up so early these days?
  요즘 왜 그렇게 일찍 일어나니?

Dialog

A: Do you need to get up early tomorrow morning?
B: Yeah. Please set the alarm for 5 a.m.

A: 내일 아침 일찍 일어나야 돼?
B: 어. 5시로 알람 좀 해줘.

Did you stay up late last night?

너 어젯밤에 안자고 있었어?

stay[be] up late는 '늦게까지 안자다,' '깨어있다.'

Example
- Are you going to stay up and watch the sunrise?
  밤을 새고 일출을 지켜볼거니?
- It's not good for you to stay up too late.
  너무 늦게까지 안자고 있는 건 좋지 않아.

Dialog

A: Did she stay up late last night?
B: No, she went to bed early.

A: 어젯밤에 늦게까지 안자고 있었냐?
B: 아니, 일찍 자던데.

Let's wait up for him to get here

걔가 올 때까지 자지말고 기다리자

wait[stay] up for sb는 '…을 자지 않고 기다리다.'

💡 **Example**
- I'll be late so don't wait up for me.
  나 늦을거니까 기다리지마.
- Wait up for the members of the tour group.
  투어 그룹 사람들을 기다리자.

 Dialog

A: Paul won't be back until midnight.
B: Let's wait up for him to get here.

A: 폴은 자정까지 돌아오지 않을 거야.
B: 걔가 올 때까지 자지말고 기다리자.

I'm going to take a shower

샤워할거야

take a shower는 '샤워하다.' take a bath는 '목욕하다.'

💡 **Example**
- I feel like taking a shower.
  샤워하고 싶어.
- It's been eight days since I took a shower.
  내가 샤워한 지 8일이 지났어.

 Dialog

A: What happened?
B: Nothing. I'm going to take a shower.

A: 무슨 일야?
B: 아무 일도 아냐. 샤워나 해야겠어.

Get dressed for the party

파티에 가게 옷입어라

get dressed는 '옷을 입다' <=> get undressed는 '옷을 벗다.'

 Example

- Now get dressed, we're going to the gym.
  체육관에 가게 옷입어.

- How long does it take to get dressed?
  옷을 입는데 얼마나 걸려?

 Dialog

A: Get dressed for the party.
B: What time are we going there?

A: 파티에 가게 옷을 입어라.
B: 언제 도착할거예요?

It's cold outside. Put on a jacket

밖에 추워. 재킷 입어

put on은 옷을 입다로 have, wear보다 입는 '동작'을 강조.

 Example

- I'll put on some shorts to exercise.
  난 운동을 하려고 반바지를 입을 거야.

- Go ahead and put on something comfortable.
  그렇게해. 편안한 옷을 입어라.

Dialog

A: Should I wear my red dress?
B: No, you should put on your black skirt.

A: 내 붉은 드레스를 입어야 하나요?
B: 아니, 검은 스커트를 입어야 해.

Take off your coat and sit down

코트를 벗으시고 앉으시죠

take off는 '옷을 벗다'라는 의미.

💡 **Example**

- Take off your coat and sit down.
  코트를 벗으시고 앉으시죠.
- Well, take off your shirt and lie down.
  자, 윗옷을 벗고 누우세요.

 Dialog

A: It seems to me that the room became hot.
B: I know. I have to take off my jacket.

A: 방이 무척 더워진 것 같아.
B: 알아. 윗도리를 벗어야 해.

Why don't you try it on?

한번 입어보지 그래?

try on은 옷 사기 전에 '한번 입어보는 것.' '음식을 먹어보다'는 try+음식명사.

💡 **Example**

- Can I try on one of these suits?
  이 옷들중 하나를 입어볼까요?
- Why don't you try it on?
  그거 입어봐.

 Dialog

A: Do you think this coat will fit me?
B: Why don't you try it on?

A: 이 코트 나한테 어울릴 것 같아?
B: 한번 입어보지 그래?

Good morning. Please take a seat

안녕하세요. 앉으세요

take a seat은 굳이 차이점을 말하자면 have a seat보다 좀 더 격식있는 표현.

 Example

- Take a seat and tell me about your day.
  앉아 그리고 오늘 하루 어땠는지 말해봐.
- Please have a seat in the reception area.
  접견실에 앉아 계세요.

 Dialog

A: Can I sit at this table with you?
B: Of course you can. Have a seat.

A: 이 테이블에 너와 같이 앉아도 되니?
B: 당연하지. 앉아.

Everyone laughed at him

모두 다 걔를 비웃었지

laugh at은 '소리내서 웃다,' 문맥에 따라 '비웃다.'

 Example

- I laugh at Jim Carrey movies.
  난 짐 캐리가 나오는 영화들을 보면서 웃어.
- We laughed at her arrogant behavior.
  우린 걔의 건방진 행동을 비웃었지.

Dialog

A: What happened when Ron fell down?
B: Everyone laughed at him.

A: 론이 넘어졌을 때 무슨 일이 생겼니?
B: 모두 다 걔를 비웃었지.

Didn't you clean up the kitchen?

부엌청소 안했어?

clean up+장소는 '…을 청소하다,' '치우다.'

 Example

- Didn't you clean up the kitchen?
  부엌을 청소했니?
- We need to clean up the room as quickly as possible.
  가능한 한 빨리 이 방을 치워야 해.

Dialog

A: I can't clean up this place alone.
B: That's why we're here. We'll help you.

A: 나 혼자서는 여기 못 치워.
B: 그래서 우리가 왔잖아. 우리가 도와줄게.

I don't like to do the dishes

설거지하기 싫어

do the dishes는 '설거지하다,' do the laundry는 '빨래하다'(get the laundry washed).

 Example

- I don't like to do the dishes.
  설거지하기 싫어.
- Let me help you finish washing the dishes.
  설거지 도와줄게.

Dialog

A: Your kitchen is pretty dirty.
B: I know. I don't like doing the dishes.

A: 너희 집 부엌 굉장히 지저분하구나.
B: 맞아. 내가 설거지하는 걸 싫어해서.

138

What will it cost to fix the car?

그 차를 고치는데 얼마나 들겠니?

fix the car는 '차를 수리하다,' fix the computer는 '컴퓨터를 수리하다.'

Example

- What will it cost to fix the car?
  그 차를 고치는데 얼마나 들겠니?
- Can you come into the living room and help me fix the TV?
  응접실에 와서 TV 고치는 걸 도와줄 수 있겠니?

A: You never fixed the broken window in your car.
B: That's because I don't have enough money.

A: 차에 깨진 유리창을 안바꿨네.
B: 그야 그럴 돈이 없으니까.

139

How about going out for lunch?

점심 먹으러 나갈까?

go to lunch는 '점심 먹으러 나가다' = go out to[for] lunch.

Example

- Where do you want to go for lunch?
  점심 먹으러 어디 가고 싶어?
- How about going out for lunch?
  점심 먹으러 나갈까?

A: May I speak to Bill, please?
B: He just stepped out for lunch.

A: 빌 좀 바꿔 주시겠어요?
B: 점심 식사하러 방금 나가셨는데요.

Do you have time to have dinner?

저녁 먹을 시간 있어?

have dinner (with sb)는 '…와 함께 저녁먹다.' have 대신 get, do, eat을 써도 된다.

 Example

- Do you have time to have dinner?
  저녁 먹을 시간 있어?
- Where are you going to eat dinner?
  저녁 먹으러 어디로 가니?

Dialog

A: **Do you have time to have dinner?**
B: **Not really. I think I must be going now.**

A: 저녁 먹을 시간 있어요?
B: 실은 안 돼요. 지금 가봐야 될 것 같아요.

Help yourself to the cake

케익 드세요

help yourself to+음식명사는 '…을 편하게 먹다.'

 Example

- Help yourself to the cake.
  케익 드세요.
- He helped himself to a bottle of beer.
  걘 맥주 한 병을 가져다 마셨어.

Dialog

A: **Angela, please help yourself to the cake.**
B: **I will. It looks quite delicious.**

A: 안젤라, 케익 갖다 먹어라.
B: 네. 되게 맛있어 보이네요.

Have a drink with us after work

퇴근 후 우리랑 술 한잔하자

have a drink는 물이나 주스를 마시다이지만 술을 뜻할 때가 많다. = go for a drink

 Example

- Have a drink with us after work.
  퇴근 후 우리랑 술 한잔하자.

- You're not allowed to have drinks out here.
  음료는 밖으로 가지고 나가실 수 없어요.

 Dialog

A: I've really got to go home now.
B: Have a drink with me before you leave.

A: 난 이제 정말로 집에 가야 해.
B: 떠나기 전에 나랑 술 한잔하자.

Don't drink and drive!

음주운전하지마!

drink and drive[drive drunk]는 '음주운전하다,' '음주운전'은 drunk driving이라고 한다.

 Example

- The accident happened when he was drinking and driving.
  걔가 음주운전했을 때 사고가 났어.

- It is illegal to drink and drive in this country.
  우리나라에서 음주운전은 불법야.

Dialog

A: Why are the police stopping cars?
B: They want to catch people who drink and drive.

A: 왜 경찰이 차들을 세우는 거야?
B: 음주운전자 단속하려고.

144

You seem a little drunk tonight
오늘 밤 너 좀 취한 것 같아

get[be] drunk는 '취하다' = be loaded. get tipsy는 '알딸딸하게 취하다.'

💡 **Example**

- I heard you were drunk and broke a window yesterday.
  듣자 하니 너 어제 취해서 창문을 깼다면서.
- How did Ted get so drunk on Friday night?
  테드가 금요일 저녁에 어떻게 해서 그렇게 고주망태가 된거니?

 Dialog

A: You seem a little drunk tonight.
B: It has been a while since I had beer.

A: 오늘 밤 너 좀 취한 것 같아.
B: 맥주 마신지 좀 됐는데.

 145

I'll have the same as you
난 너랑 같은 걸 먹을래

have the same은 음식주문시 '같은 걸로 하다.' Make it two! 역시 "같은 걸로 주세요!"

💡 **Example**

- Do you want to have the same thing?
  너도 같은 걸 원하니?
- I'll have the same as she's having.
  나도 걔가 먹는 것과 같은 걸로 할래.

 Dialog

A: Give me some bacon and eggs.
B: I'll have the same as you.

A: 베이컨과 계란을 좀 주세요.
B: 난 너랑 같은 걸 먹을래.

I'll have a salad and a burger

샐러드하고 햄버거를 먹을래요

I'll have+음식은 식당 주문시 쓰는 표현 = I'd like to order+음식.

💡 **Example**

- **I'll have** a salad and a burger.
  샐러드하고 햄버거를 먹을래요.
- **I'll have** a steak and some potatoes.
  스테이크하고 감자를 먹겠습니다.

 Dialog

A: Can I get you some food to eat?
B: **I'll have** a sandwich and some milk.

A: 먹을 음식을 좀 드릴까요?
B: 샌드위치하고 우유 약간 주세요.

Who's going to pay for dinner?

누가 저녁식사를 내나요?

pay for dinner는 '저녁 식사비를 내다.'

💡 **Example**

- Who's going to **pay for** dinner?
  누가 저녁식사를 내나요?
- Can you **pay for** dinner? I can't afford it.
  저녁값 낼래? 내가 돈이 없어서.

 Dialog

A: Did Harry make you **pay for** dinner?
B: He tried to get me to **pay for** it, but I refused.

A: 해리가 저녁값을 네가 내게 했단 말야?
B: 내가 돈내게끔 하려고 하더라구. 하지만 싫다고 했어.

I am too full to eat anything else

너무 배가 불러서 아무것도 못 먹겠어

be full은 '배가 부르다' = be stuffed = have enough.

💡 **Example**

- John was full after eating at the buffet.
  존은 부페에서 먹고서 완전 배가 불렀어.
- Gerry is full and wants to lie down.
  게리는 배가 불러서 눕고 싶어해.

 Dialog

A: How about something for dessert?
B: I am too full to eat anything else.

A: 디저트 좀 할래요?
B: 너무 배가 불러서 아무 것도 못 먹겠어요.

She loves to cook Korean food

걘 한국 음식을 요리길 좋아해

cook+음식은 '…음식을 요리하다,' cook sth for dinner, cook sth for sb도 알아둔다.

💡 **Example**

- Please cook something for my dinner.
  내 저녁 식사로 요리 좀 해줘라.
- She'll cook something for lunch soon.
  걔가 곧 점심 음식을 준비할거야.

 Dialog

A: What are you doing in the kitchen?
B: I'm going to cook something for dinner.

A: 부엌에서 너 뭐하니?
B: 저녁 식사로 뭔가를 요리하고 있어.

150

Got to make dinner for the kids

애들 저녁을 만들어 줘야 돼

make dinner for sb는 '···을 위해 저녁을 준비하다.'

💡 **Example**

- It's time to make dinner for the guests.
  손님들을 위해 저녁을 준비할 시간이야.
- We can make dinner for Jason.
  우린 제이슨을 위해 저녁식사를 준비할 수 있어.

 Dialog

A: Well, I must be off. Got to make dinner for the kids.
B: What are you making tonight?

　A: 그만 가야 돼. 애들 저녁을 만들어 줘야 하거든.
　B: 오늘밤엔 뭘 만들어 줄거지?

151

He is on leave

걘 휴가중이야

be on leave는 '휴가중이다'라는 말. = be on vacation[holiday]

💡 **Example**

- I'll take care of your dog when you're on vacation.
  너 휴가가면 강아지를 맡아줄게.
- I met Herman when he was on leave.
  헐만이 휴가 중일 때 내가 만났어.

 Dialog

A: I saw Jim working in the office today.
B: That's weird. He is supposed to be on a vacation.

　A: 오늘 짐이 사무실에서 일하고 있더라.
　B: 거 이상하네. 그 친구는 휴가중일텐데.

152

I'm thinking of going on a vacation
휴가갈까 생각중야
go on a vacation 역시 '휴가가다' = go on a holiday.

 **Example**

- You'll be sorry if you don't come on a vacation with me.
  나랑 휴가가지 않으면 후회하게 될거야
- I'm thinking of going on a vacation.
  휴가갈까 생각중야.

Dialog

A: Shall we go on a vacation together?
B: I'm not sure. Let's talk about it.
  A: 함께 휴가갈까?
  B: 몰라. 얘기해보자.

153

I have the whole week off
난 일주일 전부 쉴거야
have[take]~ off는 '…만큼 쉬다.' on one's days off는 '쉬는 날에.'

 **Example**

- Will he have the Christmas holiday off?
  갠 크리스마스 휴일에 쉴거니?
- I have the whole week off.
  난 일주일 전부 쉴거야.

Dialog

A: Why don't you take the rest of the day off and go home?
B: God bless you!
  A: 오늘은 그만 하고 집에 가지 그래요?
  B: 이런 고마울 데가!

Why don't you take a break?

쉬지 그래.

take a break는 '휴식을 취하다' = take five. break는 '휴식시간.'

💡 **Example**

- Why don't you take a break?
  쉬지 그래.
- Take a break from your work.
  일을 잠시 중단하고 휴식을 취하자.

A: Shall we take a break now?
B: No, let's keep going.

A: 지금 잠시 좀 쉴까?
B: 아니, 계속하자.

He went on a trip to Japan

걘 일본으로 여행갔어

go on a trip to~는 '…로 여행을 가다' = take off on a trip.

💡 **Example**

- The class went on a trip to the zoo.
  학급은 동물원으로 실습여행을 했어.
- Our family went on a trip to Sweden.
  우리 가족은 스웨덴으로 여행을 갔어.

A: Where do you want to visit most?
B: I want to go on a trip to Australia.

A: 넌 어딜 가장 가고 싶니?
B: 난 호주 여행을 하고 싶어.

I enjoyed talking with you
너랑 얘기해서 즐거웠어
enjoy 다음에는 ~ing가 많이 오지만 명사도 많이 쓰인다는 점을 알아둔다.

💡 Example
- I enjoyed talking with you.
  너랑 얘기해서 즐거웠어.
- Enjoy your stay in Chicago.
  시카고에 있는 동안 즐거운 시간 되길 바래.

A: Did you enjoy walking around today?
B: Yes, but I'd like a guide tomorrow.

A: 오늘 둘러보는 거 좋았어?
B: 어, 하지만 내일은 가이드가 필요해.

I had a good time at the party
난 파티에서 즐거운 시간을 보냈어
have a good time은 '즐거운 시간을 보내다.' Have a nice day[one]!도 기억해둔다.

💡 Example
- I wonder if she had a good time.
  걔가 즐겁게 지냈는지 모르겠네.
- You'll have a good time at the nightclub.
  넌 나이트클럽에서 즐겁게 보낼 수 있을 거야.

A: Sandy is back from her date.
B: I wonder if she had a good time.

A: 샌디가 데이트 하고 돌아왔어.
B: 즐거운 시간 보냈는지 모르겠네.

Have much fun at the party!
파티에서 아주 재밌게 놀아!
have fun은 have a good time보다 좀 더 가볍고 캐주얼한 표현이다.

💡 **Example**
- I want you to feel free to have fun while you're on vacation.
  휴가 때 마음편히 재미있게 보내길 바래.
- I'd rather have fun than save money.
  난 저축을 하느니 즐기고 싶어.

 Dialog

A: Oh boy, we're going to have fun tonight!
B: What are you guys doing?
  A: 야! 우리 오늘밤에 재미있게 놀거다!
  B: 너희들 뭘 할건데?

She got a ticket for the concert
걘 그 연주회 입장권을 구했어
get a ticket는 '표를 구하다,' 어떤 표인지는 for~이하에 말하면 된다.

💡 **Example**
- Did you get a ticket for the flight?
  그 항공편 표를 받았니?
- Laura got a ticket for the concert.
  로라는 그 연주회 입장권을 받았어.

 Dialog

A: I got a ticket for the Lakers game.
B: Let's go to the game together.
  A: 레이커스 팀의 경기 표를 하나 얻었어.
  B: 그 경기 같이 가자.

I just came to listen to music

단지 음악을 들으려고 왔어

listen to~는 '주의를 기울여 듣는' 것을 말한다.

 Example

- The audience sat down to listen to music.
  청중들은 음악을 감상하려고 앉았다.
- I would listen to music when I rode the subway.
  난 지하철을 탈 때 음악을 들어.

Dialog

A: Did you come here to dance?
B: No, I just came to listen to music.

A: 너 여기 춤추러 왔니?
B: 아니, 단지 음악을 들으려고 왔어.

Would you like to go watch a movie?

영화보러 갈래?

watch a movie는 굳이 구분하자면 집중해서 보는 행위를, see a movie는 극장에서 보는 것.

 Example

- We went to watch a movie at the shopping mall.
  우린 쇼핑몰에서 영화를 보러 갔어.
- Would you like to go watch a movie?
  영화보러 갈래?

Dialog

A: I can't watch a movie without popcorn.
B: Don't be so picky.

A: 난 팝콘 없이는 영화를 못봐.
B: 너무 까다롭게 굴지 마.

I'm having a party tonight

오늘밤에 나 파티해

have a party는 '파티를 하다.' ~with sb, for sb가 이어진다.

💡 **Example**

- We're having a party for Tom. Hope you can make it.
  탐을 위해서 파티여는데, 올 수 있었으면 좋겠어.

- He might have a party at home.
  걘 집에서 파티를 할 것 같아.

A: **I'm having a party** tonight. Can you come?
B: I'm sorry, I can't. I have to study for my exams.

A: 오늘 밤 파티 할건데. 올래?
B: 미안하지만 못가. 시험공부 해야 해.

I hope you get well soon

곧 낫기를 바래

get well은 '병에서 회복되다.' 여기서 well은 형용사로 '건강한'이란 뜻.

💡 **Example**

- How long did it take you to get well?
  네가 회복하는데 얼마나 걸렸니?

- I hope you get well soon.
  곧 낫기를 바래.

A: Simon has been in the hospital for a week.
B: I think he will **get well** soon.

A: 사이몬은 일주간 병원에 입원해있어.
B: 난 걔가 조만간 회복할 것으로 생각해.

She has pain in her hand

갠 손에 통증이 있어

have pain in+신체부위는 '…가 아프다'라는 의미. have 대신 feel도 가능.

Example

- Mom has pain in her hand.
  엄마는 손에 통증이 있어.
- Older people have pain in their joints.
  노인들은 관절에 통증을 가지고 있지.

Dialog

A: Why are you walking so slowly?
B: I have a pain in my foot today.

A: 넌 왜 그렇게 천천히 걷고 있니?
B: 오늘 발이 좀 아파서.

I caught a cold yesterday

어제 감기에 걸렸어

catch[get] a cold는 '감기에 걸리다.' 심한 정도는 bad, light를 쓴다.

Example

- Many children caught colds at school.
  많은 애들이 학교에서 감기에 걸렸어.
- Stay inside or you'll catch a cold.
  안에 들어가 있어 아니면 감기걸린다.

Dialog

A: What's wrong with you?
B: I caught a cold yesterday.

A: 어디 아파요?
B: 어제 감기에 걸렸어요.

Does he have a fever?

걔가 열도 나?

have[run] a fever는 '열이 나다.' 강조하려면 have a high fever.

💡 **Example**
- You feel hot. I think you have a fever.
  몸이 뜨겁지. 열이 나는 것 같아.
- Pam took aspirin because she has a fever.
  팸은 열이나 아스피린을 먹었어.

 **Dialog**

A: The kid has a runny nose and is coughing a lot.
B: Does he have a fever?

A: 애가 콧물이 나고 기침을 많이 해요.
B: 열도 나나요?

I've got a splitting headache

머리가 빠개질 것 같아

have[get] a headache는 '머리가 아프다.' give A a headache는 'A의 머리를 아프게 하다.'

💡 **Example**
- I've got a splitting headache.
  머리가 빠개질 것 같아요.
- I can't work because I have a headache.
  두통으로 일을 할 수 없어요.

 **Dialog**

A: I have a severe headache and I need some medicine.
B: Do you want Tylenol or aspirin?

A: 두통이 심해. 약을 좀 먹어야겠어.
B: 타이레놀이나 아스피린 줄까?

Are you suffering from diarrhea?

설사가 있으신가요?

have diarrhea는 '설사하다' = have the runs.

🔆 **Example**

- Kate had diarrhea after eating spicy food.
  케이트는 매운 음식을 먹은 후 설사했어.
- Some international travelers have diarrhea.
  해외여행자들중 일부는 설사를 해.

 Dialog

A: **Are you suffering from diarrhea?**
B: **No, but I have a stomachache.**

A: 설사가 있으신가요?
B: 아니요, 위통예요.

 Guess What?

He swept off her feet

걔는 그녀의 맘을 사로잡았어

sweep sb off sb's feet하게 되면 sb의 마음을 사로잡다, sb가 사랑에 빠지게 하다라는 뜻이다. 특히 만나자마자 바로 사랑에 빠지게 하다(cause someone to fall in love quickly, a short time after meeting)라는 의미로 쓰인다.

093

169

Hurry and go to see a doctor
어서 병원에 가봐

see a doctor는 '진찰받는' 것. 일반적으로 병원간다고 할 때 쓴다. = go to a doctor.

Example
- I need to go to see a doctor.
  의사한테 가봐야겠어.
- Shelly saw a doctor about her cough.
  셀리는 기침문제로 진찰을 받았어.

 Dialog

A: The rash on my skin keeps getting worse.
B: Hurry and go to see a doctor.

A: 피부에 뾰루지가 점점 심해지고 있어.
B: 어서 병원에 가봐.

170

How about we take a walk tonight?
오늘 저녁 산보하자

go for a walk는 '산보하다' = take a walk[take walks].

Example
- How about we take a walk tonight?
  오늘 저녁 산보하자
- I don't want to go for a walk in the rain.
  비맞으며 산책하고 싶지 않아.

 Dialog

A: Where are you going?
B: I want to take a walk around the park.

A: 어디 가니?
B: 공원 근처에 산책하러 가려고.

She's getting fat

걘 점점 살이 찌고 있어

get fat는 '살이 찌다.' 다소 직설적인 표현. =gain[put on] weight(일상표현).

💡 Example

- I would be unhappy if I got fat.
  내가 살이 찌면 난 불행할 거야.

- No wonder they're getting so fat.
  걔네들이 그렇게 살찔 만도 하군

A: **Stella got fat after eating a lot of ice cream.**
B: **She has to eat fruits and vegetables instead.**

A: 스텔라는 아이스크림을 먹은 후 살이 쪘어.
B: 걘 과일과 야채를 대신 먹어야 해.

Are you on a diet right now?

지금 다이어트 중이야?

be[go] on a diet는 '다이어트하다.' diet는 일반적인 '식사,' '음식물'의 의미도 있다.

💡 Example

- Many people go on a diet after the holidays.
  많은 사람들이 휴일이후에 다이어트를 하지.

- I went on a diet before my wedding.
  난 결혼식 전에 다이어트를 했어.

A: **My mom has gotten kind of heavy.**
B: **She needs to go on a diet for a while.**

A: 우리 엄마는 약간 무거워지고 있어.
B: 잠시 다이어트를 하실 필요가 있을 걸.

173

It's so hard to lose weight

몸무게를 줄이기가 굉장히 어려워

lose weight는 '살이 빠지다.' '날씬해졌다'는 become thin[slim].

Example

- It's so hard to lose weight.
  몸무게를 줄이기가 굉장히 어려워.

- It looks like you've lost weight lately.
  너 최근에 살이 빠진 것 같아.

A: I wish I could lose some weight.
B: It's what's inside that counts.

A: 살을 좀 빼고 싶어.
B: 중요한 건 육체의 내면이라구.

174

I've heard so much about you

너에 대해 많은 얘기 들었어

hear about은 '…에 관한 말을 듣다.' hear from(…로부터 듣다), hear of(…의 소식을 듣다).

Example

- I heard about your daughter.
  네 딸 얘기 들었어.

- I heard about your wedding the other night.
  지난 밤에 너 결혼식 얘기 들었어.

A: Nice to meet you, Sam.
B: I've heard so much about you.

A: 만나서 반가워, 샘.
B: 너에 대해 많은 얘기 들었어.

175

Did you hear if he got the job?

걔가 취직했는지 소식 들었어?

hear의 목적어로 절이 오는 경우로 that이 오거나 혹은 what, who, how 등이 올 수 있다.

💡 Example

- I hear that the weather there is very nice.
  그곳 날씨가 아주 좋다고 하던대.
- I heard that he moved to Philadelphia.
  걔가 필라델피아로 이사갔다며.

 Dialog

A: Did you hear if Mark got the job?
B: Judging by the look on his face, I'd say yes.

A: 마크가 일자리를 얻었는지 소식 들었어요?
B: 얼굴 표정으로 봐선 그런 것 같던데요.

176

He looked at me and smiled

걔가 나를 보고 웃었어

look at~은 '…을 쳐다보다' = take a look at.

💡 Example

- She is afraid to look at snakes.
  걘 뱀 쳐다보는 걸 무서워해.
- Do you mind if I take a look around here?
  내가 여기 좀 둘러봐도 괜찮겠니?

 Dialog

A: Look at this. It's a picture of my boyfriend.
B: Wow, he looks like a movie star.

A: 이것 좀 봐. 내 남친 사진이야.
B: 와, 영화배우처럼 생겼네.

177

We need to wait and see

기다려봐야 돼

wait and see what[how~] S+V는 '상황이나 결과 등을 지켜보다.'

🔆 **Example**

- Let's wait and see how things go.
  일이 어떻게 돼가는지 지켜보자.
- Just wait and see what she has to say.
  걔가 무슨 말을 할지 지켜보자

 Dialog

A: When will the festival begin?
B: We need to wait and see.

A: 축제가 언제 시작돼?
B: 기다려봐야 돼.

178

I'm aware of the situation

난 그 상황을 알고 있어

be aware of that S+V[what~]은 '…을 알고 있다.'

🔆 **Example**

- You were both aware of the situation.
  너희 둘 모두 상황을 알고 있었잖아.
- Are you aware of what's going on with Jim?
  짐이 어떻게 지내는지 알아?

 Dialog

A: Are you aware of what she said about you?
B: No. Did she say something bad?

A: 걔가 너에 대해 무슨 말했는지 알아?
B: 아니. 뭐 나쁜 말을 한거야?

I know the answer to this question

그 문제의 답을 알고 있어

know the answer to sth은 '…에 대한 답을 알고 있다.'

💡 **Example**

- Please just level with me. I want to know the truth.
  솔직히 말해. 사실 그대로 알고 싶어.
- I think I know the answer to this question.
  그 문제의 답을 알 것 같아.

 Dialog

A: The teacher might not know the answer.
B: It doesn't hurt to ask.

A: 선생님도 그 해답을 모를 수 있어.
B: 물어봐야 손해볼 것 없잖아.

I have no idea

모르겠어

have no idea = don't know. have no idea that[what, how~] S+V처럼 뒤에 절.

💡 **Example**

- I had no idea you were from New York.
  네가 뉴욕 출신이라는 걸 몰랐어.
- I have no idea what you're talking about.
  네가 무슨 말을 하는 건지 모르겠어.

 Dialog

A: How was your trip to Toronto?
B: You have no idea how exciting it was.

A: 토론토 여행은 어땠어?
B: 얼마나 신났었는지 넌 모를 거야.

Can I ask you a question?

질문해도 돼?

ask (sb) a question은 '(…에게) 질문하다.'

💡 **Example**

- Can I ask you a question? It's urgent.
  질문해도 돼? 급한건데.
- Feel free to ask me any questions you might have.
  질문 있으면 편하게 해.

 Dialog

A: Can I **ask you a few questions**?
B: You can ask me anything you want to.

A: 질문 몇 개 좀 해도 돼?
B: 뭐든 물어봐.

Is it too early to check in?

체크인하기엔 너무 이른가요?

check in은 '체크인하다,' '탑승수속하다.' check the baggage, check in one's baggage는 '짐을 부치다.'

💡 **Example**

- Is it too early to check in?
  체크인하기엔 너무 이른가요?
- She checked in yesterday and paid with a credit card.
  어제 투숙했고 카드결재했어요.

 Dialog

A: We have to **check in** our bags at least half an hour before our flight.
B: Let's do that now and then go for a coffee.

A: 최소 비행기 출발 30분 전에 가방을 부쳐야 해.
B: 지금 하고 나서 커피 마시러 가자.

183

I'd like to check out now

첵아웃을 하고 싶은데요

check out은 '퇴실절차를 밟다,' '확인하다,' '책을 대출받다.'

💡 **Example**

- Check out all the houses decorated with lights for Christmas.
  성탄불빛으로 장식된 집들 살펴봐.
- We need to check out your office.
  당신 사무실을 살펴봐야겠어요.

 Dialog

A: I'd like to check out now.
B: Could you tell me your room number please?

A: 첵아웃을 하고 싶은데요.
B: 방 번호를 말씀해 주시겠습니까?

184

Let me check the schedule

일정 확인해볼게요

let me check~ 다음에 명사나 if S+V절이 온다.

💡 **Example**

- Let me check your temperature.
  체온 재볼게요.
- Let me see if I can reschedule the appointment.
  약속을 다시 조정할 수 있는지 알아볼게.

 Dialog

A: Do you know when the next train leaves?
B: Just a moment. Let me check.

A: 다음 열차는 언제죠?
B: 잠깐만요. 확인해볼게요.

185

You need to look over this e-mail
넌 이 이메일을 살펴봐야 돼

look over는 많은 주의를 기울이지 않고 빨리 검토해보는 것을 뜻. 자세히는 go over.

💡 **Example**
- Karen looked over the new rules.
  캐런이 새로운 규칙을 살펴봤어.
- You need to look over this e-mail.
  넌 이 이메일을 살펴봐야 돼.

 Dialog

A: James gave me the report this morning.
B: Let's look over what it says.

A: 제임스가 오늘 아침 보고서를 줬어.
B: 뭐라 썼는지 훑어보자고.

186

I heard a rumor that you got married
너 결혼했다는 소문들었어

hear a rumor about[that S+V]은 '…라는 소문을 듣다.'

💡 **Example**
- I heard a rumor that the store's going to shut down.
  가게가 문닫을거란 소문야.
- I heard some negative rumors about the election.
  선거에 관한 부정적인 소문을 들었어.

 Dialog

A: Annie, I heard a rumor that you got married.
B: That's not true. I'm so embarrassed.

A: 애니야, 너 결혼했다는 소문들었어.
B: 사실이 아냐. 정말 당황스러워.

I just found out the results

난 방금 그 결과를 알았어

found out은 '정보나 사실을 알아내다,' find sth은 '…을 발견하다.'

 **Example**

- When you find out the results, please give me a call.
  결과 알게 되면 전화해줘라.
- I'm calling to find out if the meeting has been postponed.
  회의연기여부 확인차 전화했어.

 Dialog

A: How did you find out about this concert?
B: There was a newspaper ad describing it.

A: 이 콘서트 정보 어떻게 알아낸거야?
B: 콘서트에 대한 신문광고가 있었어.

She mistook me for a teacher

걘 나를 선생님으로 착각했어

mistake A for B는 'A를 B로 잘못 오해하다.' 사람, 사물 다 가능하다.

 **Example**

- Jerry mistook a stranger for one of his friends.
  제리는 낯선이를 친구중 하나로 착각했어.
- He was so drunk that he mistook the student for his wife.
  걘 너무 취해 그 학생을 자기 아내로 착각했어.

Dialog

A: Why are you eating the tomato sauce?
B: Oh my, I mistook the tomato sauce for soup.

A: 왜 토마토 소스를 먹는거야?
B: 이런, 토마토 소스를 수프로 봤네.

Could you keep a secret?

비밀 지킬 수 있어?

keep (sth) secret은 '(…을) 비밀로 지키다.' 비밀로 해야 되는 것은 keep 다음에 넣는다.

💡 **Example**

- Could you keep a secret?
  비밀 지킬 수 있어?

- Don't worry. I can keep a secret.
  걱정마. 비밀 지킬 수 있어.

 Dialog

A: Can I trust you to keep a secret?
B: Sure, you can count on me.

A: 비밀 지킬거라고 믿어도 돼나요?
B: 물론, 날 믿어.

Keep your mouth shut

입다물고 있어

keep one's mouth shut (about)은 '(…에 관한 것을) 비밀로 하다.'

💡 **Example**

- Paul should really keep his mouth shut.
  폴은 정말 입을 다물어야 될거야.

- You keep your mouth shut about the document.
  그 서류에 대해 누구에게도 말하면 안돼.

 Dialog

A: Is this a secret?
B: Yes, it is. Keep your mouth shut.

A: 이거 비밀야?
B: 어 그래. 입다물고 있어.

191

You need to keep quiet about it

그거 비밀 지켜야 돼

keep quiet about sth은 '…을 함구하다,' '비밀을 지키다.'

💡 **Example**

- Keep quiet about the money I gave you.
  내가 준 돈에 대해 함구해.

- Why do you keep quiet about it?
  왜 그거에 대해 입다물고 있는거야?

 **Dialog**

A: Tell me what Joseph did last night.
B: OK, but you need to keep quiet about it.

A: 조셉이 간밤에 뭘했는지 말해줘.
B: 좋아, 하지만 그거 비밀 지켜야 돼.

192

Watch your tongue!

말 조심해!

watch[hold] one's tongue은 '말을 그만하다,' '함구하다.'

💡 **Example**

- Watch your tongue, or I'll beat you up.
  말 조심해 아님 패버릴거야.

- Hold your tongue! The walls have ears!
  말 조심해! 낮말은 새가 듣고 밤말은 쥐가 듣잖아!

 **Dialog**

A: I think my teacher is kind of nasty.
B: Watch your tongue. You're going to be punished.

A: 선생님이 좀 치사한 것 같아.
B: 말 조심해. 혼나겠다.

Don't lie to me!

거짓말하지마!

lie to sb는 '…에게 거짓말하다' = tell a lie to sb. liar는 '거짓말쟁이.'

 Example

- If you lie to me, I will lie to you.
  네가 거짓말하면 나도 할거야.
- Don't lie to me. I've seen you kissing him.
  거짓말 마. 네가 그 남자랑 키스하는 걸 봤어.

 Dialog

A: Don't lie to me. I'm not that stupid.
B: I'm not kidding. I'm dead serious.

A: 거짓말하지마. 내가 그렇게 바보는 아니라고.
B: 농담아냐. 진심야.

Let me explain why I did it

내가 왜 그랬는지 설명할게

explain sth to sb는 '…에게 …을 설명하다.' explain that[why~] 형태도 가능.

 Example

- Would you mind explaining it to me?
  이것 좀 설명해줄래?
- Let me explain why I did it.
  내가 왜 그랬는지 설명할게

Dialog

A: I've got to tell you something.
B: No, no. You don't have to explain yourself to me.

A: 얘기할 게 있어.
B: 아냐. 내게 심중을 털어놓을 필요는 없어.

What does the FBI stand for?

FBI는 무엇을 상징해?

stand for는 '…을 의미하다,' '상징하다.' 약자 등을 풀어서 설명하는데 주로 사용한다.

Example

- This is symbolic of impressionist art.
  이건 인상주의 미술의 상징이야.

- He implied that we were lazy.
  걘 우리가 게으르다는 점을 넌지시 비췄어.

Dialog

A: Tell me what this means.
B: It is a symbol that stands for quiet.

A: 이게 뭘 의미하는 지 말해줘.
B: 이건 조용히 하라는 것을 의미하는 상징이야.

Guess What?

Hold your horse!

진정해!

달려가는 말을 세우라는 뜻으로 뭔가 천천히 하고, 인내심을 가져(a way of saying slow down and be more patient)라고 말하는 표현이다. 진정해, 흥분하지 말고 침착해 등의 의미인 이 표현은 Hold your horses!의 명령문 형태로 많이 쓰인다.

Feel free to give me a call
아무 때나 편하게 전화해

feel free to+V는 '편하게 …을 하다.' don't hesitate to+V와 비슷한 표현.

Example
- Feel free to stay here as long as you like.
  원하는 만큼 자유롭게 여기에 머무세요.
- Feel free to pick out whatever you need.
  필요한 거 아무 것이나 골라.

A: Thank you for your help with this report.
B: If there's anything else you need, feel free to ask.

A: 내 보고서 도와줘서 고마워.
B: 필요한 거 있으면 바로 말해.

Can I offer you some help?
제가 좀 도와드릴까요?

offer sb sth = offer sth to sb는 '…에게 …을 제안하다.'

Example
- Are you going to offer me a chance to work here?
  여기서 일할 기회를 줄건가요?
- I think we need to make an offer on the house.
  우리가 그 집 구매제안을 해야 될 것같아.

A: Why did you choose to take the job?
B: They offered a high salary to me.

A: 왜 일을 맡으려고 선택했니?
B: 걔들은 나한테 높은 봉급을 제의했어.

She almost forgot to come

걘 오는 것을 거의 잊을 뻔했어

almost forget은 잊지는 않은 경우. before I forget은 '내가 잊기 전에'라는 의미.

💡 **Example**

- Helen almost forgot to come.
  헬렌은 오는 것을 거의 잊을 뻔했어.
- Kevin totally forgot about the meeting.
  케빈은 그 회의에 대해 완전히 잊어버렸어.

A: Christmas day will be here soon.
B: I almost forgot to buy Christmas presents.
   A: 조만간 크리스마스가 될 거야.
   B: 크리스마스 선물 사는 걸 거의 잊을 뻔했어.

I forgot about our date

데이트하는 걸 잊었어

forget sth은 기억을 하지 못하는 경우, forget about~은 '신경쓰지 않고 잊어버리다.'

💡 **Example**

- I forgot about our date. I'm so sorry.
  데이트하는 걸 잊었어. 미안해.
- Don't let me forget her birthday.
  걔 생일을 내가 잊지 않게 해줘.

A: Will we be getting some ice cream?
B: Forget about it. We're going straight home.
   A: 우리 아이스크림 좀 먹어볼까?
   B: 잊어버려. 집으로 바로 갈 거야.

I forgot to lock the door

문 잠그는 것을 잊었어

forget to+V는 깜박 잊고 하지 못한 일을 말할 때. Don't forget to+V는 '…하는 것을 잊지 않다.'

💡 Example

- Please don't forget to make a backup of those files.
  그 파일들 복사본 꼭 만들어 놔.
- I forgot to tell you that the boss called.
  사장이 전화했다는 걸 말하는 걸 잊었어.

Dialog

A: Don't forget to fill out those forms today.
B: I'll leave them on your desk before I go.

A: 가기 전에 이 양식을 다 채우는 것 잊지마.
B: 제가 가기 전에 책상 위에 둘게요.

I'm sorry you feel that way

네가 그렇게 생각한다니 유감이네

feel that way는 '그렇게 생각하다.' that way는 '그런 식,' '그렇게'라는 말이다.

💡 Example

- I'm not at all surprised they feel that way.
  걔들이 그렇게 생각한다고 전혀 놀랍지는 않아.
- Not all married women feel that way.
  결혼한 여성들이 모두다 그렇게 생각하지는 않아.

Dialog

A: I think you're the most beautiful woman in the world.
B: Really? I'm surprised you feel that way.

A: 난 네가 이 세상에서 가장 아름다운 여자라고 생각해.
B: 정말? 그렇게 생각하다니 놀랍군.

Why didn't I think of that?

내가 왜 그 생각을 못했을까?

think of[about]은 '…을 생각하다,' think of[about] ~ing는 '…할 생각을 하다'(예정).

 Example

- What do you think of the new guy?
  새로 들어온 그 사람을 어떻게 생각해?
- Give me a few days to think about it.
  며칠 더 두고 볼게.

 Dialog

A: What do you think of cloning humans?
B: It is totally crazy. It seems immoral to me.

A: 인간복제에 대해서 어떻게 생각해?
B: 완전히 미친 짓이야. 도덕적으로 옳지 않은 것 같아.

I need to think it over

난 그걸 다시 생각해봐야 돼

think over sth or think sth over는 '신중히 생각하다' = think twice.

 Example

- You think it over. Call me back.
  신중히 생각해봐. 전화해.
- You need to think carefully before starting your own business.
  자영업을 시작하기 전에 신중하게 생각해야 해.

Dialog

A: I need to think over my choices.
B: You'll have to decide soon.

A: 난 내 선택에 대해 생각해볼 필요가 있어.
B: 넌 조만간 결정해야만 할 거야.

You should be more careful

좀 더 신중해야 돼

should+V는 강제성이 약한 의무조동사로 '…해야지' 정도로 생각하면 된다. = ought to+V

💡 Example

- You should put on a sweater. It's cold outside.
  스웨터입어. 밖에 날씨가 쌀쌀해.
- You should be more careful.
  좀 더 신중해야 돼.

 Dialog

A: You shouldn't put off that work for much longer.
B: I'll try and finish it before I go.

A: 그 일을 너무 오랫동안 미루어 두지 마라.
B: 열심히 해서 퇴근하기 전에는 끝내 놓을게.

You're meaner than I thought

넌 내가 생각했던 것보다 더 야비해

~than I thought[imagined, expected]는 뭔가 '예상보다 정도가 심할' 때 사용한다.

💡 Example

- You're not stupid. You're meaner than I thought.
  넌 멍청하지 않아. 내 생각보다 넌 더 야비해.
- My teacher is a lot smarter than I imagined.
  선생님이 내 생각보다 훨씬 더 똑똑하셔.

 Dialog

A: Your apartment is bigger than I thought.
B: Yeah, there's a lot of room in here.

A: 네 아파트는 내가 생각한 것보다 더 크구나.
B: 그래, 여기 공간이 많이 있네.

Do you believe in ghosts?

넌 유령이 있다고 믿어?

believe sth은 어떤 '사실을 믿다,' believe in~은 '존재를 믿다' 혹은 '…의 능력을 믿다.'

💡 **Example**

- Do you believe in ghosts?
  유령이 있다고 생각해?

- Is it still possible to believe in love at first sight?
  아직도 첫 눈에 반한다는 걸 믿을 수 있나?

 Dialog

A: I don't believe in our boss.
B: I know. I don't trust him either.

A: 난 보스에 대해 믿음이 없어.
B: 알아. 나도 보스를 신뢰하지 못해.

You can always depend on me

넌 언제나 나를 믿어도 돼

depend on은 '의존하다,' '…에 달려있다,' '신뢰하며 믿다' 등의 의미 = count[rely] on.

💡 **Example**

- I have a responsibility to those who depend on us.
  난 우리를 의존하고 있는 사람들에게 책임감을 갖고 있어.

- I usually read a book each month, depending on how busy I am.
  얼마나 바쁘냐에 따라 다르지만, 나는 대체로 매달 한 권 정도의 책을 읽어요.

 Dialog

A: Could you tell me where the closest subway station is?
B: It depends. Where do you want to go?

A: 제일 가까운 지하철역이 어딘가요?
B: 경우에 따라 다르죠. 어디에 가실 건데요?

I hope you like it

네 맘에 들었으면 좋겠어

hope to+V[that S+V]는 충분히 가능성이 있는 일이 일어나길 '희망하다.'

Example

- We hope they will attend our party.
  걔들이 우리 파티에 참석할 것을 바래.

- The win-win situation is what we all hope for.
  윈윈 상황은 바로 우리 모두가 바라던 거야.

Dialog

A: Thank you for the gift you sent on my birthday.
B: Oh, it was my pleasure. I hope you like it.

A: 내 생일에 보내준 선물 고마워.
B: 뭘 그런 걸 갖고. 네 맘에 들었으면 좋겠다.

I wish you good luck

행운을 빌어

wish to~는 hope to~와 달리 좀 형식적이고 공식적 상황에서 자주 쓰인다.

Example

- We wish to apologize for the late arrival of this train.
  기차 연착을 사죄 드립니다.

- I wish you good luck.
  행운을 빌어.

Dialog

A: I'll be starting my new job next week.
B: I wish you all the best at your new job.

A: 다음 주부터 새 직장에 출근해.
B: 새 직장에선 모든 게 잘 되길 빌어.

I'm responsible for customer service
난 고객서비스를 담당하고 있어
be responsible for sth[to sb]는 '…에 책임을 지다[…에게 책임이 있다].'

💡 **Example**

- I don't hold her responsible for the accident.
  쟤에게 그 사건의 책임이 있다고 생각하지 않아.
- We all should be responsible for our own children.
  우리 모두는 우리 자녀들에 대해 책임을 져야만 해.

 Dialog

A: My mother-in-law was responsible for breaking up our marriage.
B: How did she do that?

A: 시어머니가 우리 결혼을 깨트린 책임이 있었죠.
B: 시어머니가 뭘 했는데?

She's in need of a vacation
걘 휴가가 필요해
be in need of+N[~ing]는 '…을 필요로 하다.'

💡 **Example**

- They are in need of help studying.
  걔들은 공부에 도움을 필요로 해.
- I have patients in need of medical attention right now.
  나에겐 지금 치료가 필요한 환자들이 있어.

 Dialog

A: Can I get something for you?
B: I am in need of something to eat.

A: 뭐라도 갖다 드릴까요?
B: 난 뭔가 먹을 것이 필요해.

212

You need to get some rest
넌 좀 쉬어야 해

need to+V는 '스스로 필요성'을 인식하다이고, have to+V는 '외부적 요인'으로 해야 됨을 강조.

💡 **Example**

- I think you need to talk with the boss about it.
  이 문제로 사장과 얘기해야 될 것 같아.
- I need you to sign the document.
  서류에 서명을 해줘.

 Dialog

A: I need you to copy the minutes and distribute them.
B: To everybody or just the board members?

A: 이 의사록을 복사해서 나눠주도록 하게.
B: 모두에게요, 아니면 이사회 임원들에게 만요?

213

I don't need to pay for it
내가 그 비용을 지불할 것까진 없잖아

don't need to+V = don't have to+V. '…할 필요가 없다'라는 의미.

💡 **Example**

- I don't need to pay for it.
  내가 그 비용을 지불할 것까진 없잖아.
- You're right, I don't have to apologize.
  네 말이 맞아. 난 사과할 필요가 없어.

 Dialog

A: Have you asked to borrow her phone?
B: I don't need to borrow a phone now.

A: 걔 전화를 빌려달라고 요청했니?
B: 이제는 전화를 빌릴 필요가 없어.

214

Are you sure about that?
너 정말 그거 확실해?
be sure of[about]+N[~ing]는 '…을 확신하다.' be sure to+V는 '반드시 …하다.'

💡 **Example**

- You seem sure about the decision.
  그 결정에 확신이 있는 것 같은데요.

- I'm sure she's going to be all right.
  쟤는 괜찮아 질거라고 확신해.

 Dialog

A: I'm sure he wants to live with you.
B: You're sure? You're absolutely sure?

A: 걔가 너랑 살고 싶어하는 게 확실해.
B: 정말이야? 정말 확실한거야?

215

Korea is famous for K-pop
한국은 케이팝으로 유명하다
be famous for+N[~ing]는 '…으로 유명하다.' <=> be notorious for.

💡 **Example**

- The criminal is notorious for killing people.
  저 범죄인은 살인범으로 악명 높아.

- You know what the British people are famous for?
  영국인들이 뭐로 유명한지 아니?

 Dialog

A: Who is that tall man?
B: He is famous for being a basketball player.

A: 저기 키 큰 친구 누구야?
B: 걘 농구 선수로서 유명해.

216

He's known for helping others

걘 다른 사람들을 돕는 것으로 알려져 있어

be (well-)known for+N[~ing]는 '…로 (잘) 알려져 있다.'

💡 **Example**

- This restaurant is known for its spaghetti.
  이 식당은 스파게티로 알려져 있어.
- The electoral system is known for being corrupt.
  선거체계가 부패한 것으로 알려져 있어.

A: He's known for his smooth talk.
B: I'll keep that in mind when I run into him.
  A: 걘 부드러운 말로 사람을 홀리는 것으로 유명해.
  B: 다음에 만나게 되면 그 말 명심할게.

217

Seoul is popular with tourists

서울은 관광객들에게 인기가 있다

be popular with~는 '…에게 인기가 있다,' 즉 '유명하다'라는 의미이다.

💡 **Example**

- The Eiffel Tower is popular with tourists.
  에펠 타워는 관광객들에게 인기가 있어.
- Jan is the most popular girl in our school.
  얀은 학교에서 가장 인기가 높은 여자애야.

A: Rolex makes very nice watches.
B: They are popular with people who are rich.
  A: 롤렉스는 아주 좋은 시계를 만들어.
  B: 그 시계는 부자들에게 인기가 있지.

They are mean to Chris

걔네들은 크리스에게 짓궂게 대해

be mean to sb에서 mean은 형용사로 '비열하다'라는 의미 = nasty, gross.

Example

- It was a mean trick to steal her money.
  걔 돈을 훔치다니 정말 비열한 짓이었어.
- The smell near the toilet was gross.
  화장실 주변 냄새가 지독했어.

 Dialog

A: The kids were mean to Teddy.
B: Yeah, but I don't feel sorry for him.

A: 애들은 테디에게 짓궂게 대했어.
B: 그래, 하지만 테디가 불쌍하다는 생각이 들지 않아.

Don't be so cheap

치사하게 그러지마

be so cheap 역시 '치사하게 굴다,' '인색하다.'

Example

- Carl is so cheap that he doesn't buy presents.
  칼은 인색해서 선물을 사지 않아.
- My uncle was so cheap he never went on vacation.
  삼촌은 너무 지독해서 결코 휴가를 가지 않았어.

 Dialog

A: Are you going to pay for my dinner?
B: Don't be so cheap. Pay for yourself.

A: 저녁 식사비를 낼래?
B: 치사하게 그러지 마. 네 것은 네가 내.

I can't put up with his attitude

걔 태도는 도저히 못 참겠어

put up with~는 유명숙어로 '…을 참다.' 동의어 tolerate, endure는 좀 formal하다.

Example

- They can no longer put up with the cold temperatures.
  걔들은 추위를 더 이상 참을 수가 없어.
- Tom can't tolerate the slow Internet service.
  탐은 느린 인터넷서비스를 참을 수가 없어.

 Dialog

A: Is your shower still broken?
B: Yes, we can't put up with it anymore.

  A: 네 샤워기 아직도 고장 나있니?
  B: 어, 더이상 못참겠어.

I'm against the new proposal

새로운 제안에 난 반대야

be[go] against sb[sth]은 '…에 반대하다.' '찬성하다'는 be for~라고 하면 된다.

Example

- Stealing things is against the law.
  물건을 훔치는 일은 위법이지.
- I am against the new proposal.
  난 새로운 제안에 대해 반대야.

 Dialog

A: Everyone in class wants to take the exam today.
B: You can't go against your classmates.

  A: 학급 모두가 오늘 시험을 치르기를 원해.
  B: 넌 학급 아이들의 의견에 반대할 수 없어.

She refused to help me

걘 날 도와주지 않겠다고 했어

refuse to+V는 다른 사람의 요청이나 부탁을 '단호히 …하는 것을 거절하다.'

Example

- She refused to go swimming with me.
  걘 나랑 수영하러 가는 것을 거절했어.

- I refused to complete the assignment.
  난 그 과제를 완수하기를 거절했어.

A: Are you still angry at Mark?
B: Yeah, I refuse to answer his calls.

A: 넌 여전히 마크에게 화나 있니?
B: 응, 난 걔 전화를 받지 않아.

I agree with you

네 말에 동의해

agree with+sb/의견/생각은 '…에 동의하다,' agree to+제안/계획/요구는 '받아들이다.'

Example

- The company made an agreement with another firm.
  그 회사는 다른 회사와 합의를 했어.

- What I'd like to say is we agreed on a plan.
  내 말은 우리가 어떤 계획에 동의했다는거야.

A: We should try to improve our school.
B: I agree with you. What should we do first?

A: 우린 우리 학교를 개선하려고 노력해야 돼.
B: 동의해. 우리가 뭐부터 먼저 해야 돼?

You've got a point

일리가 있어

have a point는 '일리가 있다,' 상대방의 말이 good idea이거나 good suggestion일 때.

💡 Example

- That's right. You've got a point.
  맞아. 일리가 있어.

- I have a point to make about our workplace.
  난 우리 작업장에 대해 할 말이 있어.

A: My father told me to quit smoking.
B: He has a point. You'll be healthier.

A: 아버지는 내게 담배를 끊으라고 말했어.
B: 일리가 있는 말이지. 그러면 더 건강해질거야.

Be careful of scams on the internet

인터넷 사기를 조심해

be careful of~는 '…을 조심하다,' be careful to+V는 '…하도록 조심하다.'

💡 Example

- Be careful about driving too fast.
  과속하지 않도록 조심해.

- Be careful when you are out after dark.
  어두워진 후에 외출할 때 조심해.

A: Be careful of people selling things on the subway.
B: I know. Some of the items are really junk.

A: 지하철에서 물건을 파는 사람들을 조심해.
B: 알아요. 일부 물건들은 정말로 쓰레기죠.

Look out for cars!

차를 조심해!

look out (for)~는 '주의를 경계하다,' '찾다', '돌보다' 등의 의미로도 쓰인다.

💡 **Example**

- Look out for cars when you cross the street.
  길을 건널 때 차들을 조심해.
- Look out for the construction site.
  건축 현장 주변에서는 조심해라.

 Dialog

A: I'm going to visit several different countries.
B: Look out for thieves near your hotel.

A: 난 여러 다른 나라들을 방문할 거야.
B: 네 호텔 주변에 있는 도둑들을 조심해.

Don't pay attention to rumors

루머는 신경쓰지마

pay attention to~는 '…에 주의를 기울이다' = give attention to.

💡 **Example**

- I told you not to pay attention to rumors.
  루머 신경쓰지 말라고 말했잖아?
- Pay attention to the things I tell you.
  내가 너한테 말한 것에 주의를 기울여라.

 Dialog

A: Pay attention to this part of the textbook.
B: Are we going to be tested on it?

A: 교재 중 이 부분에 주의를 기울여.
B: 이 부분에 대해 시험을 볼 건가요?

Watch out when you cross the street

길 건널 때 조심해

watch out (for)~는 '조심하다,' '경계하다.' 상대방에게 충고할 때 사용한다.

Example
- Watch for the water that spilled on the floor.
  바닥에 흘린 물을 조심해.
- Watch out when you cross the bridge.
  다리를 건널 때 조심해.

A: We're going out to a nightclub tonight.
B: Watch out if Dave starts drinking whiskey.

A: 우린 오늘 밤 나이트클럽에 갈 거야.
B: 데이브가 위스키를 마시기 시작하는지 지켜봐.

He's likely to get the job

걘 그 일을 얻을 가능성이 있어

be likely to+V는 '…하기 쉽다.' likely 앞에 more[less]를 넣어 가능성의 정도를 표현한다.

Example
- They are likely to attend the meeting together.
  걔들이 함께 회의에 참석하기 쉬워.
- I am likely to travel to Washington, D.C. next month.
  난 다음 달 워싱턴 DC로 여행할 것 같아.

A: Jonas has a very good singing voice.
B: He is likely to become a successful singer.

A: 요나스는 노래하는 목소리가 무척 좋아.
B: 성공적인 가수가 될 가능성이 커.

It may be worth a try
그렇게 해볼 가치가 있을거야
be worth+N[~ing]는 '…할 가치가 있다,' be worthy of+N은 '…할만한 가치가 있다.'

💡 **Example**

- It may be worth a try.
  그래도 해봄직 할거야.

- It's not worth the trouble to complete the report.
  고생해서 보고서를 끝낼 가치가 없어.

 Dialog

A: Is this old coin valuable?
B: No, it is worth very little.
  A: 이 오래된 동전은 가치가 있니?
  B: 아니, 가치가 거의 없어.

I don't have an interest in art
난 예술에 관심이 없어
be interested in(감정 등) = have a interest(관심분야, formal) = take an interest(새롭게 관심 갖다)

💡 **Example**

- Are you interested in working some overtime?
  초과근무 좀 할 생각 있어?

- She's not interested in working for us.
  걘 우리와 일하는 것에 관심이 없어.

 Dialog

A: I'm interested in the new golf class.
B: Me too! Why don't we join together this Saturday?
  A: 난 새로 생긴 골프 교실에 관심이 있어.
  B: 나도! 이번 토요일에 같이 가보는 게 어때?

She's anxious to meet me

걘 나를 만나고 싶어 안달이야

be anxious to+V는 '…을 무척 하고 싶어하다,' be anxious about[for]~는 '…을 걱정하다.'

Example

- Mom is anxious to finish paying the taxes.
  엄마는 세금을 완납하고 싶어 안달이셔.

- I'm so anxious to hear your decision
  네 결정을 무척이나 듣고 싶구나.

 Dialog

A: Have the exam results been announced?
B: No, I'm anxious to see my score.

A: 그 시험결과가 발표가 되었니?
B: 아니, 내 점수를 무척 알고 싶어.

We're willing to help you

우린 너를 기꺼이 도와줄게

be willing to+V는 '기꺼이 …하다,' '흔쾌히 …하다.'

Example

- I'm willing to do anything to help her career.
  걔 경력에 도움된다면 뭐라도 하겠어.

- I'm willing to work on Saturdays until my vacation.
  휴가까지 토요일마다 일할 용의 있어.

 Dialog

A: Now let's talk turkey.
B: We're willing to pay you half the asking price.

A: 이제 솔직히 이야기해 봅시다.
B: 제시한 금액의 반이라면 두말 않고 내겠어요.

I don't feel like eating now

난 지금 먹고 싶지 않아

feel like ~ing는 '…하고 싶다,' feel like+N[S+V]는 '…와 같은 느낌이다.'

💡 **Example**

- I feel like having a nice cold beer right now.
  지금 시원한 맥주가 당기는데.
- So what do you feel like having for lunch?
  그래 점심으로 뭘 하고 싶니?

A: Do you feel like shopping with me?
B: Sure! I need to buy some new clothes.

A: 나랑 쇼핑하고 싶어?
B: 그럼. 새 옷을 몇 벌 사야 돼.

Do you want to come with me?

나와 함께 가고 싶어?

want to+V는 '…하고 싶다,' want sb to+V는 '…가 …하기를 바라다.'

💡 **Example**

- What do you want to have for lunch?
  점심으로 뭘 먹고 싶니?
- You want me to lie to my boss?
  나보고 사장한테 거짓말을 하라는거야?

A: Everyone wants you to sing a song.
B: I'm not going to sing tonight.

A: 모두가 네가 노래하는 것을 원해.
B: 난 오늘 밤 노래하지 않을 거야.

I'd like to ask you a question

질문 하나 하고 싶어

would like to+V는 '지금 …을 하고 싶다,' like to+V는 '일반적으로 좋아한다.'

Example

- I'd like you to think about that.
  그거에 대해 생각해 보라고.
- I'd like a nice notebook computer.
  난 좋은 노트북 컴퓨터를 원해.

A: I've heard about the Great Wall of China.
B: Would you like to go and visit it?

A: 난 만리장성에 대해 들었어.
B: 가고 싶지 않니?

Who is your favorite player?

어느 선수를 제일 좋아하니?

be one's favorite는 '…가 가장 좋아하는 것이다'라는 의미.

Example

- LA Dodgers is my favorite team.
  LA 다저스가 내가 가장 좋아하는 팀이야.
- Documentaries are also one of my favorite things to watch.
  다큐멘터리도 역시 내가 선호하는 프로 중 하나야.

A: I really love the Argentina soccer team.
B: That's great! Who is your favorite player?

A: 난 아르헨티나 축구팀을 정말로 좋아해.
B: 훌륭해! 어느 선수를 제일 좋아하니?

It's like talking to a wall

벽하고 얘기하는거 같아

be like+N[~ing] 혹은 be like S+V는 '마치 …와 같다,' '…처럼 느껴진다'라는 의미.

💡 Example

- It's like prices go higher every year.
  매년 가격이 오르는 것 같아.
- It's like work is becoming more difficult.
  일이 계속 어려워지는 것 같아.

A: Have you eaten at the new restaurant?
B: Sure. It's like my mom's cooking there.

A: 그 새 식당에서 먹어봤니?
B: 그럼. 마치 엄마가 요리한 것 같아.

I feel like such a loser

난 실패자로 느껴져

feel like+N[S+V]은 '…처럼 느껴진다'라는 의미.

💡 Example

- I feel like he doesn't like me.
  걔가 날 싫어하는 것 같아.
- I feel like fast food is making me fat.
  패스트푸드가 날 살찌게 만드는 것 같아.

A: I feel like such a loser. I have no friends.
B: That's not true. I'm your friend.

A: 난 실패자로 느껴져. 친구가 없어.
B: 사실이 아냐. 내가 친구잖아.

240

It seems like we can leave
우리가 떠날 수 있을 것 같아
seem like+N[S+V]는 '…인 것 같다'라는 빈출표현이다.

Example
- It seems like his mood is good.
  걔 기분이 좋은 것 같아.
- She seems like she will quit school.
  걔 학교를 그만둘 것 같이 보여.

A: Are you ready to start our trip?
B: Yes, it seems like we can leave.
  A: 넌 우리 여행을 떠날 준비가 되었니?
  B: 응, 우리가 떠날 수 있을 것 같아.

241

She seems to be ready to start
걔 시작할 준비가 되어 있는 것 같아
seem to+V는 '…하는 것 같다,' seem that S+V는 '…인 것 같아,' seem+형용사는 '…처럼 보인다.'

Example
- It seems that George doesn't want to study.
  조지는 공부를 원치 않는 것 같아.
- She seems to be ready to start.
  걔 시작할 준비가 되어 있는 것 같아.

A: What is Brian's favorite food?
B: He seems to like ice cream the best.
  A: 브라이언이 좋아하는 음식은 뭐니?
  B: 아이스크림을 가장 좋아하는 것 같아.

Sounds like a plan

좋은 계획같아, 좋아

sound like+N[S+V]는 '…인 것처럼 들린다.' sound+형용사는 '…한 것처럼 보인다.'

 Example

- You sound angry with your boyfriend.
  넌 남친한테 화난 것처럼 보이네.
- You sound sick today. Are you OK?
  넌 오늘 아픈 것처럼 보이는데 괜찮니?

Dialog

A: It sounds like a storm is coming.
B: I hear thunder in the distance too.

A: 폭풍이 오고 있는 것 같아.
B: 나도 멀리서 천둥소리가 들려.

Guess What?

So you're off the hook for now?
그럼 이제 거기서 벗어난거야?

"낚시 고리(hook)에서 벗어난"이라는 의미로 비유적으로 뭔가의 책임을 지지 않다, 혹은 받아야 했을지도 모를 벌을 받지 않다(a person no longer is responsible for something, or will not receive some punishment that might have been given out)라는 뜻으로 사용된다. get sb off the hook도 많이 쓰이는데 …을 살려주다, 봐주다라는 의미.

243

Sure thing. I'll email it right away
알겠어. 지금 바로 이메일 보낼게
sure thing은 '확실하지,' '그럼'이란 의미로 '형용사+명사' 형태의 표현이 부사처럼 쓰이는 경우.

Example
- **Sure thing,** she is coming over now.
  확실해, 걔가 이제 올 거야.
- Can you give me a hand moving it? – **Sure thing.**
  그것 옮기는데 도와줄 수 있니? – 그럼.

**Dialog**

A: Yeah, we have to make an effort to stay in touch.
B: **Sure thing.** Bye!

　A: 그래 서로 만나도록 노력하자.
　B: 물론, 잘 가!

244

I'm so excited to see you again
너 다시 보게 되어 넘 좋아
be excited about[to+V]~은 '…에 무척 좋아하다,' '들뜨다.'

Example
- **Are** you **excited about** celebrating Christmas?
  성탄절 축하파티를 하는 게 좋아?
- **I'm so excited to** see you again.
  너 다시 보게 되어 넘 좋아.

**Dialog**

A: They **are excited about** going overseas.
B: I think it will be a fun trip.

　A: 걔네들은 해외 가는데 들떠 있어.
　B: 재미 있는 여행이 될 거야.

Are you happy with that?

거기에 대해 만족해?

be happy with~는 '…에 만족하다.' be happy 다음에 with, about, for 및 to+부정사가 올 수 있다.

💡 **Example**

- Are you happy with that?
  거기에 대해 만족해?

- You sound happy about your meeting.
  회의에 만족스러운 것 같아.

 Dialog

A: I wanted to let you know I'm getting divorced.
B: But why? You seemed so happy with your husband.

　A: 이혼한다고 알려주고 싶었어.
　B: 왜? 남편과 행복해 보였는데.

I'm feels comfortable in casual clothes

난 캐주얼한 옷을 입을 때 편안함을 느껴

feel comfortable with는 '…에 기분이 좋다.' feel comfortable with sb ~ing는 '…가 …하는걸 편하게 생각하다.'

💡 **Example**

- Do you feel uncomfortable with those shoes?
  저 신발 불편해?

- He feels comfortable with his kind boss.
  걘 상냥한 사장에 기분이 편해.

 Dialog

A: I'd like you to sing a song for us.
B: I feel uncomfortable with so many people here.

　A: 우릴 위해 노래를 불러줘.
　B: 난 여기 많은 사람들 앞이라 불편해.

I feel much better now

이제 기분이 더 좋아

feel much better about[A ~ing]은 '기분이 더 좋다.'

💡 Example
- She was just trying to make you feel better.
  걘 널 기분좋게 해주려는 거였어
- I'll feel much better in the morning.
  아침에 기분이 더 좋아질 거야.

 Dialog

A: I certainly hope you are feeling better.
B: I am. Thank you so much.

A: 난 진짜 네 기분이 나아졌으면 좋겠어.
B: 그래. 정말 고마워.

I feel sad about her dying.

걔가 죽어서 슬퍼

feel[bad] sad about~는 '…에 슬퍼하다,' feel sad about A ~ing는 'A가 …해서 슬프다.'

💡 Example
- Jane felt sad about the movie's ending.
  제인은 영화의 마지막에 슬퍼했어.
- I feel sad when the Christmas holiday ends.
  성탄절 휴가가 끝났을 때 슬펐어.

 Dialog

A: I feel sad about my uncle dying.
B: Yes, he was a good man and we'll miss him.

A: 내 삼촌이 돌아가셔서 슬퍼.
B: 그래, 좋은 분이셨는데 그리울 거야.

Why are you so angry with me?

왜 나한테 그렇게 화가 난거야?

get[be] angry with[at, about sb ~ing]는 '화나다.' 사람이 올 때는 at이나 with를 쓴다.

Example
- I don't have any reason to be angry at you.
  난 네게 화날 아무런 이유가 없어.
- The problem is that the boss is still angry with you.
  문제는 사장이 아직도 너한테 화가 나있다는 거야.

 Dialog

A: Why are you so angry with me?
B: Because you always take his side.

A: 왜 나한테 그렇게 화가 난 거야?
B: 네가 항상 그 친구 편만 들잖아.

I'm mad at my boss

나 사장한테 화났어

get[be] mad at[about]~은 '화나다.' 단 ~mad about sb는 문맥에 따라 '무척 좋아하다.'

Example
- I got mad at him because he took my money.
  걔가 내 돈을 가져가 화났어.
- Don't worry, I'm not going to get mad.
  걱정마, 화 안낼게

 Dialog

A: I'm mad at my boss.
B: Oh? Why is that?

A: 나 사장한테 화났어.
B: 이런, 뭣 때문에?

251

She's worried about losing her job

걘 직장을 잃을까 봐 걱정하고 있어

be worried about~[that S+V]은 (감정/상태) '걱정하다.' worry about은 행동에 중점을 둔 표현.

Example
- I'm a little worried about my singing ability.
  내 노래 실력이 좀 걱정돼.
- I'm worried you might be little cold.
  네가 좀 춥지 않을까 걱정돼.

 Dialog

A: I'm worried Pam won't come to the party.
B: Why? Is she still angry with you?

A: 팸이 파티에 못 올까 봐 걱정돼.
B: 왜? 아직도 너한테 화나 있어?

252

Never mind that

그거 신경쓰지마

never mind A는 'A를 신경쓰지 않다,' '걱정하지 않다.'

Example
- Never mind that.
  그거 신경쓰지마.
- Does it bother you to go to the store every day?
  매일 가게 가는거 귀찮지?

 Dialog

A: My friend was saying that I'm ugly.
B: Never mind. He's just teasing.

A: 친구가 내가 못생겼다고 그래.
B: 너무 신경쓰지마. 그냥 놀리는거야.

Don't worry about me

내 걱정하지마

worry about은 걱정하는 '행동'을 의미하며 주로 명령문 등 조언을 할 때 사용된다.

💡 Example

- You don't need to worry about that.
  그거 걱정할 필요없어.

- I'm not going to die that easy. Don't worry about that.
  난 그렇게 쉽게 죽지 않을 거야. 걱정마.

🧠 Dialog

A: This is dangerous. You've got to be careful.
B: Don't worry about me.

A: 이 일은 위험해. 조심해야 한다구.
B: 내 걱정하지마.

I regret the day I met you

널 만난 날이 후회된다

regret sth[~ing]은 '…을 후회하다.' regret the day S+V는 '…한 날을 후회하다.'

💡 Example

- I regret the day I met you.
  널 만난 날이 후회된다.

- I'm sure he doesn't regret it that much.
  걔가 그렇게까지 후회하지는 않을거야.

🧠 Dialog

A: Don't you regret anything about your past?
B: No. If I had the chance, I'd do it all over again.

A: 넌 지난 과거가 후회되지 않니?
B: 아니. 기회가 온다면 또 다시 그렇게 할거야.

Say thank you to your wife

네 아내에게 고맙다고 해

say thank you to sb[for sth]는 '…에(게) 감사하다'는 말을 하다.

Example

- You must say thank you for his help.
  걔 도움에 넌 감사해야 돼.
- Say thank you for the new cell phone.
  신형 핸드폰에 감사하라고.

Dialog

A: Say thank you to your grandfather.
B: Grandpa, thanks for buying me a birthday gift.

A: 할아버지께 감사하다고 해라.
B: 할아버지, 생일 선물 사주셔서 감사해요.

I'm sorry what I said

내가 한 말에 미안해

be[feel] sorry for+N[~ing]는 '…에 미안해하다,' '유감이다.' be sorry what~도 가능하다.

Example

- I'm sorry for being late to work.
  출근이 늦어서 미안하다.
- He is sorry for making everyone angry.
  걘 모두를 화나게 해서 미안하대.

Dialog

A: I feel so sorry for my mother. She's all alone.
B: That must be difficult at her age.

A: 어머니가 참 안돼 보여. 항상 혼자시거든.
B: 그 연세엔 그게 견디기 힘들지.

I'm a big fan of LA Dodgers

난 LA 다저스 광팬이야

be a big fan of~는 '…을 무척 좋아하다.' 뒤에 음식이나 사물 등이 올 수도 있다.

 Example

- He's not a big fan of fried foods.
  걔는 튀김류 음식을 크게 좋아하지는 않아.
- We are big fans of our local football team.
  우린 동네 축구팀의 열렬 팬들이야.

 Dialog

A: **I'm a big fan of Justin Beiber.**
B: **Really? I've never heard of him.**

A: 난 저스틴 비버를 무척 좋아해.
B: 정말로? 난 이름도 못 들어 봤는데.

I like to jog in the morning

난 아침에 조깅하는 걸 좋아해

like to+V는 would like to+V와 달리 '…하는 것을 일반적으로 좋아하는' 것을 말한다.

 Example

- I like to jog in the morning.
  난 아침에 조깅하는 걸 좋아해.
- I like to get outdoors too.
  난 외출하는 것도 좋아해.

Dialog

A: **What do you do on Saturdays?**
B: **I stay at home. I like to watch soccer games.**

A: 토요일마다 뭘 하세요?
B: 집에 있어요. 축구경기 보는 걸 좋아하거든요.

139

I prefer to be alone

혼자 있고 싶어

prefer N[~ing]는 '…을 더 좋아하다,' prefer A to B는 'B보다 A를 더 좋아하다.'

💡 **Example**

- I prefer indoor sports to outdoor one.
  실외 운동보다는 실내 운동을 좋아해
- I prefer to be alone. Please leave.
  혼자 있고 싶어. 그만 가줘.

 Dialog

A: Why are you always here in the library?
B: I prefer studying rather than going out.

A: 넌 왜 항상 이 도서실에 있니?
B: 난 외출하는 것 보다 공부하는 것을 더 좋아해.

I'm surprised to see you smoking

네가 담배피는거 보고 놀랐어

be surprised at[by]는 '…에 놀라다,' be surprised to see~는 '…을 보고 놀라다.'

💡 **Example**

- He was surprised at Sarah's anger.
  걘 사라의 분노에 대해 놀래 버렸어.
- Don't be surprised by the strange costumes.
  이상한 옷차림에 대해 놀라지마.

 Dialog

A: Many people came to our rally today.
B: Yeah, I'm surprised by how many are here.

A: 많은 사람들이 오늘 집회에 참석했지.
B: 그래, 얼마나 많이 참석했는지 놀랬어.

I feel sympathy for fat people

난 뚱뚱한 사람들에 동정심을 느껴

feel[have] sympathy for~는 '…을 동정하다.'

💡 **Example**

- She felt sympathy for her younger sister.
  걘 자신의 여동생에 대해 동정심을 느꼈지.
- I feel sympathy for the newest students.
  난 가장 신참 학생들에 대해 동정심을 느껴.

A: I don't have sympathy for fat people.
B: I know. They should go on a diet.

A: 난 뚱뚱한 사람들에겐 동정을 할 수 없어.
B: 알고 있지. 걔들은 다이어트를 해야 돼.

I'm fed up with this weather

이런 날씨 정말 지긋지긋해

be fed up with+N[~ing]는 '…에 질리다,' '지겹다,' '싫증나다.'

💡 **Example**

- Everyone is fed up with the freezing temperatures.
  모두가 영하의 기온에 질렸어.
- Lisa is fed up with her noisy neighbors.
  리사는 시끄러운 이웃들에 진절머리가 났어.

A: I'm fed up with the food in this cafeteria.
B: It really needs to be improved.

A: 이 카페테리아 음식에 완전히 질렸어.
B: 정말로 질적으로 나아져야 해.

I'm sick of her lies

걔 거짓말에는 넌더리가 나

be sick of+N[~ing] 역시 '질리다,' '넌더리가 나다'라는 의미.

💡 Example

- You said you were sick of this.
  이건 지겹다고 했잖아.

- I'm sick of her lies.
  걔 거짓말에는 넌더리가 나.

 Dialog

A: I'm really getting sick of winter.
B: I don't like winter all that much myself.

A: 난 정말 겨울이 지겨워.
B: 나도 겨울이 그렇게 좋지는 않아.

I'm ashamed of you

난 네가 부끄러워

be ashamed of+N[~ing, to+V]는 '…를 부끄러워하다,' '창피해하다.'

💡 Example

- You stole the money. I'm ashamed of you.
  넌 돈을 훔쳤어. 부끄러운 일이야.

- I am ashamed of the problems I created.
  난 내가 자초한 문제들로 부끄럽게 생각해.

 Dialog

A: You should be ashamed of cheating on your exam.
B: What's the big deal? A lot of students do it.

A: 컨닝한 걸 수치스러워해야지.
B: 뭘 그런 걸 갖고? 학생들 많이 그래.

I feel humiliated now

난 지금 굴욕적인 느낌이야

feel[be] humiliated는 '굴욕을 당하다,' '수치스럽다.'

💡 Example

- The team felt humiliated after losing the game.
  그 팀은 경기에서 진 후 망신을 당했어.
- I felt humiliated when I failed the exam.
  난 시험에 떨어져서 창피를 당했어.

Dialog

A: So, your boyfriend was seeing other women?
B: It's true. I feel humiliated now.

A: 그래, 네 남친이 딴 여자를 만나고 있다며?
B: 사실이야. 난 지금 굴욕적인 느낌이야.

He is too shy to do that

걘 그러기에는 너무 수줍음을 타

be shy to~는 '수줍어 …하지 못하다,' be shy of[about] ~ing은 '…까지는 하지 않다.'

💡 Example

- I was too shy to accept a date with him.
  너무 수줍어 걔의 데이트신청을 거절했어.
- The children are too shy to talk to me.
  얘들은 너무 부끄러워 내게 말을 못 걸어.

Dialog

A: Is Melissa going to sing for the crowd?
B: No, she is too shy to do that.

A: 멜리사가 사람들을 위해 노래를 부를 거니?
B: 아니, 걘 그러기에는 너무 수줍음을 타.

I'm so proud of you

네가 정말 자랑스러워

be proud of~는 '…을 자랑스러워하다.' of 이하에는 자랑스러워하는 사람[사물]을 넣는다.

Example

- I'm so proud of your recent promotion. Here's to you!
  얼마 전 승진한 거 정말 축하해요. 위하여!

- I'm proud of you all. You make me proud.
  여러분 모두가 자랑스러워. 너희들 때문에 내가 뿌듯해.

Dialog

A: I got the highest score in the class!
B: Way to go! I'm so proud of you.

A: 내가 우리 반에서 제일 좋은 점수를 받았어!
B: 잘했구나! 네가 정말 자랑스러워.

I'm impressed with your hard work

열심히 일하는 모습이 인상적이네

be impressed by[with]~는 '…에 감동받다,' make an impression upon은 '인상을 남기다.'

Example

- I'm impressed with the amount of money you made.
  네가 번 돈 규모가 매우 인상적이야.

- You did a good job! I was very impressed.
  정말 잘 했어! 매우 인상적이었어.

Dialog

A: I'm impressed with your hard work.
B: Really? Do you think I'm ready for a promotion?

A: 열심히 일하는 모습이 인상적이네요.
B: 정말인가요? 제가 곧 승진할 것 같아요?

Are you crazy? That's dangerous!

너 미쳤어? 그건 위험해!

be crazy는 기본적으로 '미치다'이지만 be crazy about+N하면 '…에 푹 빠지다'라는 뜻.

💡 **Example**

- The old woman down the street was crazy.
  저 길 끝에 있는 여자는 제 정신아냐.
- You're crazy if you don't plan your future.
  미래를 계획하지 않으면 넌 정신이 나간거야.

 Dialog

A: The World Cup fans spent thousands of dollars to attend.
B: They are crazy to spend that much money.

A: 월드컵 팬들은 경기를 참관하려고 수천 불을 지불했어.
B: 그렇게 많은 돈을 쓰다니 미쳤구만.

Try to calm down. OK?

진정하라고. 알았어?

calm down은 '진정하다'라는 의미의 대표 구동사. 명령형으로 많이 쓰인다.

💡 **Example**

- It was raining hard, but now it has calmed down.
  비가 많이 오다 이제 좀 그쳤어.
- Look guys, try to calm down. OK?
  얘들아, 진정해. 알았어?

 Dialog

A: Some of my friends got really angry today.
B: How long did it take them to calm down?

A: 일부 내 친구들은 오늘 정말로 화를 냈어.
B: 걔들이 진정하는데 얼마나 걸리디?

271

Keep cool and don't yell

침착해, 소리 지르지마

keep[stay] cool은 흥분과 초조하지 않고 안정된 상태를 유지하다.

💡 **Example**

- It's best to keep cool when you're in trouble.
  어려움에 처했을 때 침착한 게 최고야.

- I kept cool when my boss visited my office.
  보스가 내 사무실을 방문했을 때 난 침착을 유지했지.

 Dialog

A: Randy is always making me angry.
B: Keep cool. Don't let him bother you.

A: 랜디는 항상 나를 화나게 해.
B: 침착해라. 걔에 대해 신경쓰지마.

272

Just take it easy and try to relax

걱정하지 말고 긴장을 풀어봐

take it easy는 '서두르지 않다,' '화내지 않다,' 헤어질 때 say goodbye라는 의미.

💡 **Example**

- Take it easy when you're driving on the highway.
  고속도로 운전할 때 편안하게 해.

- Just take it easy and try to relax.
  걱정하지 말고 긴장을 풀어봐.

 Dialog

A: I'm looking forward to getting to know you.
B: Take it easy. We have a lot of time.

A: 널 빨리 알게 되고 싶어.
B: 진정하라고. 우리 시간이 많잖아.

It's going to be all right
괜찮아 질거야

be all right (with/for/to~)은 '괜찮다,' '좋다,' go all right은 문제없이 '잘 되다'라는 뜻.

💡 **Example**

- It's all right with me.
  난 괜찮아.

- It's going to be all right.
  괜찮을거야.

 **Dialog**

A: Honey, everything's going to be all right.
B: What do you know?

A: 자기야, 다 잘 될거야.
B: 네가 그걸 어떻게 알아?

Guess What?

I got it straight from the horse's mouth
당사자로부터 직접 들었어

말의 이빨을 보면 말의 정확한 나이를 알 수 있다는 것에서 발전한 이 표현으로 뭔가 정보를 믿을 만한 사람이나 당사자로부터 직접 들었다(get information directly from the main person or people involved)는 것을 뜻한다. 동사로는 hear나 get이 쓰인다.

It's not that bad

그렇게 까지 나쁘지 않아

be not bad(괜찮은 편이다)에서 that이 추가된 것으로 '그렇게까지 나쁘지 않다'라는 의미.

 Example

- Studying English is not that bad.
  영어를 공부하는 것은 그리 어렵지 않아.
- This old movie is not that bad.
  그 흘러간 영화가 그렇게 나쁘지는 않아.

Dialog

A: Many people said they don't like McDonald's food.
B: It's not that bad. You should try it.

A: 많은 사람들이 맥도날드 음식을 싫어한다고 말했어.
B: 그리 나쁘지 않아. 한번 먹어 봐.

I'm okay with that

그거 좋아

be okay with+N[~ing]는 '좋다,' be okay with sb ~ing는 '…가 …하는게 괜찮다,' '좋다.'

 Example

- All of the people in the accident are okay.
  사고를 당한 사람들 모두 괜찮아.
- It is okay for you to go out with my sister.
  내 여동생과 데이트해도 괜찮아.

Dialog

A: Look, Charlie, it's going to be okay.
B: That's easy for you to say.

A: 자, 찰리야, 잘 될거야
B: 넌 그렇게 말하기 쉽겠지.

I have no problem with that

난 괜찮아

have no problem with~는 '별 문제없다.' with 이하에는 사람이나 일.

- I have no problem with people who have different religions.
  난 다른 종교를 가진 사람들과 아무런 문제가 없어요.
- We have no problem with waiting for you.
  우린 널 기다리는데 아무런 문제가 안돼.

Dialog

A: Is it OK if I come to work ten minutes late?
B: Sure. I have no problem with that.

A: 10분 정도 늦게 출근해도 되나요?
B: 그럼요. 괜찮아요.

If it's okay with you, I'm leaving

네가 괜찮으면 난 갈게

if it's okay with you는 (부탁하면서) '네가 괜찮다면' = if you don't mind.

- I'll come at eleven thirty if that's okay with you.
  괜찮다면 11시 반에 오겠습니다.
- If it's okay with you, I'll take tomorrow off instead of Monday.
  괜찮다면 월요일 대신 내일 쉬었으면 해.

Dialog

A: If it's okay with you, I'll take tomorrow off.
B: Let me check the schedule.

A: 괜찮으면 내일 쉬고 싶은데요.
B: 일정 좀 보고.

You had better take this book
이 책을 가져가는게 좋을거야
had better는 친구나 아랫사람에게 하는 말로 '…해라.' 충고나 경고할 때.

Example
- You had better finish the report soon.
  보고서를 빨리 완성하는 편이 나아.
- They had better pay me my money.
  걔들은 내 돈을 갚는 편이 좋아.

A: We had better do the dishes tonight.
B: Yeah, otherwise the kitchen will be dirty.
  A: 우린 오늘 밤 설거지하는 게 나아.
  B: 그래, 안 그러면 주방이 더러워질 거야.

I have to go now
난 이제 가야 돼
have to+V = have got to+V는 '…을 해야 한다.' 과거는 had to~, 미래는 will have to.

Example
- Do you have to work this weekend?
  이번 주말에 일해야 돼?
- I don't have to pay him any money.
  난 걔한테 어떤 돈도 갚을 필요가 없어.

A: I have to leave right away for the meeting.
B: I'll catch up with you later.
  A: 회의가 있어서 지금 당장 가봐야겠는데.
  B: 나중에 다시 전화하지 뭐.

You must keep trying

계속 시도해봐야 돼

must는 의무 조동사중 가장 '강제성'이 강하다.

Example

- You must do the laundry tonight.
  너 오늘 밤 세탁해야 해.

- Each student must do extra homework.
  학생들 모두 다 추가 숙제를 해야 돼.

A: I can't find a good job.
B: Never say die. You must keep trying.

A: 적당한 일자리를 찾을 수가 없네.
B: 약한 소리 마. 계속 시도해봐야 한다구.

He was forced to cancel the trip

걘 여행을 취소할 수밖에 없었어

be forced to+V는 본인 의지와 상관없이 '억지로, 강제적으로 …하다.'

Example

- He was forced to listen to the music.
  걘 음악을 억지로 들었어.

- They were forced to help with the crime.
  그들은 그 범죄를 방조해야만 했어.

A: What happened when you didn't get a visa?
B: I was forced to leave the country right away.

A: 비자를 얻지 못해서 어떻게 됐니?
B: 즉시 그 나라를 떠나야 했어.

I can't help thinking about her

걔를 생각하지 않을 수가 없어

can't help+N[~ing] = can't help but+V는 '…하지 않을 수 없다.'

💡 **Example**
- She can't help drinking so much alcohol.
  갠 술을 많이 마시지 않을 수가 없어.
- I can't help being cautious.
  조심할 수밖에 없어.

 **Dialog**

A: Just forget about your ex-girlfriend.
B: I try, but I can't help thinking about her.

A: 옛 여친을 그냥 잊어버려라.
B: 해보는데, 그녀를 생각하지 않을 수가 없어.

I can't stop eating junk food

난 정크푸드를 끊을 수가 없어

can't stop ~ing는 하던 것을 끊을 수가 없음을 말한다.

💡 **Example**
- John can't stop eating junk food.
  존은 정크 푸드를 끊을 수가 없어.
- My son can't stop playing video games.
  내 아들은 비디오 게임을 중단할 수가 없어.

 **Dialog**

A: Could you just shut up for a little while?
B: I can't stop singing to myself.

A: 잠시만이라도 입을 닥쳐줄래?
B: 흥얼거리지 않을 수가 없어.

Things will get better soon
곧 더 나아질거야
get better는 '좋아지다,' '나아지다' <=> get worse는 '상태가 더 나빠지다.'

 **Example**

- There's a chance he can get better.
  걔가 나아질 가능성이 있어.
- I'd like to get better at speaking English.
  영어회화 실력이 나아지면 좋겠어.

Dialog

A: Some days I just feel like giving up.
B: Be strong. Things will get better soon.

A: 언젠가 그냥 내가 포기하고 싶어.
B: 강해져야지. 곧 더 나아질 거야.

I am in the same situation
나도 같은 처지야
be in the same situation은 다른 사람과 마찬가지의 처지에 놓이다.

 **Example**

- She is in the same situation as her sister.
  걔는 여동생하고 같은 처지에 있어.
- Everyone in the class is in the same situation.
  학급 전 학생들이 같은 상황에 처해있어.

Dialog

A: It's been very difficult for me this year.
B: I know. I am in the same situation.

A: 나에겐 금년도가 무척 힘들었어.
B: 알아. 나도 같은 처지야.

I have trouble with studying here

난 여기서 공부하는데 어려움이 있어

have trouble with[~ing]는 '…하는데 애를 먹다,' '어려움을 겪다.'

Example

- She had trouble with making a living.
  생계를 꾸리는데 애먹고 있어.
- They have trouble with playing their instruments.
  걔들은 악기연주에 애먹고 있어.

Dialog

A: I have trouble with studying here.
B: It's noisy. Let's go to the library.

A: 난 여기서 공부하는데 어려움이 있어.
B: 시끄럽지. 도서관으로 가자.

Do you suffer from insomnia?

불면증에 시달리나요?

suffer from~은 어떤 힘든 일이나 '병으로 고생하다,' '병을 앓다.'

Example

- Some men are also suffering from sexual harassment.
  성희롱으로 고통받는 남성들도 있단 말이야.
- Do you suffer from insomnia?
  불면증에 시달리나요?

Dialog

A: Do you suffer from back pain?
B: Only if I lift heavy objects.

A: 등 통증에 시달립니까?
B: 무거운 물건을 들어올릴 때만 그래요.

288

Do you have a problem with that?
그거 뭐 문제라도 있어?

have a problem with sb[sth]는 '…에 문제가 있다.'

💡 Example

- I have a problem with people who are rude.
  난 무례한 사람들에 대해 거부감이 있어.

- Do you have a problem with that?
  그거 뭐 문제라도 있어?

A: How long have you had a problem with indigestion?
B: Ever since I started my new job.

A: 소화불량으로 얼마 동안이나 고생했나요?
B: 새 일을 시작한 후로 줄곧 그래왔어요.

289

You're out of luck
넌 운이 없나 봐

be out of luck은 '운이 없다'는 표현이다.

💡 Example

- He was out of luck after missing the last bus.
  막차를 놓치다니 걘 운이 없었어.

- The stores are closed, so we're out of luck.
  가게들이 문을 닫아 버렸어, 우린 운이 없나 봐.

A: I want to buy a TV that is on sale.
B: You're out of luck. We sold the last one.

A: 난 세일 중인 TV를 사길 원해.
B: 넌 운이 없나 봐. 우리가 마지막 남은 것을 팔았어.

I had a rough day at work

직장에서 힘든 하루를 보냈어

have a rough day는 '지치고 힘든 하루를 보내다'라는 의미 = have a bad day.

💡 Example
- This extra work means we'll have a rough week.
  더 일한다니 이번주 힘들겠구만.
- Did you have a rough day at your school?
  오늘 학교에서 힘들었니?

 Dialog

A: You look very tired tonight.
B: I had a rough day on the job.

A: 오늘 너 무척 피곤해보여.
B: 일이 무척 힘든 날이었어.

It's just not my day

운이 없는 날이야

not be one's day는 '…에게 안좋은 일들이 일어나 …의 날이 아니다'라는 뜻.

💡 Example
- It wasn't Page's day, because she had many problems.
  페이지가 운이 없는 날이었어. 문제가 많이 생겼거든.
- The teacher just punished me. It isn't my day.
  선생님이 날 처벌했지. 운이 없는 날이야.

 Dialog

A: Albert said you were two hours late to work.
B: I overslept. It's just not my day.

A: 알버트는 네가 2시간 늦게 출근한다고 말했어.
B: 내가 늦잠을 잤어. 운이 없는 날이야.

292

I had a chance to talk to my boss

상사와 얘기할 기회가 있었어

have[get] a chance to+V는 '…할 기회를 갖다.'

💡 **Example**

- Did you have a chance to check it?
  확인할 기회가 있었어?

- I am glad that we finally had a chance to talk.
  마침내 얘기 나눌 기회가 생겨 기뻐.

 Dialog

A: Come and see my new apartment when you have a chance.
B: Can I come over on Wednesday night?

A: 기회가 있으면 내 새 아파트를 보러 와라.
B: 수요일 밤에 한번 가도 되겠니?

293

Give him a chance to do his job

걔에게 자기 일을 할 기회를 줘라

give sb a chance는 '…에게 기회를 주다' = give a chance to sb.

💡 **Example**

- Give them a chance to finish the project.
  걔들에게 그 프로젝트를 끝낼 기회를 줘라.

- Give Susan a chance to do her job.
  수잔에게 자신의 일을 할 기회를 줘라.

 Dialog

A: I don't like the new student in our class.
B: Give her a chance to become your friend.

A: 난 우리 학급의 신참 학생을 좋아하지 않아.
B: 네 친구가 될 기회를 한번 줘봐라.

294

My cell is different from Tim's

내 핸폰은 팀의 것과는 다른거야

be different from~는 '…와 다르다' = differ from.

💡 **Example**

- This food is different from the type I normally eat.
  이 음식은 내가 통상적으로 먹는 타입과 다른 거야.
- My computer is different from Tim's.
  내 컴퓨터는 팀의 것과는 다른 거야.

 Dialog

A: Is that coat made by Burberry?
B: No, it is different from Burberry coats.

A: 그 코트는 버버리 회사에서 만든 거니?
B: 아니, 버버리 코트와 다른거야.

295

Your earphones are similar to mine

네 이어폰은 내 것과 비슷해

be similar to+N은 '…와 유사하다'로 두개가 거의 비슷한 경우에 쓴다.

💡 **Example**

- Cheju Island is similar to the Hawaiian Islands.
  제주도는 하와이와 비슷해.
- In what ways is it similar?
  어떤 점에서 이것이 비슷해?

 Dialog

A: Are you carrying a Louis Vuitton suitcase?
B: No, but it is similar to a Louis Vuitton suitcase.

A: 넌 루이 비통 가방을 들고 있니?
B: 아니지만 루이 비통 가방과 비슷한거야.

He looks like a movie star

갠 영화배우처럼 생겼어

look like+N[S+V]은 겉모습이 '…처럼 보인다'라는 뜻.

💡 **Example**

- This food looks like it is spoiled.
  이 음식은 부패한 것처럼 보여.

- You look like you stayed up late.
  넌 늦게까지 잠을 자지 않은 것처럼 보여.

 Dialog

A: What does your uncle look like?
B: I think he looks like Tom Cruise.

A: 네 아저씨는 어떻게 생겼니?
B: 그는 탐 쿠르즈 같이 생겼어.

How can you say something like that?

어떻게 그런 말을 할 수가 있어?

do[say] something like that은 '그런 말[행동]을 (말)하다.'

💡 **Example**

- I didn't think something like that would happen.
  그런 일이 생길 지 생각도 못했어.

- Brenda always does something like that.
  브렌다는 항상 그런 일을 해.

 Dialog

A: How could you do something like that?
B: I promise I won't let it happen again.

A: 어떻게 그럴 수가 있죠?
B: 다신 그런 일 없을 거예요. 약속해요.

298

He takes after his father

걘 아버지를 닮았어

take after는 혈연 중에 생김새가 비슷할 때, be the spitting image of~는 '빼닮다'(혈연/비혈연).

💡 **Example**

- Mike takes after his father's side of the family.
  마이크는 아버지 쪽을 닮았어.
- She takes after her great aunt.
  걘 고모 할머니를 닮았어.

 Dialog

A: Your daughter seems very smart.
B: Well, she takes after her grandmother.

A: 네 딸은 무지 똑똑한 것 같아.
B: 그래? 걘 할머니를 닮았어.

299

He's familiar with K-pop

걘 케이팝에 익숙해

be familiar with sth은 '…을 잘 알다[이해하다]', be familiar to sb는 '주어가 sb에게 익숙하다.'

💡 **Example**

- Sherry was not familiar with the school's classrooms.
  쉐리는 학교의 교실에 익숙하지 않았어.
- Are you familiar with using computers?
  넌 컴퓨터를 사용하는데 익숙하니?

 Dialog

A: This music was composed by Chopin.
B: I am not familiar with his music.

A: 이 음악은 쇼팽이 작곡했지.
B: 난 그의 음악이 익숙하지 않아.

It's difficult to cook this food

이 요리를 하는 건 어려워

be difficult to+V는 '…하기 어렵다,' It's difficult to+V의 형태로 자주 쓰인다.

💡 Example

- It is not difficult to see the ocean from here.
  여기서 바다를 보는 건 어렵지 않아.

- It is not difficult to cook this food.
  이 음식은 요리하기가 어렵지 않아.

 Dialog

A: I don't like the notebook computer I have.
B: It is not difficult to buy a different model.

A: 난 내가 가진 노트북 컴퓨터를 싫어해.
B: 다른 모델을 사는 것은 어렵지 않아.

They are easy to work with

그들과 같이 일하는 것은 쉬워

be easy to+V는 '…하기 쉽다'로 <=> be difficult to+V(…하기 어렵다).

💡 Example

- It is easy to fix this problem.
  이 문제를 고치는 것은 쉽지.

- They are easy to work with.
  그들과 같이 일하는 것은 쉬워.

 Dialog

A: It's easy to talk to my girlfriend.
B: You have a good relationship with her.

A: 내 여친에게 말하는 것은 쉬워.
B: 여친과 관계가 좋구나.

I'm cool with that plan

난 그 계획 괜찮아

be cool은 '침착하다,' '멋지다,' be cool about은 '괜찮다,' be cool with는 '동의하다,' '괜찮다.'

 Example

- Be cool and try not to get so stressed.
  냉정해, 그렇게 스트레스 받지 말고.

- The art class is cool and a lot of fun.
  미술 시간은 신나고 재미가 많아.

 Dialog

A: How are things going in your school?
B: My classes are cool. I really like my teachers.

A: 학교에서 어떻게 지내니?
B: 수업들이 마음에 들어. 선생님들을 진짜 좋아해.

They are doing okay

걔네들은 잘 지내고 있어

be doing okay는 '잘 지내다' = be doing fine[good, great].

 Example

- I'm glad to see you're doing okay.
  네가 잘 지낸다니 좋아.

- You're doing great.
  너 잘하고 있어.

Dialog

A: I haven't seen your parents in a while.
B: My dad and mom are doing okay.

A: 난 한동안 네 부모님을 뵙지 못했어.
B: 제 부모님은 잘 지내고 계세요.

I chose to stay home tonight

난 오늘밤에 집에 있기로 했어

choose to+V는 여러가지 가능성 중에 '하나를 선택하다'라는 의미.

💡 **Example**

- We can choose to do what is right.
  우린 옳은 것을 하기로 선택할 수 있지.
- Tell me why you chose to pursue a career in engineering.
  네가 공학분야 경력을 갖기로 선택한 이유를 말해봐.

Dialog

A: What is Ken going to do tomorrow?
B: I think he'll choose to go to the park.

A: 캔은 내일 뭘 할거야?
B: 걘 공원을 가기로 할거야.

I changed my mind

나 마음이 변했어

change one's mind (about~)는 이미 결정한 것을 변심해서 바꾼다는 의미.

💡 **Example**

- I changed my mind. I'll have dinner with you.
  마음을 바꿨어. 너랑 저녁식사 할게.
- I had to change my plans for the summer.
  난 여름 계획을 바꿔야 해.

Dialog

A: I thought you were going to go on leave.
B: I was thinking about that, but I changed my mind.

A: 난 네가 쉴 거라고 생각했는데.
B: 그렇게 생각했었는데 마음이 변했어.

I decided to quit my job
난 직장을 그만두기로 결정했어
decide to+V[that S+V]는 '…을 결정[결심]하다' = make a decision.

💡 **Example**
- I decided I wanted to come to your party.
  네 파티에 가기로 결정했거든.
- What made you decide to quit your job?
  왜 회사를 그만둘 결심을 한거예요?

A: **I decided to** leave early in the morning.
B: You should get a good night's sleep.

   A: 난 아침 일찍 떠나기로 결정했어.
   B: 넌 숙면을 해야겠구나.

Her drunk driving led to an accident
걔의 음주운전으로 사고가 났어
lead to+N는 주어로 인해서 '…으로 이어지다,' '…한 결과가 나오다,' '…로 이끌다.'

💡 **Example**
- Poor planning leads to failure.
  기획을 부실하게 하면 실패로 이어져.
- Ted and Betty's friendship led to romance.
  테드와 베티간 우정은 사랑으로 이어졌어.

A: I decided to study harder in school.
B: That will **lead to** better grades.

   A: 난 학교에서 열심히 공부하기로 결정했어.
   B: 그러면 학점이 좋아질거야.

How did the meeting turn out?

회의 어떻게 됐어?

turn out to be+명사/형용사는 '~로 드러나다,' turn out+형용사/부사는 '결국 …하게 되다.'

 Example

- Everything turned out alright at the office.
  사무실에서 모든 것이 잘 되었어.
- We'll wait to see how the meeting turns out.
  회의가 어떻게 끝날지 우린 지켜볼거야.

 Dialog

A: How did your blind date turn out?
B: It was terrible. I never want to see her again.

   A: 네 소개팅은 어떻게 되었니?
   B: 끔찍해. 다시는 걜 만나고 싶지 않아.

I provided support to the workers

난 노동자들에게 지지를 보냈어

give support to[=be supportive of]는 '지지하다,' 공식적인 표현은 provide support to~.

 Example

- I provided support to the workers.
  난 노동자들에게 지지를 보냈어.
- She supported her husband when he went to school.
  걘 남편이 학교를 다녔을 때 남편을 부양했어.

Dialog

A: Are you giving that food to poor people?
B: Yes, we've got to give support to them.

   A: 그 음식을 가난한 사람에게 줄거니?
   B: 예, 그들을 지원해야만 해요.

Tell him to bring me a drink

걔에게 마실 것 좀 내게 갖다 주라고 해

tell sb to+V는 (좀 지시적으로) '…에게 …하라고 말하다,' be told to+V는 '…라고 지시받다.'

💡 Example

- Erica was told to go to bed early.
  에리카는 일찍 잠자리에 들라고 말을 들었어.
- He told me to cut down on my intake of fast food.
  나보고 패스트푸드섭취를 줄이래.

 Dialog

A: **Tell Katie to** bring me a drink.
B: I think she's busy right now.

A: 케이티에게 마실 것 좀 나한테 갖다 주라고 말해라.
B: 걔가 지금은 바쁜 걸로 생각되는데.

He asked me to attend the meeting

걘 나보고 회의에 참석해달라고 요청했어

ask sb to+V는 tell sb to+V와 달리 '부탁하다,' '청하다'라는 의미.

💡 Example

- Ambrosia asked another student for help.
  암브로시아가 다른 학생에게 도움을 청했어.
- We have a favor to ask of you.
  너한테 부탁이 있는데.

 Dialog

A: Dana **asked me to** find a nice hotel.
B: Why don't you check the Internet?

A: 데이나는 나한테 좋은 호텔을 찾아달라고 부탁했어.
B: 인터넷으로 찾아보면 어때?

312

I can't be helpful in giving tips

난 팁을 줌으로써 도움이 될 수 있어

be helpful (in ~ing)는 '도움이 되다' = be supportive. with the help of~는 '…의 도움으로.'

Example

- The money you gave us was helpful.
  네가 나한테 준 돈이 도움이 되었어.
- They were supportive when Fred had problems.
  프레드에게 문제가 생겼을 때 걔들이 도움이 되었어.

Dialog

A: I'm not sure what I should study in school.
B: I can be helpful in giving you advice.

A: 학교에서 뭘 공부해야 할지 잘 모르겠어.
B: 내가 도움이 되는 충고를 해줄 수 있어.

313

Do you mind giving me a hand?

좀 도와주면 안될까?

give sb a hand with[~ing]는 '…하는 것을 도와주다.'

Example

- Why don't you give me a hand?
  나를 좀 도와주라.
- Could you give me a hand watering the flower?
  꽃에 물주는 거 도와줄래?

Dialog

A: Would you mind giving me a hand?
B: Sorry, but I'm really busy at the moment.

A: 좀 도와주면 안될까?
B: 미안하지만 지금은 정말 바빠.

Let me help you do that

내가 도와줄게

help sb+V는 '…가 …하는 것을 돕다,' 동사 앞에 'to'는 거의 쓰지 않는다. = help sb with+N

💡 **Example**

- You should help move that desk.
  저 책상을 옮기는데 네가 도와줘야 해.
- Can you help me finish this work?
  이 일을 끝내는데 네가 날 도와줄 수 있니?

 Dialog

A: I have difficulty turning this knob.
B: Let me help you do that.

A: 난 손잡이를 돌리는데 어려움이 있었어.
B: 내가 도와줄게.

I need some help with moving

이사하는데 좀 도움이 필요해

need some help는 '도움이 좀 필요하다,' 뒤에 with+N 혹은 (with) ~ing를 붙여 말한다.

💡 **Example**

- We need some more help fixing this.
  우린 이것을 고치는데 좀 더 도움이 필요해.
- I'll let you know if I need help.
  도움이 필요하면 알려줄게.

 Dialog

A: Do you need some help with this work?
B: No, I've got it all taken care of.

A: 이 일을 하는데 좀 도움이 필요하니?
B: 아니, 잘 처리해 놓았어.

He's learning about programming
걘 프로그래밍에 대해 배우고 있어

learn about~은 '…에 대해 배우다,' give a lesson은 '가르치다,' learn a lesson은 '교훈을 얻다.'

 **Example**

- Ms. Thompson gave a lesson to the elementary students.
  톰슨 씨는 초등학생들을 가르쳤어.
- I spent a lot of time learning about fashion.
  난 패션 배우는데 많은 시간을 보냈어.

Dialog

A: What did you learn about today?
B: The teacher taught us about European history.

A: 오늘 뭐에 대해서 배웠니?
B: 선생님은 유럽역사에 대해 가르쳤어.

Guess What?

Has the cat got your tongue?
너 왜 꿀먹은 벙어리가 된거야?

좀 불리하거나 안좋은 상황에 처한 사람이 말을 하지 못하고(the person is being unusually quiet) 있을 때 사용하는 표현으로 "왜 꿀먹은 벙어리?," "왜 말이 없는거야?"라는 뜻이다. 원래는 Has the cat got your tongue?이다.

I'm learning to cook Korean food

난 한국음식 요리하는 것을 배우고 있어

learn to+V는 '…하는 것을 배우다' = learn how to+V.

💡 Example

- Gina learned the song by heart.
  지나는 그 노래를 외웠어.

- Lenny learned to fly an airplane.
  레니는 비행조종을 배웠어.

 Dialog

A: I am broke again this week.
B: You should learn to manage your money.

A: 이번주 돈이 바닥났어.
B: 너 돈관리하는 것 좀 배워야겠다.

He taught us about camping

걘 우리에게 캠핑에 대해 가르쳤어

teach sb about~는 '…에게 …에 관해 가르치다,' teach sb to+V는 '…에게 …하는걸 가르치다.'

💡 Example

- Walter taught us about camping.
  월터는 캠핑에 대해 우리에게 가르쳤어.

- I hope to teach at a college in a few years.
  몇 년 후에 대학에서 가르치기를 바래.

 Dialog

A: Sharon taught us to cook Italian food.
B: You can make a meal for me then.

A: 샤론은 우리에게 이태리 요리를 가르쳐줬어.
B: 그러면 나한테 이태리 음식을 해줄 수 있겠네.

You shouldn't treat me like this

날 이런 식으로 대하면 안돼

treat sb like~는 '…을 …처럼 대하다,' treat sb very well은 '…을 잘 대하다.'

💡 Example

- Dave treated me like a brother.
  데이브는 날 남동생처럼 대해줬어.
- You shouldn't treat me like this.
  날 이런 식으로 대하면 안돼.

 Dialog

A: Is your boss tough to work for?
B: Yes, he treats his workers like slaves.

A: 네 보스랑 같이 일하기 힘드니?
B: 응, 보스는 직원들을 노예처럼 대해.

He's waiting on customers right now

걘 지금 손님들을 응대하고 있어

wait on sb는 '접대하다,' '시중들다,' 혹은 '기다리다,' wait on sth은 '…에 달려있다.'

💡 Example

- Sarah had to wait on her mother-in-law hand and foot.
  사라는 시어머니를 정성을 다해 돌봤어.
- I won't wait on you even if you are sick.
  네가 아프더라도 난 네 시중들지 않을거야.

 Dialog

A: Is this restaurant even open?
B: Someone will wait on us soon.

A: 이 식당 문을 열기나 한 거에요?
B: 조만간 누가 접대를 할 겁니다.

I always keep my word

난 항상 약속을 지키잖아

keep one's word는 '자기가 한 약속을 지키다' <=> break one's word.

 Example

- You'd better honor your promise to our kids.
  넌 우리 애들에게 약속을 지키는 게 좋을 거야.
- She had to go to her hometown to fulfill a promise.
  걘 약속을 지키기 위해 고향으로 가야만 했어.

 Dialog

A: Are you still coming to my party?
B: Sure. I always keep my word.

A: 내 파티에 올 거니?
B: 그럼, 난 항상 약속을 지키잖아.

I promise to keep your secret

너의 비밀을 지키겠다고 약속할게

I promise to+V는 내가 to 이하를 하기로 약속[다짐]하다.

 Example

- I promised myself that I will exercise more.
  내가 운동을 좀 더 할 것을 다짐해.
- You need to give me the money like you promised.
  네가 약속한대로 나한테 돈을 줘야 해.

Dialog

A: I promise to make you a happy woman.
B: Well, then I will be glad to marry you.

A: 널 행복한 여자로 만들 것을 약속해.
B: 그렇다면 기꺼이 즐겁게 결혼하겠어.

323

I swear to run as fast as I can
내가 가능한 한 빨리 뛸 것을 맹세해
sweat to+N는 '…가 진실임을 보증하다,' swear to+V는 '…을 하겠다고 다짐하다.'

Example
- The soldiers swore allegiance to each other.
  병사들은 서로에게 충성을 맹세했어.
- The ex-president swore to stay out of politics.
  전직 대통령은 정치에서 벗어나 있겠다고 맹세했어.

A: Are you going to win the race?
B: I swear to run as fast as I can.
  A: 넌 경주에서 이길 거니?
  B: 내가 가능한 한 빨리 뛸 것을 맹세해.

324

We arranged for a place to stay
우린 머물 곳을 마련해놓았어
arrange to+V[for sth]는 '…할 준비를 하다' = make some arrangements for.

Example
- We arranged for a place to stay.
  우린 머물 곳을 마련해놓았어.
- The company arranged a meeting for tomorrow.
  회사는 낼 열릴 회의를 준비했어.

A: Are you traveling to your hometown?
B: Yeah, I've arranged to meet some of my old teachers.
  A: 네 고향으로 여행가니?
  B: 그래, 내 옛날 선생님 몇 분을 만나게 되어 있어.

He's preparing for a job interview

갠 취업면접을 준비하고 있어

prepare for[to+V]는 '앞으로 할 일을 준비하다,' prepare oneself for는 '…에 대비하다.'

 Example

- My sister prepared to make some food.
  여동생이 음식을 좀 만들려고 준비했어.

- It will take time for us to prepare the report.
  그 보고서 준비하는데 시간이 걸릴거야.

 Dialog

A: What is taking you so long?
B: I'm preparing for my interview tomorrow.

A: 왜 이렇게 오래 걸리는 거야?
B: 난 내일 인터뷰를 준비하고 있어.

Where is this vase from?

이 꽃병은 어디에서 난거니?

come[be] from~은 '…의 출신이다,' '생겨나다,' '유래하다.'

 Example

- The groceries came from the corner store.
  그 식품점은 코너가게에서 시작되었어.

- Where did this pair of socks come from?
  이 양말은 어디에서 난거니?

Dialog

A: Where is this vase from?
B: I bought it when I was in Israel.

A: 이 꽃병은 어디에서 난거니?
B: 내가 이스라엘에 있을 때 산거야.

327

I got a ring from my boyfriend

난 남친으로부터 반지를 받았어

get sth from~은 '…에서 …을 가져오다[사다, 얻다],' get A B=get B for A는 'A에게 B를 주다.'

💡 **Example**

- Get a chair for her to sit in.
  걔가 앉도록 의자를 가져와라.

- Get a new shirt for him to wear.
  걔가 입도록 새 셔츠를 가져와라.

 Dialog

A: Did you have a good holiday?
B: Sure. I got a ring from my boyfriend.

A: 휴일 잘 지냈니?
B: 그럼. 난 남친으로부터 반지를 받았어.

328

He handed over the keys to the realtor

걘 부동산중개인에게 열쇠를 건네주었어

hand over는 '건네주다,' '양도하다,' hand over sth to sb는 '…에게 …을 넘겨주다.'

💡 **Example**

- The teacher provided the students with exams.
  선생님이 학생들에게 시험을 치렀어.

- The manager presented one of his workers with an award.
  매니저는 직원 한 명에게 상을 주었어.

 Dialog

A: Are you finished moving your things?
B: Yeah, but I need to hand over my apartment key.

A: 네 물건 다 옮겼니?
B: 응, 다만 내 아파트 열쇠를 넘겨줘야 해.

I want you to take it back

그거 다시 가져가, 그 말 취소해

take sth back은 '다시 가져가다[오다],' 말(word)일 경우에는 '이미 한 말을 취소하다.'

💡 Example

- Take this paperwork back to Mary.
  이 서류작업을 메리한데 돌려줘라.
- We need to take the defective items back to the store.
  하자 있는 물품은 가게로 반품해야 돼.

 Dialog

A: Peter had many problems with his new car.
B: He said he wants to take it back.

A: 피터는 자신의 새 차에 문제가 많았어.
B: 걘 차를 돌려주기를 원한다고 말했어.

I want my old boyfriend back

내 옛 남친하고 다시 사귀었으면 해

want sth[sb] back은 '돌려받기를 원하다,' give back sth to sb는 '…에게 …을 돌려주다.'

💡 Example

- Larry would like his i-pod back.
  래리는 자기의 아이팟을 돌려받기를 원해.
- She said she wants her necklace back.
  걘 자기 목걸이를 돌려받기를 원한대.

 Dialog

A: I want my old boyfriend back.
B: But you broke up with him a year ago.

A: 내 옛 남친하고 다시 사귀었으면 해.
B: 그렇지만 1년전에 걔랑 헤어졌잖아.

Keep your dogs off my lawn

네 강아지들을 내 잔디에 못오게 해

keep A off B는 'A를 B로부터 떼어놓다,' 다시 말해 A와 B를 떨어진 상태로 유지하다라는 말.

 Example

- We have to take your watch apart to fix it.
  네 시계를 고치려면 분해해야 돼.
- Keep your feet off the coffee table.
  커피 테이블에서 네 발을 치워라.

Dialog

A: **Keep** your dogs **off** my lawn.
B: I'm sorry, I'll move them.

A: 네 강아지들을 내 잔디에 오지 못하게 해.
B: 미안해. 강아지들을 데려갈게.

I have experience in teaching French

난 프랑스어를 가르친 경험이 있어

have experience in+N[~in]/with~는 '(분야/활동) 경험이 있다,' '…을 다뤄본 경험이 있다.'

 Example

- The computer repairman had more experience with IBM.
  그 컴퓨터 수리공은 IBM과 일한 경험이 더 많아.
- We had a bad experience with that company.
  우린 그 회사와 나쁜 경험이 있어.

Dialog

A: Have you worked in an office before?
B: Yes, **I have a lot of experience with** businesses.

A: 전에 사무실에서 일해본 적이 있나요?
B: 예, 사업에 경험이 많아요.

333

I need to solve this problem

난 이 문제를 해결해야 돼

solve a problem은 '문제를 해결하다,' fix a problem은 주로 '기계 등을 고치거나 수리하다.'

💡 **Example**

- It takes time to solve a math problem.
  수학문제를 푸는데 시간이 걸려.

- I have to fix a problem with this computer.
  난 이 컴퓨터 문제를 해결해야만 해.

 **Dialog**

A: I heard you spent a lot fixing your car.
B: Yeah, but it didn't solve the problem I was having.

　A: 네 차를 고치는데 돈을 많이 썼다고 들었어.
　B: 그래, 그래도 문제를 해결하지 못했어.

334

Don't make fun of disabled people

장애인들을 놀리지 마라

make fun of~는 '조롱하다,' '비웃다' = make a fool of.

💡 **Example**

- My ex-boyfriend made a fool of me.
  내 옛 남친은 나를 놀렸어.

- Don't make fun of disabled people.
  장애인들을 놀리지 마라.

 **Dialog**

A: Many people make fun of beggars.
B: That seems very unkind.

　A: 많은 사람들이 거지들을 놀려.
　B: 그건 매우 친절하지 못한 행동이야.

Don't be so hard on me
나 좀 심하게 대하지마
be hard on sb는 '심하게 다루다,' '나무라다,' be hard on sth은 '무리하게 하다.'

💡 **Example**

- Too much running is hard on the body.
  너무 많이 뛰면 몸에 무리가 돼.
- The busy schedule was hard on everyone.
  그 바쁜 스케줄로 모두에게 무리가 되었어.

A: Our new manager really doesn't like you.
B: Yes, she has been very hard on me.
  A: 새로 온 매니저는 너를 정말 싫어해.
  B: 맞아, 걘 나한테 무지 심하게 해.

Don't give her a hard time
걔 너무 심하게 대하지마
give sb a hard time은 '…을 부당하게 대하거나 괴롭히다,' '힘들게 하다.'

💡 **Example**

- The policeman gave me a hard time.
  경찰은 나를 힘들게 했어.
- He gave Cecil a hard time until he quit.
  걘 그만둘 때까지 세실을 힘들게 했어.

A: Andrea has made many mistakes.
B: She's new. Don't give her a hard time.
  A: 안드레아는 많은 실수를 범했어.
  B: 걘 새로 왔어. 너무 심하게 대하지 마.

337

The thief robbed her of her purse
도둑은 걔의 지갑을 훔쳤어

rob 사람[은행] of~는 '…에게서 …을 훔치다' = steal sth from+사람[은행].

🔆 **Example**
- Someone robbed a bank downtown.
  누군가 시내 은행을 털었어.
- The tourists were robbed of their money.
  관광객들의 돈이 털렸어.

 Dialog

A: The thief robbed us of our Christmas presents.
B: Wow, that's a terrible thing to do.
  A: 우리가 강도한테 크리스마스 선물들을 털렸어.
  B: 와, 끔찍한 일을 저질렀군.

338

I don't want to argue about it
그 문제로 다투고 싶지 않아

argue about[over]는 '…에 대해 다투다,' argue with sb about sth는 '…와 …에 대해 다투다.'

🔆 **Example**
- Can we argue about this later?
  이거 나중에 언쟁하자, 응?
- You really want to argue with me about this?
  너 정말 나랑 이것 갖고 말다툼할거야?

 Dialog

A: My car is much nicer than yours.
B: I don't want to argue about it.
  A: 내 차가 네 것보다 훨씬 나아.
  B: 그 문제로 다투고 싶지 않아.

339

They had a really big fight

걔네들 정말 크게 싸웠어

have a fight는 '싸우다'(fight with sb) = get into a fight.

💡 Example

- Tom and I had a really big fight.
  탐과 내가 정말 크게 싸웠는데.
- My parents got into a big fight and got divorced.
  부모님은 크게 싸우고 헤어졌어.

 Dialog

A: What happened to Sylvester?
B: I think he got into a fight.

A: 실베스타에게 무슨 일이 생겼니?
B: 걔가 싸움을 했던 것 같아.

340

I'll pay you back 100 dollars today

오늘 네게 100달러 갚을게

pay back은 '빚이나 돈을 갚다,' 혹은 '보복[복수]하다,' '되갚아주다.'

💡 Example

- You must pay back the money within a week.
  넌 일주 안에 그 돈을 갚아야 해.
- Sarah got payback by breaking his cell phone.
  새라는 걔 휴대폰을 부셔 복수했어.

 Dialog

A: Why did you cut up my clothes?
B: It was pay-back for you cheating on me.

A: 왜 내 옷을 잘랐니?
B: 나를 속인 보복이었어.

181

341

I want to make up with my wife

난 아내와 화해하고 싶어

make up with sb는 '…와 화해하다' = patch things up with sb(구어체).

💡 **Example**

- You should make up with your brothers and sisters.
  네 여자, 남자 형제들과 화해해야 해.
- I couldn't make up with my worst enemy.
  난 최악의 적과 화해를 할 수가 없어.

A: Polly and her boyfriend made up with each other.
B: So they are not fighting anymore?

A: 폴리와 걔의 남친은 서로 화해했어.
B: 그래서 더 이상 안 싸우니?

342

I decided to give up drinking

난 술을 끊기로 했어

give up+N[~in]은 '그만두다,' '중단하다,' give up on+N은 '…에 대한 희망[기대]을 버리다.'

💡 **Example**

- Jean gave up working daily.
  진은 매일 일하는 것을 포기했어.
- Don't give up. Things will get better.
  포기하지마. 상황이 좋아질거야.

A: Why did you give up drinking?
B: It was making me very unhealthy.

A: 왜 술을 끊었는데?
B: 술이 내 건강을 해쳤거든.

What made you quit your job?

어째서 일을 그만둔거야?

quit+N[~ing]는 '…을 그만두다,' '중단하다,' 목적어 없이 quit 단독으로도 많이 쓰인다.

 Example

- Bill quit school last year.
  빌은 작년에 학교를 그만 두었어.

- Didn't you quit smoking last year?
  넌 작년에 금연하지 않았어?

 Dialog

A: What made you quit your job?
B: I really hated to wake up early.

A: 어째서 일을 그만둔 거야?
B: 일찍 일어나기가 정말 싫더라고.

I stopped smoking last year

난 작년에 담배끊었어

stop ~ing는 행위자체를 '그만두다,' stop to+V는 '…하기 위해 잠시 멈추다.'

 Example

- I have tried every year since 2005 to stop smoking.
  난 2005년 이래 매년 금연을 시도해왔어.

- Stop complaining and get back to work.
  불평 그만하고 일해.

Dialog

A: Let's stop working and finish this tomorrow.
B: That's a good idea. I'm tired.

A: 그만 일하고 내일 마무리하자.
B: 좋은 생각이야. 나 피곤해.

345

The court set the prisoner free
법정은 그 죄수를 석방시켰어
set sb[sth] free는 '풀어주다,' '석방하다,' 비유적으로 '…을 해방시키다.'

💡 **Example**

- The court set the prisoner free.
  법정은 그 죄수를 석방시켰다.
- The boat was lost when it got free of the dock.
  배는 선창에서 풀리자 사라졌어.

 Dialog

A: What will happen to the animals in this zoo?
B: They will be set free in the future.
  A: 이 동물원 동물들 어떻게 될까?
  B: 앞으로 자유롭게 풀려날거야.

346

Don't act like a single guy
총각처럼 행동하지마
act like+N[S+V]는 '…같이 행동하다,' act+부사는 '…하게 행동하다.'

💡 **Example**

- Gina just acted like she didn't know me.
  지나는 나를 모르는 것처럼 행동했어.
- Tony acts like he has a lot of money.
  토니는 마치 돈이 많은 것처럼 행동해.

 Dialog

A: You're married. Don't act like a single guy.
B: I'm not. I was just talking to these girls.
  A: 넌 결혼한 몸이야. 총각처럼 행동하지마.
  B: 안 그래. 그냥 이 여자분들하고 얘기 좀 나눴을뿐야.

347

I'm not in danger. I'm the danger

난 위험에 처하지 않았어. 내 자체가 위험이야

be in the danger of ~ing는 '…할 위험에 놓이다,' put sb in danger는 '…을 위험에 빠트리다.'

💡 **Example**
- The city's water **is in danger of** being polluted.
  도시수질이 오염될 위험에 처해있어.
- Joe **is in danger of** failing math class.
  조는 수학 수업에서 낙제할 위험에 처해있어.

 Dialog

A: You **are in danger of** getting fired.
B: Is there anything I can do to save my job?

A: 넌 해고당할 위험에 처해있어.
B: 직장에 남도록 할 수 있는 방안이 있을까?

348

I don't want to risk losing my money

내 돈을 잃을 위험을 감수하고 싶지 않아

risk ~ing는 '…할 위험을 감행하다,' risk it은 '위험을 감수하다,' at the risk of~는 '위험을 무릅쓰고.'

💡 **Example**
- He **risked falling** off the side of the cliff.
  걘 절벽 한쪽으로 떨어질 위험을 무릅썼지.
- You **risk hurting** someone with that knife.
  넌 그 칼로 누군가를 해칠 위험을 감수하는거야.

 Dialog

A: Lucy brought all of her money to the casino.
B: Is she going to **risk losing** it all?

A: 루씨는 카지노에 가진 모든 돈을 가져갔어.
B: 걘 모든 돈을 잃을 위험을 감수하겠다는거야?

Would you fill out this form?

이 서식을 써넣어 주시겠어요?

fill out+N은 '양식서를 채우다,' '작성하다,' fill in은 '빈칸을 채우다.'

💡 **Example**

- Would you fill out this form, please?
  이 서식을 써넣어 주시겠어요?
- I'd like you to fill out this questionnaire for me.
  이 질문서를 작성해 주셨으면 하는데요.

A: Don't forget to fill out those forms before you go.
B: I'll leave them on your desk before I go.

A: 가기 전에 이 양식을 다 채우는 것 잊지마.
B: 제가 가기 전에 책상 위에 둘게요.

I got him to turn in the report

난 걔가 레포트를 제출하도록 했어

hand in sth은 '…을 건네주다,' '제출하다' = turn in = give in = submit. hand out은 '나눠주다.'

💡 **Example**

- I got him to turn in the report.
  난 걔가 레포트를 제출하도록 했어.
- Make sure that you turn in your keys at the end of the day.
  일과가 끝나면 열쇠를 확실히 돌려줘.

A: Before I go any further, Bill has something to say.
B: I handed in my resignation this morning.

A: 제가 더 얘기를 하기 전에 빌이 뭔가 할 말이 있답니다.
B: 전 아침에 사직서를 제출했어요.

351

Don't **break the law** here

여기서는 법을 어기지마

break the law는 '법을 어기다' <=> keep the law는 '법을 지키다.'

💡 **Example**

- The little boy felt guilty about stealing candy.
  어린 애가 캔디를 훔친 데 대해 죄의식을 느꼈어

- New traffic laws go into effect this year.
  새로운 교통법이 금년에 발효돼.

 Dialog

A: It is illegal to throw garbage in the street.
B: I think we shouldn't **break the law**.

A: 거리에 쓰레기를 버리는 것은 불법이야.
B: 우린 법을 어기면 안 된다고 생각해.

352

We're **making a profit**

우리는 이익을 내고 있어

make a profit는 '이익을 내다'로 make 대신에 turn이나 earn을 써도 된다.

💡 **Example**

- You can't make a profit selling vitamins.
  비타민을 팔아서 이윤을 낼 수가 없어.

- I need to make a profit this month.
  난 이번달에 이익을 내야 돼.

 Dialog

A: How is your company doing?
B: It's fine. We're **making a profit**.

A: 네 회사는 어떠니?
B: 괜찮아. 이익을 내고 있어.

353

I'll **make up for** it tomorrow
내일 보상해줄게
make up for sth은 피해나 뭔가 잘못된 것을 '보상해주다' = make it up to sb.

💡 **Example**
- We talked for hours, making up for lost time.
  놓친 시간을 보충하려 몇 시간 얘기했어.
- Is this your first step to make up for it?
  이게 네 잘못에 대한 보상 첫 단계니?

 Dialog

A: I can't believe you didn't remember our date.
B: I'll **make up for** it tomorrow, I promise.

A: 우리 데이트 날짜를 어떻게 잊을 수 있어.
B: 내일 보상해줄게, 약속해.

354

It **belongs to** my sister
그건 내 누이 것이야
belong to+sb[sth]는 '…의 것이다,' '…의 소속이다,' belongings는 명사로 '소지품'을 뜻한다.

💡 **Example**
- She gathered her belongings and left.
  걘 자기 소지품을 챙겨서 떠났어.
- These pencils belong to my students.
  이 연필들은 내 학생들거야.

 Dialog

A: Is this your suitcase?
B: No, it **belongs to** my brother.

A: 이것이 네 여행가방이니?
B: 아니, 이건 내 동생거야.

Do you own a car?
너 차 있어?

own a car는 '차를 소유하다,' lease a car는 '차를 리스하다,' rent a car는 '차를 렌트하다.'

Example
- They called the little house their own.
  걔들은 그 작은 집이 자기들거래.
- I'll own a car when I finish college.
  난 대학을 마치면 차를 가질거야.

 **Dialog**

A: Do you own a car?
B: Yes. I drive to work every day.

A: 너 차를 가지고 있니?
B: 그럼. 매일 운전하고 사무실에 가.

Guess What?

He's got some skeletons in his closet
걘 무슨 비밀이 있어

옷장 속에 해골이 있다는 말로 비유적으로 누구나 남모르는 비밀이 있게(have some deeply hidden secret) 마련이다라는 진실을 말하는 이디엄이다. 물론 이 비밀은 사람들이 알면 창피해질 수밖에 없는 것이다. Have나 got 동사를 써도 되며 또한 Everyone has a skeleton in the closet라고 쓰기도 한다.

I'm qualified for this position

나 이 직책에 자격이 있어

be qualified for sth[to+V]는 '…의[할] 자격이 있다.'

💡 **Example**

- I am qualified to teach in high schools.
  난 고등학교에서 가르칠 자격이 돼.

- She isn't qualified to write that exam.
  걘 시험문제를 낼 자격이 없어.

 Dialog

A: Bart talks like he is a lawyer.
B: He is qualified to practice law in New York.

A: 바트는 자신이 변호사인 것처럼 말해.
B: 걔는 뉴욕에서 변호사로 활동할 자격이 있어.

I deserve to have a day off

난 하루 휴가를 받을 자격이 있어

deserve to+V는 '…할 자격이 있다,' to 다음에 무슨 자격이 되는지 동사를 붙여준다.

💡 **Example**

- I deserve to have a day off.
  난 하루 휴가를 받을 자격이 있어.

- The children deserve to get ice cream.
  아이들은 아이스크림을 받을 만해.

 Dialog

A: Kevin works very hard in class.
B: He deserves to get the highest grade.

A: 케빈은 수업중 열심히 공부해.
B: 걘 최고성적을 받을 만해.

This TV is getting old
이 텔레비전은 낡았어
get old는 사람이 주어면 '나이가 들다,' 사물이 주어면 '낡다,' '오래되다.'

 Example
- Our car got old over the years.
  우리 차는 시간이 지나면서 낡아졌어.
- Are you aware of prices getting higher?
  물가가 오르고 있다는 것을 알고 있니?

 Dialog

A: My grandmother is always complaining.
B: Well, she's probably unhappy about getting old.
A: 할머니는 항상 불평을 해.
B: 글쎄, 아마도 나이가 드는 것이 불행하게 느껴지시나 봐.

I was the first to get there
내가 거기에 최초로 도착했어
be the first to+V는 '최초로 …하다'라는 의미. first 다음에 person을 넣어도 된다.

 Example
- I was the first to enter the school.
  내가 최초로 그 학교에 들어간 거였어.
- Every boy wants to be the first to kiss Vera.
  남자애들 다 베라랑 젤 먼저 키스하고 싶어해.

Dialog

A: Why does Nadine study so hard?
B: She wants to be the first to score 100 percent.
A: 나딘이 왜 그렇게 열심히 공부하니?
B: 걘 100점을 맞는 최초의 학생이 되고 싶어해.

I like fruit such as apples and kiwis

나는 사과와 키위 같은 과일을 좋아해

such as는 '…와 같은'이라는 의미. 앞서 말한 내용에 역시 구체성을 주기 위해 예를 나열할 때.

Example
- You do good work, such as in this report.
  넌 이 보고서에서 나타난 것처럼 일을 잘해.
- He sleeps too long, such as on the weekends.
  걘 주말과 같은 때 늦잠을 자.

A: How can we improve our house?
B: We can do many things, such as paint it.

A: 우리 집을 어떻게 개량할 수 있을까?
B: 페인트를 칠하든가 많은 것을 할 수 있지.

The room is full of books

그 방은 책들로 가득해

be full of~는 '…로 가득하다'란 의미로 = be filled with.

Example
- I was full of energy after drinking some coffee.
  난 커피 좀 마셨더니 활기가 넘쳤어.
- The crowd was full of excitement as they waited.
  관중은 기다리면서 흥분에 차있었어.

A: Lyman always talks about how strong he is.
B: I don't believe it. He's full of hot air.

A: 라이만은 항상 자신이 강하다고 말하고 있어.
B: 난 믿지 않아. 걘 허풍쟁이야.

362

I have enough money to pay cash

난 현금으로 결제한만큼 충분해

enough to+V는 '…하기에 충분한'이라는 의미, have enough to+V하면 '…하기에 충분하다.'

💡 **Example**

- He **is old enough to** know better.
  걘 철이 들 나이야.

- Do you **have enough to** read on the airplane?
  비행기에서 읽을 건 충분해?

Dialog

A: Will that be cash or charge?
B: I think I **have enough to** pay cash.

A: 현금, 아님 신용카드로 하시겠어요?
B: 현금이 충분한 것 같군요.

363

We ran out of gas

기름이 바닥났어

run out of~는 '…이 다 떨어지다' = run low on~(부족하다).

💡 **Example**

- The store **ran out of** ice cream.
  그 가게는 아이스크림이 다 떨어졌어.

- We're about to **run out of** gas.
  기름이 바닥 나려고 하는데.

Dialog

A: We **ran out of** paper for the copier.
B: I'll get the secretary to get some more.

A: 복사기에 종이가 다 떨어졌어.
B: 비서한테 종이를 좀 더 가져오라고 할게.

364

He stretched before running

걘 달리기 전에 스트레칭을 했어

before ~ing는 '…하기 전에,' after ~ing는 '…한 후에,' ~ing 대신 명사나 S+V절이 올 수도 있다.

💡 **Example**

- We'll wait for you to get back before we start.
  돌아오는거 기다렸다 시작할게.

- Would you like a glass of wine before dinner?
  저녁 먹기 전 와인 한잔 할래?

 **Dialog**

A: Have some dinner before you go out.
B: Mom, I'm not hungry right now.

A: 외출하기 전에 저녁을 좀 해라.
B: 엄마, 지금 배고프지 않아요.

365

I got there on time

제 시간에 도착했어

on time(정각에) = at the exact time, in time(늦지 않게) = early or soon enough.

💡 **Example**

- I got there on time.
  제 시간에 도착했어.

- You'd better be on time tomorrow.
  내일 정각에 오도록 해라.

 **Dialog**

A: Has the meeting started? Am I late?
B: No, you're just on time.

A: 회의 시작됐어요? 제가 늦었나요?
B: 아뇨, 딱 맞게 왔어요.

We'll be closed during the vacation

휴가중 문을 닫을 예정입니다

during+특정기간명사, for+숫자명사가 각각 온다.

💡 Example

- Our high school will be closed during the vacation.
  방학 중에 우리 고등학교는 문을 닫을거야.
- What will you do during your vacation?
  너 휴가기간 동안 뭐할거니?

Dialog

A: Let's go to New York during summer vacation.
B: That would be a lot of fun.

A: 여름 휴가 동안 뉴욕에 가자.
B: 재미있겠다.

I hope to visit Tokyo some day

언젠가 도쿄에 가기를 희망해

some day는 '미래의 언젠가'(=one day).

💡 Example

- Some day I'll have a lot of money.
  언젠가는 난 많은 돈을 갖게 될 거야.
- Maybe some other time we can get together.
  아마도 우린 다른 때에 만날 수 있을 거야.

Dialog

A: When are you going to make a trip to Finland?
B: Some day, I will make sure to visit Helsinki.

A: 넌 언제 핀란드를 여행할 거니?
B: 난 언젠가 분명히 헬싱키를 방문할 거야.

368

In fact, I haven't seen Sam
실은 샘을 만난 적이 없어

as a matter of fact(사실상, 사실) = in fact.

Example
- As a matter of fact I didn't go to bed last night.
  사실은 간밤에 잠 못 잤어.
- In fact, she looked forward to a quiet dinner alone.
  사실 걘 혼자 조용한 식사를 기대했었어.

Dialog

A: Have you ever been to Disneyland?
B: No, as a matter of fact, I haven't.

A: 디즈니랜드에 가본 적이 있니?
B: 아니. 실은 가본 적이 없어.

369

I have a lot of work to do
나 할 일이 많아

a lot of = many[much]. a lot of 뒤에는 셀 수 있[없]는 명사가 올 수 있다.

Example
- There is plenty of food in the fridge.
  냉장고 안에 음식이 무지 많아.
- I found plenty of errors in the article.
  난 이 기사에서 많은 오류를 찾았어.

Dialog

A: These boxes have a lot of paperwork in them.
B: We'd better put them in the closet.

A: 이 박스들에는 상당히 많은 서류가 들어있어.
B: 창고 안에 넣어두는 것이 좋겠어.

370

I am kind of busy right now

지금은 내가 좀 바빠

kind of가 동사 뒤에 오면 '약간,' '조금'이라는 부사로 쓰인다. = kinda = sort of[sorta].

 **Example**

- I'm kind of nervous about going on stage.
  무대에 올라가는 것이 좀 긴장돼.

- I've sort of hard feelings for her.
  걔한테 조금이지만 감정이 있어.

Dialog

A: Would you like to join me for dinner?
B: Well, I am kind of busy right now. How about tomorrow?

A: 저녁 함께 드실래요?
B: 글쎄요, 지금은 제가 좀 바빠서요. 내일은 괜찮을까요?

371

He was standing next to his mom

걘 엄마 옆에 서 있었어

next to는 '…의 옆에,' beside와 같은 의미인데 '게다가'라는 의미의 besides와 구분.

 **Example**

- The prettiest girl in class sat next to me.
  반에서 젤 예쁜 애가 바로 내 옆에 앉았어.

- The keys are next to my glasses.
  열쇠가 내 안경 옆에 놓여있어.

Dialog

A: Is it next to the stadium?
B: No, it is across the street, next to the post office.

A: 그건 스타디움 옆에 있니?
B: 아니, 길 건너 우체국 옆에 있어.

372

The bank is over there

은행은 저쪽에 있어

over there는 '저기에,' '저쪽에,' 현재 있는 지점에서 반대편에 있다는 의미. far away는 '멀리.'

💡 Example

- I've walked over there from here.
  여기서 거기까지 걸어갔는데요.
- Is it far away from here?
  여기서 머니?

A: The woman sitting over there is my teacher.
B: You mean the one with brown hair?

A: 저기 앉아 있는 사람이 우리 선생님이야.
B: 갈색머리 여자 말이야?

373

I'll walk with you, if you like

원하면 내가 같이 걸어갈게

if you like는 '좋다면,' '괜찮으면,' (대답) '그렇게 하세요.'

💡 Example

- If you want to meet him, I can introduce you.
  걜 만나고 싶으면 내가 소개해줄게.
- We can leave now, if you wish.
  네가 원하면 우리 지금 떠날 수 있어.

A: I'm afraid to walk home alone.
B: I'll walk with you, if you like.

A: 난 집에 혼자 걸어가기가 두려워.
B: 원하시면 제가 같이 걸어가죠.

As for me, I like to watch TV

난, 텔레비전 보는 걸 좋아해

as for sb[as to sth]는 '…으로서,' '…에 대해 말하자면.'

💡 **Example**

- **As for** Jen, she's ready to get started.
  젠은 시작준비가 되어 있어.
- **As for** him, he'll be at lunch for an hour.
  그는 1시간 동안 점심을 할거야.

 **Dialog**

A: I really like to go on long trips.
B: **As for** me, I like to stay at home.

A: 난 정말로 긴 여행을 좋아해.
B: 나로서는 집에 머무는 것을 선호해.

Guess What?

We have bigger fish to fry
우리는 더 큰 문제가 있어

"튀길 더 큰 생선이 있다"라는 말로 사소한 문제를 논하기 보다는 그 보다 더 크고 중요한 문제(there are more important things to pay attention to)를 얘기하자고 할 때 주로 쓰이는 표현이다.

MEMO

Section 02
영어회화 핵심표현

"제대로 된 영어회화문장을 만들려면
꼭 알아두어야 하는 핵심표현들"

I'm on it
지금 할게

be on it은 '바로 일을 처리하다,' 어떤 일에 '집중하다' 또는 '능숙하다'라는 의미로 쓰인다.

Example
- I'm on it. It won't take long.
  지금 할게. 얼마 걸리지 않을거야.
- I'm on it. You can count on me.
  지금 할게. 날 믿어도 돼.

Dialog

A: Have you finished cleaning up?
B: I'm on it. I'll be done in an hour.

A: 청소를 끝냈니?
B: 지금 할게. 한 시간이면 될거야.

I'll get right on it
지금 바로 할게

be on it과 같은 맥락의 표현으로 '곧바로 일을 처리하다'라는 뜻이다.

Example
- If it's urgent, I'll get right on it.
  그 일이 급하면 바로 할게.
- I understand. I'll get right on it.
  알았어. 바로 시작할게.

Dialog

A: This needs to be done quickly.
B: Don't worry, I'll get right on it.

A: 이건 빨리 처리해야 돼.
B: 걱정하지마. 바로 할게.

003

I have to get back to work

다시 일하러 가야 돼

get to work는 '일을 시작하다,' '일하러 가다[출근하다],' get back to work는 '일을 재개하다.'

💡 Example

- I have got to get to work. So can I call you back later?
  일해야 돼. 나중에 전화해도 될까?
- How long does it take for you to get to work?
  출근하는데 얼마나 걸려?

A: Hey Nick, how about we get some beer?
B: I'd like to, but I have to get back to work.

A: 야, 닉, 우리랑 맥주 좀 마시자.
B: 그러고는 싶지만 다시 일하러 가봐야 해.

004

You did a good job!

정말 잘했어!

do a good job[do good work]은 '일을 잘하다,' 강조하려면 great, super 등을 쓰면 된다.

💡 Example

- You did a good job! I was very impressed.
  정말 잘 했어! 매우 인상적이었어.
- You did a great job organizing the fundraiser.
  모금행사를 조직하는데 일을 훌륭하게 했어.

A: I thought you always did a great job on exams.
B: Yeah, but actually I cheated all the time.

A: 넌 항상 시험을 잘 봤던 것 같은데.
B: 그랬지, 하지만 항상 컨닝을 한거였어.

005

I missed work for two days
난 이틀동안 결근했어
miss work는 '결근하다'이지만, 문맥에 따라서는 '일을 그리워하다'로도 쓰인다.

Example
- You may often miss school or work.
  넌 종종 수업이나 일을 빼먹을 수 있어.
- It's unusual for you to miss work.
  네가 일을 빼먹다니 이상한 일이다.

 Dialog

A: Why are you staying at home?
B: I miss a couple of days of work.

A: 왜 집에 머물고 있니?
B: 수일 동안 일을 빼먹고 있어.

006

Keep up the good work!
계속 열심히 일해!
keep up the good work = keep it up으로 하던 일을 계속 열심히 하다라는 뜻.

Example
- This looks good. Keep up the good work.
  잘한다. 계속 수고해.
- You did a great job. Keep up the good work.
  너 참 일 잘했어. 계속 수고해.

 Dialog

A: You are doing great work. Keep it up!
B: Gee, thanks a lot for noticing all my hard work.

A: 아주 잘 하고 있어. 계속 열심히 해!
B: 뭘, 내가 열심히 하고 있다는 걸 알아주니 아주 고마운데.

I worked around the clock yesterday

난 어제 종일 일했어

work around the clock은 24시간 일한다는 의미로 비유적으로 '열심히 일하다.'

💡 Example

- Everyone at the factory works around the clock.
  공장에 있는 모든 사람들이 종일 일하고 있어.

- I'm working around the clock to get it done.
  끝내기 위해 최선을 다하고 있어.

A: You guys look really tired.
B: We **worked around the clock** yesterday.

A: 너희들 정말 피곤해 보이네.
B: 어제 종일 일했거든.

I have a lot of work to do

난 아직 할 일이 많이 남아 있어

have a lot of work (to+V)는 일이 많다로 a lot of 대신 much를 쓰기도 한다.

💡 Example

- If you don't mind, I have a lot of work to do.
  괜찮다면 난 아직 할 일이 많이 남았어.

- Don't waste your time. We've got a lot of work to do.
  시간낭비마. 할 일이 많아.

A: I came here to see if you were finished.
B: No, I still **have a lot of work to** do.

A: 난 네 일이 끝났는지 알아보려고 여기 왔어.
B: 아니, 난 아직도 할 일이 많아.

Why don't you give it a try?

한번 해보는게 어때?

give it a try는 결과에 상관없이 '한번 해보다' = give it a shot, have a shot at.

💡 Example

- I've never played baseball, but I'll give it a try.
  야구해본 적이 없는데 한번 시도해볼게.

- Come on, you have the time. Go for it!
  야, 넌 시간이 있어. 한번 해봐!

 Dialog

A: Why don't you give it a try right now?
B: Okay, let's do it.

  A: 지금 당장 한번 해 보는 게 어때?
  B: 알았어, 한번 해 보자.

Please carry on with your work

당신 일을 계속하세요

carry on with+N[carry on ~ing]는 '어떤 일을 계속 지속적으로 하다.' 지시적 성격이 강하다.

💡 Example

- Please carry on with the presentation.
  발표를 계속해 주세요.

- They carried on kissing when there was a knock at the door.
  걔들은 누군가 문을 두들겼을 때 키스를 계속하고 있었어

 Dialog

A: Andy can't carry on with so much stress.
B: So, do you think he's going to quit?

  A: 앤디는 그렇게 많은 스트레스를 계속 받을 수 없어.
  B: 그래서 걔가 그만둘 것으로 생각하니?

011

You must keep trying

넌 계속 시도해봐야 돼

keep ~ing는 '계속해서 …하다'라는 의미. keep going는 일반적으로 '(일, 말) 계속하다'란 뜻이다.

Example

- Do you think the stock market will keep going up?
  주식시장이 계속 오를 것 같아?

- Never say die. You must keep trying.
  약한 소리 마. 계속 시도해봐야 한다고.

Dialog

A: I don't think I can finish this race.
B: Come on! Keep on running!

A: 난 이 경주를 마칠 수 없을 것 같아.
B: 왜 그래! 계속 뛰어!

012

I'll do my best

최선을 다할게

do one's best는 '최선을 다하다,'로 do 대신에 try를 써서 try one's best라고도 한다.

Example

- I'll do my best to remember your birthday next year.
  내년엔 네 생일 꼭 기억할게.

- You just have to be brave and try your best.
  용기를 갖고 최선을 다해봐.

Dialog

A: You'll have a good job interview. Cheer up.
B: Thanks. I'll do my best.

A: 면접을 잘 볼 거야. 기운 내.
B: 고마워. 최선을 다할게.

013

I made an effort to keep going

난 계속해나가려고 노력했어

make an effort to+V[at+N]는 '…하려고 적극적으로 노력하다.'

💡 **Example**

- I need to **make an effort to** exercise.
  난 운동을 하려고 노력을 해야 해.
- You have to **make an effort to** make your wife happy.
  넌 아내를 행복하게 해주려는 노력을 해야만 해.

 Dialog

A: We have to **make an effort to** keep those receipts.
B: I'll ask everyone to submit the ones that they have.

A: 영수증들을 보관하는 데 노력해야 돼.
B: 다 얘기해서 갖고 있는 영수증을 제출하라고 할게.

 014

I'm just trying to focus on this

이거에 집중하려고 하고 있는거야

concentrate[focus] on~는 '…에 노력을 집중하다,' 뒤에는 명사나 ~ing가 이어진다.

💡 **Example**

- You need to **concentrate on** being a better person.
  좋은 사람되기 위해 노력을 집중해.
- I'm just trying to **focus on** this.
  이거에 집중하려고 하고 있는 거야.

 Dialog

A: What are your plans for the new year?
B: I'm going to **concentrate on** losing some weight.

A: 너의 신년계획은 무엇이니?
B: 우선 체중 감량에 집중하려고 해.

I'm tied up all day

온종일 바빠 꼼짝 못해

be tied up (with sth)는 다른 아무것도 못하도록 꼼짝달싹 바쁜 상태를 말한다.

💡 **Example**

- I'm tied up with something urgent.
  급한 일로 꼼짝달싹 못해.

- I'm tied up all day. How about tomorrow?
  온종일 바빠 꼼짝 못해. 내일은 어때?

Dialog

A: When can I stop by to pick up those books?
B: Well, I'm kind of tied up all day. How about next week?

   A: 그 책들을 픽업하러 언제 들를 수 있을까?
   B: 저, 하루 종일 바쁠거야. 다음주가 어떨까?

I think it's good to take it slow

천천히 하는게 좋을거야

take it slow는 서두르지 말고 천천히 하다 = slow down.

💡 **Example**

- Take it slow and do a good job.
  천천히 일을 잘 해야지.

- I think it's good to take it slow.
  천천히 하는게 좋을거야.

Dialog

A: I've got to get this work done quickly.
B: Slow down. You're going to make mistakes.

   A: 이 일을 빨리 끝내야 돼.
   B: 천천히 해. 실수하겠다.

Take your time. It's not urgent

천천히 해. 급한 일 아냐

take one's time (~ing) 역시 서두르지 말고 천천히 신중하게 일을 하다.

Example

- Hold your horses, honey. I'll be home in 30 minutes.
  진정해. 30분 후에 도착해.

- Just hold your horses! We have a lot of time.
  천천히 해! 우리 시간 많다고.

A: I'll be back in ten minutes.
B: Take your time. It's not that busy.

A: 10분 후에 돌아올 거에요.
B: 여유 있게 하세요. 그렇게 바쁜 일은 아니니까.

I know how to play this game

이 게임 어떻게 하는지 알아

know how to+V는 '…하는 방법을 안다'라는 빈출 표현.

Example

- Do you know how to get there?
  거기 어떻게 가는지 알아?

- I know how to play this game.
  이 게임 어떻게 하는지 알아.

A: Do you know how to make cheese from milk?
B: Not really. But I'm sure it's difficult.

A: 우유로 치즈를 어떻게 만드는지 아니?
B: 글쎄. 하지만 분명히 어려울 거야.

Easy does it! That sofa is heavy

살살해! 그 소파는 무거워

Easy does it은 '진정해,' '서두르지마,'라는 의미외에 물건을 나를 때 조심히 다루라는 뜻으로도 쓰인다.

💡 Example

- **Easy does it.** We've got plenty of time.
  살살해. 우린 시간이 충분해.

- Stop driving so fast. **Easy does it.**
  그렇게 빨리 운전하지 마. 살살해.

 Dialog

A: I could work all night long.
B: **Easy does it.** You're going to get tired.

A: 난 밤새 일할 수 있어.
B: 살살해. 피곤해질 거야.

Let me take care of it

내가 이거 처리할게

take care of sb = 돌보다, (조폭) 죽이다, take care of sth = 처리하다, 다루다 = deal with.

💡 Example

- Who's going to **take care of** your kids while you're away?
  너 없는 동안 누가 너희 아이들을 돌봐 주게 되니?

- Can you **take care of** my work while I'm away?
  나 없을 때 내 일 좀 맡아줄래?

 Dialog

A: I can't find the time to make a dentist appointment.
B: Let me **take care of** it for you. You're too busy.

A: 치과에 전화 예약할 짬이 안나.
B: 나한테 맡겨. 넌 너무 바쁘잖아.

I can't get through the traffic jam
교통혼잡을 뚫고 갈 수가 없어

get through는 '작업을 마치다,' '어려운 시기를 넘기다,' '뚫고 가다.'

💡 **Example**

- Did you get through the DVD yet?
  그 DVD를 다 보았니?

- You need to get through this course.
  넌 이 과정을 통과해야만 해.

Dialog

A: Should we drive to the party?
B: We can't get through the traffic jam.

A: 우리 파티장까지 운전해갈거니?
B: 교통 혼잡을 뚫고 갈 수가 없어.

I'll catch up with you later
곧 따라 갈게

catch up with는 '..을 따라잡다,' 열심히 해서 앞선 사람과 동일한 수준에 도달하다.

💡 **Example**

- She needed to work hard to catch up with her classmates.
  걘 반친구들을 따라잡기 위해서 열심히 공부할 필요가 있었어.

- You go ahead. I'll catch up with you later.
  먼저가. 곧 따라 갈게.

Dialog

A: Are you planning to catch up with your high school friends?
B: Yeah, I'm going to have to run after them.

A: 넌 고등학교 친구들을 따라잡을 계획이니?
B: 응, 난 걔들 뒤를 따라가야만 해.

I can't keep up with Tina's studying

난 티나의 공부를 따라갈 수 없어

keep up with는 '…에 뒤쳐지지 않다,'로 keep up with the Joneses는 '남들처럼 하며 살다.'

 Example

- Try to keep up with the fastest runner.
  가장 빠른 주자를 따라가도록 노력해라.
- I can't keep up with Tina's studying.
  난 티나의 공부를 따라갈 수 없어.

Dialog

A: How's your new job going?
B: It didn't work out. I couldn't keep up with all the work.

A: 새로운 일은 어때?
B: 잘 되지 않았어. 모든 일을 따라갈 수가 없었어.

I didn't get it right

내가 제대로 하지 못했어

get it right은 '일을 제대로 하다,' '성공하다,' 혹은 '이해하다'라는 의미로 쓰인다.

 Example

- If you try to do something, get it right.
  뭘 하려고 노력한다면 제대로 해라.
- He quit because he couldn't get it right.
  걘 일을 제대로 할 수가 없어서 그만두었어.

Dialog

A: Did you answer her question?
B: I did, but I didn't get it right.

A: 걔의 질문에 대답을 했니?
B: 하긴 했지만 제대로 못했어요.

025

I managed to catch the last train
난 막차를 간신히 탔어

manage to+V는 어려움 속에서 노력하여 '가까스로 해내다,' '그럭저럭 해내다'라는 뉘앙스를 갖는다.

 Example

- I didn't manage to find a dance partner.
  난 댄스 파트너를 찾아내지 못했어.
- You'll have to manage to buy another car.
  넌 다른 차를 사보도록 해야 할 거야.

 Dialog

A: Did you manage to lose some weight?
B: Yeah, but I have to continue my diet.

A: 약간 체중 감량을 해냈나요?
B: 예, 그렇지만 다이어트는 계속해야만 하죠.

026

I applied for a visa last week
난 지난주에 비자를 신청했어

apply for+N(직책, 기회)는 …에 지원하다. N이 기관[학교]일 때는 apply to~를 쓴다.

 Example

- I applied for some jobs over the Internet.
  난 인터넷으로 일자리에 지원했어.
- You need to apply for a job to get hired.
  넌 고용되려면 먼저 일자리에 지원을 해야 돼.

Dialog

A: That's a nice suit you're wearing.
B: I'm going to apply for a job.

A: 매우 좋은 옷을 입었네.
B: 일자리에 지원하려고.

I sent my resume to Amazon

난 아마존에 이력서를 보냈어

send one's resume는 단순히 이력서를 보냈다는 사실 뜻함. resume는 [rezumei]로 발음한다.

💡 Example

- Randy sent his resume to IBM.
  랜디는 IBM 사에 자신의 이력서를 보냈어.

- I've sent out over one hundred resumes!
  난 이력서를 100통도 넘게 보냈다고!

A: I'd like to apply for a job here.
B: You need to send us your resume first.

A: 난 여기 자리에 지원하고 싶어요.
B: 먼저 이력서를 우리한테 보내야 합니다.

I got a job as a car designer

난 자동차 디자이너로 취직을 했어

get a job as+직종은 '…로 취직하다'라는 의미로 구체적으로 무슨 직종으로 취직했는지 말할 때 쓴다.

💡 Example

- He couldn't get a job as a garbage man.
  걘 쓰레기 청소부로 취업을 할 수 없었어.

- I want to get a job as an actor in Hollywood.
  난 헐리우드 배우로 취직하길 원해.

A: I got a job as a car designer.
B: That's great! I hope you'll be successful.

A: 난 자동차 디자이너로 취직을 했어.
B: 아주 좋아! 성공하길 바래.

029

They offered me a high-paying job
그들은 내게 고연봉 일자리를 제안했어

offer sb a job은 '…에게 일자리를 제안하다,' 이렇게 채용제안을 받다는 get a job offer from~.

💡 **Example**
- We want to offer you a job as a general manager.
  당신에게 총지배인 자리를 권하고 싶어.
- He was offered a job post in Chicago.
  걘 시카고에서 일자리를 제안 받았어.

 **Dialog**

A: Who is offering you the job with such a high salary?
B: Guess who? The CEO of the company himself.

  A: 누가 네게 그런 고임금의 일자리를 권하고 있어?
  B: 누구게? 그 회사 총괄사장 자신이야.

030

I work for the government
난 공무원이야

work for sb는 '…에서 일하다.' 물론 work at[in]~도 쓰이지만 work for~의 형태가 많이 쓰인다.

💡 **Example**
- Jason works for his father.
  제이슨은 자기 아버지를 위해 일해.
- I want to work for a university.
  난 대학에서 일하고 싶어.

 **Dialog**

A: Do you enjoy your job?
B: Yes, I work for a television station.

  A: 네 직업을 즐기고 있니?
  B: 응, TV 방송국에서 일해.

I work part-time as a driver

난 시간제 운전기사로 일해

work part-time at+직종은 '시간제로 …일을 하다,' work part-time at+장소는 '…에서 시간제로 일하다.'

💡 **Example**

- Gary works part-time at the department store.
  게리는 백화점에서 파트타임으로 일해.
- I work part-time as a French tutor.
  난 프랑스어 가정교사로 파트 타임으로 일해.

 **Dialog**

A: I never see your daughter anymore.
B: She goes to college and also works part-time.

A: 난 네 딸은 더이상 볼 수가 없구나.
B: 걘 대학에 진학하는 한편 파트 타임으로 일하고 있어.

Let's call it a day

오늘 그만 일하자

call it a day[night]은 '일을 그만하고 퇴근하다,' '오늘은 여기까지만 하다' = call it quits.

💡 **Example**

- Let's call it a day and get some beer.
  일끝내고 맥주 좀 먹자.
- Would you like to have a drink after work?
  퇴근 후 한잔 할 테야?

 **Dialog**

A: I'm so exhausted. Let's call it a day.
B: Sounds good to me.

A: 넘 지쳤어. 퇴근하자.
B: 좋은 생각이네.

033

I need to give her a raise
걔 급여를 올려줘야겠어

get a (pay) raise는 '급여가 오르다,' 반대로 회사가 급여를 올려준다고 할 때는 give sb a raise.

💡 **Example**
- I'm curious whether I will get a raise next year.
  내년에 급여가 인상될 지 궁금해.
- I'm hoping to get a raise at work in the spring.
  봄에 직장에서 임금인상이 있길 바래.

 Dialog

A: We need to give the secretary a raise.
B: When was the last time we gave her one?

A: 비서에게 봉급을 올려줘야겠어요.
B: 마지막으로 그녀의 급여를 올려준 게 언제죠?

 034

I'm going to quit this job
나 회사 그만 둘래

quit one's job은 '직장을 그만두다,' 자의로 회사를 그만두는 것을 말한다.

💡 **Example**
- Joan hated her boss and quit her job.
  조앤은 보스를 증오해서 직장을 그만두었지.
- I'm going to quit this job. I mean it.
  그만 둘래. 진심이야.

 Dialog

A: What would you do if you had a lot of money?
B: The first thing I'd do is quit my job.

A: 네가 돈을 많이 갖고 있으면 뭘 할거니?
B: 가장 먼저 할 일은 직장을 그만두는거야.

035

He's on a business trip
걔는 출장중이야

go[be] on a business trip (to~)은 '출장을 가다[출장중이다]'라는 의미 = go on a trip for business.

 **Example**

- My uncle went on a business trip to Japan.
  삼촌은 일본으로 출장갔어.
- Can you take your wife on the business trip?
  출장에 아내도 같이 가도 되는 거야?

 Dialog

A: Jack is about to **go on a business trip**.
B: Where is he going to travel?

   A: 잭은 출장을 떠나려고 해.
   B: 어디로 가는데?

036

I can't do business with my friends
난 친구들과 거래를 할 수는 없어

do business with+회사[사람]은 '…와 거래하다,' '…와 사업을 하다'라는 의미.

 **Example**

- I can't **do business with** my friends.
  난 친구들과 거래를 할 수는 없어.
- We stopped **doing business with** that firm.
  우린 저 회사와 사업관계를 중단했어.

Dialog

A: Is your company international?
B: We **do business with** people in many countries.

   A: 네 회사는 국제적이니?
   B: 우린 여러 나라들에서 사업을 해.

037

I'm afraid we'll go bankrupt
우리가 파산할 까 두려워
go bankrupt는 '파산하다,' file for bankruptcy는 '파산신고를 하다.'

💡 **Example**

- Our store needs business or we'll go bankrupt.
  우리 가게는 사업이 돼야지 아니면 파산할거야.
- The company went bankrupt last September.
  이 회사는 지난 9월 파산해버렸어.

 Dialog

A: You and your wife spend a lot of money.
B: I'm afraid we'll go bankrupt.

A: 너와 네 부인은 돈을 무지 쓰네.
B: 우리가 파산할 까 두려워.

038

I went out of business
난 사업접었어
go out of business는 '사업을 접다,' '폐업하다'라는 의미이다.

💡 **Example**

- It went out of business because there was no money.
  걔들은 자금이 없어서 파산했어.
- Many Internet companies went out of business this year.
  올해 파산한 인터넷 기업들이 많아.

 Dialog

A: No one ever goes into that store.
B: They'll probably go out of business.

A: 누구도 저 가게에 들어가질 않아.
B: 아마도 파산할 것 같아.

We're running a small business

우리는 작은 회사를 운영하고 있어

run a business는 '회사를 운영하다,' '경영하다.' business는 사업(체)를 말한다.

💡 Example

- Mike's family ran a small business.
  마이크 가족은 소규모 사업을 운영했어.

- She decided to run a business with her partner.
  걘 파트너와 함께 사업을 하기로 결정했어.

💡 Dialog

A: Maybe we should start our own company.
B: No, I don't know how to run a business.

A: 아마도 우리 자신 회사를 창업해야 할거야.
B: 아냐, 난 경영법을 몰라.

I started a new business

난 새로운 사업을 시작했어

start a new business는 '새로운 사업을 시작하다,' start up a business는 '새 사업을 창업하다.'

💡 Example

- It takes a lot of money to start a new business.
  신규사업을 하려면 많은 돈이 들어.

- I think this is a good time to start our own business.
  내 생각에는 지금이 우리가 사업을 시작하기에 좋은 기회라고 봐.

💡 Dialog

A: Are you going to get a job after you graduate?
B: No, I'm going to try starting up my own business.

A: 졸업 후엔 취업할 거니?
B: 아니, 사업을 시작해볼까 해.

📎 041

I didn't complete the work
난 그 일을 끝내지 못했어
complete the work는 '일을 완수하다.' 여기서 complete는 동사로 '끝내다,' '완수하다.'

💡 **Example**
- You can complete the work tomorrow.
  넌 내일 일을 끝낼 수 있어.
- Jay completed the work his boss gave him.
  제이는 보스가 준 일을 완수했어.

 Dialog

A: Have you finished your report?
B: I worked all night, but I didn't complete the work.

A: 보고서를 끝냈나요?
B: 밤새 일했는데도 끝내지 못했어요.

📎 042

I'll give her that task
난 걔에게 그 일을 줄거야
give sb a task는 '…에게 업무를 부여하다.' task 대신에 job이나 assignment를 사용해도 된다.

💡 **Example**
- He gave his students a difficult assignment.
  그가 학생들에게 어려운 과제를 내줬어.
- Let's give her a fun task to complete.
  걔한테 일하기 재미있는 과제를 내주자.

 Dialog

A: Can someone clean up this room?
B: I'll give Elaine that job.

A: 누가 이 방 청소를 할 수 있니?
B: 일레인에게 시킬 게.

We must cancel the meeting

우리는 그 회의를 취소해야 돼

cancel the meeting은 '회의를 취소하다,' 특히 "회의+be cancelled"라고 많이 쓰인다.

💡 **Example**

- I couldn't believe that Jack left in the middle of the meeting.
  잭이 회의 중간에 나가서 얼마나 놀랐는데.

- I don't want to be late to the meeting again.
  난 다시는 그 회의에 늦고 싶지 않아.

A: The manager had to leave suddenly.
B: That means we must cancel the meeting.

A: 매니저가 갑자기 떠나야만 했어.
B: 그렇다면 우린 회의를 취소해야만 해.

Let's not schedule a meeting today

오늘은 회의를 잡지 말자

schedule a meeting은 '회의일정을 잡다'로 회의하는 사람은 뒤에 with sb로 붙인다.

💡 **Example**

- Schedule a meeting with my secretary.
  내 비서와 회의일정을 잡으세요.

- I need to schedule a meeting with you.
  당신과의 회의일정을 짜야 돼요.

A: What time is the meeting scheduled for?
B: It will be at 5 P.M. this afternoon.

A: 회의가 몇 시에 예정되어 있나요?
B: 오늘 오후 5시에 열릴 거예요.

045

We lost the contract
우리가 계약을 놓쳤어
lose the contract는 '계약을 놓치다'라는 의미.

Example
- The firm lost their contract in Japan.
  그 회사는 일본에서 계약을 잃게 되었어.
- If you fail again, you'll lose the contract.
  네가 한번 더 실패하면 넌 계약을 잃게 될 거야.

A: I'm not kidding, we lost the contract.
B: What are we going to tell the boss?

A: 그 계약을 따내지 못했어, 정말이야!
B: 사장한테 뭐라고 하지?

046

I opened an account at this bank
난 이 은행에 계좌를 개설했어
open an account는 '계좌를 개설하다,' 혹은 '계약을 트다.' 이때 account = business account(거래선).

Example
- I need to talk to you about the Halverson account.
  할버슨 거래선에 대해 얘기하자.
- Tom opened an account at the stockbroker's firm.
  탐은 증권사에 계좌를 개설했어.

A: Tony just has opened the first account in China.
B: That'll really open up the Chinese market to us.

A: 토니가 중국에 첫 번째 거래선을 텄어.
B: 그로 인해 중국 시장이 우리에게 개방될거야.

I got it on sale

난 그걸 세일 때 샀어

get sth on sale은 '세일 때 …을 사다,' get sth at~은 '…을 …에서 사다[구하다].'

Example

- Kelly got a Rolex watch on sale.
  켈리는 세일하는 로렉스 시계를 샀어.
- I got it on sale at a department store.
  백화점에서 염가 판매하는 걸 샀어.

Dialog

A: Honey, this is for you. I got it on sale.
B: You're so sweet.

A: 이거 너 줄려고. 세일 때 샀어.
B: 정말 친절도 해라.

Guess What?

Money doesn't grow on trees!
돈을 아껴 써라!

"무성한 나뭇가지에서 가지를 쉽게 따듯 돈은 나무에서 나뭇가지처럼 자라는 것이 아니다"라는 말이다. 비유적으로 돈은 벌기 힘드니까 신중하게 사용하여서 낭비하지 않도록(money is hard to get and should be used carefully so it isn't wasted) 해야 된다는 좋은 교훈이다.

048

Let's cut back on eating out

외식비를 줄이자

cut back on+N[~ing]은 '(규모나 빈도) 줄이다,' cut down on은 주로 건강을 위해 '수량'을 줄일 때.

💡 **Example**

- Maybe next month we can cut back on a few things.
  우리는 다음 달에 아마도 몇 가지 줄여야 될지 몰라.

- We're going to cut back on shopping too.
  우린 쇼핑도 역시 줄일 거야.

 **Dialog**

A: Let's cut back on eating out.
B: But I really like eating in restaurants.

A: 외출을 줄이자.
B: 그런데 난 식당에서 식사하는 것을 정말 좋아해.

049

I earned a lot of money working here

난 여기서 일해서 많은 돈을 벌었어

earn a lot of money[~ing]는 '많은 돈을 벌다' = make a fortune.

💡 **Example**

- You won't earn a lot of money working here.
  넌 여기서 일해서 많은 돈을 벌 수는 없어.

- Korea earned a lot of money exporting items.
  한국은 수출로 많은 돈을 벌었어.

 **Dialog**

A: James earned a lot of money as a lawyer.
B: We should have gone to law school.

A: 제임스는 변호사로 많은 돈을 벌었어.
B: 우리도 법대를 갔어야 하는데.

I'll pay for the coffee

커피값은 내가 낼게

pay for+돈을 내야 되는 이유는 '…의 대금을 지불하다,' 추상적으로 '대가를 치르다.'

💡 Example

- Can you pay for our dinner?
  우리 저녁 식사비를 지불할 수 있나요?
- Charlie needs to pay me the money he owes.
  찰리는 내게 빚진 돈을 갚아야 돼.

A: We would like to pay for your airline ticket.
B: That's wonderful. I don't know how to thank you.

A: 저희가 비행기표 값을 지불하겠습니다.
B: 정말이요. 어떻게 감사 드려야 할 지 모르겠네요.

I'd like to pay in cash

난 현금으로 계산하고 싶어요

pay in cash는 '현금으로 내다.' 현금일 때는 in cash, 수표나 카드일 때는 by[with]~을 쓴다.

💡 Example

- I'd like to pay in cash. How much is it?
  난 현금으로 계산하고 싶어요. 얼마죠?
- I'm going to pay for this with a check.
  수표로 낼게요.

A: Will you pay for this in cash or by check?
B: Let me pay for it with my credit card.

A: 현금과 수표 중에 어떤 걸로 지불하시겠어요?
B: 신용카드로 계산하겠어요.

I'll get a loan from a bank

은행에서 융자를 받을거야

get a loan (from a bank)는 '(은행에서) 융자를 받다,' apply for a loan은 '융자를 신청하다.'

Example

- Jay got a loan from his bank to pay for school.
  제이는 학비를 은행에서 융자받았어.
- Joan applied for a loan to start a business
  조앤은 사업을 시작하려고 사업자금 대출을 신청했어.

Dialog

A: Will you be able to buy that new house?
B: Yeah, I'll get a loan from a bank.

A: 저 새 집을 구매할 수 있니?
B: 그럼, 은행에서 융자를 받을거야.

I can't afford to buy a new car

난 새 차를 살 여유가 안돼

can't afford to+V[can't afford+N]는 '…할 여유가 없다,' 비금전적인 상황에서도 쓰인다.

Example

- I can't afford to buy you a house.
  네게 집을 사줄 여력이 없어.
- How much can you afford to spend?
  예산은 얼마쯤 잡고 있는데?

Dialog

A: I can't afford to buy a new coat.
B: I can give you one of my brother's coats.

A: 난 새 코트를 살 여유가 없어.
B: 내 남동생 코트 중 하나를 네게 줄 수 있어.

I reduced the cost of the project

난 그 프로젝트비용을 줄였어

reduce the cost of~는 '…의 비용을 줄이다.' of 이하에 비용을 절감하는 대상을 써주면 된다.

Example

- The store reduced the cost of the jackets.
  그 가게는 재킷 만드는 비용을 줄였어.
- Can you reduce the cost of school?
  학비를 줄일 수 있겠니?

Dialog

A: These school books are so expensive.
B: I wish we could reduce the cost of buying them.

A: 이 학교 교재들이 무척 비싸네.
B: 우리가 교재 구입비용을 줄일 수 있으면 좋겠어.

I transferred money to her today

난 오늘 걔에게 송금했어

transfer money to sb[sb's account]는 '…에게[…의 계좌로] 송금하다.'

Example

- I transferred money to my son's account.
  난 내 아들 구좌로 돈을 이체했어.
- You need to transfer money to the company's account.
  넌 회사 구좌로 돈을 송금해야 해.

Dialog

A: How did you sell the computer on the Internet?
B: The buyer transferred money to my account.

A: 어떻게 컴퓨터를 인터넷으로 팔았니?
B: 매수자가 돈을 내 구좌로 이체해주었어.

056

He attended a good university
갸는 좋은 대학에 다녔어

attend a good university는 '좋은 대학에 다니다,' attend class는 '수업에 참석하다.'

 Example

- My friend Laura attended a good university.
  내 친구 로라는 좋은 대학에 다녔어.
- I told my kids to attend a good university.
  난 내 애들에게 좋은 대학에 다니라고 말했지.

Dialog

A: It's important to attend a good university.
B: I know. It helps people get high paying jobs.

A: 좋은 대학에 다니는 것이 중요해.
B: 알아. 높은 봉급의 직업을 구하는데 도움이 돼.

057

She was admitted to Yale
갠 예일대에 입학했어

be admitted to+대학하면 '…대학교에 입학하다.' to 다음에 합격한 대학을 말하면 된다.

 Example

- Only one of my classmates was admitted to Princeton.
  내 학급생 중 단지 1명만 프린스턴 대에 입학했어.
- They said I'll never be admitted to Yale.
  걔들은 내가 예일대에 떨어질거라고 말했어

Dialog

A: Were you admitted to Harvard?
B: No, I had to apply to other schools.

A: 너 하버드 대에 입학되었니?
B: 아니, 다른 학교에 지원해야만 했어.

I failed the entrance exam

난 입학시험에 떨어졌어

fail the entrance exam은 '입학시험에 떨어지다,' fail the class는 '낙제하다' = get an F in the class.

💡 Example

- Ray failed the entrance exam three times before he gave up.
  레이는 3번이나 입학시험에 떨어지고서야 포기했어.
- Don't fail the entrance exam for the university.
  대학 입학시험에 떨어지지 마라.

Dialog

A: John has been up drinking all night.
B: Oh, God, he's going to fail the entrance exam.

A: 존은 밤새 술을 마시느라 깨어 있었어.
B: 아이고, 걔 입학시험에 떨어질 거야.

Don't drop out of school

중퇴하지 말아라

drop out of school은 '중퇴하다,' dropout은 '중퇴생,' 그리고 be expelled from school은 '제적[퇴학]당하다.'

💡 Example

- Work hard and don't drop out of school.
  열심히 공부해 그리고 중퇴하지 마.
- Jane dropped out of school after failing several exams.
  제인은 몇 번의 시험에 떨어진 후 학교를 중퇴했어.

Dialog

A: Bill dropped out of school this year.
B: He'll have trouble finding work.

A: 빌은 금년에 중퇴했어.
B: 걘 직업을 찾는데 어려움이 있을거야.

060

It takes time to finish law school
법대를 마치는데는 시간이 걸려

finish law school은 '법대를 마치다,' finish grad school은 '대학원을 마치다.'

💡 **Example**
- It may take five years to finish grad school.
  대학원을 마치는데 5년 걸릴 수도 있어.
- Aaron finished medical school when he was 30.
  애론은 30세에 의대를 마쳤어.

 **Dialog**

A: How long does it take to finish law school?
B: It takes about three or four years.

  A: 법대를 마치는데 몇 년이 걸리니?
  B: 3년 내지 4년이 걸리지.

061

I graduated from Yale in 2024
난 2024년에 예일대를 졸업했어

graduate from+대학은 '…대학교를 졸업하다.' a graduate는 '졸업생,' undergraduate는 '학부생.'

💡 **Example**
- I think my secretary graduated from your university.
  내 비서가 네 대학교를 졸업한 것 같아.
- When did you graduate from university?
  대학교 언제 졸업했어요?

 **Dialog**

A: When did you graduate from high school?
B: I graduated about five years ago.

  A: 고등학교는 언제 졸업하셨어요?
  B: 한 5년쯤 전에 졸업했지.

I majored in computer science

난 컴퓨터 공학을 전공했어

major[specialize] in+과목하면 '…을 전공하다.' What's your major?처럼 명사로도 쓰인다.

💡 Example

- Ellie majored in communication studies.
  엘리는 커뮤니케이션 학을 전공했어.

- Britt can't decide what to major in.
  브리트는 뭘 전공할 지 결정하지 못했어.

Dialog

A: Many students want to major in liberal arts.
B: Science and math are more difficult to study.

  A: 많은 학생들이 교양과목을 전공하고 싶어해.
  B: 과학과 수학은 공부하기가 더 어려워.

She skips class almost every Monday

걘 거의 매주 월요일마다 수업을 빼먹어

skip class[cut class]는 '수업을 빼먹다,' skip school은 '학교를 빼먹다,' skip work는 '결근하다.'

💡 Example

- We skipped class and played computer games.
  수업을 빼먹고 컴퓨터 게임을 했어.

- Perry skipped class on the day of the test.
  페리는 시험 당일 수업에 빠졌어.

Dialog

A: How did they get in trouble?
B: They tried to skip class and got caught.

  A: 걔들에게 어떤 문제가 생겼대?
  B: 수업을 빼먹으려다 잡혔대.

He helped me with my homework

걘 내가 숙제하는걸 도와줬어

help sb with sb's homework는 '…의 숙제를 도와주다.' help sb+V, help sb with sth 형태를 익혀둔다.

Example

- Mr. Sampson helped me with my homework.
  샘슨 부인은 내 숙제를 도와주었어.

- Our best student helps others with their homework.
  우리 중 가장 똑똑한 학생이 나머지 학생들의 숙제를 도와주고 있어.

A: I don't think Bob is very smart.
B: You should help him with his homework.

A: 밥이 아주 똑똑하다고 생각하지 않아.
B: 넌 걔가 숙제 하는데 도와줘야 할거야.

I can't submit this report

난 이 리포트를 제출할 수가 없어

submit the report는 '보고서[논문]를 제출하다.' submit = turn in. '논문쓰다'는 write a paper.

Example

- Submit this report in the morning.
  이 리포트를 아침에 제출해라.

- Let's submit this report to our boss.
  이 리포트를 보스에게 제출하자.

A: I can't submit this report.
B: I know. It's full of mistakes.

A: 난 이 리포트를 제출할 수가 없어.
B: 알아. 실수 투성이지.

066

You'll never pass your exam

넌 결코 시험에 합격하지 못할거야

pass the exam[test]는 '시험에 통과하다,' '합격하다.'

💡 **Example**

- Do you think she'll pass the exam?
  그녀가 시험에 합격할 것 같니?
- You will pass the exam if you study.
  넌 공부만 하면 시험에 합격할거야.

 Dialog

A: I was up drinking all night.
B: You'll never pass your exam.

A: 난 밤새 술 마시느라 깨어 있었어.
B: 넌 결코 시험에 합격하지 못할거야.

067

I got 99% on the exam

난 그 시험에서 99%를 맞혔어

get a good grade는 '좋은 학점을 받다,' 반대로 '낮은 학점을 받다'는 get a bad grade.

💡 **Example**

- I got the highest grade on the exam.
  시험에서 제일 높은 점수를 받았어.
- I got 99% on the exam.
  난 그 시험에서 99%를 맞혔어.

 Dialog

A: You've been studying very hard.
B: I need to get a good grade on this exam.

A: 넌 아주 열심히 공부했어.
B: 난 이 시험에서 좋은 학점을 받아야 하거든.

068

It doesn't work properly
그게 제대로 작동안해

be not working (properly)는 컴퓨터나 기계 등이 '제대로 작동하지 않다' = be[break] down.

💡 **Example**

- The computers aren't working.
  컴퓨터가 작동하지 않아요.

- I'm not sure if this computer program will work.
  이 컴퓨터 프로그램이 작동될지 모르겠어.

 Dialog

A: Is there a problem with the computer?
B: Yeah, the mouse doesn't work properly.

A: 컴퓨터에 문제가 있니?
B: 응, 마우스가 제대로 작동을 안해.

069

He recovered the data
그가 데이터를 복구했어

recover the data는 '데이터를 복구하다' = recover a deleted[erased] file.

💡 **Example**

- The computer repairman recovered the data.
  컴퓨터 정비사가 그 데이터를 복구해냈어.

- Can you recover the data on this disk?
  이 디스크에 있는 데이터를 복구할 수 있니?

 Dialog

A: My computer broke last night.
B: I hope you can recover the data on it.

A: 내 컴퓨터가 지난 밤 고장났어.
B: 거기 있던 데이터를 복구할 수 있기를 바래.

The files are gone

파일들이 날아가버렸어

be gone은 작업한 파일들이 '날아가다,' '사라지다.'

 Example

- The files were gone after the virus hit.
  바이러스가 공격한 후에 그 파일들이 사라졌어.

- After the computer crashed, the files were gone.
  컴퓨터가 고장나면서 파일들이 날아갔어.

Dialog

A: Can you save the reports I wrote?
B: I'm sorry, but the files are gone.

A: 내가 작성한 보고서를 저장할 수 있니?
B: 미안해, 그 파일들이 날아가버렸어.

I can't get connected to the Wi-Fi

와이파이에 연결이 안돼요

get connected to~는 (기계, 인터넷) '연결되다,' (사람과) '연락이 되다.'

 Example

- We got connected to the Internet at the coffee shop.
  우린 커피숍에서 인터넷을 연결했어.

- I will get connected to the Internet soon.
  난 조만간 인터넷 연결을 할거야.

Dialog

A: Why isn't the computer working?
B: I tried to connect to the Internet, but I did it wrong.

A: 컴퓨터가 왜 작동이 안되는거야?
B: 인터넷 연결하다 잘못했어.

072

I searched the Internet for cheap flights

값싼 항공권을 찾으려고 인터넷을 뒤졌어

search the Internet은 '인터넷을 검색하다' = surf the Net.

Example
- Don't surf the Internet during business hours.
  근무중 인터넷 검색을 하지마라.
- Younger people are using the Internet to express their opinions.
  젊은이들은 자신들의 의견을 나타내려고 인터넷을 사용하고 있어.

Dialog
A: How did you find your new car?
B: I searched the Internet for a good deal.

A: 넌 새차를 어떻게 찾았니?
B: 좋은 거래를 하려고 인터넷을 검색했지.

073

I'll add him to my Messenger list

걔를 메신저 리스트에 올릴거야

add sb to one's Messenger (list)는 '…을 메신저 리스트에 올리다,' 즉 메신저에서 친구로 추가하는 것.

Example
- Kelly added Bill to her Messenger list.
  캘리는 빌을 자신의 메신저 리스트에 추가했어.
- Should I add Max to my Messenger list?
  맥스를 내 메신저 리스트에 추가해야 되니?

Dialog
A: Are you going to chat with Abe?
B: Sure, I'll add him to my Messenger list.

A: 넌 아브라함과 채팅을 할거니?
B: 그럼, 난 걔를 메신저 리스트에 올릴거야.

Attach the file you just finished

네가 방금 끝난 파일을 첨부해라

attach the file은 이멜에 '파일첨부하다,' 첨부된 파일은 attached file, 이를 열어보는 건 open the attached file.

💡 **Example**

- **Attach the file** you just finished.
  네가 방금 끝난 파일을 첨부해라.
- **Attach the files** so I can look at them.
  내가 볼 수 있도록 파일들을 첨부해.

 **Dialog**

A: How can I get this information to Barry?
B: **Attach the file to** an e-mail for him.

A: 이 정보를 배리에게 어떻게 줄 수 있을까?
B: 걔한테 가는 이메일에 파일을 첨부해줘.

He wrote a note to his boss

걘 보스에게 메모를 썼어

write a note to sb = write sb a note는 '…에게 메모적다.' 메모를 받아적다[남기다]는 take[leave] a note.

💡 **Example**

- I'll **write a note to** my mom tonight.
  난 오늘 밤 엄마에게 메모를 쓸거야.
- I'll **send a note** around letting everyone know.
  난 모든 사람이 알도록 메모를 돌릴거야.

 **Dialog**

A: How did Carey quit her job?
B: She **wrote a note to** her boss.

A: 어떻게 케어리가 직장을 그만 두었니?
B: 걘 보스에게 메모를 썼나봐.

I have to go make a call

나 가서 전화를 걸어야 돼

make a call은 '전화를 걸다,' 반대로 '전화를 받다'는 take the[a, this] call.

Example

- I have to go make a call. I'll be back.
  전화 좀 걸고, 곧 돌아올게.
- She took out her phone and made a call.
  걘 전화기를 꺼내서 전화를 걸었어.

A: I've got to make a call right now.
B: Here, you can use my cell phone.

A: 난 바로 지금 전화를 해야 해.
B: 여기 내 휴대폰을 사용해라.

I've got another call

다른 전화가 왔어

have (got) another call은 '다른 전화가 오다.' 진행형으로 be getting another call이라고 쓰기도 한다.

Example

- I have another call. Can I call you back later?
  다른 전화가 왔어. 나중에 전화할게.
- Can you hold on a moment? I have another call.
  잠깐 기다려 줄래? 다른 전화가 왔어.

A: Hold on, I've got another call.
B: Don't keep me waiting for you.

A: 잠깐, 다른 전화가 왔어.
B: 너를 기다리게 하지 마라.

I can't take her call right now

난 지금 전화를 받을 수 없어

take this call은 걸려오는 전화기 화면을 보며 '전화를 받아,' this 대신 take a[the] call이라고도 한다.

💡 **Example**

- Would you excuse me for a second while I take this call?
  전화 받는 동안 잠시만 양해를 구할게요.

- I will take the call in my office.
  내 사무실에서 전화를 받을게.

Dialog

A: Your mom is on the line.
B: I can't take her call right now.

A: 네 엄마가 전화에 나와 계셔.
B: 난 지금 전화를 받을 수 없어.

There's a phone call for you

전화왔어

There's a는 생략된 Phone call for you의 형태로 '전화가 왔다'로 전할 때 사용된다.

💡 **Example**

- Hey Cindy! Phone call for you!
  야 신디야! 전화왔어!

- Excuse me. There's a phone call for you.
  실례합니다. 전화왔어요.

Dialog

A: There's a phone call for you.
B: Thank you. I'll take it in my office.

A: 전화 왔어요.
B: 고마워요. 내 사무실에서 받을게요.

I'll get her for you

(전화) 바꿔드리죠

get A for B는 구어체로 쓰는 표현으로 전화를 건 B를 위해 'A를 바꿔준다'는 말. Give me A는 'A를 바꿔주세요.'

Example

- Just a moment. Let me get the manager for you.
  잠시만요. 매니저 불러올게요.

- Give me Natalie in sales, please.
  영업부의 나탈리 부탁합니다.

Dialog

A: I'd like to speak with Joanna, please.
B: I'll get her for you.

A: 조앤나와 통화하고 싶은데요.
B: 바꿔드리죠.

You can reach me at 010-3794-5450

010-3794-5450으로 연락해

reach sb at+전화번호는 '…에게 …번호로 연락하다' = contact sb.

Example

- How should I contact you to arrange another meeting?
  다시 만나려면 어떻게 연락해야 하나요?

- My name is Lee, and I would like to contact Sam.
  내 이름은 리인데 샘하고 연락하고 싶은데요.

Dialog

A: How can I get in touch with you?
B: You can reach me at 010-3794-5450 any time.

A: 어디로 통화할까요?
B: 아무때나 010-3794-5450으로 해.

We get bad reception on the elevator

엘리베이터에서는 수신상태가 안 좋아

get[have] bad reception = have a bad connection은 '수신상태가 안좋다.'

💡 **Example**

- Jim got bad reception while he was hiking.
  짐은 하이킹중 전화상태가 아주 안좋았어.

- He said his cell phone wasn't getting good reception.
  걘 전화수신상태가 안좋았대.

A: I've been calling your cell.
B: Well, we get bad reception on the elevator.

A: 핸드폰으로 계속 전화했었는데.
B: 저기, 엘리베이터에서는 수신상태가 안 좋아.

He's expecting your call

걔가 네 전화를 기다리고 있어

wait for one's call = expect one's call (from)은 '…전화를 기다리다.'

💡 **Example**

- I spent all night waiting for her call.
  난 걔 전화를 기다리느라 밤샜어.

- She was waiting for your call. Hold on a moment.
  걘 네 전화를 기다리고 있어. 조금 기다려.

A: Mr. Johnson, please. It's Bob from New York.
B: He's expecting your call. I'll connect you.

A: 존슨 씨 부탁해요. 뉴욕의 밥예요.
B: 전화 기다리고 계셨어요. 돌려드릴게요.

084

Did you miss a call just now?

너 방금 전화를 놓쳤니?

miss a call은 '부재중 전화가 있다'라는 말. get caller-ID는 발신자번호 서비스를 받다.

Example

- Did you miss a call just now?
  너 방금 전화를 놓쳤니?
- Mark missed a call from his girlfriend.
  마크는 여친으로부터 오는 전화를 놓쳤어.

 Dialog

A: I missed a call when I was in the movie.
B: Was it someone whose number you recognize?

A: 내가 영화관에 있을 때 전화통화를 놓쳤어.
B: 네가 알고 있는 번호였니?

085

I installed the Mentors app on my phone

핸드폰에 멘토스북 어플을 깔았어

install applications on a Smartphone은 '스마트폰에 어플을 깔다.'

Example

- I can use my Smartphone as a camcorder or fax machine if I want.
  난 원하면 스마트폰을 팩스나 캠코더로 사용할 수 있어.
- I enjoy exploring the various functions of my Smartphone.
  난 스마트폰이 가지고 있는 다양한 기능을 탐색하는 것을 즐겨.

 Dialog

A: Which applications did you install on your Smartphone?
B: Applications like Smartbanking, twitter, YouTube and so on.

A: 네 스마트폰에 어떤 어플들을 설치했니?
B: 어플들은 스마트 뱅킹, 트위터, 유튜브 등이야.

I took a selfie with my friend

친구와 셀카를 찍었어

take a selfie (with sb)는 '(…와 함께) 셀카를 찍다.'

💡 **Example**

- I want to take a selfie with my friend.
  난 내 친구과 셀카를 찍고 싶어

- We used a selfie stick to take a picture of everyone.
  우리는 다들 나오게 사진찍기 위해 셀카봉을 이용했어.

A: What were you doing in the museum?
B: I decided to take a selfie before leaving.

A: 박물관에서 뭐하고 있었어?
B: 떠나기 전에 셀카를 찍기로 했어.

Are you wearing a smartwatch?

너 스마트워치 차고 있는거야?

wear smart watch는 '스마트워치를 손에 차다'라는 의미.

💡 **Example**

- Could you check the time on your smartwatch?
  네 스마트워치로 몇시인지 볼래?

- She was wearing a purple smartwatch at school.
  걔는 학교에서 보라색 스마트워치를 차고 있었어.

A: Are you wearing a smartwatch?
B: Yeah, I got it as a birthday present.

A: 너 스마트워치 차고 있는거야?
B: 어, 생일선물로 받았어.

088

I got into a car accident today

난 오늘 차사고 났어

get into a car accident = have a car accident = be in a car accident는 '교통사고를 당하다.'

💡 **Example**

- I got into a car accident a few days ago.
  며칠 전에 차 사고를 당했어.
- Did you hear she got into a car accident today?
  걔 오늘 차 사고 난 거 알아?

 **Dialog**

A: I was in a car accident this morning.
B: Oh no! Are you okay?

   A: 오늘 아침에 차 사고를 당했어.
   B: 저런! 괜찮아?

089

He wrecked his car in an accident

걘 사고로 차를 크게 망가뜨렸어

wreck a car = crash a car = damage a car는 모두 다 '차를 망가트리다.'

💡 **Example**

- Don't fall asleep behind the wheel.
  운전 중에 잠들지 마라.
- I think someone damaged your car in the parking lot.
  누군가 주차장에서 네 차를 손상시킨 것 같아.

 **Dialog**

A: Jim crashed his car and is in the hospital.
B: What a shame!

   A: 짐이 차사고 나서 병원에 입원했어.
   B: 안됐네!

You'd better buckle up

안전벨트를 매는게 좋겠어

buckle up은 구어체로 '안전벨트를 매다' = fasten[wear] one's seatbelt <=> undo one's belt.

💡 **Example**

- Please fasten your seat belt, we're going for a ride.
  안전벨트 매요, 드라이브 갈거니까.

- You'd better buckle up in case we get stopped at a police checkpoint.
  불시검문을 당할 경우에 대비해서 안전벨트를 매는게 좋을거야.

A: Please wear your seatbelt in my car.
B: Is this really necessary?

A: 내 차에서는 안전벨트를 매 줘.
B: 꼭 이래야 하니?

I think we have a flat tire

펑크가 난 것 같아

have a flat tire는 '펑크나다.' (Tire) blow out 역시 '펑크나다.' (Tire) be low는 타이어 '바람이 빠지다.'

💡 **Example**

- Thomas had a flat tire on the freeway.
  토마스는 고속도로에서 펑크가 났어.

- We had a flat tire while driving to New York.
  뉴욕으로 운전하다가 펑크가 났었어.

A: Why is the car making that noise?
B: I think we have a flat tire.

A: 왜 차에서 그런 소리가 나는 거야?
B: 펑크가 난 것 같아.

We had car trouble on our trip
우린 여행 중에 차에 문제가 생겼어
have car trouble는 '차량에 문제가 있다 = have a (big) trouble with one's car.

💡 Example
- Renee had car trouble this summer.
  르네는 이번 여름에 차에 문제가 생겼어.
- He was late because he had car trouble.
  걘 차에 문제가 생겨서 늦었대.

A: We had car trouble on our trip.
B: Were you able to fix it?

A: 우린 여행 중에 차에 문제가 생겼어.
B: 고칠 수 있겠니?

This car needs a tune up
이차는 튠업이 필요해
tune up은 '엔진을 정비하다,' '악기를 조율하다.' change the oil은 '엔진오일을 교체하다.'

💡 Example
- This car runs poorly and needs a tune up.
  이 차가 형편없이 달리는데 튠업이 필요해.
- Would you change the oil, please?
  엔진오일 좀 바꿔주세요.

A: What would you like done to your car?
B: Would you change the oil, please?

A: 차 어떻게 해드려요?
B: 엔진 오일 좀 갈아줄래요?

I'll give you a ride

내가 차로 데려다줄게

give sb a ride (to~)는 '…을 차로 데려다주다 <=> get a ride(차를 얻어타다). 영국에선 ride 대신 lift.

💡 **Example**

- How about I give you a ride home?
  내가 집까지 데려다 줄까?

- Do you want me to give you a ride to the airport?
  내가 공항까지 태워다 줄까?

 Dialog

A: Are you going downtown right now?
B: Yes, I am. Get in and I'll give you a ride.

  A: 지금 시내에 가?
  B: 어 그래. 어서 타, 데려다 줄게.

Why don't we go for a drive?

우리 드라이브 갈까?

go for a drive[ride]는 '드라이브하다,' take sb for a drive[ride]는 '…을 드라이브시켜주다.'

💡 **Example**

- They went for a drive on Sunday.
  걔들은 일요일에 드라이브했어.

- I took him for a ride.
  난 걜 드라이브 시켜줬어.

 Dialog

A: Why don't we go for a drive?
B: That's a great idea. I'm a little bored.

  A: 우리 드라이브 갈까?
  B: 그거 좋은 생각이야. 좀 따분했는데.

096

You can board the plane now
지금 탑승하시면 됩니다

board the plane은 '탑승하다.' bus, train, plane을 탄다고 할 때는 board를 쓴다.

Example
- You can board the plane now.
  이제 탑승해주십시오.
- I'm flying to Boston next Saturday.
  나 다음 주 토요일에 비행기 타고 보스턴에 가.

 Dialog

A: If you have your boarding pass, you can board the plane now.
B: Is there a place that I can store my carry-on?

A: 탑승권 소지하신 분은 지금 탑승하십시오.
B: 짐을 놔둘 곳이 있나요?

097

You can check the baggage here
여기서 수화물을 부치시면 됩니다

check the baggage는 '짐을 부치다,' '짐을 검사하다,' check in baggage는 탑승수속시 '짐을 부치다.'

Example
- You can check in luggage at this desk.
  이 데스크에서 짐을 부칠 수 있어요.
- The group had a lot of luggage to check in.
  그 그룹은 부칠 짐이 아주 많았어.

 Dialog

A: How many pieces of luggage are you checking in?
B: I would like to check three pieces.

A: 부치실 짐이 몇 개죠?
B: 세 개를 부치려고 하는데요.

It's located in our lobby

그건 로비에 있어요

be located in~은 '…에 위치해 있다,' be in a suburb of~는 '…의 근교에 있다.'

Example

- It's located about 10 kilometers from Ilsan.
  일산에서 한 10킬로 미터 지점에 있어.

- You are in a suburb of Seoul.
  서울 근교에요.

Dialog

A: Where's the tourist information center?
B: It's located in our lobby.

A: 관광 안내센터가 어디에 있어요?
B: 로비에 있어요.

Guess What?

If the shoe fits, wear it

사실이 맞으면 받아들여라

"신발이 맞으면 그냥 신으라"는 말로 어떤 비판이 옳다면 듣기 싫더라도 받아들이라(if a criticism is accurate, it should be accepted, even if it seems unkind to hear)는 표현이다. 우리말로는 "사실이 옳다면 받아들여라," "그 말이 사실이면 받아들여라" 등으로 생각하면 된다.

Let's get into an elevator

엘리베이터를 타자

get into an elevator = get in the elevator. 에스컬레이터의 경우는 get on the escalator.

💡 **Example**

- Kevin has to get into an elevator to go to his apartment.
  케빈은 자기 아파트로 가려면 엘리베이터를 타야 해.

- I got into an elevator to reach Steve's office.
  난 스티브의 사무실로 가기 위해서 엘리베이터를 탔어.

 **Dialog**

A: **I want to go to the top of the Empire State Building.**
B: **Let's get into an elevator and go up.**

A: 난 엠파이어 스테이트 빌딩 꼭대기로 올라가길 원해.
B: 엘리베이터를 타고 올라가자.

Are we going the right way?

우리 제대로 가고 있는거야?

go the right way는 '길을 제대로 가다,' Coming through!는 '길 좀 비켜주세요!' = Clear the way.

💡 **Example**

- I have hot coffee. Please move out of my way.
  뜨거운 커피를 들고 있어. 비켜주라.

- We moved out of her way because she was running.
  걔가 뛰어가고 있어 길을 비켜줬어.

 **Dialog**

A: **Turn right at the next traffic light.**
B: **Are you sure we're going the right way?**

A: 신호등 있는 데서 우회전해.
B: 우리, 제대로 가고 있는거 맞아?

Do you have a minute?

시간 좀 있어?

get[have] a minute은 '잠깐 시간이 되다.' minute 대신 second를 써도 된다.

💡 Example

- I need to talk to you, if you have a minute.
  시간 좀 있으면 얘기할게 있어.

- Hold on a second. I have a question for you.
  잠깐만. 너에게 질문이 있어.

 Dialog

A: Do you have a minute?
B: Well yeah, sure, what's up?

  A: 시간 좀 있어?
  B: 그럼, 뭔데?

I can't make time for this

이걸 할 여유는 없어

make time to+V[for sth]은 '…할 시간을 내다'라는 의미.

💡 Example

- Make time to pack up your suitcase.
  네 옷가방을 꾸릴 시간을 내라.

- I'll make time to come down and see you.
  시간을 내 내려가서 널 만날게.

 Dialog

A: I'm going to see my grandmother this weekend.
B: It's good you make time to visit her.

  A: 난 이번주말 할머니를 만나볼 거야.
  B: 할머니를 방문할 시간을 내는 것은 좋은 일이야.

It took an hour to walk home

집까지 걸어가는데 한시간 걸렸어

take+시간명사+to+V는 '…하는데 시간이 …걸리다'로 It takes+시간+to+V의 형태로 많이 쓰인다.

Example

- It takes time to cook a big meal.
  푸짐한 식사를 요리하려면 시간이 걸리지.

- It took an hour to walk home.
  집까지 걸어가는데 한시간이 걸렸어.

A: I thought you were going to leave.
B: It took me a while to find my keys.

A: 네가 떠날 것으로 생각했어.
B: 내 열쇠를 찾는데 시간이 좀 걸렸어.

By the time he's here, we'll have left

걔가 여기 올 때쯤이면, 우린 떠나고 없을거야

by the time S+V는 '…할 때쯤에'라는 빈출 부사구. every[each] time S+V는 '매번 …할 때마다.'

Example

- By the time Karen arrives, we will be ready.
  카렌이 도착할 때까지 우린 준비되어 있을 거야.

- Every time I turn around, Hal is looking at me.
  내가 돌아설 적마다 할이 날 쳐다보고 있어.

A: Is it possible for me to become rich by the time I'm thirty?
B: It would be difficult, but you can never tell.

A: 30살에 부자될 수 있을까?
B: 어렵겠지만, 그야 알 수 없는 일이지.

It didn't go as planned

그건 계획대로 되지 않았어

go as planned는 '계획대로 되다' = go as scheduled.

💡 **Example**

- The English class didn't go as planned.
  영어 수업이 계획대로 이루어지지 않았어.

- If everything goes as planned, we're going to make a killing.
  모든 일이 계획대로 된다면 한 몫 긁어모을 수 있을거야.

A: Did you have a good time on your date?
B: No, it really didn't go as planned.

A: 데이트에서 좋은 시간을 보냈니?
B: 아니, 계획대로 되지 않았어.

I have no plans to visit Busan

부산을 방문할 계획이 없어

have no plans to+V는 '…할 계획이 없다,' have no plans for+N로 써도 된다.

💡 **Example**

- They have no plans to go out tonight.
  걔들은 오늘 밤 외출할 계획이 없어.

- We have no plans to visit Joe and Elaine.
  우린 조와 일레인을 방문할 계획은 없어요.

A: Are you going home for the holiday?
B: No, I have no plans to travel home.

A: 휴일 때 집에 갈거니?
B: 아니, 집에 갈 계획은 없어.

Let's make a plan for the weekend

주말 계획을 세우자

make a plan to+V[for+N]은 '계획을 세우다' = make plans.

💡 **Example**

- They made a plan to meet in a week.
  걔들은 일주일 후에 만날 계획을 세웠어.
- Alan made a plan to complete the report.
  알란은 그 보고서를 끝낼 계획을 세웠어.

 Dialog

A: I don't know what I want to study.
B: You should make a plan for your future.

A: 뭘 공부하길 원하는지 나도 모르겠어.
B: 넌 미래를 위해 계획을 세워야해.

I can't change my schedule

내 스케줄을 바꿀 수가 없어

change one's schedule은 '일정을 바꾸다,' move up the meeting schedule은 '회의일정을 앞당기다.'

💡 **Example**

- Abe will change his schedule to meet his friend.
  에이브는 스케줄을 바꿔서 자기 친구들을 만날거야.
- They changed their schedule during the summer.
  걔들은 여름 스케줄을 바꿨어.

 Dialog

A: Are you going to join us for dinner?
B: No, I can't change my schedule.

A: 만찬에 우리랑 함께 할래?
B: 아니, 내 스케줄을 바꿀 수가 없어.

He was 15 minutes late for class

걘 수업시간에 15분 늦었어

be+시간명사+late for~는 '…에 …만큼 늦다.' 늦기는 늦었는데 얼마나 늦었는지 함께 말할 때.

💡 Example

- He was 15 minutes late for class.
  걘 수업시간에 15분 늦었어.

- We were an hour late for the movie.
  우린 영화시간에 1시간 늦었어.

 Dialog

A: Do you care if we're late?
B: I don't care if we are a little late for the party.

A: 늦을 까봐서 걱정되니?
B: 파티에 조금 늦는다고 해도 신경안써.

I didn't mean to hurt you

널 다치게 하려고 한 건 아냐

mean to+V는 '…을 하려고 하다,' '작정하다,' 그래서 didn't mean to+V는 '…할 의도는 아니었다.'

💡 Example

- They didn't mean to come late.
  걔들은 늦게 올 뜻은 없었대.

- Henry didn't mean to break your watch.
  헨리는 네 시계를 깨뜨릴 의도는 아니었어.

 Dialog

A: Hey, you just stepped on my toe.
B: Sorry, I didn't mean to hurt you.

A: 야, 네가 방금 내 발끝을 밟았잖아.
B: 미안해, 널 다치게 하려고 한 것은 아냐.

I ran into Chris this morning

오늘 아침에 크리스를 우연히 만났어

run into sb = come across sb = bump into sb는 '…을 우연히 만나다.'

💡 **Example**

- He ran into his ex-girlfriend at the market.
  걘 시장에서 옛 여친과 우연히 마주쳤어.

- We ran into our former math teacher.
  우린 옛날 수학 선생님과 우연히 마주쳤어.

A: **I ran into Chris this morning.**
B: **How's he doing?**

A: 오늘 아침에 크리스를 우연히 만났어
B: 어떻게 지낸대?

He didn't show up

걘 오지 않았어

show up은 모임, 회의 또는 약속장소에 '나타나다,' '오다' = turn up. no show는 약속을 깨고 안나타나는 것을 말함.

💡 **Example**

- How come he didn't show up at the seminar this morning?
  왜 그가 아침 세미나에 참석하지 않았지?

- I might show up at the end of the meeting.
  회의가 끝날 때 쯤에 나타날 수 있어.

A: **What made you think that I wasn't going to show up?**
B: **I just thought you had other more important plans.**

A: 왜 내가 나타나지 않으리라고 생각했지?
B: 네가 다른 중요한 약속이 있을 거라고 생각했지.

I invited Jerry to our party

제리를 우리 파티에 초대했어

invite sb to+장소[파티]는 '…을 …에 초대하다,' invite sb to+V는 '…을 …하도록 초대하다.'

💡 Example

- No wonder she didn't invite you to her birthday party.
  걔가 생일파티에 널 초대하지 않은 건 당연해.
- I am thrilled to be invited to the party.
  난 그 파티에 초대되어 무척 흥분돼.

 Dialog

A: I invited Jerry to our wedding.
B: That's great! I hope he will come.

A: 제리를 우리 결혼식에 초대했어.
B: 잘했어! 걔가 오면 좋겠다.

Just make yourself comfortable

그냥 편히 계세요

make oneself at home = make oneself at home은 '집에 있는 것처럼 편하게 지내다.'

💡 Example

- Make yourself at home while you wait.
  기다리는 동안 편안히 계세요.
- Come in and make yourself at home.
  들어와서 편히 쉬세요.

 Dialog

A: Wow! This is a great place.
B: Thank you. Just make yourself comfortable.

A: 야, 집이 아주 멋지네요.
B: 고마워요. 그냥 편히 계세요.

I turned down her invitation

난 걔의 초대를 거절했어

turn down one's invitation은 '…의 초대를 거절하다.'

💡 Example
- We **turned down** David's **invitation**.
  우린 데이비드의 초대를 거절했어.
- Dick **turned down** Harriet's **invitation**.
  딕은 해리엇의 초대를 거절했어.

 Dialog

A: Are you coming to her New Year's party?
B: No, I had to **turn down her invitation**.
  A: 넌 걔의 신년파티에 올거니?
  B: 아니, 걔의 초대를 거절해야만 했어.

He stopped over at my place

걘 우리집에 잠시 들렀어

stop over는 '잠시 들르다,' 특히 비행중에 '경유하다'라는 의미로 쓰인다. stopover[layover]는 '경유.'

💡 Example
- Our **stopover** will last 2 hours.
  우리 기착은 2시간 정도 걸릴거야.
- My flight **has a stopover** in Iceland.
  내가 탄 항공편은 아이슬랜드에서 기착해.

 Dialog

A: Do you have a direct flight to LA?
B: No, I **have a stop over** in New York.
  A: LA까지 직항이 있니?
  B: 아니, 뉴욕에 잠시 기착할거야.

117

I kept you waiting so long
너무 오랫동안 기다리게 했네

keep sb waiting(+시간부사구)는 '…을 (…동안) 기다리게 하다.'

Example
- She kept me waiting for an hour.
  걘 내가 한시간이나 계속 기다리게 했어.
- Sorry to keep you waiting, I had a call on the other line.
  기다리게 해서 미안해요. 다른 전화가 와서요.

Dialog
A: I have been here for twenty minutes.
B: I'm sorry. I kept you waiting so long.

A: 제가 여기 20분 정도 있었어요.
B: 미안합니다. 너무 오랫동안 기다리게 했군요.

118

You'll have to take turns driving
너희들 교대로 운전을 해야 돼

take turns ~ing은 '교대로 …을 하다,' in turn은 '교대로'라는 의미.

Example
- We took turns using the computer.
  우린 교대로 컴퓨터를 사용했지.
- You'll have to take turns driving.
  너희들 교대로 운전을 해야 돼.

Dialog
A: The children are very polite.
B: They take turns playing with toys.

A: 얘들이 무척 공손해.
B: 걔들은 교대로 장난감을 가지고 놀고 있어.

119

Wait your turn!
차례를 기다려!
wait one's turn은 '차례를 기다리다.' 여기서 turn은 '차례,' '순번'을 의미함.

 Example

- The man didn't wait his turn to get on the bus.
  걘 버스 타는 순서를 지키지 않았어.
- I can wait my turn to turn in my exam.
  난 시험지 제출 순서를 지킬 수 있어요.

Dialog

A: I have to buy this dress right now.
B: Come on lady, wait your turn.

A: 난 이 옷을 바로 사야돼.
B: 아가씨, 순서 좀 기다려주세요.

120

Give my best to your Mom
네 엄마에게 안부를 전해줘
give one's best (regards) to sb는 '…에게 안부를 전하다'라는 의미의 표현이다.

 Example

- Give my best to Uncle John.
  존 아저씨에게 안부를 전해줘.
- Give my best regards to him for me when you see him.
  그를 만나면 안부 좀 전해 주세요.

Dialog

A: Give my best to everyone at the school.
B: I'll tell them you said hello.

A: 학교에 계신 모두에게 안부를 전해주세요
B: 모든 분들에게 안부를 전할 게요.

I can't. I have an appointment

안돼. 선약이 있어

have an appointment는 '약속이 있다,' make an appointment는 '약속을 하다.'

💡 Example

- I can't. I have an appointment.
  안돼. 선약이 있어.

- You have a dental appointment today.
  오늘 치과 예약이 되어있지.

A: So what did you do today?
B: Oh, I had an appointment to get my hair cut.

A: 그래 오늘 뭐했어?
B: 어, 머리깎기로 약속이 있었어.

I'll take a rain check

다음으로 미룰게

take a rain check은 우천시 다음 경기를 볼 수 있는 교환권으로 비유적으로 '다음으로 미루다.'

💡 Example

- Sarah took a rain check on the invitation.
  새라는 초대를 다음으로 미뤘어.

- I'm very busy, so I'll take a rain check.
  지금 무지 바빠서 다음 번에 초대해주면 좋겠어.

A: Come on upstairs for some coffee.
B: I can't, but I'll take a rain check.

A: 커피 마시게 2층으로 올라와.
B: 지금은 안되는데 다음에 해줘.

Did you get in touch with him?

걔하고 연락해봤어?

get in touch with sb는 '연락을 취하다,' keep in touch with sb는 '연락을 하고 지내다.'

💡 **Example**

- Where can I get in touch with her?
  어디로 연락해야 걔와 연락이 될까요?

- I got back in touch with old friends through a web site.
  사이트로 예전 친구들에게 연락을 취했어.

 Dialog

A: I heard that John is coming to town this weekend.
B: Did you get in touch with him?

A: 이번 주에 존이 올라온데.
B: 걔하고 연락해봤어?

I don't get along with my father

난 아버지하고 사이가 좋지 않아

get along with sb는 '…와 사이좋게 지내다.'

💡 **Example**

- The children got along with each other.
  얘들이 서로서로 잘 지냈어.

- It's easy to get along with your friends.
  네 친구들과 잘 지내는 것은 쉽지.

 Dialog

A: I don't get along with my roommate.
B: Maybe you should move elsewhere.

A: 난 룸메이트와 사이가 좋지 않아.
B: 아무래도 딴 곳으로 이사해야 겠구나.

He made friends with the neighbors

걘 이웃들과 친해졌어

make friends with sb는 '…와 친해지다,' be friends with sb는 '…와 친한 상태이다.'

 Example

- She made friends with everyone in class.
  걘 학급내 누구와도 사이가 좋았어.

- I don't want to make friends with anyone here.
  난 여기 누구와도 친구가 되고 싶지 않아.

 Dialog

A: Did you enjoy your visit to Europe?
B: Yes, I made friends with some people there.

A: 유럽 방문을 즐겼니?
B: 그럼, 거기서 친구 몇 명을 사귀었어.

We chatted about the weather

우리는 날씨에 대해 수다를 떨었어

chat about sth는 '…에 관해 수다떨다,' chat with[have a chat with] sb는 '…와 수다떨다.'

 Example

- Let's chat about next month's schedule.
  다음 달 일정에 대해 얘기를 나눠보자.

- Some people enjoy chatting about the weather.
  어떤 사람들은 날씨에 대해 잡담하는 것을 즐겨.

Dialog

A: Did you meet your friends from grade school?
B: Yes, we chatted about our lives and families.

A: 년 초등학교 친구들을 만나보았니?
B: 응, 우린 인생과 가족에 대해 수다를 떨었지.

Can I have a word with you?

얘기 좀 할 수 있어?

have a word with sb는 '…에게 말하다,' have words with sb는 '…와 다투다.'

💡 **Example**

- You should have a word with Melanie.
  넌 멜라니와 말을 나눠봐야해.

- May I have a word with you?
  잠깐 얘기할 수 있을까요?

💡 **Dialog**

A: Umm, Jimmy. May I have a word with you?
B: Yeah, of course.

A: 저기, 지미야. 얘기 좀 해보자.
B: 응, 물론이지.

I consulted with my parents

부모님과 상의했어

consult (with) sb는 '…와 상의하다.' 조언을 받을 때 사용한다.

💡 **Example**

- I consulted with my parents about my school.
  학교문제에 대해 부모님과 상의했어.

- She consulted her boyfriend about the party.
  걘 파티와 관련 남친과 협의했어.

💡 **Dialog**

A: Timothy is getting a divorce from his wife.
B: He needs to consult with his lawyer about it.

A: 티모시는 부인과 이혼을 할거야.
B: 걘 이혼과 관련해서 변호사와 상담을 해야할거야.

I told you to get out of here!

나가라고 말했잖아!

get out of here는 '여기서 나가다'로 주로 명령문 형태로 상대방이 말도 안되는 소리를 할 때 쓰는 표현.

💡 **Example**

- Would you like me to get out of here?
  여기서 나가줄까?
- I can't wait to get out of here.
  여기서 나가고 싶어 죽겠어.

 Dialog

A: I thought I told you to get out of here.
B: You did, but I don't want to.

A: 나가라고 말했던 것 같은데.
B: 그랬지, 하지만 싫은 걸.

I'm coming as quickly as I can

최대한 빨리 갈게

I'm coming은 상대방이 있는 곳으로 갈 경우로 come이 '가다'라는 의미로 쓰인다.

💡 **Example**

- I'm coming to your birthday party.
  네 생일파티에 갈게.
- I'm coming to class in ten minutes.
  10분안에 수업에 들어갈게.

 Dialog

A: Come on, or we're going to be late.
B: I'm coming as quickly as I can.

A: 서둘러, 안그러면 우린 늦는다구.
B: 최대한 빨리 갈게.

I'll ask her to come along

걔에게 같이 가자고 할게

come along (with sb)는 '…와 함께 가다.'

💡 **Example**

- Celia decided to come along with us.
  셀리아는 우리랑 함께 가기로 결정했어.
- Do you want to come along?
  같이 갈래?

 Dialog

A: I would like to go out for lunch on Friday.
B: Sounds good to me. I'll ask Greg to come along.

A: 금요일에 같이 점심 먹으러 갔으면 하는데.
B: 좋지. 그렉에게도 같이 가자고 할게.

Let's go together to the concert

같이 콘서트에 가자

go together with sb는 '…와 함께 가다(강조).' 보통 go together~ 혹은 go with~로 쓰인다.

💡 **Example**

- I can't go together with everyone here.
  여기 모든 분들과 같이 갈 수는 없어요.
- Let's go together and grab dinner before.
  같이 가서 그 전에 저녁부터 먹자.

 Dialog

A: Would you like to get a drink?
B: Sure, let's go together with our friends.

A: 술 한잔 할래요?
B: 좋죠, 친구들하고 같이 갑시다.

Can you move over a little bit?

조금만 비켜줄래?

move over는 '자리를 비키다,' '옆으로 가다'의 의미. move A over to+장소는 'A를 …로 옮기다.'

Example

- No one on the subway would move over.
  지하철에서 어느 누구도 자리를 옮기지 않아.

- I asked each person to move over.
  난 각자에게 자리를 옮기라고 요청했지.

Dialog

A: Can you move over and give me some space?
B: Sure, I'd be glad to give you more room.

A: 좀 옮겨서 나한테 공간을 좀 줄 수 있니?
B: 그럼요, 기쁜 마음으로 공간을 생기게 해드릴게요.

Guess What?

You're walking on air today
너 오늘 기분이 되게 좋은 것같네

"하늘 위를 걷고 있다"라는 표현으로 하늘을 나는 것 같은 마음이다라는 말. 비유적으로 무척 기분이 좋을 때(the person feels very happy and is in a very good mood) 사용하는 표현이다.

I'll take you to lunch

데리고 나가 점심사줄게

take sb to+장소명사는 '…을 …로 데리고 가다.'

💡 Example

- You told me you were going to take me to lunch.
  나 점심 사준다고 했잖아.

- I wanted to take you to one of my favorite restaurants.
  내가 자주 가는 식당으로 당신을 데려가고 싶었어요.

A: Wow, it's really late right now.
B: Shall I take you to your place?

A: 어휴, 이제 정말 늦었네요.
B: 집까지 바래다줄까요?

We named our dog Ari

강아지 이름을 아리라고 지었어

name sb+이름은 '…라고 이름짓다.' be named for~는 '…라고 불리다.'

💡 Example

- We named our dog Henry.
  우린 강아지 이름을 헨리라고 지었어.

- We'll name the baby Fred.
  우린 그 아이 이름을 프레드라고 부를거야.

A: Leo and Madge have a new child.
B: I heard they named him Phil.

A: 레오와 매지는 새 아이를 낳았어.
B: 아이 이름이 필이라고 들었어.

He behaved himself at the party

걘 파티에서 예의바르게 행동했어

behave oneself at[in]~는 '…에서 예의바르게 행동하다'라는 표현.

Example

- I always **behave myself** when I drink.
  난 음주할 때 항상 예의가 바르지.

- Did Fara **behave herself** at the party?
  파라가 파티에서 예의 바르게 행동했니?

Dialog

A: Why is Bart sitting over in the corner?
B: He didn't **behave himself** in class.

A: 바트가 왜 코너에 앉아있니?
B: 걘 수업시간에 행실이 좋지 않았어.

I hope to go steady with her

난 걔와 지속적으로 사귀기를 바래

go steady with sb는 '…와 지속적으로 꾸준히 만나다.'

Example

- I haven't **gone steady with** anyone.
  난 누구와도 지속적으로 사귀지 못하고 있어.

- Patty **is going steady with** a businessman.
  패티는 사업가와 계속 사귈 거야.

Dialog

A: Have you asked Andrea out yet?
B: No, but I hope to **go steady with** her someday.

A: 안드레아에게 데이트를 신청했니?
B: 아니지만 언젠가 걔랑 지속적으로 사귀면 좋겠어.

She is my type

걘 내 타입이야

be one's type은 '…가 좋아하는 스타일이다'라는 의미. type 대신에 style을 써도 된다.

Example

- The handsome actor is my type.
  저 잘 생긴 배우는 바로 내 타입이야.

- All of those girls are my type.
  저기 모든 여성들은 바로 내가 좋아하는 타입이야.

A: Elsie is tall and has dark hair.
B: That's great! She is my type.

A: 엘시는 키가 크고 까만 머리야.
B: 대단해. 걘 내가 좋아하는 타입이야.

I have a crush on her

나 걔한테 푹 빠졌어

have a crush on sb는 '…에게 반하다.' 일시적으로 홀딱 빠진 상태를 말한다. 강조하려면 crush => major crush.

Example

- It's common to have a crush on someone in school.
  학교에서 누군가에 반하는 것은 흔한 일이야.

- She had a crush on a boy in her apartment building.
  걘 자기 아파트 빌딩에 사는 한 소년에게 반했어.

A: You keep looking at Doris tonight.
B: I think I have a crush on her.

A: 넌 오늘 밤 도리스를 계속 쳐다보고 있네.
B: 난 걔한테 반한 것 같아.

He came on to me last night

갠 어젯밤 내게 추파를 던졌어

come on to sb는 '추파를 던지다,' '집적대다' = make a move on = hit on = make a pass at.

💡 **Example**

- Don't **come on to** every girl you know.
  네가 아는 모든 여성들에게 추파를 던지지마.

- He **came on to** Steph while they worked together.
  갠 같이 일하면서 스테파니에게 추파를 던졌어.

A: You seem very angry with Rick.
B: Yeah. He **came on to** me last night.

A: 넌 릭한데 무지 화난 것처럼 보이네.
B: 그래. 갠 어제 밤 나한테 추파를 던졌어.

Chris breaks many girls' hearts

크리스는 많은 여성들의 마음을 아프게 해

break one's heart는 '…의 가슴을 찢어 놓다,' '아프게 하다,' 이렇게 맘을 아프게 하는 사람은 heartbreaker.

💡 **Example**

- That girl will **break his heart**.
  저 여자 애가 그의 마음을 비통하게 만들거야.

- Bud **breaks many girls' hearts**.
  버드는 많은 여성들의 마음을 찢어놓고 있어.

A: Why are you so sad about your girlfriend?
B: She said goodbye and **broke my heart**.

A: 왜 네 여친에 대해 슬퍼하니?
B: 갠 이별하자고 해서 내 가슴을 찢어 놓았어.

I had to break up with her

난 걔와 헤어져야 했어

break up with sb는 '…와 헤어지다' = break off with sb = break it off with sb.

Example

- It seems like it's time to break up with her.
  헤어질 때가 된 것 같구나.

- I'm sorry but I have to break up with you.
  미안한데 너랑 헤어져야해.

A: I heard you had some trouble with your girlfriend.
B: I had to break up with her. We were fighting a lot.

A: 네 여친과 문제가 좀 있다고 들었어.
B: 난 헤어져야 했어. 우린 많이 싸웠거든.

Chris cheated on his girlfriend

크리스는 여친속이고 바람폈어

cheat on A with B는 'A를 속이고 B와 바람피다.' on~ 다음에 배신당한 애인이나 배우자를 쓴다.

Example

- Greg was caught when he cheated on his wife.
  그렉은 부인을 속이고 바람을 피다 잡혔어.

- She cheated on her boyfriend twice.
  걘 자기 남친을 두번이나 속이고 바람을 폈어.

A: What caused the big fight between them?
B: Bill cheated on his girlfriend.

A: 걔들이 왜 그렇게 크게 싸웠대?
B: 빌이 자기 여친을 속이고 바람폈대.

You should dump Mindy
넌 민디를 차버리라고

dump sb는 사귀고 있는 이성을 '차버리다.' get dumped by~는 '…에게 차이다.'

💡 **Example**

- I'd dump my girlfriend for a date with you.
  난 너와 데이트하려고 내 여친을 버리겠어.

- You should dump her and get someone else.
  그 여자 차버리고 다른 애 사귀어.

A: **What did Carole do when her boyfriend cheated?**
B: **She dumped him and found someone else.**

A: 캐롤은 남친이 바람을 필 때 어떤 반응을 보였니?
B: 걘 남친을 버리고 새 사람을 찾았어.

She's going to ask him to divorce
걘 이혼을 요구할거야

get a divorce는 '이혼하다' = be divorced from sb. file for divorce는 '이혼소송을 하다.'

💡 **Example**

- It took two months to get a divorce.
  이혼하는데 2달이나 걸렸어.

- I have no other choice but to file for divorce!
  난 이혼 소송을 낼 수 밖에 없어!

A: **I'm worried about Dick. He doesn't look good these days.**
B: **I heard his wife is asking him to divorce.**

A: 딕이 걱정야. 요즘 안좋아 보여.
B: 아내가 이혼하자고 그런대.

I'm ready to start a family

난 가정을 꾸밀 준비가 되었어

start a family는 엄밀히 말해서 '결혼 후 아이를 갖다,' '가정을 꾸리다'이지만 '결혼하다'라는 의미로도 쓰인다.

 Example

- People are more focused on their careers than on starting a family.
  다들 자식을 낳아 가정을 이루는 것보다는 일에 더 초점을 맞추잖아.

- Maybe now is not the right time to be starting a family.
  아마도 지금이 아이를 가질 적기야.

Dialog

A: Why did you decide to get married?
B: I am ready to start a family.

A: 왜 결혼하기로 결정을 했니?
B: 가정을 꾸밀 마음의 준비가 되었어.

June is engaged to Rob

준은 롭과 약혼한 사이야

be engaged to sb는 '…와 약혼하다,' be engaged in~는 '…에 종사하다,' '몰두하다'라는 의미.

 Example

- My best friend got engaged to the biggest loser.
  내 절친이 아주 머저리와 약혼했어.

- I've never been engaged in my life.
  난 내 생애 한번도 약혼을 한 적이 없어.

Dialog

A: Are June and Rob still dating?
B: Yes, June is engaged to Rob.

A: 준과 롭은 아직도 데이트하고 있니?
B: 그럼, 준은 롭과 약혼한 사이야.

Are you involved in anyone?

짐 누구 사귀는 사람있어?

be[get] involved in sth은 '…에 연루되다'이지만 ~in sb가 되면 '…와 사귀다'라는 의미.

Example

- She's getting more involved in school activities now.
  걘 이제 학교활동에 좀 더 참여하고 있어.

- Are you married or involved with anyone?
  결혼했니 아님 누구랑 사귀고 있니?

A: Why was Nate sent to jail?
B: He got involved in illegal activities.
  A: 왜 네이트가 감옥에 갔니?
  B: 걘 불법활동에 관여했어.

The files got mixed up on my desk

책상 위 파일들이 뒤섞였다

get mixed up하면 '연루되다,' '어울리다,' '뒤섞이다' get mixed up in sth 형태로 '나쁜 일에 연루되다.'

Example

- The exam papers got mixed up on the desk.
  시험지가 책상위에서 뒤섞여 버렸어.

- I got mixed up in some really bad stuff.
  난 아주 나쁜 일에 연루되었어.

A: Why was Paul expelled from school?
B: He got mixed up in drug dealing.
  A: 폴이 왜 퇴학 당했어?
  B: 마약거래에 연루되었대.

150

It's got nothing to do with age
그건 나이와 관련이 없어
have nothing to do with+N[~ing]하면 '…와 아무 관련이 없다'라는 의미.

Example
- It's got nothing to do with age.
  그건 나이와 관련이 없어.
- This has nothing to do with me and my family.
  이건 나와 내 가족과는 무관한 일이야.

 **Dialog**

A: You made me hurt my leg.
B: I had nothing to do with hurting you.
  A: 넌 내 다리를 다치게 했어.
  B: 난 너를 다치게 한 것과 전혀 관련이 없었어.

151

That's none of your business
네가 상관할 바가 아냐
be none of one's business는 '…가 상관할 일이 아니다' = keep one's nose out of one's business.

Example
- Their relationship is none of your business.
  걔들의 관계는 네가 상관하지마.
- Our conversation is none of their business.
  우리의 대화는 걔들이 상관할 일이 아니야.

 **Dialog**

A: David was curious about how much money you make.
B: That is none of his business.
  A: 데이빗은 네가 얼마나 버는지 호기심이 나나봐.
  B: 걔가 상관할 일이 아니지.

I don't care if she's fat or thin

난 걔가 뚱뚱하든 날씬하든 상관안해

not care if[who~] S+V는 '…을 상관하지 않다.' not care the less는 '조금도 개의치 않다.'

 Example

- I don't care if she's fat or thin.
  난 걔가 뚱뚱하든 날씬하든 상관안해.

- I don't care who he sleeps with.
  걔가 누구랑 자는지 관심 없어.

 Dialog

A: What do you think about the situation?
B: I don't care if we go on strike or not.

　A: 이 상황, 어떻게 생각해?
　B: 우리가 파업을 하든 안하든 난 상관없어.

I didn't get out of bed until noon

난 정오가 될 때까지 침대에서 안 일어났어

get out of bed는 잠에서 깨어 침대에서 일어나는 물리적인 동작을 뜻한다.

 Example

- I didn't want to get out of bed this morning.
  난 오늘 아침 잠자리에서 나오고 싶지 않았어.

- Get out of bed and get ready for school!
  잠자리에서 일어나 학교갈 준비를 해라!

Dialog

A: Arthur is going to be late for work.
B: Tell him to get out of bed right now.

　A: 아더는 출근이 늦어질 것 같아.
　B: 지금 바로 일어나라고 말해.

She didn't wear her makeup today

걘 오늘 화장을 하지 않았어

wear[put, do] one's makeup은 '화장을 하다' <=> wash one's make up off(화장을 지우다)

🔆 Example

- Carly wore her makeup when she went shopping.
  칼리는 쇼핑갈 때 화장했어.
- She didn't wear her makeup during the meeting.
  걘 회의중 화장을 하지 않았어.

 Dialog

A: Why does Dana look so nice?
B: She wore her makeup to the dance.

A: 다나는 왜 그렇게 멋있게 보이지?
B: 걘 무도회가려고 화장을 했어.

Why are you all dressed up?

왜 그렇게 차려 입었어?

dress up은 '차려입다,' '정장을 입다'라는 의미. get all dressed up은 '옷을 잘 차려입다.'

🔆 Example

- Why are you all dressed up?
  왜 그렇게 차려 입었어?
- I plan to dress up for the talent show.
  장기자랑 쇼에 나갈 때 성장할 계획이야.

 Dialog

A: Why are you dressed up tonight?
B: I've got a date that I want to impress.

A: 오늘 왜 그렇게 차려입었어?
B: 데이트가 있는데 강한 인상을 주고 싶어.

Your hat goes well with your coat

네 모자는 네 코트와 잘 어울려

(옷 등이) go well with sth하면 '…가 …와 잘 어울리다'라는 의미의 표현.

💡 **Example**

- Your hat and gloves go well with your coat.
  네 모자와 장갑은 네 코트와 잘 어울려.

- Does this scarf go well with my outfit?
  이 스카프가 내 옷과 잘 어울리니?

 Dialog

A: I'm going to wear my black shirt.
B: That shirt goes well with blue jeans.

A: 난 검은 셔츠를 입을 거야.
B: 그 셔츠에는 청바지가 잘 어울려.

He blew his nose at the table

갠 테이블에서 코를 풀었어

blow one's nose하면 '코를 풀다,' pick one's nose하면 '코를 후비다.'

💡 **Example**

- Kevin blew his nose at the table.
  케빈은 테이블에서 코를 풀었어.

- Cindy went to the bathroom to blow her nose.
  신디는 코를 풀려고 화장실로 갔어.

 Dialog

A: Excuse me, I have to blow my nose.
B: Oh, did you catch a cold?

A: 죄송합니다, 코 좀 풀겠습니다.
B: 오, 감기 걸리셨나요?

The bus broke down

버스가 고장났어

break down은 컴퓨터나 자동차 등의 기능이 멈추어서 작동하지 않는 것을 말한다.

 Example

- Did your car break down again?
  네 차 또 고장났어?

- I can't believe the bus broke down.
  버스가 고장났다니 믿을 수가 없어.

 Dialog

A: You are late for class.
B: It's not my fault I'm late. The bus broke down.

A: 수업에 늦었구나.
B: 지각한 건 제 잘못이 아니에요. 버스가 고장났다구요.

The old car didn't work well

그 중고차가 잘 달리지 않아

not work well[properly]은 장비나 기계 등이 제대로 돌아가지 않을 때 사용한다.

 Example

- The old car didn't work well.
  그 중고차가 잘 달리지 않아.

- Does the machine work well?
  이 기계는 작동이 잘 되나요?

Dialog

A: Why did you return your new TV?
B: It did not work well when I used it.

A: 새로운 TV를 왜 반환했니?
B: 써보니까 잘 작동이 되지 않았어.

160

Did you help her fix the problem?

걔가 그 문제 해결하는데 네가 도와줬어?

fix the problem은 '문제를 해결하다,' fix the car는 '차를 수리하다.'

 Example

- Did you help Jan fix the problem?
  얀이 그 문제를 해결하는데 네가 도와주었어?

- Let me see if I can fix the problem.
  내가 그 문제 해결할 수 있는지 볼게.

Dialog

A: Do you think that she will be able to fix the problem?
B: If she can't do it, nobody can.

A: 걔가 그 문제를 해결할 수 있을 거라고 생각하니?
B: 걔가 할 수 없으면 아무도 못하거든.

161

Let's grab a bite to eat

뭐 좀 먹으러 가자

grab a bite (to eat)은 '재빨리 먹다,' '간단히 들다,' '요기하다'라는 표현이다.

 Example

- Let's grab a bite to eat.
  뭐 좀 먹으러 가자.

- Could you grab me a coffee when you go to the coffee shop?
  커피 숍 갈 때 커피 한 잔만 사다 줘.

Dialog

A: I feel hungry. Let's eat.
B: Do you want to grab some snacks?

A: 배가 고파. 우리 뭐 좀 먹자.
B: 간식 좀 먹을까?

I'd like to have a light meal

난 가볍게 먹고 싶어

have a light meal은 '식사를 가볍게 하다,' 반대표현은 have a big meal이라고 하면 된다.

 Example

- Curtis had a big meal at the airport.
  커티스는 공항에서 과식했다.
- She had a light meal because she's on a diet.
  걘 다이어트중이라 가벼운 식사를 했어.

 Dialog

A: Can I get you a plate of food?
B: Sure, I'd like to have a light meal.

A: 음식 한 접시 드릴까요?
B: 그럼요, 난 가볍게 먹고 싶어요.

I have a hangover

숙취가 심해

have a hangover는 술을 많이 마셔 '숙취가 심하다'라는 뜻으로 강조하려면 huge hangover라 한다.

 Example

- John got a hangover after drinking soju.
  존은 소주를 마신후 숙취를 겪었어.
- You'll get a hangover if you drink too much.
  과음하면 숙취를 겪을거야.

Dialog

A: I have never seen Peter drink that much.
B: I bet he has a huge hangover today.

A: 피터가 그렇게 마셔대는 건 처음 봤다니까.
B: 오늘 분명히 엄청난 숙취를 느낄 거야.

Let me pick up the tab

내가 낼게, 내가 계산할게

pick up the tab에서 tab은 '식당에서 계산해야 할 계산서'를 말한다 = It's on me(내가 낼게).

💡 **Example**

- I don't have enough money to pick up the tab.
  내가 낼만큼 돈이 충분치 않아.

- She picked up the tab for everyone.
  걘 모두를 위해 식당에서 계산을 했어.

A: Michael said that he'd pick up the tab.
B: In that case I'll have another drink.
   A: 마이클이 자기가 계산한다고 했어.
   B: 그러면 한 잔 더 해야지.

Is that for here or to go?

여기서 드시나요, 아니면 가져 가시나요?

(For) Here or to go?는 '여기서 드시겠어요 아니면 포장요?' 간단히 "포장인가요?"는 Is this to go?라 한다.

💡 **Example**

- Is your food for here or to go?
  음식을 여기서 드실래요 아니면 가져가십니까?

- I'll take it home with me.
  집에 가져갈 겁니다.

A: Is that for here or to go?
B: To go, please.
   A: 여기서 드시겠어요, 아니면 가져 가시겠습니까?
   B: 가져갈 거예요.

Try to cut down on your smoking

담배를 좀 줄이도록 노력해봐

cut down on smoking은 '담배를 줄이다.' ~on 다음에 줄이고 싶은 drinking, expenses, fat 등을 쓴다.

💡 **Example**

- Phil cut down on smoking because of the cost.
  필은 비용 때문에 흡연량을 줄였어.

- The doctor said to cut down on smoking.
  의사가 흡연을 줄이라고 권했어.

 Dialog

A: I can't run as fast as I used to.
B: Try to cut down on your smoking.

A: 난 과거처럼 빨리 뛸 수가 없어.
B: 담배를 좀 줄이도록 노력해봐.

I'm off until later this afternoon.

난 오늘 늦은 오후까지 출근하지 않아

be off는 '비번이다,' '쉬다'이며, 반대표현인 be on duty는 '근무중이다'.

💡 **Example**

- They are off from work today.
  걔들은 오늘 출근하지 않는 날이야.

- I am off until later this afternoon.
  난 오늘 늦은 오후까지 출근하지 않아.

 Dialog

A: I see your brother is around these days.
B: He is off from school until January.

A: 네 동생이 요즘 잘 보이네.
B: 걘 1월까지 학교를 쉬고 있어.

Go home and get some rest

집에 가서 좀 쉬어라

get some rest는 빈출표현으로 '좀 쉬다'라는 의미 = take a rest = take time to relax.

💡 **Example**

- Go home and get some rest.
  집에 가서 좀 쉬어라.

- I'll take a nap and get some rest.
  낮잠을 자면서 좀 쉴게.

 Dialog

A: It's getting to be pretty late.
B: I'm going upstairs to get some rest.

A: 아주 늦을 거야.
B: 좀 쉬려고 위층에 올라갈 거야.

Guess What?

It takes two to tango
손바닥도 마주쳐야 소리가 나는 법이지

"탱고를 추려면 두 명이 필요하다"라는 말로 손바닥도 마주쳐야 소리가 나는 법이라는 우리말을 연상하면 된다. 두 사람이 어떤 안 좋은 일을 만들어 놨을 때 어느 한쪽이 아니라 양쪽 모두 다 책임을 져야 한다(a bad situation between two people is created by both of them, and it is not fair to blame only one of them)는 것이다.

169

He did some camping last weekend
갠 지난 주말에 캠핑을 했어

do some camping은 '캠핑가다.' = go camping = be on a camping trip.

Example

- You can do some camping this spring.
  넌 이번 봄 캠핑을 할 수 있어.

- Norman did some camping with his friends.
  노먼은 친구들하고 캠핑을 했어.

 Dialog

A: Where are you off to this weekend?
B: We're going to do some camping in the mountains.

A: 이번 주말 어디로 뜰건대?
B: 우린 산에서 캠핑 좀 할려구.

170

Let me show you around here
내가 여기 안내해줄게

show sb around+장소는 '…에게 …를 구경시켜주다.'

Example

- The kind man showed me around.
  친절한 사람이 나에게 주변을 구경시켜줬어.

- I can show you around this place.
  내가 이곳 주변을 보여줄 수 있어.

 Dialog

A: I grew up in Los Angeles.
B: Could you show me around the city?

A: 난 LA에서 성장했어.
B: 나한테 도시 구경 좀 시켜줄래?

Turn off the lights before you sleep
자기 전에 불을 꺼라

turn A off는 전기, TV, 가스 등을 끄는 것을 말하며 반대로 켤 때는 turn on.

💡 **Example**

- It's okay to turn off the radio.
  라디오를 끄는 것도 좋아요.

- I'm not sure how to turn on this phone.
  이 전화를 어떻게 켜는지 자신이 없네요.

 Dialog

A: I'm going to bed in a while.
B: Turn the lights off when you do.

A: 조금 있다가 잠자리에 들거야.
B: 그때 전등들을 꺼라.

Turn the volume up a little
소리 조금만 키워봐

turn A up은 '…의 소리를 키우다,' 반대로 '소리를 줄이다'는 turn A down.

💡 **Example**

- Turn the heat up before it gets cold.
  추워지기 전에 온도를 좀 올려.

- Turn the radio up so we can dance.
  라디오 소리 좀 키워라. 우리 춤 좀 추게

 Dialog

A: I can't hear the television.
B: Turn the volume up a little.

A: 난 TV 소리를 들을 수가 없어.
B: 볼륨을 조금 올려라.

I forgot to celebrate Tom's birthday

난 탐의 생일을 축하하는걸 깜빡했어

celebrate one's birthday는 '생일축하하다,' celebrate의 목적어로는 생일, 기념일, 성탄절 등이 온다.

Example
- We went to a bar to celebrate her birthday.
  우린 걔 생일을 축하해주려고 술집에 갔어.
- I forgot to celebrate my brother's birthday.
  난 남동생 생일을 축하하는걸 깜빡했어.

Dialog
A: What is the special event tomorrow?
B: We're going to celebrate Daniel's birthday.
  A: 내일 특별행사가 뭐니?
  B: 우린 다니엘의 생일을 축하할거야.

Let's throw a party for Sam

샘을 위한 파티를 하자

throw a party는 '파티를 열어주다' = give a party. '파티에 참석하다'는 attend one's party.

Example
- Shouldn't we give a party for him?
  그를 위해 파티를 열어줘야 하지 않을까요?
- Helen threw a party in her new apartment.
  헬렌은 새 아파트에서 파티를 열었어.

Dialog
A: I'm going to throw a party this Friday.
B: We have a test on Monday. I wonder how many people will come.
  A: 요번 주 금요일에 파티를 열 거야.
  B: 월요일에 시험이 있잖아. 몇명이나 올지 모르겠네.

I'm allergic to peanuts

난 땅콩 앨러지가 있어

be allergic to+음식명사는 '…에 앨러지 반응이 있다.'

🔆 Example

- Maybe you're allergic to something in the room.
  년 이 방의 뭔가에 앨러지가 있을지 몰라.

- I'm allergic to peanuts.
  난 땅콩 알레르기가 있어.

 Dialog

A: Come here and try some of this.
B: I can't. I'm allergic to peaches.

A: 이리 와서 이것 좀 먹어봐.
B: 안돼. 난 복숭아 알레르기가 있어.

It'll develop into a serious illness

그건 심각한 병으로 악화될거야

develop into~는 '병에 걸리다,' 혹은 '병이 다른 병으로 커지다.'

🔆 Example

- The doctor thinks it will develop into a serious illness.
  의사는 그게 심각한 질환으로 발전할 수 있다고 생각해.

- The scratch developed into a painful problem.
  찰과상이 통증문제로 발전해버렸어.

 Dialog

A: Why is Andy in the hospital?
B: His cold developed into pneumonia.

A: 앤디가 왜 병원에 있는거니?
B: 걔 감기가 폐렴으로 발전했대.

177

My ear really hurts

귀가 무지 아파

get hurt는 '아프다.' hurt의 동사변화는 hurt-hurt-hurt이며 여기서는 과거분사로 쓰인 get+pp이다.

Example

- My ear really hurts.
  귀가 무지 아파.

- I've got a terrible headache today and my back hurts.
  두통이 엄청나고 허리도 아파.

Dialog

A: It looked like you injured your leg.
B: I'm pretty sure I did. It hurts!

A: 다리가 다친 것 같네요.
B: 정말 그랬어요. 아파요!

178

I got injured in the car wreck

난 사고 난 차속에서 부상을 당했어

get injured는 '부상당하다.' injure는 사고나 천재지변 등으로, wound는 총, 칼에 의해 부상당하다.

Example

- Annie got injured in the car wreck.
  애니는 사고 난 차속에서 부상을 당했어.

- I heard that John was injured in a car accident.
  존이 교통사고 나서 다쳤다며.

Dialog

A: I used to play football for my university.
B: It's so easy to get injured doing that.

A: 난 대학에서 미식축구를 하곤 했어.
B: 운동중에 부상당하기가 무지 쉬워.

179

He came down with a cold
걘 감기에 걸렸어

come down with+병명은 '…에 걸리다.' 주로 가벼운 병을 말할 때 사용한다.

 Example

- I must be coming down with a cold.
  감기 걸린 게 분명해

- Lisa came down with malaria in Indonesia.
  리사는 인도네시아에서 말라리아에 걸렸어.

 Dialog

A: Where's Bill today?
B: He came down with a cold and called in sick.

A: 오늘 빌은 어디있니?
B: 그 친구 감기에 걸려서 병가냈어.

180

His feet felt heavy during the race
걔의 발은 경주중에 무겁게 느껴졌어

feel heavy는 '무겁게 느껴지다'로 뭔가 상태가 안좋아 무겁게 느껴지는 것으로 주어자리에 무거운 신체부위를 써준다

 Example

- His heart felt heavy when he left his girlfriend.
  여친과 헤어졌을 때 걔 마음이 무거웠어.

- The runner's feet felt heavy during the race.
  그 주자는 경주도중 발이 무겁게 느껴졌어.

Dialog

A: You know, my arms feel heavy.
B: I think you need to get some sleep.

A: 내 팔이 무겁게 느껴져.
B: 네가 좀 자야될거야.

She had a nervous breakdown

걘 신경쇠약에 걸렸어

have a breakdown은 '신경쇠약에 걸리다' = have a nervous breakdown.

 **Example**

- Zelda had a nervous breakdown and was hospitalized.
  젤다는 신경쇠약으로 입원했어.

- Relax or you'll have a nervous breakdown.
  느긋해봐 안그러면 신경쇠약에 걸릴 거야.

 Dialog

A: Why did Karen stop working here?
B: I heard she had a nervous breakdown.

A: 카렌이 여기서 왜 일을 그만두었니?
B: 걔가 신경쇠약에 걸렸다고 들었어.

Don't forget to take your medicine

약 먹는 것을 잊지마라

take one's medicine은 '약을 먹다,' take medication은 '약물치료받다.' medication은 특정병을 치료로 처방된 약물.

 **Example**

- You should take medication for your headache.
  넌 두통약을 먹어야해.

- Henry took medication in the hospital.
  헨리는 병원에서 약을 복용했어.

Dialog

A: I've been feeling very sick lately.
B: Are you taking any medication?

A: 요즘 계속 속이 메슥거려.
B: 약은 먹고 있는거니?

They cured his cancer

그들은 그의 암을 치료했어

cure a disease는 '병을 치료하다.' 목적어로는 병 혹은 사람이 온다. 두통을 치료하다는 treat the headache.

 Example

- The doctors have drugs to cure malaria.
  의사들은 말라리아를 치료할 약을 가지고 있어.

- We don't know how to cure stomach cancer.
  우린 위암 치료법을 모르고 있어.

 Dialog

A: Has Danny been in the hospital yet?
B: Yeah, they cured his cancer.

   A: 대니가 아직 병원에 있니?
   B: 그래, 걔 암을 치료했지.

I'm going through physical therapy

난 물리치료를 받고 있어

go through physical therapy는 '물리치료를 받다.' 물리재활치료는 physical rehab treatment.

 Example

- She needs to go through physical therapy for her hand.
  걘 손때문에 물리 치료를 받아야 돼.

- Many injured people go through physical therapy.
  많은 부상자들이 물리치료를 받아.

Dialog

A: My mom had to go through physical therapy.
B: Has it helped her to feel better?

   A: 어머니가 물리치료를 받아야 했어.
   B: 좋아지시는데 도움이 됐어?

I have a checkup every year

난 매년 건강검진을 받아

have a checkup은 '진찰받다' = get a checkup = have a medical checkup.

💡 **Example**

- You must have a checkup before playing sports.
  스포츠를 하기 전에 검진을 받아야 돼.

- My grandparents have a checkup every year.
  조부모님들은 매년 검진을 받으셔.

 Dialog

A: What brings you to the doctor's office today?
B: I need to have my yearly checkup.

A: 병원엔 웬일이세요?
B: 매년 건강진단을 받아야 하거든요.

She had plastic surgery on her nose

걘 코에 성형수술을 했어

have plastic surgery는 '성형수술을 받다' = cosmetic surgery. get a nose[boob] job은 코[유방]수술을 받다.

💡 **Example**

- Sue had plastic surgery on her nose.
  수는 코에 성형수술을 했어.

- He had plastic surgery to become more handsome.
  걘 좀 더 멋있게 보이려고 성형수술을 했지.

 Dialog

A: Is it a good idea to have plastic surgery?
B: Only after someone is forty years old.

A: 성형수술을 받는게 좋은 생각이니?
B: 40세만 넘으면 괜찮아.

From what I hear, she died

내가 듣기로 걘 죽었대

from what I hear[heard]는 '내가 들은 바에 따르면,' '내가 듣기로는.'

💡 **Example**

- From what I hear, that's going to take a while.
  내가 듣기로는 시간이 좀 걸릴거야.

- From what I hear, it's supposed to rain tomorrow.
  내가 들은 바로는 내일 비가 올거래.

 Dialog

A: Is Mrs. Carlson going to continue working?
B: From what I hear, she plans to retire.

A: 칼슨 부인이 계속 일을 할까요?
B: 내가 듣기로는 은퇴할 계획이래요.

I didn't hear you come in

네가 들어오는 소리 못 들었어

hear sb ~ing는 '…가 …하는 것을 듣다.' hear sb+V도 강조하는 표현이다.

💡 **Example**

- Have you ever heard him talk about his father?
  걔가 자기 아빠에 대해 얘기하는 거 들어본 적 있어?

- I didn't hear you come in.
  네가 들어오는 소리 못 들었어.

 Dialog

A: I heard you and Justin talking.
B: Talking about what?

A: 너하고 저스틴이 이야기하는 거 들었어.
B: 무슨 이야기를?

I saw you eating some cake

난 걔가 케익 먹는 걸 봤어

see[watch] sb+V[~ing]는 '…가 …하는 것을 보다.' ~ing가 좀 더 동적이다.

- I saw him working in the office today.
  오늘 그가 사무실에서 일하는거 봤어.
- You saw her dancing in the street?
  걔가 거리에서 춤추는거 봤어?

Dialog

A: Are you still dieting? I saw you eating some cake.
B: I gave up. I couldn't turn away delicious food.

A: 아직도 너 다이어트해? 케익 먹는 걸 봤어.
B: 포기했어. 맛난 음식을 외면할 수 없었어.

As far as I know, Chris left

내가 알기로는 크리스는 떠났어

as far as I know는 '내가 알고 있는 한'이라는 표현이다. as you know[see]는 '알다[보다]시피.'

- As far as I know, he didn't show up at the party.
  내가 아는 한 걘 파티에 오지도 않았어.
- As you know, a lot of people are not familiar with Korean food.
  알다시피 많은 사람들이 한국 음식에 익숙하지 않아.

Dialog

A: As far as I know, they sent it yesterday.
B: Then it should arrive later today.

A: 내가 아는 바로는 그 사람들이 어제 그걸 보냈다던데.
B: 그럼 오늘까지는 도착하겠군요.

I'd like to get to know you better

너를 더 알아가고 싶어

get to know는 '알게 되다.' 모르지만 만나서 친해지거나 혹은 직접 가서 경험해서 알게 되고 싶다고 할 때.

 **Example**

- You can take this opportunity to get to know her well.
  이 기회를 통해 걜 잘 알아봐.
- Do you happen to know if there is a good restaurant around here?
  이 근처에 혹 좋은 식당 아시나요?

Dialog

A: Can you recommend a good therapist to me?
B: Yes, I happen to know a very good psychiatrist.

A: 좋은 심리 치료사 좀 추천해 줄래요?
B: 예, 마침 아주 훌륭한 정신과 의사를 알고 있어요.

I know nothing about it

난 그것에 대해 전혀 몰라

know nothing about은 '…에 대해 전혀 모르다' = don't know anything about.

 **Example**

- You don't know anything about her, do you?
  걔에 대해 아무것도 모르지, 그지?
- I don't know the first thing about the stock market.
  난 주식시장에 대해 아무것도 몰라.

Dialog

A: Did those kids break the window?
B: No, they know nothing about it.

A: 저 애들이 유리창을 깬거야?
B: 아니, 걔네들은 그것에 대해 아무 것도 몰라.

I don't know for sure

난 확실히 몰라

not know for sure는 '확실히 모르다.' sure 대신 certain를 써서 not know for certain이라고 해도 된다.

💡 **Example**

- I think she might be a little late but I don't know for sure.
  걔가 좀 늦을 수도 있는데 확실히 몰라.

- I really don't know for sure, but I'm willing to give it a try.
  확실히는 잘 모르겠지만, 노력을 해볼려구.

A: How long is the storm going to last?
B: Maybe an hour. I don't know for sure.

A: 폭풍이 얼마나 갈거래?
B: 한 시간정도. 나도 잘 몰라.

Not that I know of. Why?

내가 알기로는 아냐. 왜?

Not that I know of는 '내가 알기로는 아냐.' know of 대신 remember, recall 등 동사를 바꿔 써도 된다.

💡 **Example**

- Not that I know of, but I'll go and check.
  내가 알기로는 아냐, 하지만 가서 확인해볼게.

- Not that I know of. Why?
  내가 알기로는 아냐. 왜?

A: Are you allergic to any kinds of medication?
B: **Not that I know of.**

A: 특정 약에 대해 앨러지 반응이 있나요?
B: 제가 알기로는 없어요.

Please give me your answer today
오늘까지 답해 줘

give sb an answer는 '…에게 답을 주다,' give a firm answer는 '확답을 주다,' get an answer는 '답을 받다.'

💡 **Example**

- I'd like to give you an answer after work.
  퇴근 후에 답을 줄게.

- You don't have to give me an answer right now.
  지금 당장 대답해야만 하는 건 아냐.

 Dialog

A: Could you give me an answer by tomorrow?
B: Sure, I'll let you know by then.

A: 내일까지 알려주시겠어요?
B: 그러죠, 그 때까지 알려드릴게요.

Please check on what was going on
무슨 상황인지 알아봐

check on sb[sth]은 '제대로 돌아가고 있는지 확인하다' = check up on.

💡 **Example**

- Sam ran forward to check on what was going on.
  샘은 무슨 일인지 확인하러 뛰어갔어.

- I checked on him but he's a little busy today.
  걜 확인해봤더니 오늘 좀 바빠.

 Dialog

A: The chair I ordered has not yet arrived.
B: I can check on your order for you.

A: 주문한 의자 아직 못받았어요.
B: 주문서 확인해볼게요.

Let's go over the budget

예산을 검토해보자

go over는 '정밀하게 조사하다.' 하지만 go over to+장소는 '…로 가다.'

Example

- They didn't go over the schedule.
  걔네들은 일정을 조사하지 않았어.
- Let's sit down and go over the budget.
  함께 앉아서 예산을 검토해보자.

 Dialog

A: Why did Jeremy call the meeting?
B: He wants to go over our future plans.

A: 제레미가 왜 회의를 소집한거야?
B: 향후 우리 계획을 면밀히 검토하고 싶어해.

Let's look into getting a dog

강아지를 구할 수 있는지 알아보자

look into는 '조사하다(examine carefully)'로 look into+N[~ing]로 쓰인다.

Example

- Let's look into getting a dog.
  강아지를 구할 수 있는지 알아보자.
- We have to look into the matter right now.
  우린 지금 당장 그 문제를 조사해야 돼.

 Dialog

A: Did you ever look into that stock I told you about?
B: I did and I bought some of it.

A: 내가 너한테 말했던 그 주식 잘 살펴봤니?
B: 응, 살펴보고 그 주(株)를 좀 샀어.

Let's look it up in the dictionary

사전에서 찾아보자

look up은 '(사전, 컴퓨터 등에서) 찾아보다,' 혹은 '방문을 목적으로 찾아가다'라는 의미로 쓰인다.

 Example

- We can look up his name in the phone book.
  전화번호부책에서 걔 이름을 찾을 수 있어.

- I want to look up a friend who lives in Seoul.
  난 서울에 사는 친구를 찾아보고 싶어.

 Dialog

A: I don't know what this word means.
B: Let's look it up in the dictionary.

A: 이 단어 뜻이 뭔지 모르겠어.
B: 사전에서 찾아보자.

Make sure the door is locked

문이 잠겼는지 꼭 확인해

make sure는 '확실히 하다.' 뭔가를 확실히 하라는 말로 주로 조언이나 충고를 할 때 많이 쓰인다.

 Example

- We need to make sure that the CEO is able to attend.
  CEO가 참석할 수 있도록 조치할 필요가 있어.

- I'll make sure that I'll keep in touch.
  내가 꼭 연락할게.

Dialog

A: Make sure that you log off when you're through.
B: Don't worry, I will.

A: 끝나면 접속을 끊는 거 잊지마.
B: 걱정마, 그럴게.

201

She informed us of her resignation
걘 우리에게 사임소식을 알렸어
inform sb of sth은 '…에게 …을 알리다.' of 대신에 about을 쓰기도 한다.

 Example

- Sandy informed us she was quitting school.
  샌디는 학교를 그만둔다고 알려줬어.
- She came by to inform us of her resignation.
  걘 들러서 사임소식을 알려줬어.

 Dialog

A: I'm here to tell you that we're cutting 100 jobs.
B: Why didn't you inform us earlier?

A: 100개의 일자리를 줄인다고 말하려 왔어요.
B: 왜 더 일찍 알려주지 않았죠?

202

I didn't mean to hurt you
너에게 상처 줄 의도가 아니었어
didn't mean to+V는 '…하려는게 아니었어'라는 의미. 자신이 한 언행에 대한 오해를 풀기 위한 표현.

 Example

- I'm sorry! I didn't mean to do that!
  미안! 그럴려고 그런게 아니었어!
- I didn't mean to hurt you.
  너에게 상처 줄 의도가 아니었어.

Dialog

A: How could you do this to me?
B: I really didn't mean to make you miserable.

A: 어떻게 내게 그럴 수 있어?
B: 널 비참하게 할려고 한 건 아냐.

Don't get me wrong
오해하지마

get sb wrong은 '…을 오해하다.' get 대신 take을 써서 take sb wrong이라고 해도 된다.

💡 **Example**

- Don't get me wrong, I'd love to work with you.
  오해마. 너랑 같이 일하고 싶어.

- Don't get me wrong. I'm trying to help you.
  오해마. 그냥 도와주려는 것 뿐이야.

 Dialog

A: Do you really hate my shoes?
B: Don't get me wrong. I think they are OK.

A: 내 신발이 그렇게 마음에 안들어?
B: 오해하지마. 괜찮은 것 같아.

Guess What?

Pardon my French
욕설해서 미안해

"프랑스어를 써서 미안하다," 혹은 "내 프랑스어가 미숙해 미안하다"라고 생각하면 안된다. 영국과 프랑스 사이의 오랜 악연을 떠올리면 이해가 되는 표현이다. 뭔가 상스러운 욕을 하고(a way of asking someone to excuse profanity or rude language) 나서 하는 말로 "욕을 해서 미안해"라는 의미이다. Pardon 대신에 Excuse~를 써도 된다.

No hard feelings on my part

기분나쁘게 생각하지마

have no hard feelings는 '악의는 없다,' '나쁜 감정은 없다.' There are no hard feelings on my part.

💡 **Example**

- It was a mistake, and he has no hard feelings.
  실수였고 그리고 걘 악의는 없었어.

- No hard feelings about you leaving me behind.
  날 두고 간 거 기분 나쁘게 생각안해.

 **Dialog**

A: I'm sorry that we argued.
B: There are no hard feelings on my part.

A: 다투어서 미안해.
B: 기분 나쁘게 생각하지마.

Don't take it personally

기분나빠 하지마

take it personally는 '개인적으로, 사적으로 감정을 갖고 받아들이다'라는 표현. 기분 나빠할 수 있는 얘기를 꺼낼 때.

💡 **Example**

- Don't take it personally, but I really don't like your new haircut.
  기분나쁘게 생각하지마, 네 새로운 머리스타일 정말 맘에 안들어.

- I can't help but take it personally.
  기분나쁘게 받아들이지 않을 수 없어.

 **Dialog**

A: What did she say about me?
B: Don't take it personally, but she said you were a jerk.

A: 걔가 나에 관해 뭐래?
B: 기분나빠 하지마, 네가 멍청이래.

I have no doubt about his loyalty

난 걔의 충성심을 의심하지 않아

have no doubt about[of]~는 '확신하다,' 반대는 have doubts about~.

💡 Example

- Tim had no doubt about his future plans.
  팀은 자신의 미래계획에 대해 확신하고 있어.

- I have no doubt you'll get better.
  분명 네가 나아질거야.

Dialog

A: Are you sure our basketball team will win?
B: I have no doubt about the outcome.

A: 우리 야구팀이 이기리라고 확신해?
B: 결과에 난 확신해.

Don't give me an excuse

내게 변명하지마

give (sb) an excuse는 '변명을 하다.' 변명하게 된 이유는 for~로 써준다.

💡 Example

- She gave another excuse for not paying me.
  걘 내게 돈을 주지 않는 다른 변명을 댔어.

- The student gave her teacher an excuse for being late.
  학생은 선생님께 지각사유를 댔어.

Dialog

A: What do you think of John's excuse?
B: To be frank, I don't buy it at all.

A: 존의 변명에 대해 어떻게 생각해?
B: 솔직히 말해서 전혀 믿기지 않아.

Schools are closed due to the heavy rains

폭우로 학교는 휴교합니다

due to+N[~ing]는 '…때문에.' = owing to. 캐주얼하게 쓰려면 because of. thanks to~담에는 좋은 일.

💡 **Example**

- We're going inside due to the rainy weather.
  비가 와서 안으로 들어갈거야.

- Thanks to you I'm not single anymore.
  네 덕에 난 더 이상 혼자가 아니야.

 Dialog

A: Why did the health club close?
B: It closed due to having very few members.
   A: 왜 헬스클럽이 문을 닫았어.
   B: 회원이 별로 없어서 닫았어.

He has no reason to hurt me

걘 날 해칠 이유가 없어

have no reason for~는 '…에 대한 이유가 없다,' have a good reason for~는 '납득할 만한 이유가 있다.'

💡 **Example**

- Andy didn't have a reason for breaking the mirror.
  앤디는 거울을 깰 이유가 없었어.

- She has no reason to hurt me.
  걘 날 해칠 이유가 없어.

 Dialog

A: Do you have a reason for acting so badly?
B: I'm sorry, but I am in an angry mood.
   A: 그렇게 못되게 행동한 이유가 있어?
   B: 미안, 하지만 화가 난 상태였어.

That's why I decided to quit

그래서 내가 그만 두려고 하는거야

That's why S+V는 '바로 그래서 …하다,' That's because S+V는 '…하기 때문이다.'

Example

- I hate you and that's why I'm leaving.
  널 싫어해서 내가 떠나는 거야.
- That's why I wanted to talk to you.
  바로 그래서 너하고 얘기하고 싶었어.

A: That business is really cut-throat.
B: That's why I decided to quit.

A: 그 사업은 정말 치열해.
B: 그래서 내가 그만 두려고 하는 거야.

He gave specifics about his plans

걘 자신의 계획에 대해 상세하게 말했어

go into details는 '자세히 말하다' = give specifics about~ = tell sb some details about~.

Example

- Jerry gave specifics about his plans.
  제리는 자신의 계획에 대해 상세하게 말했어.
- Tell us the details of your wedding.
  네 결혼식의 상세내용을 우리한테 말해줘.

A: I have some real estate you should look at.
B: Can you tell me some details about it?

A: 살펴보셔야 할 부동산을 좀 갖고 있는데요.
B: 자세하게 얘기해 보실래요?

I don't get it

이해가 안돼

get it은 '이해하다' = understand. 아주 구어적인 표현으로 "I get it"과 "I don't get it"은 꼭 외워두자.

💡 **Example**

- I don't understand why they don't get it.
  난 걔들이 왜 그걸 모르는 지 이해가 안돼.

- All right. I get it. I see what's going on here.
  좋아요. 알았어. 여기 상황을 알겠네요.

 Dialog

A: What's wrong with you today?
B: I don't get it. This stuff is too hard.

   A: 오늘 안 좋은 일 있니?
   B: 이해가 잘 안돼. 이 일은 너무 어려워.

We should give it top priority

우린 이 일을 최우선시해야 돼

give sth top priority는 '…을 최우선시하다.' 많은 일들 중에서 가장 최우선시해야 한다고 할 때.

💡 **Example**

- I'd like you to give this top priority.
  이 일에 최우선을 두게.

- I'd like to make it my top priority.
  난 이 일에 최우선권을 주고 싶어.

 Dialog

A: We have to get this homework done.
B: You're right. We should give it top priority.

   A: 우린 이 숙제를 끝마쳐야 해.
   B: 맞아. 우린 이 일을 최우선시해야 돼.

It doesn't matter to me
그건 나한테 상관없어

Sth matters (to sb)는 '…가 …에게 중요하다.' <고질라> 홍보문구인 Size does matter는 "크기가 중요하다."

💡 **Example**
- It matters to me. We should try to conserve things.
  내겐 중요해. 물건을 아끼도록 노력해야 돼.
- How can you say that it doesn't matter to me?
  어떻게 그게 나한테 상관없다고 말할 수 있어?

 Dialog

A: Your kitchen is very clean.
B: Keeping the area where you eat clean matters.

A: 네 부엌은 무지 깨끗하구나.
B: 먹는 곳을 청결하게 하는 것은 중요해.

He claimed that the money was his
걘 그 돈이 자기 것이라고 주장했어

claim that S+V는 '…을 주장하다.' claim은 절뿐만 아니라 명사나 to do를 목적어로 받을 수 있다.

💡 **Example**
- Jack claimed that she started the fight.
  잭은 걔가 싸움을 시작했다고 주장했어.
- Ray claimed he acted in a Hollywood movie.
  레이는 할리웃영화에 출연했다고 주장했어.

 Dialog

A: Melissa claims that Brian started a fight.
B: That's not true. Brian is a nice guy.

A: 멜리사는 브라이언이 싸움을 시작했다고 주장해.
B: 사실이 아니야. 브라이언은 좋은 친구야.

Can I make a suggestion?

제가 제안 하나 해도 될까요?

make a suggestion은 '제안하다' = suggest+N[~ing]. 제안받는 사람은 to sb, 제안내용은 about sth.

- Why don't you make a suggestion to your boss?
  네 보스에게 제안을 하지 그래?
- No one takes my brilliant suggestions seriously.
  아무도 내 멋진 제안을 진지하게 안받아.

A: I want to make a suggestion about your clothes.
B: Do you think I should change them?

A: 네 의상에 대해 제안을 하고 싶어.
B: 내가 옷을 바꿔 입어야 한다고 생각하니?

I have a very good memory

난 기억력이 아주 좋아

have a good memory는 '기억력이 좋다,' '잘 기억하다' <=> have a bad memory.

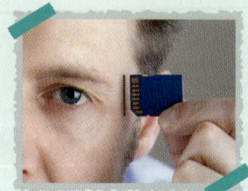

- My grandfather has a bad memory now that he's old.
  할아버지는 이제 연세가 드셔서 기억력이 좋지 않아.
- He knows all of the poems by heart.
  걘 그 모든 시들을 암기하고 있어.

A: How did you remember that?
B: Oh, I have a very good memory.

A: 어떻게 그걸 기억했어?
B: 오, 난 기억력이 매우 좋아.

I'll keep that in mind

명심할게

keep sth in mind는 '…을 명심하다.' sth이 길면 뒤로 빼서 that S+V의 형태로 써주면 된다.

💡 Example

- Keep in mind that Mindy is always late.
  민디는 항상 늦는다는 것을 기억해.

- Please keep in mind that this is your last chance.
  이게 네 마지막 기회라는 걸 명심해.

 Dialog

A: Let's buy a lot of Christmas presents.
B: Keep it in mind that we have to save money.

A: 크리스마스 선물을 많이 사자.
B: 우리가 절약해야 한다는 사실을 명심해.

Try not to look back on the past

과거를 회상하지 않도록 노력해라

look back on sth은 '회상하다.' 과거의 일이나 사건들을 think about한다는 이야기.

💡 Example

- Vera looked back on her childhood with happiness.
  베라는 행복하게 자신의 어린 시절을 회상했어.

- Try not to look back on the past.
  과거를 회상하지 않도록 노력해라.

 Dialog

A: I like to look back on my school days.
B: Yeah, we had a lot of good friends then.

A: 난 학교시절을 회상하고 싶어.
B: 응, 그때엔 좋은 친구들이 많았어.

220

You remind me of my wife

넌 내 아내를 생각나게 해

remind A of B는 'A에게 B를 생각나게 하다.' A는 사람, B는 주어 때문에 생각나는 것을 말하면 된다.

Example

- You remind me of my daughter.
  넌 내 딸을 생각나게 하는구나.
- You remind me of myself when I was an intern.
  널보면 내 인턴때 날 보는 것 같아.

 Dialog

A: The building looks very strange.
B: Yes, its shape reminds everyone of a cell phone.

A: 그 빌딩이 아주 이상하게 보여.
B: 그래, 모양이 휴대폰을 상상케 해.

221

Jim finds hiking difficult

짐은 하이킹이 힘들다고 생각해

find sth+형용사는 '…라고 생각하다, '…라고 보인다.' sth 다음에 형용사 및 ~ing형태를 쓰면 된다.

Example

- Jenna found James very interesting.
  제나는 제임스가 꽤 재미있다고 생각했어.
- Jim found hiking up the mountain difficult.
  짐은 산에서 하이킹하는게 어렵다고 생각했어.

 Dialog

A: What's taking so long?
B: I'm finding our homework difficult.

A: 뭐가 그렇게 시간이 걸리니?
B: 숙제가 어려워서.

222

Don't give it a second thought
다시 생각하지마

give it a second thought는 '다시 생각하다.' '재고하다' = have second thoughts.

💡 **Example**

- We had second thoughts about renting the apartment.
  아파트임대문제를 재고했어.
- Jim is having second thoughts about going to China.
  짐은 중국 방문문제에 대해 다시 생각하고 있어.

 Dialog

A: Don't give it a second thought. I'm always glad to help.
B: Thanks so much.

A: 걱정하지 말아요. 언제나 기꺼이 도와드리죠.
B: 정말 고맙습니다.

223

I regard my sister as a genius
난 누이를 천재로 여겨

regard A as B는 'A를 B로 여기다' = consider A (as) B = think of A as B.

💡 **Example**

- Most people regard artwork as worthwhile.
  대부분 미술품은 살 가치가 있다고 여겨.
- He regarded the meeting as a waste of time.
  갠 회의를 시간 낭비로 간주했어.

 Dialog

A: I regard Alfred as a genius.
B: Yes, he's the smartest guy in class.

A: 난 알프레드를 천재로 여겨
B: 그럼, 학급에서 가장 똑똑해.

224

What do you take me for?

날 뭘로 보는거야?
take A for B는 'A를 B로 잘못알다.' '틀리게 알고 있는 것'에 초점을 맞춘다.

 Example

- They took Cami for a fool.
  걔들은 카미를 바보로 잘못 여겼어.
- I took his story for a lie.
  난 걔 이야기를 거짓말로 잘못 생각했어.

 Dialog

A: Mr. Johnson has a lot of money.
B: Really? We took him for a poor person.
   A: 존슨 씨는 돈이 아주 많아.
   B: 정말? 우린 걔를 가난한 사람으로 잘못 알았어.

225

He hit on a new idea

걘 새로운 아이디어를 생각해냈어
hit on sth은 '…한 생각이 떠오르다,' '생각해내다.' hit on sb = come on to sb(집적대다).

 Example

- He hit on a new idea at the meeting.
  걘 회의에서 새로운 아이디어를 생각해냈어.
- I hit on the plan of creating a website.
  웹사이트를 만드는 계획이 떠올랐어.

Dialog

A: How did you figure out the math problem?
B: We hit on the answer after a few hours.
   A: 그 수학문제를 어떻게 알아냈니?
   B: 우린 몇 시간 이후에 답을 생각해냈어.

He doesn't have any faith in me

걘 날 전혀 신뢰하지 않아

have faith in~는 '…을 믿다.' faith는 강한 신뢰감을 말하는 것으로 in 다음에 사람이나 사물이 온다.

 Example

- I know you put a lot of faith in me, Jim.
  짐, 네가 나한테 큰 신뢰를 갖고 있다는 점을 알고 있어.

- My father doesn't have any faith in me.
  우리 아빠는 나한테 아무런 신뢰를 갖고 있지 않으셔.

 Dialog

A: Is Erin a good carpenter?
B: I have faith in her ability to build things.

A: 에린은 유능한 목수니?
B: 난 걔가 물건을 만드는 능력에 대해 믿음이 있어.

I have hope for better days ahead

난 앞으로 더 좋은 날이 올거라 희망해

have hope for sth은 '…에 희망을 갖다.' 희망의 크기를 말할 때는 hope 앞에 high나 big을 쓴다.

 Example

- I have big hopes for her. She's going to be a doctor.
  난 걔한테 큰 희망을 가지고 있어. 걘 의사가 될 거야.

- I had high hopes for a relationship with you.
  난 너와의 관계에 큰 기대를 했었어.

Dialog

A: You lost a lot of money this year.
B: I have hope for a better time next year.

A: 넌 금년에 많은 돈을 잃었어.
B: 내년에 상황이 나아지길 희망해.

I'm looking forward to English class
난 영어수업이 기다려져

look forward to+N[~ing]는 '…을 기대하다.' 학수고대한다는 의미로 to 다음에는 명사나 동사의 ~ing가 온다.

- I look forward to talking with you this afternoon.
  오늘 오후에 당신네들과 얘기하기를 기대합니다.
- I'm looking forward to English class.
  난 영어수업이 기다려져.

Dialog
A: I'll give you a call when things cool down.
B: I look forward to hearing from you.

A: 일이 좀 정리되면 제가 전화하겠습니다.
B: 그럼 연락 기다릴게요.

I'll take charge of the office
내가 사무실을 책임질게

take charge of~는 '…의 책임을 지다,' '통제권을 갖다.' charge 대신에 control을 사용해도 된다.

- I took control of the business when my father died.
  아빠가 돌아가셨을 때 난 사업을 책임졌어.
- Sally will take charge of planning the party.
  샐리는 파티를 기획하는 책임을 질거야.

Dialog
A: Our boss is out sick this morning.
B: OK, I'll take charge of the office.

A: 보스가 오늘 아침 아파서 결근했어.
B: 오케이, 내가 사무실을 책임질게.

My wife complains all the time

내 아내는 항상 불평해

complain about[of]~는 '…을 불평하다.' complain 뒤에 about, of, to 등 다양한 전치사가 온다.

 Example

- She complained to me about her parents.
  걘 자기 부모에 대해 내게 불평했어.
- My wife complains all the time.
  내 아내는 항상 불평해.

 Dialog

A: My neighbor's TV is too loud.
B: Have you complained about the noise?

  A: 내 이웃의 TV가 너무 시끄러워.
  B: 소음에 대해 불만을 표했었니?

I can't stand him complaining

걔가 불평하는 걸 참을 수가 없어

not stand sb[sth] ~ing는 '…가 …하는 것을 참지 못하다.'

 Example

- Sheila can't stand dating short guys.
  쉴라는 키작은 남자들과 데이트하는 걸 못참아.
- I can't stand his singing.
  난 걔가 노래하는 것을 듣고 있을 수가 없어.

Dialog

A: I cannot stand the smell of garlic.
B: Really? I love the way it smells.

  A: 난 마늘 냄새를 참을 수가 없어.
  B: 정말? 난 그 냄새 나는 게 좋은데.

I cannot take it anymore

더 이상 못 참겠어

can't take it anymore는 '더 이상 참지 못하다.'

 Example

- Stop talking. I cannot take it anymore.
  그만 말해라. 더 이상 못 듣겠어.

- He quit because he could not take it anymore.
  걘 더 이상 참지 못해서 그만뒀어.

 Dialog

A: So you decided to stop going to church?
B: Right. I could not take it anymore.

A: 그래 넌 예배 보는 것을 중단하기로 결정했니?
B: 예, 더 이상 할 수가 없어요.

Say no to drugs

마약은 거절해라

say not to sth은 '…을 거절하다,' '거부하다.'

 Example

- She said no when I asked her to marry me.
  내가 걔한데 청혼할 때 걔가 거절했어.

- Say no to drugs or you will ruin your life.
  마약을 거절해라 그렇지 않으면 네 삶이 망해.

Dialog

A: I don't want to help my friend skip class.
B: You can say no to her if she asks you to help her.

A: 난 내 친구가 수업빠지는 걸 도와주고 싶지 않아.
B: 걔가 너한테 도움을 청하면 거절해.

📎 234

He approves of them helping each other
걘 그들이 서로 돕는 것을 좋게 생각해
approve of는 '…을 찬성하다.' approve of sb ~ing은 '…가 …하는 것을 좋게 생각하다.'

💡 Example
- Everyone approves of my choice of a sports car.
  다들 내가 선택한 스포츠카를 좋아해.
- This heater is approved for use in bedrooms.
  이 히터는 침실용으로 승인된 거야.

 Dialog

A: Did you introduce your boyfriend to your parents?
B: Yes. They told me that they approve of him.
   A: 네 부모님께 네 남친을 소개했니?
   B: 네, 부모님들이 걔를 허락한다고 제게 말했어요.

📎 235

Are you with me?
너도 같은 생각이지?
be with sb (on~)은 '(…에 대해) …와 생각이 같다,' '…와 동의하다.'

💡 Example
- We're with Tom on his project.
  우린 톰의 프로젝트에 대해 그와 같은 생각이야.
- I'll go talk to the teacher. Are you with me?
  내가 선생님께 말할 거야. 너도 같은 생각이지?

 Dialog

A: Do you think Karen and Anna will help us?
B: Yes, they are both with us.
   A: 카렌과 애나가 우릴 도와줄 것으로 생각하니?
   B: 그럼, 걔들은 우리 편이야.

236

I'll go along with her on that
그점에 난 걔 말에 동의해

go along with sb는 '…에 동의하다,' go along with sth은 '…과 일치된다.'

💡 **Example**

- It's difficult to go along with the president's ideas.
  사장님의 생각에 동의하기가 어려워.

- He didn't go along with me on this.
  걔 이 문제에 대해 나하고 견해가 틀려.

 Dialog

A: Terry wants us to go out tonight.
B: That's great. I'll go along with her on that.

A: 테리는 오늘 밤 우리가 외출하기를 원해.
B: 훌륭해. 테리 말에 동의해.

237

He tends to lie to me
걔 내게 거짓말하는 경향이 있어

tend to+V는 '…하는 경향이 있다,' '…하기 쉽다'라는 의미 = have a tendency to+V

💡 **Example**

- That dog tends to bark all night long.
  저 강아지는 밤새 짖는 경향이 있어.

- Dave tends to drive fast in his car.
  데이브는 차를 너무 빨리 운전하는 경향이 있어.

 Dialog

A: I don't trust anything that Rachel says.
B: She also tends to lie to me.

A: 난 레이첼이 말하는 것은 아무것도 믿지 않아.
B: 걔 나한테도 거짓말을 하는 경향이 있어.

This shirt is your style
이 셔츠는 네 스타일이다

be one's style[type]는 '…의 스타일이다.' That's not my style은 "이건 내 스타일이 아냐."

💡 **Example**

- It's my style to come late to parties.
  파티에 늦게 오는게 내 스타일이야.
- This shirt is your style.
  이 셔츠는 네 스타일이다.

 Dialog

A: Cheryl always wears black clothes.
B: She told me that's her style.

A: 셰릴은 항상 검은 옷을 입어.
B: 걘 그게 자기 스타일이래.

I get the feeling she likes me
난 걔가 나를 좋아하는 것 같아

get[have] the feeling that S+V는 '…인 것 같다,' '…라는 기분이 들다.' have a hunch는 '예감이 들다.'

💡 **Example**

- Jimmy had a hunch that we were here.
  지미는 우리가 여기 있을 것 같은 예감이 들었대.
- We had a feeling that the movie was exciting.
  그 영화가 재미있을 것 같은 느낌을 가졌어.

 Dialog

A: Barney came over to talk to me.
B: I have the feeling he'll ask you out on a date.

A: 바니가 나한테 말하려고 왔어.
B: 걔가 너한테 데이트를 신청할 것 같은 느낌이 드네.

240

I mean she's a workaholic
내 얘긴 걔가 일벌레라는거야
I mean that S+V는 '내 뜻은 …이야.' 말중간에 I mean이라고 하면 자기 말을 강조하거나 명확히 말할 때.

Example
- **I mean** she's a workaholic.
  내 얘긴 걔가 일벌레라는거야.
- **I mean** which country you come from.
  내 말은 네가 어느 나라 출신이라는거야.

A: Don't try to take care of me. **I mean,** I'm okay.
B: Are you sure you're okay?

A: 날 돌봐주려 애쓰지 마. 난 괜찮다니까.
B: 정말 괜찮아?

241

I was frustrated with you!
너 땜에 지쳐버렸어!
get frustrated with[at]~은 '…에 좌절하다, '…에 지치다.' 뜻대로 되지 않는 상황에 크게 좌절했을 때.

Example
- I'm **frustrated with** my lack of options.
  선택할 수 있는 것이 너무 없어서 힘이 빠져.
- She's **frustrated with** her computer's problems.
  걘 컴퓨터가 문제를 일으켜 지쳤어.

A: Why did you leave the meeting so suddenly?
B: I **was frustrated with** you! You talk too much!

A: 왜 그렇게 급히 회의에서 나간 거야?
B: 너 땜에 지쳐버렸어! 넌 말이 너무 많아!

242

You hurt my feelings
너 때문에 기분 상했어

hurt one's feelings는 '…의 기분을 나쁘게 하다,' '기분을 상하게 하다.'

💡 **Example**

- It hurt my feelings that I wasn't invited.
  내가 초대받지 못해 감정이 상했어.

- It hurt Mom's feelings when we forgot her birthday.
  우리가 엄마생일을 깜박했을 때 엄마감정이 상했어.

 Dialog

A: Is Harry sad because I broke up with him?
B: I'm sure that you hurt his feelings.

A: 내가 해리랑 헤어져 걔가 슬퍼해?
B: 네가 걔 감정을 아프게 한 게 맞아.

243

It's driving me crazy
그것 때문에 미치겠어

drive sb crazy =drive sb up the wall은 '주어가 …을 미치게 만들다,' '…을 화나게 하다.'

💡 **Example**

- The traffic jam was driving everyone crazy.
  교통체증이 모두를 미치게 해.

- The media really went crazy covering that case.
  언론은 그 사건을 취재할 때 난리였어.

 Dialog

A: Can you shut off that radio? It's driving me crazy.
B: Why are you so sensitive to noise?

A: 라디오 좀 끌래? 미치겠다.
B: 왜 그리 소음에 민감한거야?

244

Are you upset about something?
뭐 화나는 일 있니?

get[be] upset about~는 '…으로 화나다,' '…에 속상하다.' 화남의 정도는 upset <angry<furious.

💡 Example

- I'm really upset that he did that.
  그런 짓을 했다니 정말 화가 나는 걸.

- I'm so upset that you forgot our anniversary.
  당신이 우리 결혼 기념일을 잊어버려서 너무 속상해.

 Dialog

A: Are you upset about something?
B: I feel awful. I got fired today.

A: 뭐 화나는 일 있니?
B: 기분 더러워. 오늘 해고당했다구.

245

I lost my temper with my wife
난 아내에게 화를 벌컥 냈어

lose one's temper (with sb)는 '화를 벌컥 내다' = lost one's cool   keep one's cool.

💡 Example

- She lost her temper when her boyfriend lied.
  걘 남친이 거짓말할 때 화를 벌컥 냈어.

- I lost my temper because she was so late.
  걔가 너무 늦어 내가 화를 냈어.

 Dialog

A: The boss is going to lose his temper when he sees this report.
B: I know. It has too many mistakes in it.

A: 사장이 이 보고서보고 엄청 화낼 거야.
B: 알아. 보고서에 실수가 너무 많아.

I have no regrets about quitting

난 그만둔거에 후회없어

have no regrets about~는 '…에 후회가 없다' <=> be full of regrets(후회막심이다).

Example

- They had no regrets about getting married.
  걔네들은 결혼한거 후회하지 않았어.
- I had no regrets about spending all of my money.
  돈 다 쓴거에 대해 후회 없어.

A: Are you sorry that you dropped out of college?
B: I have no regrets about quitting school.

A: 대학 중퇴해서 후회돼?
B: 학교 그만둔 거 후회 없어.

You shouldn't have

(선물) 그러지 않아도 되는데

should have+pp는 '…을 했어야 했는데,' shouldn't have+pp는 '…을 하지 말았어야 하는데.'

Example

- I should have gotten up early this morning.
  오늘 아침 일찍 일어났어야 했는데.
- I shouldn't have bought this new car.
  이 새 차를 사지 말았어야 했는데.

A: You should have been here hours ago.
B: Sorry. I got held up at work.

A: 몇시간 전에 도착했어야 하잖아.
B: 미안. 일에 잡혀서 말야.

You'll be sorry about teasing me

날 놀린 걸 후회하게 될거야

You'll be sorry about~은 '넌 …을 후회하게 될거야.' 상대방의 행동에 후회하게 될거라며 주의나 경고를 줄 때.

 Example

- You'll be sorry about teasing me.
  날 놀린 걸 후회하게 될거야.
- You'll be sorry if you don't obey your parents.
  부모말씀 안들으면 후회하게 될거야.

 Dialog

A: You'll be sorry if you don't prepare for the test.
B: Are you saying that I should study?

A: 시험준비를 하지 않으면 후회하게 될거야.
B: 내가 공부해야 된다고 말하는거야?

She is grateful to Chris

걘 크리스에게 고마워해

be grateful to sb (for ~ing)는 '…는 …에게 (…해준거에) 고마워하다.'

 Example

- I am grateful to everyone who gave money.
  돈을 준 모든 사람에게 감사해.
- She was grateful to her school's English teacher.
  걘 학교 영어선생님에게 감사했어.

 Dialog

A: Why did George give his mom a necklace?
B: He is grateful to her for raising him.

A: 왜 조지가 걔 엄마에게 목걸이를 선물했어?
B: 키워주신 거에 대해 감사해하고 있어.

I'm afraid you're wrong

네가 틀린 것 같아

I'm afraid (that) S+V는 상대방에게 미안한 얘기를 할 때 쓴다. '무서워하다'의 be afraid of와 구분한다.

Example

- I'm afraid you have the wrong number.
  전화 잘못 거신 것 같네요.
- I'm afraid I've got some bad news.
  좀 안 좋은 소식이 있어.

Dialog

A: You always drink my Kiwi juice.
B: I'm afraid I didn't do it this time.

  A: 넌 늘 내 키위 주스만 마시더라.
  B: 미안하지만 이번엔 안그랬어.

Guess What?

They fell head over heels for each other
걔네들은 서로 정신없이 빠져들었어

"머리가 구두 위로 떨어지다"라는 말로 미래의 결과에 대해서는 별로 신경쓰지 않고 빠르게 그리고 깊이 사랑에 빠지는 것(to fall in love with someone quickly and deeply, without regard for the future consequences)을 뜻한다. 서로 사랑에 빠져 정신 못차리는 경우를 떠올려보면 된다.

251

I was so embarrassed
난 정말 당황했어

be embarrassed at[about, over, to+V]는 '…을 창피해하다.' 실수하거나 당황한 상황에 처해 있을 때.

💡 Example

- This is really embarrassing. I'm really embarrassed about that.
  정말 당황하게 하네. 정말 당황했어.
- I was too embarrassed to tell you.
  너무 당황스러워서 네게 말할 수 없었어.

A: I heard you farted in front of your mother-in-law.
B: That's true. I was so embarrassed.

A: 장모님 앞에서 방귀꼈다며.
B: 맞아. 정말 당황했어.

252

My stomach feels weird
배가 이상해

feel[get] weird는 '기분이나 상태가 이상하다.'

💡 Example

- It felt weird to leave school in the morning.
  아침에 조퇴하니 좀 기분이 이상했어.
- Don't you think it's going to be weird?
  좀 이상할거라고 생각하지 않아?

A: Ray, what's the matter with you?
B: My stomach feels weird. I think I'm getting sick.

A: 레이, 무슨 일이야?
B: 배가 이상해. 아프려나 봐.

He seemed confused by the question

걔 그 질문에 당황한 것 같았어

be[get] confused (by)는 '…에 혼란스럽다,' '…에 당황하다.'

💡 Example

- I was confused by the signs on the road.
  도로상에 있는 광고 사인들로 혼란스러워.

- She was confused when she visited Tokyo.
  걔 도쿄를 방문했을 때 혼란스러웠대.

 Dialog

A: The menu has so many choices that I'm confused!
B: I know but nothing appeals to me today.

A: 음식 종류가 너무 많아서 고민이야.
B: 그래, 하지만 오늘은 딱히 끌리는 게 없는 걸.

She seems nervous

걔가 신경이 날카로와

be[get, look, seem] nervous는 '불안해하다,' '초조해하다.'

💡 Example

- I got so nervous that I was not able to talk then.
  초조해서 그때 말을 제대로 할 수 없었어.

- I remember how nervous I was for my first interview.
  처음 면접 때 얼마나 떨었었는지 생각나.

 Dialog

A: He seems nervous. What's wrong?
B: He's had a lot of stress lately.

A: 걔가 신경이 날카로운 것 같은데. 무슨 일 있어?
B: 요새 스트레스를 많이 받아서 그래.

255

I can't believe she got divorced

걔가 이혼했다니 믿기지 않아

I can't believe S+V는 '…라는게 말이 돼?'라는 말로 믿을 수 없다라는 부정의 표현이 아니라 놀람과 충격의 표현.

💡 Example

- I can't believe Mom slapped me in the face.
  엄마가 내 뺨을 때렸다는 게 말이 돼!

- I can't believe that she treated me that way.
  걔가 날 그렇게 취급했다니 믿어지지 않아.

 Dialog

A: **I can't believe** they didn't give us a raise.
B: I guess we'll all be on strike tomorrow.

A: 봉급을 안 올려주다니 기가 막혀.
B: 내일 우리 모두 파업에 들어가야 할 것 같아.

256

I take pity on poor people

난 가난한 사람들을 동정해

take pity on sb는 '…을 불쌍히 여기다,' '동정하다.'

💡 Example

- I take pity on poor people in my neighborhood.
  난 이웃의 가난한 사람들을 동정해.

- Take pity on the students who are failing.
  난 낙제하는 학생들이 안쓰러워.

 Dialog

A: How did you get home from the party?
B: Someone **took pity on** me and gave me a ride.

A: 넌 파티 끝나고 집에 어떻게 왔니?
B: 누군가 날 불쌍히 여겨 태워줬어.

I am scared of cockroaches

난 바퀴벌레가 무서워

be[get] scared of~는 '…을 무서워하다.' be scared to death는 '무척 무서워하다.'

- The baby is scared to sleep in the dark.
  그 애기는 어두운 데서 자는 것을 무서워해.

- I am scared of flying on airplanes.
  난 비행기를 타는 것이 무서워.

Dialog

A: I am scared of gangsters.
B: They can be very violent.

A: 난 갱들이 무서워.
B: 갱들은 매우 폭력적일 수 있지.

Shame on you!

부끄러운 줄 알아!

shame on sb는 '부끄러운 줄 알아라,' '안됐다.' sb가 행동한 것으로 창피함을 느껴야 한다고 말할 때.

- Shame on everyone for not helping the blind girl!
  그 맹인 소녀를 돕지 않다니 모두들 창피한 줄 알아라!

- Shame on you! You shouldn't be taking things from children.
  창피해라! 애들한테 물건을 빼앗아선 안되지.

Dialog

A: I stole this paper from the school.
B: Shame on you! You know it's wrong to steal.

A: 나 학교에서 이 시험지를 훔쳤어.
B: 부끄러운 줄 알아! 너도 훔치는게 나쁜거라는 건 알잖아.

259

He showed his new car off
걘 자신의 새 차를 자랑했어
show A off는 '…을 자랑해보이다,' '드러내다,' '과시하다' = make a boast of.

Example
- I wanted to show my high grades off.
  내가 받은 높은 학점을 자랑하고 싶었어.
- Did you show your diamond ring off?
  네 다이아몬드 반지를 자랑했니?

A: Where is Anna tonight?
B: She went out to show her new car off.
   A: 오늘 밤 애나는 어디에 있어?
   B: 걘 자신의 새 차를 자랑하려고 나갔어.

260

I was touched by the poem
난 그 시에 감동받았어
be touched by~는 '…에 감동받다.' touching은 '감동적인' = moving.

Example
- She was touched by the starving people in Africa.
  그녀는 아프리카의 굶주린 사람들에 의해 감정이 복받쳤어.
- Young people are often touched by Michael Jackson's songs.
  젊은이들은 종종 마이클 잭슨의 노래에 감동을 하지.

A: Everyone was touched by the poem.
B: It was so beautifully written.
   A: 모두가 그 시에 감동되었죠.
   B: 아주 아름답게 쓰여진 것 같아요.

261

Chris drives you nuts?

크리스가 널 화나게 하지?

drive sb nuts는 '…을 화나게 하다,' be nuts about~은 '무척 좋아하다.'

💡 Example
- Carla **is nuts for** turning down the job.
  칼라 그 직업을 거절하다니 미쳤구만.
- The politicians in this country **are nuts**.
  이 나라 정치인들은 다 미친 놈들이야.

 Dialog

A: Doesn't Rick **drive you nuts**?
B: Sometimes he can be a little annoying.

A: 릭이 널 화나게 하지 않니?
B: 가끔씩 약간 짜증나게 하긴 해.

262

He has a lot of stress these days

걘 요즘 무척 스트레스가 많아

have a lot of stress는 '스트레스를 많이 받다' = be under a lot of stress.

💡 Example
- She **has a lot of stress** in her classes.
  걘 수업시간에 많은 스트레스를 받고 있어.
- The soldiers at the border **have a lot of stress**.
  국경근무병사들은 많은 스트레스를 받아.

 Dialog

A: It's not fun to hang around with Barry.
B: He **has a lot of stress** these days.

A: 배리와 같이 다니는 것은 재미없어.
B: 걘 요즘 무척 스트레스가 많아.

263

I feel the same way about you, too

나 역시 너와 같은 생각이야

feel the same way about sb는 '…와 같은 생각이야.'

 Example

- I hope that you feel the same way about me.
  네가 나에 대해 같은 생각이길 바래.
- I'm sorry I don't feel the same way about that.
  미안하지만 그것에 대해 생각이 달라.

 Dialog

A: You're my best friend and I love you.
B: I feel the same way about you, too.

A: 넌 내 최고의 친구야 사랑해.
B: 나도 널 그렇게 생각해.

264

I was caught in a shower

소나기를 만났어

be[get] caught in~는 '…(곤란)한 상황에 처하다' = be[get] stuck with.

 Example

- I got caught in a shower on my way home.
  집에 오다 소나기를 만났어.
- She got caught in bed with his neighbor's husband.
  걔가 이웃집 남편과 침대에 있다 걸렸대.

Dialog

A: My gosh! You are really soaked.
B: Yes, I am. I was caught in a shower.

A: 세상에! 정말 흠뻑 젖었구나.
B: 응. 소나기를 만났어.

If I were you, I wouldn't go there

내가 너라면 거기에 가지 않을텐데

if I were you는 '내가 너라면' = if I were in your shoes = if I were in your places.

Example

- If I were you, I would go to see a doctor.
  내가 너라면 병원 가볼거야
- What would you do if you were in her situation?
  네가 걔처지라면 어떻게 하겠어?

 Dialog

A: If I were in your shoes, I wouldn't sell it yet.
B: Do you think the stock will bounce back?

A: 내가 너의 입장이라면 아직 팔지 않겠어.
B: 주식이 반등할 것같니?

They caused trouble in class

걔들은 수업시간에 말썽을 폈어

cause trouble는 '문제를 일으키다' = get in trouble.

Example

- The software caused trouble in my computer.
  소프트웨어가 내 컴퓨터에서 문제를 일으켰어.
- Jack causes trouble when he drinks alcohol.
  잭은 술마실 때 문제를 일으켜.

 Dialog

A: Some of the students cause trouble in class.
B: They may be asked to leave the school.

A: 일부 학생들이 수업시간에 문제를 일으키고 있지.
B: 걔들은 퇴교 조치를 권고 받을 수 있어.

267

You're in trouble

너 큰일났어

be[get] in trouble은 '곤경에 처하다,' get sb in trouble하게 되면 '…을 곤경에 빠트리다.'

💡 **Example**

- You will get in trouble if you do that.
  그렇게 하면 곤란해 질거야
- I'm not here to get you in trouble.
  널 곤란하게 하려고 여기 온게 아냐.

 Dialog

A: You're in trouble. The boss wants to see you.
B: Really? What did I do?

　A: 너 큰일났어. 사장님이 널 보자셔.
　B: 정말이야? 내가 무슨 짓을 했길래?

268

He gives her hard time in class

걘 수업시간에 그녀를 힘들게 해

give sb a hard time하면 '…을 힘들게 하다.'

💡 **Example**

- I gave the girls a hard time when they wore too much makeup.
  여자애들이 화장을 지나치게 많이 했을 때 내가 좀 괴롭혔어.
- The coach gave the player a hard time because he was lazy.
  코치는 그 선수가 너무 게을러서 무섭게 몰아세웠지.

 Dialog

A: Why is Kevin so unhappy these days?
B: His science teacher gives him a hard time in class.

　A: 왜 케빈이 요즘 기분이 안 좋은 거야?
　B: 과학선생님이 수업시간에 걔를 힘들게 하나 봐.

I have a hard time making new friends

난 새 친구 사귀는데 고생하고 있어

have a hard time ~ing은 '…하는데 힘들어하다.' time 다음 in을 넣기도 하는데 구어체에서는 생략하는 경우가 많다.

Example

- Holly has a hard time making new friends.
  홀리는 새 친구 사귀는데 고생하고 있어.
- I have a hard time following the highway signs to the airport.
  고속도로의 공항 표지판을 따라가는 게 힘들어

Dialog

A: **I'm still having a hard time accepting the decision.**
B: **I'm sure you'll be fine in a few days.**

A: 난 그 결정을 받아들이는데 아직도 어려움이 있어.
B: 며칠 지나면 괜찮아질거야.

I have no problem working late

난 야근하는데 전혀 문제가 없어

have no problem with+N[~ing]은 '…하는데 아무 문제없다.'

Example

- She has no problem working late at night.
  걔는 밤늦게 일하는데 전혀 문제가 없어.
- They have no problem donating money to the charity.
  걔들은 자선단체에 기부하는데 전혀 문제가 없어.

Dialog

A: **Can you take Logan on a tour of the building?**
B: **Sure. I have no problem showing him around.**

A: 로간에게 이 건물 구경을 시켜줄 수 있겠니?
B: 그럼요. 걔에게 구경시켜주는데 아무런 문제가 없어요.

📎 271

We really have it good here
우린 여기서 운이 좋은거야

have it good은 '운이 좋다,' '재수있다' = be in luck.

💡 Example

- Employees at Samsung have it good.
  삼성 직원들은 운이 좋은거야.
- Pop musicians really seem to have it good.
  팝 음악가들은 정말로 재주가 있는 것 같아.

 Dialog

A: So many people are starving in Africa.
B: I know. We really have it good here.

A: 아프리카에서는 많은 사람들이 굶고 있어.
B: 잘 알지. 우린 여기서 운이 좋은거야.

📎 272

Why not try your luck?
운에 맡기고 해봐

try one's luck은 '운을 시험해보다,' 즉 결과에 상관없이 그래도 운에 맡기고 해보다.

💡 Example

- Have you tried your luck at other jobs?
  다른 직업들도 시도해 보았니?
- I'll try my luck at finding a girlfriend.
  여친을 찾는데 한번 운을 걸어볼게.

 Dialog

A: We're going to try our luck at the casino.
B: I think you'll lose all of your money.

A: 우린 카지노에서 우리 운을 시험해볼 거야.
B: 아마 네가 모든 돈을 잃을 것으로 생각해.

It has been a long day
기나긴 하루였어
have a long day (at work)는 '(직장에서) 힘든 하루를 보내다.'

💡 **Example**
- Everyone is unhappy and it's going to be a long day.
  모두가 불만이야 힘든 하루가 될 거야.
- It has been a long day.
  기나긴 하루였어.

A: **We need to have this report finished by tonight.**
B: **Oh no! It's going to be a long day.**
  A: 우린 오늘 밤까지 이 보고서를 끝내야 해.
  B: 그래, 힘든 하루가 되겠네.

Give me a break!
한번만 봐줘!, 그런 소리 하지마!
give me a break는 '기회를 한번 더 주다,' '말도 안되는 얘기하지 않다.'

💡 **Example**
- Give him a break. It's his first day working here.
  걔 한번 봐줘. 첫 출근일야.
- They don't speak English well, so give them a break.
  걔들은 영어 잘못해, 기회줘봐.

A: **I can't give you a discount on this.**
B: **Come on, give me a break on the price.**
  A: 이것은 네게 할인을 해줄 수가 없어.
  B: 왜 그래. 한번 봐주라.

275

We have the same idea
우린 생각이 같아

have the same with[as]+N or have the same as S+V = …와 같다

💡 **Example**

- The temperature is the same as it was yesterday.
  오늘 기온이 어제와 같아.

- This TV show is the same as most other game shows.
  이 TV 쇼는 대부분의 여타 게임 쇼들과 같아.

A: Take a look at my diamond earrings.
B: They are the same as the pair my aunt has.
  A: 내 다이아몬드 귀걸이 좀 봐라.
  B: 우리 이모가 가진 것과 같은 거네.

276

It looks as if she's about to cry
걘 금방 울 것처럼 보여

look as if S+V는 '마치 …처럼 보이다.'

💡 **Example**

- It looks as if I need a better job.
  난 좀 더 나은 직업이 필요한 것 같아.

- It looks as if we'll be leaving tomorrow.
  우린 내일 떠날 것 같아.

A: It looks as if Henry is going home.
B: He told me he was feeling sick today.
  A: 헨리가 귀가한 것처럼 보이네.
  B: 걘 오늘 몸이 아프다고 말했어.

277

You'd better get used to it
적응하도록 해라
get[be] used to+N[~ing]는 '…에 익숙해지다' = get accustomed to.

- You need to get used to eating different foods.
  넌 다른 음식을 먹는데 익숙해질 필요가 있어.
- You'd better get used to it.
  적응하도록 해라.

 Dialog

A: Did you get used to the weather in Canada?
B: Yes, but it is awfully cold in the winter.

A: 캐나다의 날씨에 적응했나요?
B: 네, 하지만 겨울은 지독하게 춥군요.

278

It couldn't be better
더할 나위 없이 좋아
couldn't be better는 '최고다'= Never better. 부정어+비교급=최상급!

- The weather today just couldn't be better.
  오늘 날씨는 더할 나위가 없이 좋아.
- The taste of chocolate couldn't be better.
  초콜릿 맛이 더 이상 좋을 수가 없어.

Dialog

A: How are things going around here?
B: They couldn't be better.

A: 여기 일이 어떻게 돼가니?
B: 아주 좋아.

279

She picked out a dress for the party
걘 파티에 입을 드레스를 골랐어
pick out은 '고르다,' '선택하다' = single out = take one's pick.

💡 Example

- I'm going to pick out some new clothes.
  난 새 옷을 몇 벌 고를거야.

- Feel free to pick out whatever you need.
  원하는 거 아무것이나 골라.

 Dialog

A: Can you help me pick out a wedding ring?
B: I'd be happy to help you.
  A: 결혼반지 고르는거 도와줄래?
  B: 기꺼이 도와주지.

280

I'll take this one
난 이걸로 할게
take sth은 마음에 드는 것을 결정하여 '택하다.'

💡 Example

- That's my offer, take it or leave it.
  그게 내 제안이야. 받는가 말든가 해.

- You need to decide. It's now or never.
  네가 결정해야 돼. 바로 지금 해야 돼.

 Dialog

A: I'll take this one.
B: Do you want me to wrap it up for you?
  A: 이걸로 사겠어요.
  B: 포장해 드릴까요?

281

I need to get my ID renewed

신분증 갱신해야 돼

get ~ renewed는 '…을 갱신하다' = renew

💡 **Example**

- Did you renew your driver's license?
  네 운전면허증 갱신했니?

- This office is for the renewal of your passport.
  이 사무실은 네 여권을 갱신하는 곳야.

A: Why are you going to the government office?
B: I need to get my ID renewed.

A: 왜 관청에 가니?
B: 난 내 신분증을 갱신해야 되거든.

282

I'll replace it with a newer one

더 새걸로 교체해줄게

replace A with B는 'A를 B로 교체하다.' be replaced by가 많이 사용된다.

💡 **Example**

- The tires on my car need replacing.
  내 차 타이어를 교체할 필요가 있어.

- Can you replace this stove with another one?
  이 난로를 다른 걸로 교체해줄 수 있니?

A: That is a very old notebook.
B: I know. I'll replace it with a newer one.

A: 그건 아주 오래된 노트북이야.
B: 알아. 더 새 걸로 교체해줄게.

I'll take it back to the store

반품하러 가게에 가져갈거야

take it back은 '돌려주거나,' '반품하거나,' 혹은 '이미 내뱉은 말을 취소하다.'

💡 **Example**

- The TV doesn't work and I'll take it back to the store.
  TV가 작동하지 않아 가게에 반환할 거야.

- If you don't like the ring, take it back.
  이 반지를 좋아하지 않으면 돌려줘.

A: I heard that Chip gave you his i-pod.
B: No, he came and took it back.

A: 칩이 너한테 자기 아이팟을 줬다고 들었어.
B: 아니, 걘 와서 그걸 도로 가져갔어.

When will you make a decision?

너 언제 결정할래?

make a decision (on/about~)은 (…에 대해) 결정하다 = decide.

💡 **Example**

- When will you make a decision?
  너 언제 결정할래?

- We need to make a decision on who's going to be fired.
  누가 해고될 지 우린 결정을 해야만 돼.

A: I don't know if I want to marry Jen.
B: You need to make a decision about that.

A: 내가 젠하고 결혼하기를 원하는지 모르겠어.
B: 네가 그에 대한 결정을 해야 되지.

We made a resolution to go

우리는 가기로 결심했어

make a resolution (to+V)은 '(…하기로) 결심하다.'

 Example

- The ball's in your court if you want to do something.
  네가 뭘 하기를 원한다면 공이 네 코트에 있는거지.
- Let's make a resolution to meet next year.
  내년에 만나기로 약속을 하자.

Dialog

A: How are things with your boyfriend?
B: We made a resolution not to argue.

A: 네 남친하고는 어때?
B: 우린 싸우지 않기로 결심을 했어.

Guess What?

The cat is out of the bag!

비밀이 들통났어!

"고양이가 가방에서 나왔다"라는 것은 원래는 비밀이었지만 사람들에게 다 알려져 더 이상 비밀이 아니게 됐다(a secret is known by most people, and it's no longer secret)라는 뜻이다. 특히 let the cat out of the bag의 형태로 무심코 비밀을 누설하다라는 표현으로 많이 쓰인다.

286

Make up your mind
결정해
make up your mind (to+V/about~)는 '(…하기로) 결심하다.'

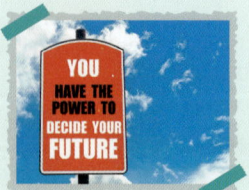

💡 **Example**
- Make up your mind. What time is okay for you?
  결정해. 몇시가 좋아?
- You have to make up your mind pretty quick.
  넌 아주 빨리 결심해야만 해.

A: Hurry up and make up your mind.
B: It's not easy. Give me more time.

A: 서둘러서 결심해라.
B: 쉽지가 않아. 좀 더 시간을 줘.

287

Please do just as you please
원하는대로 해
do as one pleases는 '…가 원하는대로 하다,'로 pleases 대신 likes를 써도 된다.

💡 **Example**
- All people have the right to do as they please.
  모든 사람들은 자신들이 원하는대로 할 권리를 갖고 있어.
- Please do just as you please.
  당신 원하는대로 하세요.

A: Maria says she will take the job she was offered.
B: Well, she can do as she pleases.

A: 마리아는 제의 받은 직업을 택할 거래.
B: 글쎄, 걘 자신이 원하는대로 할 수 있어.

288

He followed his heart

걘 맘가는대로 했어

follow one's heart는 '…의 마음이 내키는대로 하다.'

Example

- Follow your heart rather than following money.
  돈보다는 네 맘이 원하는대로 해라.

- If you want a happy life, follow your heart.
  행복한 삶을 원한다면 네 맘가는 대로 해라.

A: What has Sam decided to do?
B: He's going to follow his heart and study music.

A: 샘은 뭘 하기로 결정했어?
B: 걘 마음이 내키는대로 음악을 공부한대.

289

We all backed him up

우리 모두는 걔를 지원했어

back sb up은 뒤에서 받쳐준다는 것으로 '…을 지지[지원]하다.'

Example

- I had to back up the story with pictures.
  난 사진들로 내 이야기의 정당성을 뒷받침했어.

- Don't worry. I've got your back.
  걱정하지마. 내가 널 도와줄게.

A: Did you help Ryan out?
B: Yeah, we all backed him up.

A: 넌 라이언을 끝까지 도왔니?
B: 응, 우린 모두 걜 지원했어.

You're not allowed to smoke here

여기서는 금연이야

allow sb to+V는 '…가 …하는 것을 허용하다,' be allowed to~는 '…하는게 허용되다.'

💡 **Example**

- You're not allowed to talk in class.
  년 수업 중 말하면 안돼.

- I'm not allowed to watch TV tonight.
  난 오늘 밤 TV를 보도록 허락 받지 못했어.

 Dialog

A: Where did Cheryl stay last night?
B: We allowed her to sleep at our place.
  A: 셰릴은 어제 밤 어디에서 잤니?
  B: 우리 거처에서 자도록 해줘어.

I came to congratulate you

너 축하해주려고 왔어

congratulate (sb) on sth[sb]는 '…에 대해 (…을) 축하해주다'라는 의미.

💡 **Example**

- I never had a chance to congratulate you on the baby.
  난 그 아기에 대해 축하해줄 기회가 없었어.

- Peter, I just came here to congratulate you.
  피터, 축하해주려고 방금 온거야.

 Dialog

A: Congratulations on your graduation!
B: I'm so happy to be finished with school.
  A: 졸업 축하해!
  B: 학교 과정이 다 끝나서 너무 기뻐.

Cheer up! You look so gloomy

힘내! 너 정말 우울해 보여

cheer sb up은 '…을 기운나게 하다.' 격려할 때 Cheer up!, 술잔부딪히며 Cheers!

💡 Example

- Cheer up! You look so gloomy.
  힘 좀 내봐! 너 정말 우울해 보여.

- Do you know what might really cheer me up?
  뭐가 정말로 날 기운나게 하는지 아니?

 Dialog

A: You'll have a good job interview. **Cheer up.**
B: Thanks. I'll do my best.

A: 면접을 잘 볼 거야. 기운 내.
B: 고마워. 최선을 다할게.

I advised him to take the job

걔에게 그 일자리를 잡으라고 했어

advise sb to+V는 '…가 …하도록 충고하다,' be advised to+V는 '…하라는 권고를 듣다.'

💡 Example

- She should **be advised to** stay home.
  걘 집에 남아있으라고 권고를 받아야 해.

- Please **be advised that** I'm leaving now.
  제가 지금 떠나는 점을 숙지하세요.

 Dialog

A: **I advised** Bill **to** change jobs.
B: He's very unhappy at his work.

A: 난 빌한테 직업을 바꾸라고 조언했어.
B: 걘 자기 일에 대해 매우 불행하게 느껴.

He counseled me to follow my heart

걔 나보고 맘가는대로 하라고 했어

counsel sb to+V는 격식있는 표현으로 '…에게 …을 하도록 조언하다.'

💡 Example

- Jane counsels rape victims downtown.
  제인은 강간 피해자들을 위해 시내에서 카운슬링을 하고 있어.

- The two countries were counseled to end the war.
  양국은 종전하도록 권고를 받았어.

 Dialog

A: What did your dad say to you?
B: He counseled me to marry my girlfriend.

A: 네 아빠는 너한테 뭐라고 말했니?
B: 내 여친과 결혼하라고 조언하셨어.

Let me give you some advice

내가 조언을 좀 할게

give sb some advice (about~)는 '…에게 충고[조언]를 하다.'

💡 Example

- Heather gave me advice about how to fix the computer.
  헤더는 컴퓨터 고치는 방법을 알려줬어.

- Do you need me to give you some advice?
  내가 너한테 충고 좀 해주길 원하니?

 Dialog

A: Give Bob some advice about his future.
B: Is he confused about what he will do?

A: 밥에게 그의 미래에 대해 충고 좀 해줘라.
B: 걔가 무엇을 할지 혼란스러워하니?

He gave me a warning not to go there

걘 나보고 가지 말라고 경고했어

give sb a warning to+V는 '…에게 …을 하도록 경고하다.'

💡 **Example**

- I suppose I could give him a warning.
  걔한테 경고를 줄까?
- I just can't believe that Mike didn't give me any warning.
  마이크가 내게 아무런 경고도 하지 않다니 믿을 수 없어.

 Dialog

A: The ranger gave us a warning to put out the campfire.
B: We'd better do what he says.

A: 공원관리원이 모닥불을 끄도록 우리한테 경고를 했어.
B: 경고대로 하는 게 좋지.

I warned you not to be here

여기 오지 말라고 경고했잖아

warn sb to+V[about~]는 '…에게 …를 경고하다.' about 대신에 of나 on.

💡 **Example**

- I'm not going to warn you about that again.
  네게 다시는 그걸 경고하지 않을 거야.
- Didn't I warn you about calling me names?
  날 욕하지 말라고 경고하지 않았니?

 Dialog

A: Mickey broke my heart.
B: I warned you about dating him.

A: 미키는 내 마음을 아프게 했어.
B: 난 네가 걔하고 데이트하는 것에 대해 경고했어.

I did Sam a favor last week

지난주에 샘에게 호의를 베풀었어

do sb a favor는 '…에게 호의를 베풀다' = do something for somebody.

Example

- Could you do me a favor and get me a snack?
  부탁인데 스낵 좀 갖다 줄래요?
- Do Ryan a favor and call his mom.
  라이언에게 호의를 베푼다는 의미에서 걔 엄마에게 전화해주라.

 Dialog

A: What is this thank you card for?
B: I did Pam a favor last week.

A: 이 감사 카드는 뭐야?
B: 내가 지난 주 팜한테 호의 베푼 것이 있거든.

I need to get some help

난 좀 도움을 받아야 해

get (some) help는 '도움을 (좀) 받다'로 get help ~ing, get help for+N로 쓰인다.

Example

- Can you get help for the old woman?
  저 나이든 여성분을 위해 도움을 받을 수 있니?
- The workers got help in the doctor's office.
  직원들은 의사 진료실에서 도움을 받았어.

 Dialog

A: I need to get help carrying these boxes.
B: Some of my friends will help you out.

A: 이 박스들을 옮기는데 난 도움이 필요해.
B: 내 친구들 몇 명이 널 끝까지 도와줄 거야.

Excuse me for being so late

이렇게 늦은데 대해 미안해

excuse sb for+N[~ing]는 '…에 대해 …를 용서하다.'

Example

- Excuse me for being so late.
  이렇게 늦은데 대해 죄송해요.
- Excuse her for acting so rude.
  걔가 그렇게 무례하게 것을 용서하세요.

 Dialog

A: Please excuse me for being rude.
B: You'd better try to be nicer.

A: 무례한 데 대해 용서하세요.
B: 좀 더 착해지도록 노력하는 게 좋을 거야.

I forgive you for lying to me

내게 거짓말한거 용서할게

forgive sb for+N[~ing]는 '…가 …한 것을 용서하다.'

Example

- Do you want me to forgive you? Why should I?
  내가 널 용서하길 원하니? 왜 그래야 하는데?
- You're going to forgive me for not going to school?
  결석한거 용서해줄거죠?

 Dialog

A: Jan and Mike are staying together.
B: Did she forgive him for dating other women?

A: 잰과 마이크는 같이 머물고 있어.
B: 마이크가 다른 여자와 데이트한 걸 잰이 용서했니?

302

I never break my word

난 절대 약속을 깨트리지 않아

break one's word (to sb/on sth)은 '약속을 깨트리다' <=> keep one's word

💡 Example

- I never break my word to my friends.
  난 친구들에게 결코 약속을 어긴 적이 없어.

- The auto salesman broke his word to us.
  자동차 영업사원은 우리에게 약속을 어겼어.

 Dialog

A: Did Darlene pay you the money?
B: No, she broke her word on that.
　A: 달린이 네게 돈을 줬어?
　B: 아니. 그 약속을 안지켰어.

303

Get ready for heavy rains

폭우에 대비해

get ready for+N[to+V]는 '…을 준비하다,' '대비하다.'

💡 Example

- I came here to see if you were ready.
  네가 준비되어 있는지 보러 왔어.

- Let me make sure Mom is ready to leave.
  엄마가 떠날 준비가 되어 있는지 확인해보자.

 Dialog

A: Get ready for the snow storm.
B: It is supposed to be a very big storm.
　A: 눈 폭풍에 대비를 해라.
　B: 아주 큰 폭풍이 될 거야.

I'll bring you the bill

계산서 갖다 드릴게요

bring sb sth = bring sth to sb는 '…에게 …을 가져다 주다.'

💡 **Example**

- Don't forget to bring your girlfriend to the party.
  파티에 네 여친 데려오는 것 잊지마.

- Bring me a coffee on your way back.
  돌아 오는 길에 커피 좀 가져오세요.

A: Could you let me know the total cost?
B: I'll bring you the bill.

A: 총 합계가 얼마죠?
B: 계산서를 갖다 드리죠.

I've got a present for you

너 줄려고 선물가져왔어

have got sth for sb는 '…에게 주려고 …을 사다[구하다].'

💡 **Example**

- We have got a present for our teacher.
  우리 선생님을 위해 선물을 가져왔어.

- Here is a DVD for you to watch.
  여기 네가 볼 DVD가 있어.

A: Here is something for you to eat.
B: Thanks. I don't mean to cause extra work.

A: 이거 좀 먹어.
B: 고마워. 나 땜에 일을 더하는 것을 바라진 않아.

You'll inherit my house

넌 내 집을 물려받을거야

inherit sth from sb는 '…로부터 …을 상속[물려]받다' = hand down.

 Example

- You'll inherit my house when I die.
  내가 죽으면 넌 내 집을 물려받을거야.

- The young man inherited a fortune from his parents.
  젊은이가 부모로부터 큰 돈을 물려받았어.

 Dialog

A: Kathy is taking a trip to Europe.
B: I heard she inherited money from her grandmother.

A: 케시는 유럽 여행을 하고 있어.
B: 걔가 할머니한테서 유산을 받았다고 들었어.

It's hard to separate truth from fiction

진실과 허구를 구분하는 것은 어려워

separate A from B는 'A를 B로부터 분리하다.'

 Example

- The student was separated from his parents for a year.
  그 학생은 1년간 부모와 떨어졌어.

- The law separates politics from religion.
  법은 정치와 종교를 분리시켰어.

Dialog

A: My boss and I went out drinking twice this week.
B: You should separate your private life from work.

A: 보스와 난 일주에 2번 마시러 나갔어.
B: 너 사생활을 일과 분리해야만 해.

I don't want to go through that

난 그 일을 겪고 싶지 않아

go through sth은 '…(힘든 일)을 경험하다' = undergo.

 Example

- Our economy has gone through some very hard times.
  경제가 힘든 시기를 겪었어.
- I don't want to go through that.
  난 그 일을 겪고 싶지 않아.

Dialog

A: We had to go through three months of training.
B: Was it difficult being in the military?

A: 우린 3달에 걸친 훈련을 겪어야 했어.
B: 군대에 있는 것이 어렵니?

You'd better brief me on it

넌 내게 그에 대해 보고해봐

brief sb on sth은 '…에게 …을 브리핑[보고]하다.'

 Example

- The whole committee was briefed on the plan.
  전체 위원회가 그 계획에 대해 설명을 들었어.
- I'll brief you on what happened in the meeting.
  회의내용을 네게 브리핑해줄게.

Dialog

A: You'd better brief the president on the situation.
B: He is very worried about it.

A: 그 상황에 대해 대통령에게 보고해라.
B: 대통령이 그 상황에 대해 크게 걱정하고 있거든.

You need to register your new car
넌 네 새 차를 등록해야 해

register (for) sth은 '등록[신고]하다,' '가입하다,' '신청하다.'

💡 **Example**

- People register marriages at the courthouse.
  사람들은 법원에서 결혼을 신고해.

- The letter arrived via registered mail.
  그 편지는 등기 편으로 도착했어.

 Dialog

A: Why did you come to this office?
B: I need to register as a foreign citizen.

A: 왜 이 사무실에 왔니?
B: 난 외국시민으로 등록해야만 해.

I reported the problem to him
난 그에게 그 문제를 보고했어

report sth to sb는 '…을 …에게 신고하다.' 어떤 문제나 사고 등을 윗사람에 신고하다.

💡 **Example**

- You should report the cheating to your teacher.
  컨닝은 선생님에게 보고해야 돼.

- Leo reported the theft to the authorities.
  레오는 절도를 당국에 신고했어.

 Dialog

A: Did you tell Mason about the problem?
B: Someone reported the problem to him.

A: 메이슨에게 그 문제에 대해 말했니?
B: 누군가 걔한테 그 문제를 보고했어.

I found a solution to our problem

난 우리 문제에 대한 답을 찾았어

find a[the] solution to~는 '…에 대한 해결책을 찾다.'

💡 Example

- She couldn't find a way to go home.
  갠 집에 갈 길을 찾지 못했어.

- We need to find a solution to our problem.
  우린 우리 문제에 대한 답을 찾아야만 해.

A: Did you find the solution to the mystery?
B: No, we still don't understand what happened.

A: 그 미스터리에 대한 해법을 찾았니?
B: 아니, 우린 아직도 일어난 일을 이해하지 못하고 있어.

He blamed me for the mistake

갠 그 실수을 내탓이라고 비난했어

blame A for B는 'B에 대해 A를 비난하다,' '탓하다.' take the blame for~는 '…에 대한 책임을 지다.'

💡 Example

- Karen was to blame for ending the marriage.
  카렌이 결혼파국의 책임이 있어.

- The coach lay the blame on one of the team members.
  코치는 팀 멤버 중 한 사람에게 책임을 물었어.

A: An old stove was blamed for the house fire.
B: Wow, it burned everything to the ground.

A: 낡은 난로가 그 집 화재의 책임이었어.
B: 와, 그 난로가 모든 것을 태워 버렸구나.

Did you file a complaint against her?

너 걔를 고소했어?

file a complaint against A (for ~ing)는 '…를 (…했다고) 고소하다.' 법적, 공식적 절차.

 Example

- Madge filed a complaint against the store for poor service.
  매지는 그 가게 서비스가 형편없다고 불평을 제기했어.

- He filed a complaint against Sam for damaging his car.
  걘 자기 차를 손상시켰다고 샘을 고소했어.

 Dialog

A: The new neighbor has his music on all night.
B: Why don't you file a complaint against him?

A: 새로 온 이웃은 밤새도록 음악을 틀었어.
B: 걔한테 불평을 제기하지 그러니?

Why are you picking on me?

왜 날 괴롭히는거야?

pick on sb는 '…을 괴롭히다,' '트집잡다.'

 Example

- Some people pick on my little brother.
  일부 사람들은 내 남동생을 괴롭혀.

- Why are you picking on me?
  왜 날 괴롭히는거야?

Dialog

A: Beth has a very big nose.
B: It's not nice to pick on people.

A: 베스는 매우 큰 코를 가지고 있어.
B: 사람에게 트집잡는 것은 좋지 않아.

I finally reached a settlement

결국 해결책을 찾았어

reach a settlement는 '해결책에 이르다,' '해결방안을 찾다.'

💡 **Example**

- Joan reached a settlement with the insurance company.
  조앤은 보험회사와 합의를 했어.

- Will you ever reach a settlement with her?
  한번이라도 걔와 문제해결 한 적이 있니?

A: How is your court case going?
B: I finally reached a settlement.

A: 네 법원 사건은 어떻게 돌아가니?
B: 결국 해결책을 찾았어.

The car is getting in the way

그 차가 길을 가로막고 있어

get[be] in the way는 '…의 방해가 되다,' '막고 있다' <=> get out of the way.

💡 **Example**

- The table is in the way of the door.
  테이블이 문을 막고 있어.

- The tree is falling. Get out of the way!
  나무가 넘어져. 비켜서라!

A: Don is the worst member of our group.
B: He always gets in the way when we do things.

A: 돈은 우리 그룹 중에서 최악의 멤버야.
B: 우리가 일할 때 항상 방해가 돼.

I can't stop her from drinking

난 걔가 술마시는 것을 막을 수가 없어

stop sb from ~ing는 '…가 …하는 것을 막다,' stop 대신에 keep, prevent를 사용해도 된다.

💡 Example

- The police prevented the thief from stealing money.
  경찰은 도둑이 돈을 훔치는 것을 사전에 막았어.
- The airport stopped people from getting on the plane.
  공항 측은 승객들이 탑승하는 것을 막았어.

A: We stopped Gary from fighting with Tom.
B: Good. Those guys don't like each other.

A: 우린 게리가 톰과 싸우는 것을 막았어.
B: 잘했어. 걔들은 서로 싫어해.

I finally got out of debt

난 마침내 빚에서 벗어났어

get out of sth[~ing]는 '…하기 싫은 일을 성공적으로 피하다.'

💡 Example

- I got out of going on that blind date.
  난 그 소개팅을 성공적으로 피했지.
- You need to get out of the schedule you have.
  넌 네 스케줄을 회피할 필요가 있어.

A: We have to work all day Sunday.
B: Is there any way to get out of it?

A: 우린 일요일 하루 종일 일해야 돼.
B: 그걸 피할 수 있는 어떤 방도가 있니?

Keep off the grass

잔디에 들어가지 마시오

keep off sth은 '…에 가까이 하지 않다,' '피하다.'

💡 Example

- You'd better keep off my lawn.
  내 잔디밭에 가까이 오지 마라.
- She said to keep off the new furniture.
  걘 새로 산 가구에 가까이 오지 말라고 했어.

A: **Keep off** the sidewalk.
B: I see it is being repaired.

A: 보도에 가까이 가지마.
B: 보수공사중이네.

Stay away from there

그곳에 가까이 가지마

stay away from~은 '…로부터 떨어져 있다.' 물리적, 추상적으로 멀리하다.

💡 Example

- **Stay away from** dishonest people.
  부정직한 사람들 가까이 하지마라.
- **Stay away from** my wallet.
  내 지갑에 접근하지 마라.

A: Have you been to this neighborhood?
B: **Stay away from** there. It's dangerous.

A: 이 주변에 와본적 있어?
B: 그곳에 가까이 가지마. 위험해.

I made a move to avoid it

그걸 피하기 위해 행동을 취했어

make a move는 '움직이다,' '행동을 취하다.' 어떤 문제를 해결하거나 목적을 달성하기 위해.

Example
- Rick made a move to find a better job.
  릭은 좀 더 나은 직업을 찾으려고 행동을 취했어.
- The students made a move to join another class.
  학생들이 다른 수업에 참석하려고 조치를 취했어.

Dialog

A: I'm worried that I will lose all my money.
B: You should make a move to protect it.

A: 내 모든 돈을 잃을 까봐 걱정이 돼.
B: 그 돈을 보호할 조치를 취해야 돼.

He met the challenge head-on

걘 그 도전에 정면으로 맞섰어

meet a challenge는 '도전에 맞서다,' '도전에 대응하다,' '문제를 해결하다.'

Example
- Are you ready to meet a challenge from someone else?
  다른 사람으로부터 도전해도 대응할 준비가 되어 있니?
- We can meet a challenge from another company.
  우린 다른 회사로부터의 도전에 응할 수 있어.

Dialog

A: Our basketball team is pretty talented.
B: They can meet a challenge from any other team.

A: 우리 농구팀은 정말 재능 있어.
B: 어떤 다른 팀이 도전해도 당당히 대응할 거야.

I decided to take a chance

난 모험해보기로 했어

take a chance는 '위험을 무릅쓰다,' '모험하다,' '한번해보다.'

💡 **Example**

- **Take a chance** and do something new.
  한번 새로운 것을 운을 걸고 시도해봐라.

- Pam **took a chance** and tried Internet dating.
  팸은 운걸고 인터넷 데이트를 시도했어.

A: Do you think I should get this leather coat?
B: It may be bad quality. You'd **be taking a chance on** it.

A: 이 가죽 코트를 가져야 한다고 생각하니?
B: 질은 좋지 않을 수 있는데 한번 시도해봐라.

He got caught stealing a watch

갠 시계를 훔치다가 잡혔어

get caught ~ing는 '(나쁜 행동을) …하다 잡히다.'

💡 **Example**

- Jerry **got caught** steal**ing** a watch.
  제리는 시계를 훔치다가 잡혔어.

- I **caught** him look**ing** in my windows.
  난 걔가 내 창문을 들여다보는 것을 알아챘어.

A: I read in the paper that the police **caught** a thief.
B: Good. I feel safer hearing that.

A: 경찰이 도둑을 잡았다고 신문에서 읽었어.
B: 좋아. 그 말을 들으니 좀 더 안심이 되네.

The firm suffered a loss last year
그 회사는 작년에 손실을 보았어

suffer a loss는 '손실을 입다,' make a loss of~는 '…만큼의 손해를 보다.'

Example
- The firm suffered a loss last year.
  그 회사는 작년에 손실을 보았어.
- Many people on Wall Street suffered a loss.
  월가의 많은 사람들이 손실을 입었어.

Dialog
A: Jill seems very unhappy.
B: She suffered a loss on her investments.

A: 질은 매우 안좋아보여.
B: 투자했다가 손해봤거든.

He shared the news with me
걘 그 소식을 나와 공유했어

share sth with sb는 '…을 …와 함께 공유하다,' '전하다,' '나누다.'

Example
- She shared her textbook with her friend.
  걘 교재를 친구와 같이 보았어.
- Do you want to share this taxi with me?
  나랑 이 택시 합승할까?

Dialog
A: I forgot to bring my lunch today.
B: I could share my food with you.

A: 난 오늘 점심 가져오는 것을 잊었어.
B: 내것 같이 나눠 먹자.

328

Schools are going digital with tablets

학교는 태블릿으로 디지털화하고 있어

go digital은 '디지털화다.' go 다음에 형용사가 와서 '…하게 변하다'라는 뜻.

Example

- My cousin decided to see the green this summer.
  내 조카는 이번 여름 신록을 보기로 했어.

- Samsung went global about 30 years ago.
  삼성은 30여년 전에 국제화 했어.

Dialog

A: It's so easy to use the Internet here.
B: Korea was very quick to go digital.

A: 여기서 인터넷 쓰기가 아주 쉬워.
B: 한국은 매우 빨리 디지털화 했어.

Guess What?

She's the apple of my eye

걘 눈에 넣어도 아프지 않은 아이야

이는 '소중한 사람,' '눈에 넣어도 아프지 않을 사람'이라는 의미로 종종 부모들이 자신의 아이들을 말할 때(person is adored, or is someone's favorite person. Often we hear this used to refer to a parent's child) 사용된다.

This is the only way to go

이것이 유일한 방책이야

be the only way to+V는 '…할 유일한 방법이다.' 위에서 go는 '가다'가 아니다 '선택.'

💡 **Example**

- This is the best way to go.
  이것이 최선의 방책이야.

- Excuse me. Is this the way to the airport?
  실례해요. 공항 가는 길 맞나요?

 Dialog

A: I think you are working too hard.
B: It's the only way for me to make extra money.

A: 네가 너무 열심히 일하는 것 같아.
B: 추가적으로 돈벌려면 이게 유일한 방법이야.

He is one of my closest friends

걘 나와 절친 중 한 명이야

be one of the+최상급+복수명사는 '가장 …한 것 중의 하나이다.'

💡 **Example**

- He's one of the best painters I've ever seen.
  걘 내가 본 최상의 화가 중 한 명이야.

- I heard he was one of the best athletes in the game.
  최고의 선수 중 하나였다고 들었어.

 Dialog

A: What do you think about Hitler?
B: He's one of the most shameless men that ever lived.

A: 넌 히틀러 어떻게 생각하니?
B: 그는 지금껏 존재해온 가장 파렴치한 인물 중 한 명야.

It's raining harder than ever before
그 어느 때보다 더 비가 오네

비교급+than ever before는 '그 어느 때보다 …한'이라는 의미. 비교급+than=최상급.

 Example

- You need to study harder than ever before.
  넌 어느 때보다 더 열심히 공부해야 돼.
- My doctor told me to drink less than before.
  의사가 내게 전보다 절주하라고 했어.

Dialog

A: Wow, it's raining harder than ever before.
B: I think the river is going to overflow.

A: 와, 그 어느 때보다 더 비가 오네.
B: 강이 넘칠 것 같은데.

I have every right to complain
난 불평할 권리가 충분해

have the right to+V는 '…할 권리가 있다.' right 앞에 every를 붙이면 '…할 권리가 충분하다.'

 Example

- None of you have the right to complain.
  너희들 누구도 불평할 권한이 없어.
- You have no right to talk bad about me.
  나에 대해 나쁘게 말할 권한이 너에겐 없어.

Dialog

A: I hate working at this factory.
B: You have the right to quit your job.

A: 난 이 공장에서 일하는 것을 싫어해.
B: 넌 일을 그만둘 권한을 가지고 있어.

333

It went beyond my expectations
그건 나의 기대를 뛰어넘었어

go beyond sth은 '…을 넘어서다,' '…이상이다.' 물리적 혹은 기대, 기준, 상상을 넘을 때.

Example
- This secret goes beyond you and I.
  이 비밀은 너와 내 선을 넘는거야.
- The bills went beyond the money they had.
  청구서는 걔들이 갖고 있는 돈을 초과했어.

 Dialog

A: You can be successful in your hometown.
B: I'd like to go beyond my hometown.
  A: 넌 고향에서 성공할 수 있어.
  B: 난 고향을 넘어서고 싶어.

334

We have enough food to eat
우리는 먹을 음식이 충분해

have enough+명사+to+V는 '…하기에 충분한 …을 가지고 있다.'

Example
- They had enough work to stay busy all day.
  걔들은 종일 바쁘게 할 일이 있었어.
- Do you have enough money to start up the company?
  넌 회사창업자금이 충분해?

 Dialog

A: Would you like to go to the grocery store?
B: No, we have enough food to eat for a few days.
  A: 넌 식품점에 가길 원하니?
  B: 아니, 며칠간 먹을 음식은 충분해.

335

It was canceled as of 9 am
그건 오전 9시부로 취소됐어
as of+시점명사는 '…부로,' '…시점을 기준으로.'

Example
- You're fired, as of right now.
  넌 지금 시점에서 해고야.
- We'll be leaving, as of midnight tonight.
  우린 오늘 밤 자정 부로 떠날 거야.

A: Are classes going to begin soon?
B: No, they were canceled as of 9 am.
  A: 수업이 곧 시작될거니?
  B: 아니, 9시 부로 수업이 취소되었어.

336

To date, she hasn't been here
현재까지 갠 여기에 오지 않았어
to date는 '현재까지'라는 의미. up to now와 같은 뜻.

Example
- To date, nothing special has happened.
  현재까지 특별한 일이 생기지 않았어.
- To date, the business has been doing fine.
  현재까지 사업은 잘 되고 있어.

A: Has Alicia come to see you?
B: To date, she hasn't been here.
  A: 알리샤가 널 보러 왔니?
  B: 현재까지 갠 여기에 오지 않았어.

337

Everyone, line up in a row
모두 한 줄로 서라

in a row는 '연속적으로,' '잇따라.'

💡 **Example**
- The soldiers stood in a row for an hour.
  병사들이 1시간동안 줄 서있었어.
- This is our team's fifth win in a row.
  우리 팀이 이번에 5연승을 한 거야.

 Dialog

A: It's time to start exercising.
B: OK, everyone line up in a row.

A: 이제 운동을 시작할 시간이야.
B: 오케이, 모두 한 줄로 서라.

338

I brush them on a daily basis
난 매일 양치질해

on a daily basis는 '매일 단위로.' on a+시간명사+ basis면 주기가 '시간명사' 단위로라는 의미.

💡 **Example**
- Mom goes shopping on a weekly basis.
  엄마는 주단위로 쇼핑을 해.
- He goes to meetings on a bi-monthly basis.
  걘 한 달에 두 번씩 회의에 참석해.

 Dialog

A: Do you brush your teeth often?
B: Sure, I brush them on a daily basis.

A: 넌 자주 양치질을 하니?
B: 그럼. 매일 양치질해.

As I told you before, I'm in trouble

전에 말했듯이 난 어려움에 처해있어

as I told you before는 '이전에 말했듯이.' like I said before는 '전에 말했듯이.'

 Example

- As you've already heard, classes were cancelled.
  이미 들었겠지만 수업은 취소됐어.

- As I told you before, I am in a big trouble.
  전에 말했듯이 난 큰 어려움에 처해있어.

Dialog

A: Do you want to go to the concert?
B: As I told you before, I have no time for that.

A: 연주회에 가고 싶니?
B: 전에 말했듯이 난 그럴 시간이 없어.

Speaking of which, I'm leaving

말이 나왔으니 말인데 난 그만둬

Now that you mention it는 '그 얘길해서 말인데,' Speaking of which는 '말이 나와서 말인데.'

 Example

- Now that you mention it, I remember that event.
  네가 말하니까 그 행사가 기억나.

- Speaking of which, are you ready to go to lunch?
  말이 나왔으니 말인데, 점심 먹으러 갈 준비됐어?

Dialog

A: I'm sure we met somewhere before.
B: Now that you mention it, you look familiar.

A: 전에 우리가 만난 적이 있다고 확신해.
B: 말하니까 말인데 낯이 익어.

Let's say you're right about that

네 말이 맞았다고 쳐보자

Let's say~는 아직 일어나지 않았지만 '뭔가 일어난다면'이라는 가정을 해볼 때.

💡 **Example**

- **Let's say** you and I had a date together.
  이를테면 너하고 내가 함께 데이트를 한다면.

- **Let's say** Kim can't come with us.
  예를 들어 김씨가 우리랑 같이 갈 수 없다면.

 Dialog

A: Let's say the electricity stopped working.
B: That would mean many people would have problems.

A: 예를 들어 전기가 끊어진다면.
B: 많은 사람들에게 문제가 생긴다는 것을 의미하지.

Guess What?

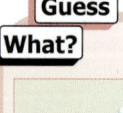

You can't just sit on the fence

넌 그냥 중립적인 태도를 취하면 안돼

직역하면 "울타리에 앉아 있다"라는 말로 사람들이 뭔가 토론이나 논쟁으로 열중하고 있을 때 어느 한 편을 들지 않고 중립적인 태도를 보이는(a person is not choosing a side in a discussion or argument, especially when people have strong feelings about a subject) 것을 말한다.

Section 03
영어회화 응용표현

"네이티브와 1분이라도 프리토킹을
가능하게 하는 영어말하기 표현들"

001

I've been swamped at my job
일에 빠져 정신없었어
be swamped at[with]~는 '…로 시달리다,' '…로 정신을 못차리다.'

Example
- I'm swamped with work for my classes.
  수업준비하느라 정신없이 바빠.
- He was swamped with dinner invitations.
  걘 저녁초대건으로 정신없었어.

 Dialog

A: You look like you need some rest.
B: We've been swamped at my job.

A: 너 좀 쉬어야 될 것 같아.
B: 우린 일에 빠져 정신 없었어.

002

I'm often up all night working
난 종종 공부하면서 밤을 새
be up all night ~ing은 '…하면서 밤을 새다'라는 표현이다.

Example
- Students are often up all night working.
  학생들은 종종 공부하면서 밤을 새지.
- Jim was up all night working on the project.
  짐은 그 프로젝트 하느라 밤새웠어.

 Dialog

A: What's wrong with you? You look tired.
B: I was up all night working on a report.

A: 무슨 일 있어? 지쳐 보여.
B: 과제물 하느라 밤을 꼬박 샜어.

003

I have my hands full
나 일이 무척 많아
have one's hands full은 '일이 무척 많다.'

 Example

- She had her hands full with the children's party.
  걘 애들 파티로 넘 바빴어.
- I've got my hands full with the project.
  난 그 프로젝트를 하느라 아주 바빠.

 Dialog

A: Can you help me with my homework?
B: I'm sorry, but I have my hands full.
  A: 내 숙제를 도와줄 수 있니?
  B: 미안해, 나도 일이 무척 많아.

004

Let's get started on the plan
그 계획부터 시작하자고
get started on sth은 뭔가 늦었어 서둘러 '시작해야 한다'는 뉘앙스.

 Example

- You need to get started on a diet.
  넌 다이어트를 시작할 필요가 있어.
- It's time to get moving. We don't want to be late.
  이동할 때야. 늦지 않아야지.

Dialog

A: I'm in. I'm always on your side.
B: Good. Let's get started on the plan.
  A: 낄래, 난 항상 네 편이잖아.
  B: 좋았어. 그 계획부터 시작하자고.

Let's hit the road

출발하자, 시작하다

hit the road는 뭔가 시작하거나 출발한다는 의미. hit the books는 '열심히 공부하다.'

💡 **Example**
- I want you to pack up your things and hit the road.
  네가 짐꾸려서 떠났으면 좋겠어.
- Let's have some food before we hit the road.
  출발하기 전에 요기 좀 하자.

 **Dialog**

A: Are you ready to start our trip?
B: I sure am. Let's hit the road.

A: 우리 여행 떠날 준비됐어?
B: 물론. 출발하자고.

He set out to become a doctor

걘 의사가 되려고 작정했어

set out to~는 분명한 계획이나 목적을 가지고 시작한다는 의미.

💡 **Example**
- Barry set out to become a doctor.
  배리는 의사가 되려고 작정했어.
- Some church members set out to help poor people.
  일부 교회 성도들은 가난한 사람들을 돕는 일에 착수했어.

 **Dialog**

A: Where is Marsha this morning?
B: She set out to buy some food.

A: 오늘 아침 마샤가 어디에 있니?
B: 걘 음식을 좀 사려고 나갔어.

You should try it out

한번 써봐

try out은 제대로 되는지 새로운 방법으로 시도해 보다. try out for~는 (팀원이 되려고)지원하다.

 Example

- Can I try out this laptop computer?
  이 랩탑 컴퓨터 한번 해봐도 되니?

- Mom is trying out different chicken salad recipes.
  엄마는 다양한 닭 샐러드 조리법을 시도하고 계셔.

Dialog

A: Is this the new smart phone?
B: Yes it is. You should try it out.

A: 이것이 새로 나온 스마트폰이니?
B: 그래. 한번 써봐.

Get on with it!

계속하라고!

get on with sth은 '계속하다,' '진행하다,' get on with sb는 '사이좋게 지내다.'

 Example

- It was difficult to get on with the gardening.
  정원 일을 계속 하기가 어려웠어.

- She decided to get on with her studies.
  걘 자신의 공부를 계속하기로 결정했어.

Dialog

A: I'm not feeling well today.
B: You've still got to work. Get on with it!

A: 오늘 몸이 좋지 않아.
B: 아직 일해야 돼. 계속하라고!

009

I did everything in my power to save him
걜 구하기 위해 할 수 있는 모든 것을 했어
do everything in one's power to+V = do (all) the best one could+V.

💡 **Example**
- I do everything in my power to be a good person.
  난 좋은 인간이 되려고 모든 힘을 다하고 있어.
- Dee did everything in her power to stay awake.
  디는 깨어있으려 안간힘을 다했어.

 Dialog

A: I can't believe that Levi died.
B: We did everything in our power to save him.
A: 리바이가 죽었다는 사실을 믿을 수가 없어.
B: 우린 걜 구하려고 모든 힘을 다했어.

010

I applied myself to finish it
난 그걸 마치는데 힘을 쏟았어
apply oneself to+N[~ing]는 '…에 힘을 쏟다,' '힘을 기울이다.'

💡 **Example**
- Tim applied himself to finishing the job.
  팀은 그 일을 끝내는데 힘을 쏟았어.
- The mechanic applied himself to fixing the car.
  정비사가 차고치는데 온 힘을 기울였어.

 Dialog

A: My math class is so difficult.
B: You must apply yourself to solving the problems.
A: 수학 수업시간이 너무 어려워.
B: 그 문제들을 푸는데 힘을 쏟아야지.

I'm devoted to my family
난 가족에 헌신하고 있어

be devoted to sth[~ing]은 '…에[…하는데] 전념하다.' devoted 대신 committed도 가능.

💡 **Example**

- Sam was devoted to his new girlfriend.
  샘은 새로 생긴 여친에게 몰두했어.

- We're devoted to our favorite teacher.
  우린 좋아하는 선생님에게 몰입해 있어.

A: My mom attends church every day.
B: She must be devoted to her religion.

A: 엄마는 매일 교회에 출석하세요.
B: 어머니께서 신앙에 전념하고 계심에 틀림이 없어.

I haven't got all day
내가 시간여유가 없어

haven't got all day는 '바쁘다,' '시간적 여유가 없다'라는 의미.

💡 **Example**

- Work faster. We haven't got all day.
  좀 더 빨리 일해라. 시간이 없어.

- Haven't you finished? We haven't got all day.
  일을 끝냈니? 우린 시간이 없어.

A: Just give me ten more minutes.
B: No way. I haven't got all day.

A: 단 10분 만 더 주실래요?
B: 안돼. 내가 시간적 여유가 없어.

013

I like to keep myself busy

바삐 생활하는 걸 좋아해

keep oneself busy는 '바쁘게 지내다,' 자기 자신을 바쁜 상태로 계속 유지.

💡 **Example**

- Sam kept himself busy at work.
  샘은 직장에서 바삐 지내.

- You can keep yourself busy using the computer.
  컴퓨터를 사용해 바쁘게 살 수 있어.

 Dialog

A: How do you avoid being bored?
B: I like to keep myself busy.

A: 어떻게 지루함을 피하고 살아?
B: 바삐 생활하는 걸 좋아해.

014

Get a move on it!

서둘러!

get a move on sth은 '…을 서두르다,' 주로 명령문형태로 상대방에게 서두르라고 말할 때.

💡 **Example**

- Get a move on it! We're already late.
  서둘러. 우린 이미 늦었어.

- Let's go! Get a move on it!
  가자! 서둘러!

 Dialog

A: Get a move on it!
B: I'm going as fast as I can.

A: 서둘러!
B: 최대한 서두르고 있다고.

I am totally burned out

난 완전히 뻗었어

be burned out은 '완전히 뻗다[지치다]' = be wiped out.

💡 **Example**

- I am totally burned out from doing this job.
  이 일하느라 완전히 뻗었어.

- I'm going to have to cancel. I'm totally wiped out.
  취소해야돼. 완전히 녹초됐어.

 Dialog

A: Burt always looks so tired.
B: He is burned out from being here.

A: 버트는 항상 무지 피곤해 보여.
B: 걘 여기 있는 것만으로 지쳐버렸어.

She was up and about

걘 상태가 호전되었어

be up and about은 '호전되다,' '일어나 돌아다니다.' 환자상태가 호전, 혹은 사람들이 활동적인 상태.

💡 **Example**

- Everyone was up and about early this morning.
  모든 사람들이 아침 일찍부터 일어나 돌아다녔어.

- The patient was up and about.
  환자 상태가 호전되었어.

 Dialog

A: Where did mom and dad go?
B: They've been up and about for a few hours.

A: 아빠, 엄마는 어디로 갔어?
B: 일어나셔서 몇 시간 동안 돌아다니셔.

I'm getting back on my feet

난 좋아지고 있어

get back on one's feet는 슬픔[질병]에서 회복하다 = get back on track.

💡 Example

- I'm weak, but I'm getting back on my feet.
  쇠약해졌지만 좋아지고 있어.

- I want you to get back on your feet.
  난 네가 빨리 재기하길 바래.

A: I have no job and no money.
B: You'll get back on your feet soon.

A: 난 직업도 없고 돈도 없어.
B: 넌 조만간 회복될 거야.

Get your act together

정신 좀 차려

get one's act together는 '기운이나 정신차리다' = pull oneself together.

💡 Example

- Shelia needs to get her act together.
  쉴라는 정신을 차려야 해.

- Stop lying and get your act together.
  그만 누워있고 정신을 차려.

A: These grades are terrible. Get your act together.
B: I'm doing the best I can.

A: 성적이 엉망이야. 정신 좀 차려.
B: 최선을 다하고 있어요

You'll get over it

넌 잊게 될거야

get over는 '(병, 힘든 상황) 극복하다,' '잊어버리다.'

💡 **Example**

- He can't get over his father's death.
  걘 아버지의 죽음을 극복하지 못하고 있어.

- Don't worry. She'll get over it in a few weeks.
  걱정마, 걘 몇 주 후면 괜찮아질 거야.

A: I'm so angry with my wife for deceiving me!
B: You'll get over it.

A: 내 아내가 날 속인 것에 대해 무지 화가 나!
B: 잊게 될 거야.

He can fix the car on his own

걘 스스로 차를 고칠 수 있어

do sth on one's own은 '…을 혼자 힘으로 하다' = do sth (by) oneself.

💡 **Example**

- He can fix the car on his own.
  걘 스스로 차를 고칠 수 있어.

- I want to do something on my own from now on.
  이제부터 뭔가 스스로 하고 싶어.

A: Have you asked your father for help?
B: No, I want to do this on my own.

A: 아버님한테 도움을 청해봤어?
B: 아니, 나 혼자 힘으로 해보고 싶어.

021

I can't stand on my own feet yet

난 아직 자립할 수가 없어

stand on one's own feet은 말 그대로 자신의 말로 일어서다, 즉 '자립하다.'

💡 **Example**

- Perry stood on his own feet after graduating.
  페리는 졸업 후 자립했어.
- I can't stand on my own feet yet.
  난 아직 자립할 수가 없어.

 **Dialog**

A: Why won't you give me any more money?
B: You need to stand on your own feet.

A: 왜 나한테 돈을 조금 더 주지 않니?
B: 넌 자립해야 할 필요가 있어.

022

I did well on the exam

나 시험을 잘 봤어

do well on~은 (주로 시험 등에서) '잘하다.'

💡 **Example**

- You must do well on the college entrance test.
  넌 대학입학 시험을 잘 봐야 해.
- We can do well on the interview questions.
  우린 인터뷰 질문에 대해 잘 할 수 있어.

 **Dialog**

A: Did you do well on the exam?
B: Yes, I think I got a high grade.

A: 너 시험 잘 봤니?
B: 응, 높은 학점을 받은 것 같아.

I don't feel up to cooking today

오늘은 요리할 기운이 없어

feel up to+N[~ing]은 '…하고 싶다,' '…을 할 수 있다.' 능력보다는 '의사[의지]'를 표현.

Example

- They didn't feel up to celebrating last night.
  걔들은 어제 밤 축하하고 싶지 않았어.

- Harry felt up to carrying the heavy bags.
  해리는 무거운 가방들을 나를 기분이 났어.

Dialog

A: Do you feel up to going for a walk?
B: Oh no, I'm feeling very sick.

A: 산책하고 싶니?
B: 아니야, 난 많이 아파.

Guess What?

I draw the line at insulting people

난 사람들 욕하는 것은 참을 수가 없어

"선을 긋다"라는 의미로 해서는 안되거나 용납할 수 없는 것에 대한 확고한 범위를 정한다(set a firm boundary of something that is not permitted or allowed to be done)는 말이다. 한 개인의 결정의 결과를 말한다. 비유적으로 "한계를 긋다," "한도를 정하다," "…넘는 건 허용하지 않다"라는 의미이다.

024

Don't get ahead of yourself
너무 앞서 가지마

get ahead of~는 '…보다 앞서가다,' '…을 피하다,' get ahead of oneself는 '너무 앞서가다.'

Example
- I got ahead of everyone else in line.
  난 줄에서 누구보다 앞에 서있었어.
- We got ahead of the big traffic jam.
  우린 교통 대 혼잡을 피해 앞서갔지.

Dialog
A: People always want to get ahead of each other.
B: Sure. Everyone wants to be the most successful.
  A: 사람들은 항상 서로 앞서가길 원해.
  B: 그래. 누구나 가장 성공하길 원하지.

025

The cook has lost his touch
주방장이 감을 잃었어

lose one's touch는 '감[요령]을 잃다' = fail at what one used to do well.

Example
- The music was terrible after the band lost its touch.
  밴드가 감을 잃은 후에 음악이 끔찍해졌어.
- You're losing your touch these days.
  넌 요즘 감을 잃은 것 같아.

Dialog
A: This food tastes pretty bad.
B: The cook here has lost his touch.
  A: 이 음식 맛은 아주 나빠.
  B: 주방장이 감을 잃었나 봐.

I can't **deal with** her anymore

난 걔 더 이상 감당못하겠어

deal with sth[sb]는 '…을 다루다,' '처리하다,' '감당하다.'

 Example

- Can you deal with those customers?
  저기 고객들을 상대해줄 수 있니?
- I am going to deal with that noisy dog.
  내가 저 시끄러운 강아지를 다뤄볼게.

Dialog

A: I'm having some problems with my girlfriend.
B: You should deal with them right away.

A: 난 여친과 좀 문제가 있어.
B: 즉시 그 문제를 처리해야지.

Go easy on punishing Chris

크리스에게 너무 심하게 벌주지마

go easy on sb[…을 살살 다루다], go easy on sth[조금만 섭취하다], go easy on ~ing[심하지 않게 하다].

 Example

- Go easy on your little sister.
  네 여동생에게 너무 심하게 하지마.
- Go easy on punishing Bill.
  빌에게 너무 심하게 벌주지마.

Dialog

A: My new assistant is really stupid.
B: Go easy on him. He will learn more.

A: 새로운 보좌관은 정말 멍청해.
B: 살살 다뤄. 배워나갈 거야.

I'll **make it through** this crisis

난 이 위기를 헤쳐나갈거야

make it through는 '어려운 시기를 견뎌내다,' '병이나 사고를 이겨내다.'

💡 **Example**

- We had to make it through a cold winter.
  우린 추운 겨울을 잘 이겨내야만 했어.

- The family made it through a hard time without money.
  그 가족은 돈 없이 어려운 시기를 잘 이겨냈어.

 Dialog

A: Jim didn't make it through the training period.
B: I guess he wasn't tough enough to finish.

A: 짐은 훈련기간을 잘 이겨내지 못했어.
B: 걔가 훈련을 잘 마칠 만큼 강인하지 못했던 것으로 추측돼.

I wasn't able to **pull through**

난 병을 이겨낼 수가 없었어

pull through는 병이나 어려움 등 매우 힘든 상황을 이겨내다.

💡 **Example**

- The old man wasn't able to pull through.
  그 노인은 병을 이겨낼 수가 없었어.

- He may not pull through after his car wreck.
  걘 차사고로 인한 부상을 잘 이겨내지 못할거야.

 Dialog

A: I heard your grandmother was in the hospital.
B: She was very sick, but she pulled through.

A: 너의 할머니가 입원했다고 들었어.
B: 아주 아프신데 잘 이겨내셨어.

030

I want to be done with it

난 그걸 끝내고 싶어

be done with st[sb, ~ing]는 '…을 끝내다.' I'm not done talking은 '내 얘기 아직 안끝났어.'

 **Example**

- Are you done with cooking for tonight?
  오늘 밤 요리를 끝냈니?
- I'm not sure if he's done with it yet.
  걔가 그걸 마쳤는지 모르겠어.

Dialog

A: Why are you working so hard on that project?
B: I just want to be done with it.

A: 왜 그 프로젝트를 그렇게 열심히 하니?
B: 난 단지 그걸 끝내고 싶어서.

031

She's through showering

걘 샤워를 끝냈어

be through with sth은 '…을 끝내다,' be through ~ing는 '…하기를 끝내다.'

 **Example**

- Sarah is through showering.
  새러가 샤워를 끝냈어.
- He is through eating his dinner.
  걘 저녁식사를 마쳤어.

Dialog

A: Can I use the exercise machine?
B: Sure, I'm through exercising right now.

A: 운동기계를 사용할 수 있나요?
B: 그럼요. 전 지금 바로 운동을 끝냈어요.

032

You should just get it over with
넌 빨리 해치우는게 좋아

get it over with는 별로 내키지 않는 일을 '빨리 해치우다.'

💡 Example

- Clean up your room and get it over with.
  네 방 청소를 해치워버려라.

- Get your studying over with before we go.
  우리가 떠나기 전에 네 공부를 해치워라.

 Dialog

A: I hate swimming in cold water.
B: Jump in the pool and get it over with.

A: 난 찬물에서 수영하는 걸 싫어해.
B: 풀장에 뛰어들어 해버려.

033

Get it done right away
바로 이거 끝내

get sth done은 finish와 같은 의미이나, 좀 더 강압적, 그리고 늦었으니 빨리 하라는 뉘앙스.

💡 Example

- I will get the homework done tonight.
  난 오늘 밤 숙제를 끝낼 거야.

- Don't worry. I'll get it done for you.
  걱정 마. 널 위해 해낼 테니까.

 Dialog

A: Please get it done right away.
B: Don't worry, you can count on me.

A: 지금 당장 이것 좀 해줘.
B: 걱정 마. 나만 믿어.

Let's wrap up the meeting

회의를 마칩시다

wrap up sth은 '…을 마무리하다,' '끝내다'라는 의미.

 **Example**

- You need to wrap up what you're doing.
  네가 하고 있는 일을 끝낼 필요가 있어.

- Let me wrap up the speech I made.
  내 연설을 끝내도록 하죠.

Dialog

A: The conference will wrap up on Saturday.
B: It will be very busy until then.

A: 그 회의는 토요일에 끝날 거야.
B: 그때까지 무지 바쁘겠네.

I think it came off well

잘된 것 같아

좀 낯설지만 come off well은 '(경쟁 등) 잘 되어가다'라는 의미.

 **Example**

- The date with Natalie came off well.
  나탈리하고의 데이트가 잘 된 것 같아.

- Everything came off well at school today.
  오늘 학교에서 모든 일이 다 잘됐어.

Dialog

A: How did your presentation go?
B: I think it came off well.

A: 프리젠테이션 어땠어?
B: 잘된 것 같아.

You can make it!

넌 해낼 수 있어!
make it은 '해내다,' '성공하다,' make it (to+ 장소명사)하면 '…에 늦지 않게 도착하다.'

 **Example**

- The basketball player wants to make it in the NBA.
  그 농구선수는 NBA에서 뛰고 싶어해.

- I tried to come to the party, but I couldn't make it.
  난 파티에 오려고 노력했지만 오지 못했어.

 Dialog

A: I can't do this any more.
B: Yes, you can. You can make it!

A: 난 이걸 더 이상 할 수가 없어.
B: 넌 할 수 있어. 해낼 수 있다고!

They pulled off a big win

그들은 큰 승리를 해냈어
pull off는 '(어려운 일을) 해내다,' '성공하다,' pull of sth = pull it off는 '…을 해내다.'

 **Example**

- You can't pull off a stunt like that.
  넌 그와 같은 스턴트를 해낼 수가 없어.

- The baseball team pulled off a big win.
  그 야구팀은 큰 승리를 해냈어.

Dialog

A: Did someone rob the bank next door?
B: Yeah, three crooks pulled off a robbery.

A: 누군가 옆에 있는 은행을 털었니?
B: 응, 3명의 범인이 은행강도를 했어.

038

It'll work out for you
너에게 잘 맞을거야
work out for sb는 '…에게 잘 되어가다,' '잘 맞다.' 주어에는 '잘 되어가는 일'이 온다.

💡 **Example**

- The schedule worked out for me.
  스케줄은 나한테 잘 맞았어.

- I'm sorry it didn't work out for you.
  네 일이 잘 안되어서 어쩌니.

 Dialog

A: I really like my new job.
B: It will probably work out for you.

A: 난 새로 구한 직업을 아주 좋아해.
B: 아마도 너에게 잘 맞을 거야.

039

He got the better of the rookie
걘 신입을 제압했어
get the better of sb는 '(경기나 논쟁) 이기다.'

💡 **Example**

- I got the better of my new teacher.
  난 새로운 선생님을 이겼어.

- You'll never get the better of me.
  넌 결코 날 이길 수 없을거야.

 Dialog

A: Did Tim win the computer game?
B: No, the other guy got the better of him.

A: 팀이 컴퓨터 게임을 이겼니?
B: 아니, 다른 친구가 이겼어.

040

You are way off base
네가 잘못 짚었어
be way off base는 '잘못되다,' '맞지 않다.'

💡 **Example**
- Jill was way off base about her friend.
  질은 자기 친구에 대해 잘못 짚었어.
- Your ideas are way off base.
  네 생각은 잘못 된 거야.

 Dialog

A: Does your family have a lot of money?
B: No. You are way off base.
  A: 네 가족은 돈이 많이 있니?
  B: 아니. 잘못 짚었어.

041

Don't blow it
일을 망치지마
blow it은 '실수하다,' 특히 실수나 부주의로 기회를 잃는 것을 말한다.

💡 **Example**
- We were winning, but we blew it.
  우린 이기고 있었는데 기회를 놓쳐버렸어.
- Jeff blew it before he finished.
  제프는 끝내기도 전에 실수해버렸어.

 Dialog

A: I am meeting Wendy for a date today.
B: She likes you. Don't blow it.
  A: 난 오늘 데이트를 위해 웬디를 만날거야.
  B: 걘 너를 좋아해. 일을 망치지 마.

042

I got nowhere asking her on a date

난 걔에게 데이트요청했지만 성과없었어

get nowhere with sb[sth]은 '…에 아무런 성과가 없다,' = get nowhere with ~ing.

Example

- You'll get nowhere with that policeman.
  저 경찰하고는 소용없을거야.

- He got nowhere asking Kim on a date.
  걘 Kim에게 데이트를 요청했으나 성과가 없었어.

 Dialog

A: Did you ask the boss for a raise?
B: Of course, but I got nowhere with him.

A: 넌 보스에게 봉급인상을 요구했니?
B: 물론, 그러나 성과는 없었어.

043

Don't mess up this chance

이번 기회를 망치지마

mess up은 '망치다,' 즉 중요한 일을 망치거나 제대로 하지 못할 때.

Example

- These new classes will mess up my schedule.
  이 새 수업들 때문에 내 스케줄이 엉망이 될 거야.

- I didn't mess up your room.
  난 네 방을 어지럽히지 않았어.

 Dialog

A: It sure is windy out today.
B: My hair is going to get messed up.

A: 오늘 밖에 바람이 정말 많이 불어.
B: 내 머리가 엉망이 되겠어.

044

He is not qualified for a job

걘 그 일을 할 자격이 없어

be qualified for (sth)은 '(일자리 등에) 자격을 갖추다.' be 다음에 well이나 highly로 강조.

💡 Example

- Tracy is qualified for a job with the airlines.
  트레이시는 항공사 일자리에 자격이 있어.

- He is not qualified for a job with the police force.
  걘 경찰 직업에 자격이 없어.

 Dialog

A: Make sure that all of the applicants are qualified for the job.
B: When are we going to schedule the interviews?

A: 지원자들 모두 그 일을 맡을 만한 자질을 갖췄는지 확인해 봐.
B: 면접 일정을 언제로 잡을까?

045

He has been in sales for 3 years

걘 3년간 판매분야에서 일하고 있어

have been in+업종+for~는 '…동안 …업계에서 종사했다.'

💡 Example

- I have been in management for a year.
  난 1년간 경영진에서 일하고 있어.

- Liz has been in therapy for seven years.
  리즈는 7년간 치료 요법을 받고 있어.

 Dialog

A: What does your husband do?
B: He has been in sales for 13 years.

A: 네 남편 직업은 뭐니?
B: 13년간 판매분야에서 일하고 있어.

She's gone for the day

걘 퇴근했어

go[leave] for the day는 '퇴근하다.' = get off work.

> **Example**
>
> - I need to get off work early on Friday.
>   난 금요일 일찍 퇴근해야 돼.
>
> - You need to get out of the office sometimes for fresh air.
>   기분전환을 위해 가끔 사무실에서 나올 필요가 있어.

A: Excuse me. Is Mr. Jones in his office right now?
B: I'm sorry, but he's gone for the day.

A: 죄송합니다. 존스 씨가 지금 사무실에 있나요?
B: 미안합니다만 퇴근했네요.

I got paid for working overtime

난 시간외 일로 수당을 받았어

get paid는 '돈을 받다,' '급여를 받다,' get promoted는 '승진하다.'

> **Example**
>
> - Hey, Tom, did you get paid this month's wages?
>   탐, 이달 치 급여를 받았니?
>
> - I don't get paid for working overtime.
>   난 시간외 일로 수당을 받지 못하고 있어.

A: I'm going to get paid on Friday.
B: You'll have money to buy Christmas presents.

A: 난 금요일에 급여를 탈 거야.
B: 넌 크리스마스 선물을 살 돈을 갖게 되겠네.

048

He was transferred to Korea

걘 한국으로 발령났어

be transferred to~는 '…로 전근가다,' 반대로 전근오는 것은 be transferred from~.

💡 **Example**

- Kathy wants to be transferred to Florida.
  캐시는 플로리다로 전근을 원하고 있어.
- Next month, I'm getting transferred to a new office location.
  다음 달에 새로운 다른 지사로 전근을 가게 됐어요.

A: I heard you will be moving.
B: My dad was transferred to England.

A: 난 네가 이사할거라고 들었어.
B: 우리 아빠는 영국으로 발령이 났어.

049

They laid off a few employees last week

그들은 지난주에 몇 명의 직원을 해고했어

lay off는 '(불황 등으로) 일시 해고하다,' 또한 '…을 그만두다,' '건드리지 않다'로도 쓰인다.

💡 **Example**

- We're going to have to lay off at least 100 people.
  적어도 100명은 해고할거야.
- We're going to be laying off people in every department.
  모든 부서별로 몇 사람씩 자를거야.

A: My company is laying everyone off.
B: Are they going out of business?

A: 회사는 모두를 정리해고하고 있어.
B: 회사가 파산할 예정이니?

050

I'm planning to resign from my job

나는 직장에서 사직할거야

resign from[as]은 '…의 직을 그만두다,' '사임하다,' retire from은 '정년퇴직하다.'

 Example

- Perry resigned from the sales department.
  페리는 판매부에서 그만두었어.

- I handed in my resignation this morning.
  나 아침에 사직서를 제출했어.

 Dialog

A: So, what brings you here at such a late hour?
B: I came by to tell you that I need to resign.

A: 이렇게 늦은 시각에 무슨 일로 오셨습니까?
B: 자리에서 물러나야겠다는 말을 하려고 들렸어요.

051

She owns her own business

걘 자영업을 하고 있어

own one's own business는 '자영업을 하다.' 앞의 own은 '소유하다,' 뒤의 own은 '자신의.'

 Example

- The businessman owned his own business.
  저 사업가는 자기 업체를 소유했어.

- I'd like to own my own business.
  난 내 사업체를 갖고 싶어.

Dialog

A: Rick always seems very busy.
B: Well, he owns his own business.

A: 릭은 항상 무지 바빠 보여.
B: 글쎄, 걘 자영업을 하고 있어.

052

He's on call 24 hours a day

걘 하루에 24시간 호출대기 중야

be on call은 '대기중이다,' '당번이다.'

💡 **Example**

- I'm on call. Let me know if there are problems.
  내가 당번야. 문제가 생기면 알려줘.

- Who is going to be on call tonight?
  누가 오늘 밤 당번할 거니?

 Dialog

A: I'd like to become a doctor.
B: Doctors are on call 24 hours a day.

 A: 난 의사가 되고 싶어.
 B: 의사들은 하루에 24시간 호출 대기 중이야.

053

Can you cover my shift tonight?

오늘밤 내 근무 대신해 줄 수 있어?

cover one's shift는 '…의 근무시간을 대신하다,' '…의 근무를 맡아주다.'

💡 **Example**

- None of the employees could cover my shift.
  어느 직원도 내 교대근무를 대신해줄 수 없어.

- If you cover my shift, I'll pay you.
  내 교대근무를 대신해주면 내가 보답할게.

 Dialog

A: I need you to drive me to the airport.
B: Someone will need to cover my shift at work.

 A: 네가 날 공항까지 운전해주면 좋겠어.
 B: 누군가 내 교대근무를 대신해줘야 해.

054

My cousin works as a temp

사촌이 임시직으로 일해

work as a temp는 '임시직으로 일하다.' temp '임시직원' 혹은 '임시직으로 일하다'라는 뜻.

💡 **Example**

- I'm only employed here on a temporary basis.
  난 여기에 단지 임시직으로 고용됐어.

- Some people work as temps until they get better jobs.
  더 나은 직장을 얻기 전까지 임시직으로 일하는 사람들도 있어.

A: My cousin works as a temp.
B: Does she have a good salary?

A: 사촌이 임시직으로 일해.
B: 급여는 괜찮아?

055

I finished giving the presentation

난 프리젠테이션을 마쳤어

give[do] a presentation on sth은 '…에 대해 발표하다.'

💡 **Example**

- Our teacher is giving a presentation on science.
  선생님이 과학에 대해 프리젠테이션을 하고 계셔.

- Let's get together after I finish giving the presentation.
  내가 프리젠테이션을 끝낸 다음 만나자.

A: What is the subject of today's meeting?
B: Someone is giving a presentation on cooking.

A: 오늘 회의 주제는 뭐니?
B: 누군가 요리에 대해 프리젠테이션을 할 야.

📎 056

I must work on my presentation

난 프리젠테이션 작업을 해야 돼

work on one's presentation은 '발표작업을 하다' = prepare for one's presentation.

💡 **Example**

- I worked on my presentation for the meeting.
  난 회의 프리젠테이션을 위해 일했어.

- Each student worked on his presentation for the class.
  학생들은 수업 중 자신들의 프리젠테이션을 위해 작업했어.

 **Dialog**

A: How long will you work on your presentation for the boss?
B: I'm going to be up all night writing it.

　A: 넌 보스 앞 프리젠테이션을 위해 얼마나 일한거니?
　B: 난 준비를 위해 밤새 깨어있을거야.

📎 057

I put together a report in two hours

난 2시간동안 한 보고서 준비했어

put together a report는 '보고서를 준비하다.'

💡 **Example**

- We put together a report in five hours.
  우리 5시간 동안 한 보고서를 준비했어.

- I need you and Gene to put together a report.
  너와 진이 보고서를 준비해.

 **Dialog**

A: What has that team been working on?
B: They are trying to put together a report.

　A: 저 팀은 무슨 일을 하고 있니?
　B: 걔들은 보고서를 준비하려고 노력하고 있어.

058

We may close the deal tonight

오늘밤 거래를 맺을지도 몰라

close a deal은 거래를 끝내는게 아니라 계약을 합의하여 성공리에 완결짓는다는 의미.

 **Example**

- You told me you were going to Chicago to close a deal.
  거래를 마무리하기 위해 시카고에 간다고 했잖아.

- I hope that she doesn't blow the deal tomorrow.
  걔가 낼 거래를 망치지 않기 바래.

Dialog

A: This is amazing! We may close the deal tonight.
B: Settle down, we have to think straight.

A: 세상에! 오늘밤 거래가 매듭지어질지도 모르겠어요!
B: 진정해요. 차분히 생각해 봐야죠.

059

He lost one of her big accounts

걘 큰 거래선 중 하나를 놓쳤어

lose an account (with~)는 '거래선을 놓치다, 잃다.'

 **Example**

- We're looking for someone to handle our account in India.
  인도 거래선을 다룰 사람을 찾고 있어.

- Why do you think we lost the Miller account?
  왜 밀러 고객을 놓쳤다고 생각해?

Dialog

A: Why does Sarah look so upset?
B: She lost one of her big accounts.

A: 왜 새라가 낙담해보여?
B: 큰 거래선 중 하나를 놓쳤거든.

060

I guess he got the contract
그가 계약을 따낸 것 같아

sign a contract for~는 '…계약을 맺다' = make a contract with.

💡 **Example**

- I'm pleased to announce that we won the contract.
  계약따냈다는 소식전하게 돼 기뻐.
- Sally came by and said that she didn't get the contract.
  샐리가 잠시 들렸는데 자기가 이번 계약 건을 따내지 못했다고 하더군.

Dialog

A: I guess he got the contract.
B: I thought he was in a particularly good mood.

A: 제 생각에는 그가 계약을 따낸 것 같아요.
B: 그가 무척 기분이 좋다고 생각했어요.

061

We trade in cars with Turkey
튀르키에와 자동차무역을 해

trade in A with B는 'B와 A를 거래[무역]하다,' trade in A for B는 '차액주고 A를 B로 교환하다.'

💡 **Example**

- The companies trade in tea with China.
  그 회사들은 중국과 차 교역을 하고 있어.
- We trade in cars with the Middle East.
  우린 중동지역과 자동차 장사를 하고 있어.

Dialog

A: What kind of sales do you do?
B: I trade in clothing with the Brazilians.

A: 넌 어떤 종류의 판매업을 하고 있니?
B: 난 브라질 사람들과 옷을 거래하고 있어.

I made an online purchase of a mouse

마우스를 온라인으로 구매했어

make an online purchase는 '온라인으로 구매하다' = purchase sth over the Net.

💡 **Example**

- Have you ever purchased anything over the Internet?
  인터넷구매 해본 적 있어?

- Why don't you buy her something online at Amazon?
  아마존에서 걔한테 뭐 사줘.

A: Many people want to make online purchases.
B: Yeah, I like shopping on the Internet.

A: 많은 사람들이 온라인 구매를 원해.
B: 그래, 난 인터넷 쇼핑을 좋아해.

I sent away for some books

책 몇 개를 우편으로 주문했어

send away for~는 '…을 우편으로 혹은 인터넷으로 주문하다.'

💡 **Example**

- The students sent away for their books.
  학생들이 책을 우편으로 주문했어.

- Did you send away for this picture?
  이 그림을 우편으로 주문했니?

A: I sent away for some new glasses.
B: Are you sure they will fit you?

A: 새 안경을 몇 개 우편으로 주문했어.
B: 너한테 맞을 거라고 확신하니?

Do you carry ink cartridges?

잉크 카트리지 있습니까?

carry+상품은 '(가게에서) …을 취급하다,' '팔다.'

💡 **Example**

- The grocery store carries our favorite foods.
  저 식품점은 우리가 좋아하는 음식을 팔고 있어.

- I'm sorry, we don't carry that brand.
  미안하지만 그 브랜드는 취급하지 않아요.

 Dialog

A: Do you carry ink cartridges?
B: Yes, are you looking for a particular kind?

  A: 잉크 카트리지 있습니까?
  B: 예, 특별히 찾는 게 있나요?

We have that kind in stock

그 종류는 재고 있어요

have sth in stock은 '제품이 있다,' '재고가 있다' <=> be out of stock.

💡 **Example**

- I'll check to see if we have any in stock.
  재고가 있는지 찾아 볼게요.

- Let me see if we have that kind in stock.
  그런 종류가 재고가 있는지 알아볼게요.

 Dialog

A: This is a hot sale item nowadays.
B: Do you have any more in stock?

  A: 이게 요즘 잘 나가는 제품이에요.
  B: 물건 재고가 있나요?

He sold the car on the Internet

걔 차를 인터넷으로 팔았어

sell sth on[over] the Internet은 '…을 인터넷으로 팔다.'

Example

- It's a good idea to sell used books over the Internet.
  중고책을 인터넷으로 파는 건 좋은 생각야.
- He's trying to sell socks on the Internet.
  걔 인터넷으로 양말을 팔려고 해.

Dialog

A: How did Don sell his sports car?
B: He sold the car on the Internet.

A: 돈은 어떻게 자기 스포츠카를 팔았니?
B: 인터넷으로 팔았대.

Guess What?

I spilled the beans about the party
내가 파티에 대해 비밀을 털어놓았어

"자루에 있던 콩을 쏟다"라는 말로 앞서 나온 let the cat out of the bag와 비슷한 의미. "무심결에 비밀을 털어놓다"(to tell others something that was supposed to have been kept secret)라는 의미가 된다.

I'd like my money back

환불해주세요

get one's money back은 '돈을 돌려받다,' '환불받다.'

💡 **Example**

- Gina got her money back from her friend.
  지나는 친구로부터 돈을 돌려받았어.

- They wouldn't give me my money back.
  걔들은 내 돈을 돌려주지 않았어.

 Dialog

A: I'd like my money back, please.
B: Was there a problem with this item?

A: 돈을 환불해주세요.
B: 이 물품에 문제가 있었나요?

Can I get a refund for this?

이거 환불받을 수 있을까요?

refund for~는 '환불받다' = get[have] a (full) refund for~.

💡 **Example**

- Rico got a refund for the broken stove.
  리코는 부서진 스토브를 환불받았어.

- Can I have a refund for this shirt?
  셔츠 환불해주시겠어요?

 Dialog

A: Can I get a full refund for this?
B: Certainly, if you have your receipt.

A: 이 물건을 전액 환불받을 수 있을까요?
B: 물론이죠, 영수증만 있으시다면요.

I enjoy playing the market
난 주식투자를 즐겨

play the market은 '주식을 하다' = invest in the stock market

💡 **Example**

- They lost their money playing the market.
  걔들은 주식 투자에서 돈을 잃었어.

- Frieda plays the market with her salary.
  프리다는 봉급으로 주식 투자를 하고 있어.

A: You always read about stocks.
B: Well, I enjoy **playing the market**.

A: 넌 항상 주식 기사를 읽고 있구나.
B: 글쎄, 난 주식투자를 즐겨.

I cut off one of his buttons
난 단추 한 개를 떼어 버렸어

cut off는 '줄이다,' '자르다' = shorten by cutting의 의미. cut corners은 '비용줄이다.'

💡 **Example**

- He is cutting corners to save cash.
  걘 현금을 아끼려고 경비를 줄이고 있어.

- Jerry cut off one of his buttons.
  제리는 단추 한 개를 떼어 버렸어.

A: How did Shelly save money this year?
B: She had to **cut off** all of her extra expenses.

A: 셸리가 금년에 어떻게 절약을 한거야?
B: 모든 추가지출을 줄여야만 했어.

071

She's cashing in on her fame
걘 자기 명성을 이용하고 있어
cash in on은 '…로 돈을 벌다,' '…을 이용하다.'

Example
- Rindy cashed in on her banking knowledge.
  린디는 자신의 금융지식을 잘 이용했어.
- I'd like to cash in on the gold coins I have.
  난 내가 보유하고 있는 금화를 현금화하고 싶어.

A: Johnny Depp does a lot of advertisements.
B: I guess he's cashing in on his fame.
  A: 조니 뎁은 광고에 많이 나와.
  B: 걘 자신의 명성을 이용하고 있다고 보여.

072

It is due next Monday
다음 월요일에 제출 예정야
be due+시간명사[be due on+요일명사]는 '…가 지불기일이다,' '…에 마감기한이다.'

Example
- The library books are due on Saturday.
  도서관 책들이 토요일에 반납예정이죠.
- The bills are due on the first day of the month.
  청구서가 그 달 첫날에 지불 기한이죠.

A: When is this report going to be finished?
B: Well, it is due next Monday.
  A: 언제 이 보고서가 마무리 될 수 있니?
  B: 글쎄요, 다음 월요일에 제출 예정이에요.

I need to pay off my debt

난 빚을 갚아야 돼

pay off one's debt는 '…의 빚을 갚다,' '청산하다' = pay back.

💡 **Example**

- It will take years to pay off this debt.
  이 빚을 갚으려면 수년이 걸릴 거야.
- When can you pay off your debts?
  언제 네 빚을 청산할 수 있겠니?

A: Students owe a lot of money after graduation.
B: They need to pay off their debt.
  A: 학생들은 졸업 후 많은 돈을 빚지게 돼.
  B: 걔들은 빚을 갚아야만 하지.

I'd like to buy a car on credit

신용대출로 차를 구매하고 싶어

pay sth on one's credit card는 '신용카드로 계산하다' = buy sth on credit.

💡 **Example**

- No one buys the newspaper with a credit card.
  신문을 신용카드로 사는 사람은 없어.
- I'd like to buy a car on credit.
  신용 대출로 차를 구매하고 싶어.

A: I'd like to buy this with my credit card.
B: I'm sorry but we don't accept credit cards.
  A: 신용카드로 낼게요.
  B: 우린 신용카드 받지 않아요.

075

How much do I owe you?

얼마죠?

owe to sb는 '…에게 빚지다.' owe A to B 이면 B에게 A를 빚지다, A는 B의 덕이다.

💡 **Example**

- How much do I owe you for the gas?
  기름 값 얼마 내면 되죠?
- Thanks for your help. How much do I owe you?
  도와줘서 고마워요. 얼마죠?

 Dialog

A: I heard you **owe a lot of money to** your father.
B: Yes, I had no choice but to borrow it from him.

  A: 네 아버지에게 돈을 많이 빚졌다며.
  B: 응, 난 아빠로부터 빌릴 수 밖에 없었어.

076

The project **is over budget** by $20,000

그 프로젝트는 예산을 2만 달러 초과했다

be over budget은 '예산넘어서다' = go over budget(예산초과하다) = be beyond one's budget.

💡 **Example**

- Hollywood movies are always over budget.
  헐리우드 영화는 항상 예산이 초과돼.
- We went over budget on our expenses.
  우린 지출이 예산 초과되었어.

 Dialog

A: This apartment building looks very expensive.
B: They **were** millions of dollars **over budget**.

  A: 이 아파트 빌딩은 무지 비싸게 보이네.
  B: 걔들은 수백만 불이나 예산이 초과되었대.

How did you get into debt?

어떻게 빚을 지게 되었니?

get into debt는 '빚지다' <=> get out of debt.

💡 **Example**

- Leon got into debt because of school costs.
  레온은 학비 때문에 빚을 지게 되었어.

- Some families got into debt by buying expensive homes.
  일부 가족들은 값비싼 집을 사느라고 빚을 지게 돼.

 Dialog

A: How did you get into debt?
B: I had too many credit cards that I used.

  A: 어떻게 빚을 지게 되었니?
  B: 내가 신용카드를 너무 많이 썼나봐.

I'd like to make a cash deposit

현금 입금을 하고 싶어요

make a (cash) deposit는 '(현금) 입금하다' = deposit.

💡 **Example**

- You can make a cash deposit at the ATM.
  ATM에서 현금입금을 할 수 있어요.

- Sam made a cash deposit after selling his car.
  샘은 차를 판 후에 현금입금을 했어.

 Dialog

A: Hello, how can I help you?
B: I'd like to make a cash deposit.

  A: 여보세요, 도움이 필요하나요?
  B: 현금 입금을 하고 싶어요.

I took money out of my account

계좌에서 돈을 인출했어

take money out of one's account는 '…의 계좌에서 돈을 인출하다' = withdraw money from.

💡 Example

- Paula took money out of her account for the ticket.
  폴라는 표를 구입하기 위해 자기 구좌에서 돈을 꺼냈어.

- He decided not to take money out of his account.
  갠 자신의 계좌에서 돈을 인출하지 않기로 했어.

 Dialog

A: I need to take money out of my account.
B: Let's stop at this bank machine.

A: 내 계좌에서 돈을 인출해야겠어.
B: 이 현금기계에서 잠깐 서자.

She got into Harvard

갠 하버드 대학에 들어갔어

get into+대학명은 '…대학에 입학하다' = be admitted to+대학명.

💡 Example

- You'll never get into Harvard with your grades.
  네 성적 가지고는 결코 하버드 대에 들어갈 수 없을 거야.

- Less than ten percent of applicants get into Yale.
  지원자중 10%이하가 예일대입학해.

 Dialog

A: Why are John's parents so happy?
B: They just found out he got into Harvard.

A: 존의 부모는 왜 그렇게 행복하니?
B: 존이 하버드 대학에 입학할 것을 방금 알았거든.

She signed up for a cooking class

걘 요리 수업에 등록했어

sign up for+수강관련명사는 '…에 등록하다,' '신청하다.'

Example

- There's only a week to sign up for our classes.
  수강 신청하는데 단 일주일 남았어.
- Is this the office where I can sign up for my classes?
  이 사무실이 내가 수강 신청하는 곳이니?

Dialog

A: I signed up for my classes this morning.
B: Which ones will you be taking?

A: 오늘 아침 내 수업에 등록했어.
B: 어떤 과목을 듣는데?

She got an A in science class

걘 과학 과목에서 A 학점을 받았어

get an A in class는 '…과목에서 A학점을 받다,' get an F on one's report는 '리포트 F학점받다.'

Example

- Ryan needs to get an A in class.
  라이언은 수업에서 A 학점을 받아야 해.
- I hope you do really well on the exam.
  시험 정말 잘 보기를 바래.

Dialog

A: Your sister is pretty smart.
B: She got an A in science class.

A: 네 여동생은 꽤 똑똑해.
B: 걘 과학 과목에서 A 학점을 받았어.

Let me turn on the computer

컴퓨터를 켜줄게

turn on the computer는 '컴퓨터를 켜다' <=> turn off the computer.

💡 Example

- Turn on the computer before we start.
  우리 시작하기 전에 컴퓨터를 켜자.
- Please go and turn on the computer.
  가서 컴퓨터를 켜라.

 Dialog

A: I need to use the Internet.
B: Let me turn on the computer.

A: 난 인터넷을 사용할 필요가 있어.
B: 컴퓨터를 켜줄게.

I did research on the Internet

난 인터넷에서 자료검색을 했어

do research on the Internet은 '인터넷에서 자료검색을 하다.'

💡 Example

- Danny did research on the Internet for class.
  대니는 수업을 위해 인터넷에서 자료를 검색했어.
- I did research on the Internet to find the best price.
  난 가장 좋은 가격을 찾으려고 인터넷을 검색했어.

 Dialog

A: Why do students go online so much?
B: Many of them do research on the Internet.

A: 왜 학생들이 그렇게 많이 인터넷을 사용하니?
B: 대다수가 인터넷으로 자료 검색을 하고 있기 때문이야.

He posted it on the Internet

걘 그걸 인터넷에 올렸어

post sth on the Internet은 '인터넷에 …를 올리다,' post one's opinion about은 '…의 의견을 올리다.'

Example

- Pam posted her phone number on the Internet.
  팸이 인터넷에 자기 전번을 올렸대.
- The company posted an ad for a job on the Internet.
  회사는 인터넷에 구인 광고를 올렸어.

Dialog

A: I'm going to post a message on the Internet.
B: What kind of message is it?

A: 난 인터넷에 메시지를 올릴 생각이야.
B: 무슨 종류의 메시지인데?

I didn't react to the Internet article

난 그 인터넷 기사에 대응하지 않았어

react to an Internet article은 '인터넷 기사에 반응하다,' '댓글을 달다.'

Example

- Many people reacted angrily to the Internet article.
  많은 사람들이 그 인터넷기사에 분노했어.
- They didn't react to the Internet article.
  걔네들은 그 인터넷 기사에 대응하지 않았어.

Dialog

A: How did Kevin react to the Internet article?
B: He didn't like what it said.

A: 케빈이 그 인터넷 기사에 어떤 반응을 보였니?
B: 걘 그 기사를 좋아하지 않았어.

He's trolling on the Internet

걘 인터넷에 악성댓글을 올려

troll on the Internet은 '악성댓글달다.' troll은 악성댓글다는 사람, cyber bullying은 넷상의 괴롭힘.

Example

- A troll on the Internet tries to make people angry.
  악성 댓글 올리는 사람은 사람들을 화나게 해.

- I think trolls on the Internet need to be banned.
  악성댓글은 금지되어야 해.

Dialog

A: This person keeps posting nasty things.
B: He's just trolling on the Internet.

A: 이 사람은 한심한 글을 계속 올리고 있어.
B: 걘 인터넷에 악성 댓글을 올리고 있어.

He used a false name

걘 가명을 사용했어

use a false name은 '가명을 사용하다,' use a nickname은 '별명을 사용하다.'

Example

- He used a false name to post in the chatting forum.
  걘 대화방에서 가명을 사용해서 의견을 올렸지.

- Able uses a false name to chat with women.
  에이블은 인터넷에서 여성들과 대화를 나누는데 가명을 쓰고 있어.

Dialog

A: Who started those rumors about you?
B: Someone using a false name on the Internet.

A: 누가 너에 대한 그런 루머를 시작했니?
B: 인터넷에서 가명을 쓴 작자야.

He's addicted to online games

걘 온라인 게임에 중독됐어

be addicted to sth은 '…에 중독되다.' 뒤에 the Internet이나 computer games가 온다.

💡 Example

- He's addicted to computer games and plays daily.
  걘 컴퓨터 게임에 중독돼서 매일 해.

- Helen is still addicted to computer games.
  헬렌은 아직도 컴퓨터 겜에 중독되어 있어.

 Dialog

A: I think I'm addicted to computer games.
B: You should spend time doing other things.

A: 난 컴퓨터 게임에 중독이 된 것 같아.
B: 넌 다른 일을 하면서 시간을 보내 봐야해.

I got an instant message from her

난 걔로부터 IM을 받았어

instant message(IM)은 '인스턴트 메신저로 보낸 메시지,' 'IM으로 메시지 보내다.'

💡 Example

- We send instant message to our overseas friends.
  해외친구들에게 IM를 보내.

- Sam just got an instant message from his wife.
  샘은 아내로부터 IM를 방금 받았어.

 Dialog

A: I use instant messenger for contacting my sister.
B: Do you do that every day?

A: 여동생과 연락하는데 인스턴트 메신저를 사용해.
B: 너 메신저 매일 하니?

She found me on Facebook

걘 나를 페이스북을 통해 찾았어

find sb on Facebook은 '페이스북에서 …을 찾다.'

💡 **Example**

- I found many classmates from high school on Facebook.
  난 페이스북을 통해 고등학교 동창을 많이 찾았어.

- Tommy hopes to find new friends on Facebook.
  토미는 페이스북을 통해 새로운 친구를 만나기를 소망해.

A: An old girlfriend found me on Facebook.
B: Are you going to meet up with her?

A: 오래된 여친이 페이스북을 통해 날 찾았어.
B: 넌 걔를 만날 거니?

I friended Cindy on Facebook

난 신디를 페이스북에 친구로 등록했어

friend sb는 '페이스북에 친구로 등록하다,' friend가 동사로 쓰인 경우이다.

💡 **Example**

- People at work want you to friend them.
  직장 사람들은 네가 자기들을 친구등록하기를 바래.

- Josh friended some of his relatives.
  조쉬는 자기 친척 몇명을 친구로 등록해놨어.

A: How did you stay in touch with your classmates?
B: I friended all of them on Facebook.

A: 넌 어떻게 네 학교 친구들과 연락을 주고 받았어?
B: 난 페이스북에 친구들 다 등록해놨어.

My e-mail got through to her

걔가 내 이멜을 받아보았대

an email got through to sb는 '…가 이멜을 받아보다,' 이멜이 주어로 쓰인 경우.

Example

- The e-mail got through to everyone on the list.
  그 이메일은 리스트에 있는 모든 사람들에게 보내졌어.

- Each e-mail got through to the addressee.
  각각의 이메일이 수신인들에게 보내졌어.

Dialog

A: The Internet was down for two hours.
B: My e-mail still got through to my girlfriend.

A: 인터넷이 2시간 동안 되지 않았어.
B: 그래도 여친은 내 이메일을 받았대.

Forward his e-mail to his teacher

걔의 이멜을 선생님에게 다시 보내줘

forward one's email to sb는 '…의 이메일을 …로 다시 보내주다.'

Example

- Forward the manager's e-mail to everyone.
  매니저의 이메일을 전부에게 재전송해줘.

- Forward this e-mail to the police.
  이 이메일을 경찰에게 재전송해라.

Dialog

A: Al's e-mail said he'll be late to class.
B: Forward his e-mail to his teacher.

A: 알은 이메일로 자기가 수업에 늦을 거라고 말했어.
B: 걔의 이메일을 선생님에게 다시 보내줘.

It went to my junk file

그게 내 스팸메일 박스로 갔어

go to one's junk file은 '이멜이 스팸박스로 들어가다.' put into a junk email folder은 '스팸폴더로 넣다.'

Example

- Twenty or thirty e-mails go to my junk file daily.
  하루에 20개에서 30개에 이르는 이메일이 내 스팸메일 박스로 들어와.

- The invitation went to Tina's junk file.
  그 초청서는 티나의 스팸메일 박스로 들어 갔어.

A: I never got the e-mail Dick sent.
B: Maybe it went to your junk file.

A: 난 딕이 보낸 이메일을 결코 받지 못했어.
B: 아마도 그것이 네 스팸메일 박스로 들어갔나봐.

I'm calling to ask you for a favor

부탁할 게 있어서 전화했어

be calling to ask~는 '…을 물어보려고 전화하다.' call to tell sb~는 '…에게 …을 말하려고 전화하다.'

Example

- I'm calling to ask you for a favor.
  부탁 하나 하려고 전화했어.

- I'm just calling to see if you received the payment.
  송금한거 받았는지 확인할려고 전화했어.

A: Chris, I'm calling to ask you for a favor.
B: I'll do my best, what would you like?

A: 크리스, 너한테 부탁할 게 있어서 전화했어.
B: 힘 닿는대로 해볼게. 부탁이 뭔데?

Please get off the phone

전화 좀 끊어

get off the phone (with sb)은 '(…와) 전화를 끊다' = hang up. hang up on은 도중에 끊다.

Example

- Please hang up the phone.
  제발 전화 좀 끊어.

- Don't hang up. Just listen.
  전화 끊지 말고 내 얘기 들어.

Dialog

A: Would you please get off the phone?
B: Why? I can use it if I want to.

A: 전화 좀 끊을테야?
B: 왜? 내가 필요하면 써도 되는 거 아냐?

Guess What?

You look down in the dumps today

너 오늘 우울해보여

be down in the dumps는 뭔가 슬프고 행복하지 않을 때(to feel sad or depressed) 사용하는 표현으로 우울하다, 울적하다라고 생각하면 된다. be 대신에 feel, look down을 써도 된다.

098

He got the phone when it rang

걘 전화가 울렸을 때 받았어

get the phone은 '전화받다' = answer the phone. get a call saying that~은 '…라는 전화를 받다.'

💡 **Example**

- Sally got the phone when it rang.
  샐리는 전화기가 울렸을 때 전화를 받았어.

- I'm sorry, but I couldn't get the phone.
  미안해, 전화를 받을 수가 없었어.

A: Hey, someone is calling us.
B: I'll get the phone and see who it is.
　A: 헤이, 누가 우리에게 전화하네.
　B: 내가 전화 받아서 누군지 볼게.

099

Did you get through to your Dad?

아빠와 연결이 되었니?

get through to sb는 '…와 연락이 통하다,' '…에 도착하다.'

💡 **Example**

- It was hard to get through to the office.
  사무실로 통화하기가 힘들었어.

- I got through to my parent's house.
  내 부모님 집으로 통화가 되었어.

A: Did you get through to your brother?
B: No, he never picked up the phone.
　A: 네 동생에게 연결이 되었니?
　B: 아니, 걘 전화를 받지 않았어.

Hold on. I'll get the manager

잠시만요, 매니저를 바꿔줄게요

hang on은 '기다리다' = wait = be patient = hold on a minute = hold on a second

💡 **Example**

- Hang on a minute. I'll get him.
  잠깐만요. 바꿔줄게요

- Can you hang on? I've got another call.
  기다릴래? 다른 전화가 와서.

 Dialog

A: Excuse me, is there someone there who can speak English?
B: **Hold on.** I'll get the manager.

　A: 실례지만, 영어하는 사람 있어요?
　B: 잠시만요, 매니저를 바꿔줄게요.

Just have him call me, okay?

걔보고 내게 전화하라고해 알았지?

have A call B는 사역동사 have의 용법으로 'A가 B에게 전화를 걸도록 하다.'

💡 **Example**

- Just have him call me, okay?
  그 사람 보고 나한테 전화하라고해 알았지?

- If she finds it, have her call me immediately.
  그걸 찾으면 내게 바로 전화하라고 해.

 Dialog

A: I'll **have her call** you back as soon as she gets in.
B: Thank you.

　A: 걔가 들어오는 대로 전화하라고 할게.
　B: 고마워요.

Put it through to my office
내 사무실로 돌려줘

put A through B는 "A를 B에게 전화 바꿔주다," put sb on the phone는 '…을 바꿔주다.'

💡 **Example**

- Would you put me through to the manager, please?
  매니저 좀 바꿔줄래요?

- I'll put you through right away.
  바로 바꿔드리죠.

 Dialog

A: Phone call for you. Are you available?
B: Sure, put it through to my office.

  A: 전화왔는데 받을 수 있어요?
  B: 그럼요, 내 사무실로 돌려줘요.

The phone is dead
전화가 먹통이야

be cut off는 '전화가 끊기다.' (battery) be dying, (the phone) go dead, It eats up batteries(빨리 닳아)

💡 **Example**

- The phone is dead.
  전화가 먹통이야.

- Here is the number in case we get cut off, 212-555-1234.
  우리 전화가 끊어질 경우에 대비해서 번호는 212-555-1234 야.

 Dialog

A: Did you break your cell phone?
B: No. My battery went dead and it stopped working.

  A: 핸드폰 망가졌어?
  B: 아니. 배터리가 다 돼서 작동이 안돼.

You're breaking up!

소리가 끊겨 들려!

break up은 '전화소리가 끊기다.'

💡 **Example**

- The cell phone call began to break up.
  휴대폰 소리가 끊어지기 시작했어.

- You're breaking up!
  소리가 끊어져서 들려요!

 Dialog

A: Your voice isn't very clear.
B: I think this line is breaking up.

A: 네 목소리가 아주 분명하지 않아.
B: 아마 전화가 끊어질 것 같아.

Call your friend over here

저기 있는 네 친구 좀 불러주라

call sb over는 '…을 오라고 부르다.'

💡 **Example**

- Call your friend over here.
  저기 있는 네 친구 좀 불러주라.

- I'm on call at the hospital all weekend.
  주말 내내 병원에서 비상 대기해야 하거든요.

 Dialog

A: Do you want to go to a movie?
B: I'd like to, but I'm on call today.

A: 영화 보러 갈거니?
B: 그러고 싶은데, 난 오늘 대기해야 돼.

Let's call her cell phone

걔 핸드폰으로 전화해보자

call sb's cell phone은 '…의 핸드폰으로 전화하다,' call sb on your cell phone은 '네 핸드폰으로 …에게 전화하다.'

💡 **Example**

- I called my supervisor's cell phone.
  난 직장 상사의 핸드폰으로 전화했어.
- Call me on your cell phone when you are free.
  시간 날 때 핸드폰으로 전화해.

A: Paula never came to dinner.
B: Let's call her cell phone.

A: 폴라는 저녁 먹으러 오지 않았어.
B: 걔 핸드폰으로 전화해보자.

I had my cell phone on vibrate

핸폰을 진동으로 해놨어

have one's phone on vibrate는 '…이 핸폰을 진동으로 해놓다' = be set to vibrate.

💡 **Example**

- The students had their phones on vibrate.
  학생들은 자신들의 핸드폰을 진동모드로 했어.
- I always have my phone on vibrate. It's more polite.
  항상 핸드폰을 진동으로 해놔. 더 예절을 지키는 거지.

A: We must be quiet during the movie.
B: I have my cell phone on vibrate.

A: 우린 영화 도중에 조용히 해야 해.
B: 내 핸드폰을 진동으로 해놨어.

I kept my cell phone charged

내 핸폰 충전시켰어

keep one's cell phone charged는 '핸드폰을 충전시키다.'

💡 Example

- Keep your cell phone charged.
  네 핸드폰 충전시켜.
- I forgot my cell phone charger.
  핸드폰 충전기를 두고 왔어.

A: My phone isn't working again.
B: You need to keep your cell phone charged.

A: 내 전화가 또 안되네.
B: 넌 핸드폰을 충전시킬 필요가 있어.

I turned my cell phone off

핸드폰을 꺼놨어

turn my cell phone off는 '핸드폰을 끄다.' turn 대신에 switch도 가능.

💡 Example

- I'm sorry to trouble you, but could I borrow a cell phone?
  미안하지만 핸드폰 좀 빌릴 수 있을까요?
- I turned my cell phone off.
  핸드폰을 꺼놨어.

A: Can you call a taxi for me?
B: Sure, I'll use my cell phone.

A: 나한테 택시를 불러줄 수 있니?
B: 그럼, 내 핸드폰으로 할게.

I left early to beat the traffic

난 교통체증을 피하려 일찍 출발했어

beat the traffic은 '교통혼잡을 피하다,' '서둘러 막히기 전에 이동하다.'

 Example

- I had no idea that traffic was this bad in Seoul.
  서울교통이 이렇게 심한줄 정말 몰랐어.

- It was raining and there was a lot of traffic.
  비가 오고 있었고 교통이 매우 혼잡했어.

 Dialog

A: I usually try to get to the office by 6:45 to beat the traffic.
B: Then what time do you leave home for work?

A: 교통혼잡을 피하려고 보통 6시 45분까지 출근하려고 해.
B: 그럼, 몇 시에 집에서 출발하는데?

We got held up in town

우린 시내에 묶여 있었어

get held up 은 '(교통혼잡 등에) 지연되다,' '막히다,' get held up at work은 일로 늦어지다.

 Example

- They got held up at the airport.
  걔들은 공항에서 발이 묶였어.

- I got held up behind a traffic accident on the highway.
  고속도로에 사고나 꼼짝못했어.

Dialog

A: Why didn't you come to the picnic?
B: I'm sorry. We got held up in town.

A: 왜 소풍에 오지 않았어?
B: 미안해. 우린 시내에 묶여 있었어.

I pulled up to Mr. Lane's house

랜씨 집에 차를 세웠어

pull up은 차가 신호등에 걸렸을 때처럼 "멈추다," pull over는 차를 '길가에 세우다.'

💡 Example

- You should pull up a little further.
  조금 더 가서 차를 세워.
- I pulled up to Mr. Lane's house.
  랜씨 집에 차를 세웠어.

A: Where should I park my car?
B: Pull up in front of the apartment building.

A: 내 차를 어디에 주차해야 돼?
B: 아파트 건물 앞에 세워.

My car won't start

자동차 시동이 안걸려

~won't start는 (차량이) '시동이 걸리지 않다,' ~doesn't work는 (브레이크 등이) 작동하지 않다.

💡 Example

- Darryl's car won't start, so he must fix it.
  다릴의 차가 시동이 안걸려, 고쳐야겠어.
- Carol's new car won't start today.
  캐롤이 새로산 차가 오늘 시동이 걸리지 않아.

A: My car won't start. What should I do?
B: Why don't you call a repair shop?

A: 자동차 시동이 안걸려. 어떻게 해야 하지?
B: 정비소에 전화해.

I have to get my car repaired
난 차를 수리해야 돼

make repairs to+차량은 '(차를) 수리하다,' make 대신 carry out, do를 써도 된다.

💡 Example
- Do you know anything about repairing a car?
  차 수리에 대해 좀 알아?
- The repairs on your car are going to be really expensive.
  차 수리비가 정말 많이 나올거예요.

 Dialog

A: I plan to get my car repaired next weekend.
B: How long will it take to get it fixed?

A: 다음 주에 차 수리 받을 거야.
B: 차를 수리하는데 얼마나 걸릴까?

I got fined $200 for driving fast
과속으로 200달러 벌금맞았어

be fined+벌금+for a traffic violation은 '교통위반으로 …벌금을 부과받다.'

💡 Example
- My dad was fined $100 for a traffic violation during the holiday.
  아버지가 휴일에 교통위반으로 벌금 백 달러를 받았어.
- The student was fined over $500 for traffic violations.
  그 학생은 교통위반으로 500 달러가 넘는 벌금을 받았어.

 Dialog

A: Why are you so unhappy today?
B: I got fined $200 for driving too fast.

A: 왜 오늘 그렇게 불행해보이니?
B: 과속으로 벌금 200달러를 받았어.

116

The valet will bring up your car
주차요원이 네 차를 갖다 줄거야

valet는 주차를 대신해주는 사람. hand the valet the ticket은 주차요원에게 주차권을 주다.

💡 **Example**

- She **handed the valet a ticket** to get her car.
  주차요원에게 차가져다 달라고 주차권줬어.
- **A valet brought up our car** from the lot.
  주차요원이 주차장에서 우리 차를 가져왔어.

A: I'm ready to go home now.
B: The valet will bring up your car.
  A: 난 지금 집에 갈 준비가 되어있어.
  B: 주차요원이 네 차를 갖다 줄거야.

117

It took us an hour to clear customs
세관통과하는데 1시간이 걸렸어

clear customs는 '통관절차를 마치다' = go through customs.

💡 **Example**

- As soon as we **clear customs**, we're going to catch a cab.
  통관절차가 끝나자 마자 즉시 우린 택시를 잡아탈 거야.
- **The customs officer** asked me if I had brought any food with me.
  세관원이 음식물 들여오는게 있는지 물었어.

A: Do you have anything to declare?
B: No, we only have personal belongings.
  A: 신고한 물건이 있나요?
  B: 아뇨, 단지 개인소지품뿐이예요.

Who is available now?

누가 시간이 돼?

be available to~는 '…할 시간이 되다. 시간을 낼 수 있다'라는 의미이다.

💡 **Example**

- I'm not sure if I am available Friday.
  내가 금요일에 시간되는지 모르겠어.

- I'd like to speak with Mark, if he is available.
  마크가 가능하면 통화하고 싶은데요.

 Dialog

A: Do you need to visit a dentist?
B: Yeah. Who is available now?

　A: 넌 치과의사를 방문해야 돼니?
　B: 그럼요. 어느 의사가 가능하니?

We have an hour before school ends

우리는 한시간 지나면 학교끝나

have+시간+to+V before S+V는 '…하기 전에 …할 시간이 있다.'

💡 **Example**

- We have a couple of hours before school ends.
  우리는 두시간지나야 학교끝나.

- I have a few hours before I need to go home.
  집에 가야할 때까지 몇시간 있어.

 Dialog

A: The movie starts at eight.
B: We have time to eat before it begins.

　A: 영화가 8시에 시작해.
　B: 시작하기 전에 먹을 시간이 있겠다.

120

We put in two hours so far
지금까지 2시간 일했어
put in+시간명사는 '…에 시간을 투자하다,' '쏟다.'

💡 **Example**

- Workers must put in thirty years before retiring.
  근로자들은 퇴직까지 30년간 일해야돼.

- The baseball players put a lot of energy into playing.
  야구선수들은 시합에 많은 에너지를 쏟는다.

 Dialog

A: How long have you been working here?
B: We put in seven hours so far.

A: 여기서 얼마동안 일한거야?
B: 지금까지 7시간 일했어.

121

I was up for an hour exercising
난 운동하면서 1시간을 보냈어
be up+시간명사+ ~ing는 '…하면서 …을 보내다' be up all night ~ing는 '밤새 …하다.'

💡 **Example**

- Jim was up all night playing computer games.
  짐은 밤새 컴퓨터게임을 했어.

- The campers were up for hours singing songs.
  캠퍼들은 수시간 노래를 불렀어.

 Dialog

A: Susan was up for an hour exercising.
B: She's always in good physical condition.

A: 수잔은 운동하면서 1시간을 보냈어.
B: 걘 항상 건강상태가 좋아.

122

It didn't take long before we broke up
오래지 않아 우리는 헤어졌어

It didn't take long before~는 '…하는데 시간이 많이 걸리지 않았다.'

💡 **Example**

- It didn't take long before the thunderstorm began.
  곧 뇌우가 시작되었지.

- It didn't take long before he finished his ice cream.
  걘 금방 아이스크림을 먹어치웠어.

 Dialog

A: Did Heather and Ralph break up?
B: Yes, but it didn't take long before they were back together.

A: 헤더와 랠프는 헤어졌니?
B: 응, 근데 곧 재결합했어.

123

It has been a week since he died
걔가 죽은지 일주일 됐어

it has been+시간명사+since~는 '…한지 시간이 …됐다.'

💡 **Example**

- It has been a week since our last rainstorm.
  마지막 폭풍우가 있은지 일주일 됐어.

- It has been six months since he joined the army.
  걔가 입대한지 6개월이 되었어.

 Dialog

A: Have you seen Gina lately?
B: It has been a few years since I've seen her.

A: 요즘 지나를 보았니?
B: 내가 걜 본지 몇 년이 되었어.

It's high time he finds a good job

걔가 좋은 직장을 잡을 호기야

It's about time S+V는 '…할 시기이다,' '…해야 할 때이다.' 좀 늦었다는 뉘앙스.

Example
- It's time for you to get married.
  네가 결혼할 시기야.
- It's high time he finds a good job.
  걔가 좋은 직장을 잡을 호기야.

A: **It's about time** we got a raise.
B: **You're telling me.**

A: 임금을 올려 받을 때야.
B: 네 말이 맞아.

I know you're up to something

네가 뭔가 꾸미는거 난 알고 있어

be up to something은 '…을 꾸미고 있다,' '…을 계획하고 있다.'

Example
- I think those teenagers are up to something.
  저 10대 애들이 뭔가 꾸미고 있다고 생각돼.
- Angelina Jolie is always up to something.
  안젤리나 졸리는 항상 뭔가를 꾸미고 있어.

A: You look like you're **up to something**.
B: I feel like selling my stocks.

A: 너 어째 뭔가 좀 다른 걸 해보려고 하는 것 같은데.
B: 내 주식을 좀 팔까 봐.

He is bound to lose the race

걔는 경주에서 질게 뻔해

be bound to+V는 '…할 예정이다,' '…하지 않을 수 없다' = be very likely to.

Example

- You're bound to get fat from eating so much.
  과식으로 뚱뚱해지지 않을 수 없어.
- This new car is bound to become popular.
  이 새 차는 인기를 얻을 수 밖에 없어.

A: Dan is a very slow runner.
B: I think he is bound to lose the race.

A: 댄은 매우 늦은 주자야.
B: 걘 경주에서 질 것으로 생각돼.

The bus is due to arrive at 7 p.m

버스는 오후 7시에 도착예정이야

be due to+V는 '…할 예정이다,' due to+N[~ing]는 '…때문에.'

Example

- Kerry can't be here due to getting sick.
  케리는 아파서 여기 올 수가 없어.
- The bus was late due to breaking down.
  버스가 고장나서 늦었어.

A: The plane is not due to arrive for another hour.
B: Then we have time for another drink.

A: 한 시간 더 있어야 비행기가 도착할 거라는 군.
B: 그럼 한 잔 더 할 시간이 있겠구나.

I'd better call and reschedule

일정을 재조정하는 편이 낫겠어

rearrange one's schedule은 '…의 일정을 조정하다,' fit sth into one's schedule는 '…의 일정에 맞추다.'

 Example

- My boss rearranged his schedule on Thursday.
  보스가 목요일 일정을 재조정했어.

- The tour company rearranged its schedule.
  관광회사가 관광일정을 다시 잡았어.

 Dialog

A: Traffic in Seoul can be a real killer.
B: I guess I'd better call and reschedule.

A: 서울의 교통은 정말 죽여줘.
B: 전화해서 일정을 재조정하는 편이 낫겠어.

We've set a date for the festival

우린 축제 날짜를 정했어

set a date (for~)는 '(약속 등의) 날짜를 잡다' = fix a date.

 Example

- Harry and Melinda set a date to get married.
  해리와 멜린다는 결혼 날짜를 잡았어.

- We've set a date for the festival.
  우린 축제 날짜를 정했어.

Dialog

A: I've got to schedule an appointment with the surgeon.
B: Well, make sure you let me know when you set a date.

A: 외과의사하고 약속시간을 정해야 해.
B: 그럼, 날짜가 잡히면 내게 꼭 알려줘야 돼.

I set up a schedule for today

난 오늘 스케줄을 잡았어

set up a schedule (for/of~)는 '…의 일정을 잡다.'

💡 **Example**

- I set up a schedule for this weekend.
  난 이번 주말 스케줄을 잡았어.

- Did Jeff set up a schedule for his schoolwork?
  제프가 학업 스케줄을 잡았니?

 Dialog

A: I'm visiting ten countries in Europe.
B: You should set up a schedule of things to see.
   A: 난 유럽 10개국을 방문할거야.
   B: 넌 관광 계획을 짜야 돼.

This car was designed to go fast

이 차는 빨리 달리게 고안되었어

be designed to+V는 특정한 용도로 '…하기로 의도되다,' '예정되다.'

💡 **Example**

- This sports car was designed to go fast.
  이 스포츠 카는 빨리 달리게 고안되었지.

- This building was designed to be comfortable.
  이 빌딩은 편안하도록 설계되어 있어.

 Dialog

A: Is this computer program useful?
B: It was designed to make work easier.
   A: 이 컴퓨터 프로그램은 유용하니?
   B: 그건 일을 좀 더 쉽게 해주기위해 만들어졌어.

He came by to keep me company

걘 나랑 같이 있어주려고 들렀어

keep sb company는 '…와 동행하다,' '같이 있어주다.' company는 다른 사람과 함께 있는 상대.

💡 **Example**

- He came by to keep me company.
  걘 나랑 같이 있어주려고 들렀어.

- My mom's dog always keeps her company.
  우리 엄마 애견은 항상 엄마랑 같이 있어.

 Dialog

A: Helen has been in the hospital since yesterday.
B: I should go there and keep her company.

　A: 헬렌은 어제 이래 입원해있어.
　B: 거기 가서 같이 있어줘야겠다.

You better buzz him in

걔한테 문을 열어줘

buzz sb in는 '인터폰이 울리면 문열어주다.'

💡 **Example**

- Sharon didn't buzz the stranger in.
  샤론은 낯선 사람에게 문을 열어주지 않았어.

- The doorman buzzed me in.
  도어맨이 나에게 문을 열어줬어.

 Dialog

A: Jerry is standing outside the door.
B: You better buzz him in.

　A: 제리가 문밖에 서있어.
　B: 걔한테 문을 열어주는게 좋아.

I'll **walk you to** your car

네 차있는 데까지 바래다 줄게

walk sb to~는 '…를 …까지 배웅하다.' walk는 타동사로 '강아지 산책시키다'라는 뜻도 있음.

💡 Example

- Jason **walked Cindy to** her home.
  제이슨은 신디를 집까지 바래다줬어.

- You don't have to **walk me home**.
  집까지 바래다줄 것까진 없는데.

A: It's time for me to drive home.
B: I'll **walk you to** your car.

A: 내가 운전해서 귀가할 시간이야.
B: 네 차있는 데까지 바래다 줄게.

It's difficult to **get a hold of** him

걔와 연락하기가 어려워

get a hold of~는 '…와 연락이 되다(get through to sb),' '…을 얻다(obtain).'

💡 Example

- She needs to **get a hold of** a lawyer.
  걘 변호사와 연락할 필요가 있어.

- I've been trying to **get a hold of** you all morning!
  아침 내내 네게 연락하려고 했어!

A: Mike never answers his e-mail.
B: It's difficult to **get a hold of** him.

A: 마이크는 이메일에 결코 답을 하지 않아.
B: 걔와 연락하기가 어렵군.

The flights are all booked

비행기가 다 예약됐어

be booked (up)은 '다 예약되다,' '예약이 끝나다.'

Example
- Every bus to Seoul was all booked up.
  서울행 버스가 모조리 예약이 끝났대.
- I tried to leave but the train was booked up.
  난 떠나려고 했는데 기차예약이 끝났어.

A: Why don't you make a reservation on Northwest Airlines?
B: I tried, but the flights are all booked.

A: 노스웨스트 항공사에 예약하는 게 어때?
B: 해봤어. 하지만 비행기가 다 예약됐대.

Do you get on well with your wife?

네 아내하고 잘 지내?

get on well with sb는 '…와 사이좋게 지내다.'

Example
- He got on well with his boss.
  걘 자기 보스하고 잘 지내.
- Try to get on well with everyone.
  누구와도 사이좋게 지내도록 노력해봐.

A: Does Dave get on well with his wife?
B: No, they are always arguing.

A: 데이브가 자기 아내하고 잘 지내니?
B: 아니, 걔들은 항상 다퉈.

Logan and I go way back

로간과 난 오랜 친구야

go way back은 '오랜 친구이다,' 즉 오래전부터 알고 지내던 막연한 친구라는 뜻.

 Example

- Their close relationship goes way back.
  걔들의 가까운 관계는 매우 오래됐지.
- Janice and Ian's friendship goes way back.
  재니스와 이안의 우정은 매우 오래 되었지.

 Dialog

A: Have you ever met my friend Logan?
B: Yes. Logan and I go way back.

A: 내 친구 로간을 만나본 적이 있니?
B: 그럼. 로간과 난 오랜 친구야.

I'll get back to you on that

나중에 그거에 대해 말해줄게

get back to sb (on sth)은 '…에게 나중에 …에 대해 연락하다[알려주다].'

 Example

- I'm sorry I didn't get back to you sooner.
  더 빨리 연락 못 줘서 미안해.
- I'll get back to you on that. I might have other plans.
  나중에 말해줄게. 다른 일이 있을지도 모르거든.

Dialog

A: I need a decision from you. Get back to me.
B: I'll call you tomorrow morning.

A: 너의 결정이 필요해. 나중에 연락해.
B: 내일 아침 연락할게.

Let me say I'm proud of you
네가 자랑스럽다고 말하고 싶어
let me say~는 '(소감을 한마디) 말하겠다,' '…에 대해 말하자면.'

💡 **Example**

- Let me say that this can be repaired.
  이건 고칠 수 있다고 말하겠어.

- Let me say that you look very nice tonight.
  말하자면 넌 오늘 밤 무지 멋있게 보여.

 Dialog

A: Are you happy about Aurora's performance?
B: **Let me say that** it was very disappointing.

A: 오로라의 공연에 만족하니?
B: 아주 실망스러웠다고 말하겠어.

Guess What?

You can't have your cake and eat it too
두마리 토끼를 잡을 수는 없잖아

직역하면 케익을 갖고 있으며 또 먹기도 한다라는 것으로 보통은 함께 갖는 것이 불가능한 좋은 일 두 가지를 차지하다(to somehow have two good or positive things that are usually not possible to have together)라는 의미이다. 굳이 우리말로 하자면 '독차지하다,' '두마리 토끼를 잡다'이다. 주로 You can't have your cake and eat it too!의 형태로 "두마리 토끼를 다 잡을 수는 없다"의 의미로 사용된다.

141

Let's put our heads together
머리를 맞대고 의논해보자

put one's heads together는 '머리를 맞대고 의논하다.'

💡 **Example**

- We put our heads together and created a program.
  우린 머리를 맞대고 프로그램을 만들어냈어.

- We can put our heads together and fix this.
  우린 머리를 맞대고 이 문제를 해결할 수 있어.

 **Dialog**

A: It's too difficult to solve this problem.
B: Let's put our heads together and figure it out.

A: 이 문제를 해결하기는 무척 어려워.
B: 머리를 맞대고 해결책을 찾아보자.

142

Run it by me one more time
한 번 더 내게 설명해봐

run it[that] by sb는 '…에게 …을 설명하다, …에 관해서 상담하다.'

💡 **Example**

- Run it by me one more time.
  한 번 더 내게 설명해봐.

- I'll run it by my wife tonight.
  난 오늘 밤 그것에 대한 아내의 의견을 들어볼 거야.

 **Dialog**

A: Do you like my new ideas?
B: I need to run them by my boss.

A: 내 새로운 아이디어가 어떠니?
B: 내 보스에게 그 아이디어를 설명할 필요가 있어요.

Speaking of health, let's go jogging

건강에 대해 말하자면 조깅을 하러 가자

speaking of sth은 '…에 대해 말한다면,' 그중 speaking of which는 '얘기가 나왔으니 말인데.'

 Example

- Speaking of your sister, how has she been?
  네 여동생에 대해 말하자면 걘 요즘 어떻게 지내니?
- Speaking of lunch, let's get something to eat.
  점심? 그러고 보니 먹으러 가자.

 Dialog

A: I just joined a health club.
B: **Speaking of** health, let's go jogging.

A: 난 방금 헬스클럽에 가입했어.
B: 건강에 대해 말하자면 조깅을 하러 가자.

She's headed for New York City

걔는 뉴욕시로 향해 가고 있어

be headed for~는 '…으로 향하다,' 여기서 head는 동사로 'go toward.'

 Example

- Bette is headed for New York City.
  베티는 뉴욕시로 향해 가고 있어.
- We're headed for a large campground.
  우린 큰 캠프장을 향하고 있어.

Dialog

A: By the way, what are you doing tonight?
B: **I'm headed to** the library.

A: 근데, 오늘 밤에 뭐할거야?
B: 도서관에 가려고.

I'm off to China in the morning

난 아침에 중국으로 떠나

be off to+장소명사[혹은 동사]는 '…로 서둘러 떠나다,' '출발하다' = take off.

💡 Example

- Well, I'm off to China in the morning.
  난 아침에 중국으로 떠나.

- I am leaving with my best friend.
  난 절친과 함께 떠날 거야.

A: I saw your kids leave in a taxi.
B: Yes, they are off to their grandmother's house.

A: 네 애들이 택시로 떠나는 것을 봤어.
B: 그래, 걔들은 할머니 댁으로 떠난거야.

I have been to the station

주유소 갔다 왔어

have been to+장소는 '…에 갔었다,' '…에 갔다 왔다.' 화장실이나 미장원같이 가까운 곳도 사용.

💡 Example

- She had been to the Lourve Museum.
  걘 루브르 박물관을 다녀왔어.

- Tad has been to the best restaurant in Busan.
  태드는 부산에서 제일 좋은 식당을 가 본적이 있어.

A: Have you traveled much internationally?
B: Yes, I have been to 36 different countries.

A: 넌 국제적으로 여행을 많이 했니?
B: 네, 36개 국을 다녀봤어요.

147

Hope you can make it

네가 오면 좋겠어

make it to+장소하면 '시간에 늦지 않게 …에 도착하다.' make it만으로도 사용가능.

💡 **Example**

- Helen can't make it to Washington DC.
  헬렌은 워싱턴 DC에 가지 못했어.

- We're having a party for Tom. Hope you can make it.
  탐에게 파티를 열어주려고 해. 너도 올 수 있었으면 좋겠다

A: I won't be able to make it to the presentation.
B: That's okay. I'll take notes for you.

A: 발표회에 가지 못할 것 같아.
B: 걱정 마. 내가 대신 노트해 줄게.

148

I'll pick you up at 9 am

아침 9시에 데리러 갈게

pick up은 '차로 …를 데려오다,' '차로 데려가다.'

💡 **Example**

- I'll pick you up tomorrow at 9 a.m.
  내일 아침 9시에 데리러 올게.

- Do you need me to pick you up from the airport?
  공항에서 널 픽업해 줄 필요가 있니?

A: We are on our way to the airport to pick up the boss.
B: Did you check to see if his flight is arriving on time?

A: 사장님 모시러 공항에 가는 길이야.
B: 비행기가 정시에 도착하는지 알아봤니?

149

I can stick around for a while

잠시 주변에 있을 수 있어

stick around는 '예정보다 좀 더 길게 주변에 머무르다.' stick with는 '…의 곁에 머물다.'

💡 **Example**

- She'll stick around until eleven tonight.
  걘 오늘 밤 11시까지 가지 않고 있을 거야.

- Greg stuck around the nightclub.
  그레그는 나이트클럽 주변에서 얼쩡댔어.

 Dialog

A: Are you in a hurry to leave?
B: No, I can stick around for a while.

A: 너 빨리 떠나야하니?
B: 아니, 잠시 주변에 있을 수 있어.

150

We are on a first name basis

우리는 친한 사이야

call by one's first name은 '이름을 부르다,' be on a first name basis는 '친한 사이다.'

💡 **Example**

- Don't call our boss by his first name.
  우리 보스의 이름을 부르지마.

- She called her mom by her first name.
  걘 엄마의 이름을 불렀어.

 Dialog

A: Do you know the manger well?
B: Yes, I do. We are on a first name basis.

A: 매니저 잘 알아?
B: 어 그래. 친한 사이야.

151

Don't talk back to our boss

보스에게 말대꾸하지마

talk back to sb는 '…에게 말대꾸하다.'

💡 **Example**

- Brett was punished when he talked back.
  브렛은 말대꾸할 때 처벌을 받았어.

- Don't talk back to our boss.
  우리 보스에게 말대꾸하지마.

A: It is very rude to talk back to teachers.
B: Parents must teach children good manners.

A: 선생님에게 말대꾸하는 것은 매우 무례한 일이야.
B: 부모님들이 애들에게 좋은 매너를 가르쳐야 해.

152

I fixed her up with my friend

난 그녀에게 내 친구를 소개시켜줬어

fix A up with B는 'A에게 B를 소개시켜주다'로 fix 대신에 set을 써도 된다.

💡 **Example**

- Lisa set Rebecca up with her friend.
  리사가 레베카에게 자신의 친구를 소개시켰어.

- Let's set my sister up with a nice guy.
  내 여동생에게 괜찮은 친구를 소개시켜주자.

A: I'm going to fix you up with a date.
B: I'd rather go to the party all by myself.

A: 내가 소개팅시켜줄게.
B: 그 파티에 그냥 혼자 갈래.

455

She finally fell for Chris

갠 마침내 크리스를 좋아하게 됐어

fall for sb는 '…에게 반하다,' fall for sth은 '…에 속아 넘어가다.'

💡 **Example**

- I fell for her while we were dancing.
  우리가 춤을 추었을 때 난 걔에게 반했지.

- Tara fell for a boy in her class.
  타라는 자기 학급의 한 남학생에게 빠졌어.

Dialog

A: I have heard Barb is in love.
B: She fell for a man who is much older than her.

A: 바브가 사랑에 빠져있다고 들었어.
B: 걘 자기보다 훨씬 나이 많은 남성에 반했어.

They ended up splitting up

걔네들은 결국 헤어졌어

split up (with sb)는 '(…와) 헤어지다' = be separated from sb.

💡 **Example**

- It's over between Jen and Terry.
  젠과 테리 관계는 끝났어.

- My girlfriend told me it's over with us.
  여친은 우리 관계가 끝이 났다고 내게 말했어.

Dialog

A: Fran and Barb are always fighting.
B: I'm thinking that they should split up.

A: 프랜과 바브는 언제나 싸워.
B: 걔들은 헤어져야 한다고 생각해.

155

She is expecting a baby
걘 임신중이야

expect a baby는 '임신중이다,' '출산예정이다.' be in labor는 '진통중이다,' deliver는 '분만하다.'

 Example

- The married couple is expecting a baby soon.
  그 결혼 커플은 조만간 출산예정이야.

- She doesn't have a stomachache, she's in labor.
  걘 복통이 아니라 산고로 진통하고 있어.

 Dialog

A: Heather looks like she is pregnant.
B: She is expecting a baby in a few months.

A: 헤더는 임신한 것처럼 보여.
B: 걘 몇 달안에 출산할거야.

156

I was a party to cheating
나도 사기에 가담했어

be a party to~은 '…에 관계[가담]하다.'

 Example

- Debbie was a party to the theft.
  데비는 절도에 관여했어.

- I'm not going to be a party to your lie.
  난 네 거짓에 가담하지 않을거야.

Dialog

A: Jacob was a party to cheating.
B: Well, we will have to punish him.

A: 제이콥은 사기에 가담했어.
B: 그래, 걘 처벌해야겠구나.

157

It has to do with our family
그건 우리 가족과 관련된 일이야

have to do with sb[sth]는 '…와 관련이 있다' = have something to do with sb[sth].

💡 **Example**

- What does stress have to do with my sickness?
  스트레스하고 내 병이 무슨 상관이 있나요?
- What does that have to do with you?
  그게 너와 무슨 관계가 있니?

 Dialog

A: What do you want to talk about?
B: It has to do with our class schedule.
　A: 넌 무엇에 대해 이야기할거니?
　B: 우리 학급 스케줄과 관련된거야.

158

Get your hands off of my car!
내 차에 손대지마!

get one's hands off of~는 '…에서 손을 떼다.' of는 생략가능하다.

💡 **Example**

- Get your hands off of that candy!
  그 캔디로부터 손을 떼!
- Get your hands off of my new car!
  내 새차에 손대지마!

 Dialog

A: Get your hands off of my money!
B: I was just counting it for you.
　A: 내 돈에서 손을 떼라!
　B: 단지 널 위해 세고 있었던거야.

159

She keeps late hours

걘 늦게 자고 늦게 일어나

keep late hours는 '늦게 자고 늦게 일어나다(저녁형 인간)' <=> keep early hours.

💡 **Example**

- I'm tired because I've been keeping late hours.
  난 늘 늦게 자기 때문에 피곤해.

- She prefers to keep late hours.
  걘 늦게 자는 것을 선호해.

 **Dialog**

A: The light in Mike's window is always on.
B: That's because he keeps late hours.

A: 마이크 집 창문 속의 불빛은 항상 켜있어.
B: 걔가 늦게 자기 때문이지.

160

We'd better turn in early tonight

우리는 오늘밤 일찍 자야 돼

turn in은 좀 의외의 표현으로 '잠자리에 들다'라는 의미.

💡 **Example**

- I'm ready to turn in for the night.
  일찍 잠자리에 들 준비가 되었어.

- When is everyone going to turn in?
  모두들 언제 잠자리에 들건가?

 **Dialog**

A: We have to leave at 4 am tomorrow.
B: I think we'd better turn in early tonight.

A: 우리 내일 새벽 4시에 떠나야해.
B: 우리가 오늘 밤 일찍 잠자리에 드는 것이 좋겠어.

I got my hair cut

나 머리잘랐어

get one's hair cut은 미장원이나 다른 사람이 머리를 잘라줬다는 의미 = have[get] a haircut.

Example

- I'll get my hair cut on Wednesday afternoon.
  난 수요일 오후에 머리를 자를 거야.

- Did you just get your hair cut?
  너 네 머리를 잘랐니?

 Dialog

A: You look different today.
B: I got my hair cut. Does it look good?

A: 너 오늘 좀 달라보인다.
B: 머리를 잘랐거든. 보기 좋아?

That shirt looks good on you

그 셔츠가 네게 잘 어울려

의상+look good[nice] on sb는 '…가 …에게 좋아 보이다,' '잘 어울리다.'

Example

- Do these glasses look good on me?
  이 안경이 내게 맞는 것 같니?

- All clothes look good on her.
  모든 옷들이 걔에게 잘 맞아.

 Dialog

A: That shirt looks good on you.
B: Thank you. I just bought it.

A: 그 셔츠가 네게 잘 어울려.
B: 고마워. 방금 산거야.

It was hard to keep a straight face

웃음을 참기 어려웠어

keep a straight face는 '웃음을 참다' = keep one's face straight= hold back one's laughter.

💡 Example

- Can you keep a straight face when Sam tells jokes?
  샘이 농담을 할 때 웃음을 참을 수 있니?
- I can never keep a straight face when I lie.
  난 거짓말을 할 때면 결코 웃지 않을 수가 없어.

A: I can't believe our teacher made that mistake.
B: I know. It was hard to keep a straight face.

A: 우리 선생님이 그런 실수를 했다는 걸 믿을 수 없어.
B: 알아. 웃음을 참기 어려웠지.

They sighed with relief

걔네들은 안도의 한숨을 쉬었어

sigh with relief는 '안도의 한숨을 쉬다' = give a sigh of relief.

💡 Example

- I'm going to sigh with relief when this report is done.
  보고서 끝나면 안도의 한숨을 쉴거야.
- Pam sighed with relief when school was canceled.
  팸은 수업이 취소되자 무지 안심했어.

A: What happened when the exam finished?
B: All of the students sighed with relief.

A: 시험이 끝날 때 어땠니?
B: 학생들 모두 안도의 한숨을 쉬었지.

I finally settled down here

난 마침내 여기에 정착했어

settle down은 '자리를 잡다,' '정착하다.' settle down to sth은 '~에 집중하기 시작하다.'

💡 Example

- I'd like to settle down somewhere in the country.
  난 시골 어딘가에 정착하길 바래.

- Jane and Dick settled down and had some kids.
  제인과 딕은 정착해 애들을 몇 낳았어.

 Dialog

A: I'm happy that I'm finished with military service.
B: Are you going to settle down now?

A: 이제 군대를 마치니 정말 행복해.
B: 이제 정착할거니?

It's gone up to 70 degrees

70도까지 기온이 올라갔어

go up to ~degrees는 '기온이 …까지 올라가다.' degrees 다음에 Fahrenheit가 생략된 것.

💡 Example

- The temperature will go up to 90 degrees today.
  오늘 기온이 90도까지 올라갈 거야.

- The temperatures on the beach went up to 87 degrees.
  바닷가 온도가 87도까지 올라갔어.

 Dialog

A: Did you turn on the heater?
B: Sure, it's gone up to 70 degrees.

A: 히터를 틀었니?
B: 그럼, 70도까지 기온이 올라갔잖아.

Come and get it

와서 식사해라

come and get it은 '와서 식사해라' = Dinner is serviced.

💡 **Example**
- Dinner is served. Come and get it.
  저녁이 준비되었어. 와서 먹어라.
- Take anything you want. Come and get it.
  원하는 것 아무거나 집어. 와서 먹어.

 Dialog

A: **Everything is ready. Come and get it.**
B: **This food looks like it will be good to eat.**

　A: 모든 것이 차려졌어. 와서 식사해라.
　B: 이 음식은 먹기에 좋아 보이네요.

Can I freshen up your drink?

술한잔 더 따라줄까?

freshen up은 '뭔가 새롭게 하다'라는 의미로 여기서는 '술잔을 새로 채우다.'

💡 **Example**
- The waiter will freshen up our drinks.
  웨이터가 우리 술잔을 다시 채워줄거야.
- Could you freshen up my tonic water?
  탄산음료 좀 새로 따라줄래?

 Dialog

A: **Can I freshen up your drink?**
B: **Sure. I'm drinking cocktails tonight.**

　A: 술한잔 더 따라줄까?
　B: 그래. 오늘밤에 칵테일을 마실게.

I feel tipsy

좀 취했어

get tipsy는 '약간 취기가 있다,'로 get 대신에 feel을 써도 된다.

💡 **Example**

- I need to go home. I feel tipsy.
  나 집에 가야 돼. 좀 취했어.

- She got tipsy after a few shots of whisky.
  위스키 몇잔 먹고 걘 취했어.

 Dialog

A: That was the best party we ever had.
B: Yeah, most of the guests got tipsy.

A: 어느때보다도 가장 멋진 파티였어.
B: 그래, 손님들 대부분 좀 취했어.

The special comes with a salad

스페셜메뉴에는 샐러드가 함께 나와

A comes with B는 'A에는 B가 함께 나온다'로 A에는 메인상품이 나온다.

💡 **Example**

- Does this vacation come with a free car rental?
  이 휴가여행에는 자동차 무료 대여도 달려있는 건가요?

- The pie comes with a scoop of ice cream.
  이 파이는 아이스크림 한 스쿠프가 같이 나와요.

 Dialog

A: All of our specials come with a salad and dessert.
B: Okay, I think I'll have special number 2, please.

A: 저희 모든 특별요리에는 샐러드와 디저트가 나옵니다.
B: 알겠습니다. 두 번째 특별요리로 하죠.

Would you care for some salad?

샐러드 좀 들래요?

Would you care for~?는 '…을 드시겠어요?' care for는 부정/의문문에서 '좋아하다'.

💡 **Example**

- Would you care for some salad dressing?
  샐러드 드레싱을 드시겠어요?

- Would you care for some chocolate ice cream?
  초코렛 아이스크림을 좀 하시겠습니까?

💡 **Dialog**

A: I would like to have a hot dog.
B: Would you care for some mustard on it?

A: 난 핫도그를 원합니다.
B: 그 위에 겨자를 좀 뿌려 드릴까요?

This one is on me

이번은 내가 낼게

be on sb는 '…가 돈을 내다' = be one's treat. be on the house는 '가게주인이 내다.'

💡 **Example**

- Order anything you want because it's on me.
  내가 쏠 테니까 먹고 싶은 거 아무거나 다 시켜.

- Let's go out for dinner and drink's on me.
  저녁식사하러 나가죠. 술을 제가 살테니.

💡 **Dialog**

A: This one is on me.
B: Thanks a lot! I'll pay for lunch tomorrow.

A: 이번은 내가 낼게.
B: 고마워! 내일 점심은 내가 내지 뭐.

Let's split the bill

각자 내자

split the bill은 '돈을 나눠서 각자 내다' = go Dutch = go fifty-fifty with.

Example
- We split the bill among five people.
  우린 5명이 계산서를 나누어 냈어.
- They split the bill for their dinner.
  걔들은 저녁식사비를 나누어 냈어.

 Dialog

A: Let's split the bill.
B: That sounds like a good idea.
  A: 각자 내자
  B: 좋은 생각이야.

I'm going to fix myself a drink

난 스스로 음료를 만들어 마실거야

fix sb sth은 '…에게 …를 준비해주다,' 여기서 fix는 '음식이나 음료를 준비하다.'

Example
- I'm going to fix myself a drink.
  난 스스로 음료를 만들어 마실 거야.
- You should fix them some coffee.
  넌 걔들에게 커피를 만들어 줘라.

 Dialog

A: Kevin is waiting in the living room.
B: Fix him some coffee while he waits.
  A: 케빈은 거실에서 기다리고 있어.
  B: 걔가 기다리는 동안 커피 좀 타줘라.

I'll set off for Hawaii soon

조만간 하와이로 떠날 예정이야

set off for~는 '…로 가기 시작하다.'

💡 **Example**

- Her mom set off for the high school.
  걔 엄마는 고등학교로 가기 시작했어.

- Each person set off for a different place.
  각각의 사람들이 서로 다른 곳으로 떠나고 있어.

 **Dialog**

A: Are you all ready to begin your vacation?
B: Sure. I'll set off for Hawaii soon.

A: 넌 휴가를 시작할 모든 준비가 되고 있니?
B: 물론이지. 난 조만간 하와이로 떠날 예정이야.

Guess What?

I try to keep my head above water
난 간신히 버티려고 노력하고 있어

경제적으로 간신히 꾸려나가다라는 의미의 표현. 다시 말해서 물에 빠지지 않고 간신히 살아 있는 그림에서 보듯 비즈니스에서 어렵게 꾸역꾸역 버티고 있다, 혹은 뭔가 어려운 상황 하에서도 뭔가 계속하다(to survive, especially as a business, or to continue doing something, even in difficult circumstances)라는 뜻으로 쓰인다.

176

Don't fool around with my car

내 차 가지고 장난하지마

fool around (with sb/sth)는 '빈둥거리다, 장난치다' = goof around.

 **Example**

- Don't fool around with my car.
  내 차 가지고 장난하지마.
- I'm going to fool around with this computer.
  이 컴퓨터를 가지고 놀거야.

 Dialog

A: Who was making all of that noise?
B: Some kids were fooling around with each other.

A: 누가 저 소음을 전부 내고 있냐?
B: 애들이 서로 떠들면서 장난치고 있었어.

177

I hung out with Chris

난 크리스와 어울려 놀았어

hang out (with sb)는 '(…와) 시간을 보내다, 어울리다.' = hang around (with sb).

 **Example**

- Stay a little longer and hang out with me.
  더 남아서 나랑 놀자.
- Do you know of any cool places to hang out?
  가서 놀 만한 근사한 데 어디 알아?

Dialog

A: What did you do Saturday night?
B: I hung out with an old friend of mine.

A: 토요일 저녁엔 무얼 하니?
B: 오랜 친구랑 시간을 보냈어.

How about we go to a movie tonight?

오늘 저녁 영화보러 가는거 어때?

go to a movie는 '영화를 보러 가다(영화에 초점)' = go to the movies는 '영화관에 가다(영화관에 초점).'

💡 **Example**

- How about we go to a movie tonight?
  오늘 저녁 영화보러 가는거 어때?
- How often do you go to the movies?
  영화 얼마나 자주 보러 가니?

A: Why don't we go to the movies tonight?
B: Why don't you get lost?

A: 오늘 영화보러 갈래?
B: 좀 사라져 줄래?

My birthday fell on a Monday

내 생일은 월요일이야

특정한 날+fall on+요일은 '…가 …요일이다.' 주어로는 기념일, 생일 등이 온다.

💡 **Example**

- Joe's birthday fell on a Wednesday.
  조의 생일은 수요일이야.
- The lunar new year falls on a different day each year.
  구정은 매년 다른 날에 돌아와.

A: What day is Christmas Eve this year?
B: I think it will fall on a Saturday.

A: 금년 크리스마스 이브는 무슨 요일이니?
B: 토요일인 것 같아.

It is difficult to keep in shape

계속 건강을 유지하는 것은 어려워

keep in shape은 '건강을 유지하다' = keep[maintain] one's health.

💡 Example

- It is difficult to keep in shape.
  계속 건강을 유지하는 것은 어려워.
- Those women do aerobics to keep in shape.
  저 여성들은 건강을 유지하기 위해 에어로빅을 하고 있어.

 Dialog

A: How are you able to keep in shape?
B: I go jogging almost every day.
  A: 어떻게 건강을 유지하는 거야?
  B: 난 거의 매일 조깅을 해.

Tony contracted a disease

토니는 병에 걸렸어

contract a disease는 '병에 걸리다' = get[catch] a disease(더 캐주얼함).

💡 Example

- I don't know when I contracted this disease.
  난 언제 이 병에 걸렸는지 모르겠어.
- Do you think he contracted the disease while in Africa?
  그가 아프리카에 있는 동안 병에 걸렸다고 생각하세요?

 Dialog

A: How was your overseas church trip?
B: One of our members contracted a disease.
  A: 교회에서 간 해외여행은 어땠어?
  B: 그룹중 한명이 병에 걸렸어.

My cold went away after a while
감기가 얼마 후에 나았어

병+go away~는 '(병이나 아픔이) 없어지다.'

💡 **Example**

- A cold will go away in about a week.
  약 1주일이면 추위도 사라질 거야.

- My sore throat went away after a while.
  목감기가 잠시 후 괜찮아졌어.

 Dialog

A: Many students start to cough in the winter.
B: It will go away when nicer weather comes.

　A: 많은 학생들이 겨울에 기침을 시작하지.
　B: 날씨가 좋아지면 기침도 사라질 거야.

I just finished working out
난 방금 운동을 끝냈어

work out은 '(특히 gym에서) 운동하다,' workout은 명사로 '운동.'

💡 **Example**

- Morning is her favorite time to work out.
  걔한테는 아침이 가장 좋은 운동시간이야.

- If you work out, you will become stronger.
  만약 네가 운동을 하면 강건해질거야.

 Dialog

A: Why are you sweating so much?
B: I just finished working out.

　A: 왜 그렇게 많이 땀을 흘리니?
　B: 난 방금 운동을 끝냈어.

Please hear me out

끝까지 들어봐

hear sb out은 '…가 말하는 것을 끝까지 듣다.'

💡 **Example**
- Hear us out and then we can talk.
  내 말을 끝까지 들어봐 그래야 얘기할 수 있지.
- I didn't even hear her out.
  난 걔 말을 끝까지 들을 수가 없었어.

 Dialog

A: Stop lying to me. I'm not stupid.
B: Please hear me out. I can explain this.

A: 거짓말 마. 내가 바보인 줄 알아.
B: 끝까지 들어봐. 내가 설명할 수 있어.

I haven't heard anything about that

전혀 그런 소식 못들었는데

not hear anything about은 '…에 관해 전혀 들어보지 못하다.'

💡 **Example**
- Are you sure? I haven't heard anything about that.
  정말? 전혀 그런 소식 못들었는데.
- Have you heard any of the current popular music?
  요즘 유행하는 음악 들어본 것 있어?

 Dialog

A: I haven't heard anything about the money.
B: Yeah, I hope they give it to us soon.

A: 그 돈에 대해서 아무 것도 듣지 못했어.
B: 그래. 걔들이 조만간 그걸 우리에게 주기를 바래.

186

I don't know. You got me
몰라. 나도 모르겠어
You got me는 '(내가 졌을 때 혹은 내가 모르는 것을 질문했을 때) 몰라' = Search[Beats] me.

💡 **Example**

- I don't know. You got me.
  몰라. 나도 모르겠어.

- What will happen? You got me.
  어떻게 될까? 나도 모르겠어

 Dialog

A: Is George coming over today?
B: You got me. I haven't heard anything.
   A: 조지가 오늘 들른대?
   B: 나도 몰라. 들은 바 없어.

187

He asked me why I did that
걘 내가 왜 그렇게 했는지 물었어
ask sb why [what~]는 '…에게 …을 물어보다.'

💡 **Example**

- The bank teller asked me if I wanted to open an account.
  은행원은 은행계좌를 개설하고 싶은지 물었다

- She asked me what I did for a living.
  걔가 내 직업을 물었어.

 Dialog

A: My boss asked me if I planned to change jobs.
B: So, what did you say to him?
   A: 사장이 내게 이직할 계획이냐고 물었어.
   B: 그래서, 뭐라고 했어?

188

I wonder if she's still angry
난 걔가 아직도 화나 있는지 궁금해
wonder if S+V는 '…인지 궁금해하다.'

 Example
- I wonder if he will finish the report on time.
  걔가 보고서를 제시간에 끝낼지 궁금해.
- I am curious whether I will get a raise next year.
  내년에 내가 급여인상이 될지 궁금해.

Dialog

A: **I wonder if** Tammy is still angry that she was fired.
B: Well, that was five years ago.
  A: 태미가 해고돼서 아직도 화나 있는지 궁금해.
  B: 글쎄, 5년전 일이잖아.

189

I'll check to see if he came in
걔가 돌아왔는지 확인해볼게
check to see if S+V는 '…인지 알아보기 위해 확인하다.'

 Example
- I'm just checking to see if she's okay.
  난 걔가 괜찮은지 확인해보는 거야.
- I'll see if she wants to come back.
  걔가 돌아오고 싶어하는지 알아볼게.

Dialog

A: Is your boss in the office?
B: **I'll check to see if** he came in.
  A: 사장님 사무실에 계셔?
  B: 돌아오셨는지 확인해볼게.

Let me get this straight

정리해보자

get sth straight는 '…을 제대로 해놓다, 바로잡다.'

💡 **Example**

- Let me get this straight. He tried to hit you?
  정리해보자. 걔가 널 치려고 했다고?

- Let's just get one thing straight. I don't want to date you.
  한가지 분명히 해두자고. 너랑 데이트하기 싫어.

A: Let me get this straight, you don't love me?
B: That's right!

　A: 정리해보자, 날 사랑하지 않는다는거야?
　B: 맞아!

I ran a check on each person

난 모든 개개인을 조사했어

run a check on sth은 '조사하다, 확인하다.' run 대신 carry out, make, do를 쓴다.

💡 **Example**

- I can run a check on the new employees.
  난 신입직원들을 조사할 수 있어.

- They ran a check on each person.
  걔네들은 모든 개개인을 조사했어.

A: Is all of this information correct?
B: We should run a check to make sure.

　A: 이 모든 정보가 정확한거야?
　B: 확실히 하기 위해 조사해봐야겠어요.

192

Rumor has it that she got pregnant
걔 임신했다고 그러던대
Rumor has it that~은 '소문에 의하면 …라고 한다' = There is a rumor that S+V.

💡 **Example**
- Rumor has it that we are going to get a 20% cut.
  20% 임금삭감소문이 있어.
- There is a rumor that Christine is pregnant.
  크리스틴이 임신했다는 소문이 있어.

 Dialog

A: **Rumor has it that** you'll be promoted next month.
B: Right. I'll become a vice president.

A: 소문듣자니 다음달에 승진한다며.
B: 맞아. 부사장이 될거야.

193

Bad news travels fast
나쁜 소식은 빨리 돌잖아
travel fast은 '(소문 등이) 빨리 돌다,' 주어로는 word, good[bad] news 등이 온다.

💡 **Example**
- Word of her accident traveled fast.
  걔의 사고 소식이 빨리 돌았어.
- News of the baby's birth traveled fast.
  애기 출산소식은 빨리 돌았어.

 Dialog

A: Did you hear Rex got engaged?
B: Yes I did. Good news **travels fast**.

A: 렉스가 약혼했다는 거 들었어?
B: 어. 좋은 소식은 빨리 돌잖아.

He filled me in on the latest gossip

걔가 최신 소문을 알려줬어

fill sb in on sth은 '…에게 …에 관한 자세한[최신] 정보를 주다.'

Example

- Well, I'll be happy to fill in the blanks.
  기꺼이 공란을 채워 드리죠.

- Please fill in all the information on the form.
  양식서의 모든 정보를 채워주세요.

Dialog

A: I have a lot to tell you about the meeting.
B: You'll have to fill me in later because I'm busy now.

A: 회의에 대해 말할게 많아.
B: 나 지금 바쁘니까 나중에 어떻게 된 건지 설명해.

I'll keep you posted, okay?

너한테 소식 전할게, 알았지?

keep sb posted는 '…에 근황을 알리다' = keep sb updated = keep me in the loof.

Example

- Keep me posted on how she's doing.
  걔가 어떻게 지내는지 소식전해줘.

- I've got to go. I'll keep you posted, okay?
  나 가야 돼. 너한테 소식 전할게, 응?

Dialog

A: Paula was taken to the hospital today.
B: Keep us posted on what happens to her.

A: 폴라가 오늘 병원에 실려갔어.
B: 걔 근황 계속 알려줘.

I mean no offense, but it sucks

기쁜나쁘게 하려는 것은 아니지만, 별로야

mean no offense는 '악의는 없다,' offense 대신 harm을 써도 된다.

Example

- No offense, but I've got to go back home.
  기분 나빠하지마, 하지만 나 집에 가야 돼

- I think that coat isn't a good match for you. No offense.
  코트가 너와 안 어울리는 것 같아. 기분 나빠하지마.

Dialog

A: I don't want to be your friend. No offense.
B: Gee, that's too bad.

A: 너랑 친구하기 싫어. 기분 나빠하지마.
B: 아이고, 안타까워라.

You have to come clean with me

넌 내게 다 털어놓아야 해

come clean with sb는 '비밀을 다 털어놓다.'

Example

- You've got to clean with me.
  나한테 다 털어놓지.

- You have got to come clean with her! This is not right!
  걔한테 털어놔! 이건 옳지 않아!

Dialog

A: You have to come clean with Judith.
B: I just can't tell her how I feel.

A: 주디스에게 다 털어놔야 돼.
B: 난 걔에게 내 감정을 말할 수 없어.

Give it to me straight

다 털어놔

give it to sb straight는 '솔직히 말하다' = tell it like it is.

💡 **Example**

- Give it to me straight. I can't wait to hear about that.
  다 털어놔. 알고 싶어 죽겠어.
- How about you give it to me straight?
  솔직하게 말해주지?

 Dialog

A: How will you tell Jim that his mom died?
B: I'll have to give it to him straight.

A: 짐에게 어머니가 돌아가셨다고 어떻게 말할거야?
B: 솔직히 털어놔야지.

Please just level with me

솔직히 말해

level with sb (on sth)는 '(특히 안 좋은 일에 관해) …에게 솔직히 말하다.'

💡 **Example**

- I think it's time to level with you.
  네게 솔직히 말할 때인 것 같아.
- I really need to level with you. I am very unhappy.
  솔직히 털어놔야겠어. 아주 우울해.

 Dialog

A: Please just level with me. I want to know the truth.
B: I'd like to, but I can't. This is a secret.

A: 솔직히 말해. 진실을 알고 싶어.
B: 그러고 싶지만 그럴 수 없어. 비밀야.

He covered up his mistake

걘 자신의 실수를 감췄어

cover up은 '숨기다, 비밀로 하다' = Your secret is safe with me = My lips are sealed.

Example
- Don't worry. Your secret's safe with me.
  걱정마. 절대 비밀 지킬게.
- You're making up new lies to cover up the old ones.
  넌 지난 거짓말을 숨기기 위해 새로운 거짓말을 꾸며내고 있어.

A: Did your boss get punished for his mistake?
B: No, he covered up everything that happened.
　A: 네 직장상사가 실수로 혼났어?
　B: 아니, 그 사람은 일어난 모든 걸 비밀로 했어.

Don't let on that he's psycho

걔가 사이코라는 걸 절대 발설하지마

let on sb은 '비밀을 누설하다,' let on that S+V는 '…라는 사실을 누설하다.'

Example
- Don't let on that you know her age.
  너 걔 나이 알고 있다고 말하지마.
- He didn't let on that he was a gangster.
  걘 자기가 갱이었다는 걸 누설하지 않았어.

A: Marsha has been pregnant for three months.
B: She never let on to me about that.
　A: 마샤는 임신 3개월이야.
　B: 걘 내게 그거에 대해 말하지 않았어.

I won't say a word

한 마디도 안할게

won't say a word (to sb/about sth)는 '(…에 관해) 아무 말도 않다.'

💡 **Example**

- I promise I won't say a word.
  정말이지 한 마디도 하지 않을게.
- You can trust me. I won't say a word.
  날 믿어. 아무 말도 안할게.

 Dialog

A: Don't ruin the surprise party.
B: I won't say a word.

A: 깜짝파티를 망치지마.
B: 한 마디도 안할게.

We'll pretend we're sick

우리는 아픈 척할거야

pretend to+V는 '…인 척하다' <=> pretend not to do(…하지 않은 척하다).

💡 **Example**

- Don't try to pretend you're best friends with the boss.
  사장과 친한 친구인 척하지마.
- We'll just pretend like it never happened.
  우린 시치미 딱 뗄거야.

 Dialog

A: How can we get a day off?
B: Here's my plan. We'll pretend we're sick.

A: 어떻게 하루를 쉴 수 있을까?
B: 내 생각은 이래. 우리 아픈 척 하는거야.

Don't give me that

그런 변명하지마

don't give me that은 '그런 말 마,' '그런 변명하지마.'

💡 **Example**

- Don't give me that. I know all the details.
  그런 말마. 속속들이 다 알고 있다고.
- Don't give me that. I'm mad at you.
  그런 말 마. 너한테 열받았어.

 Dialog

A: I can't work with that guy.
B: **Don't give me that.**

A: 그 사람이랑 같이 일 못하겠어.
B: 그 따위 소리 하지 말라구.

I couldn't account for skipping school

난 학교빼먹은거에 대해 설명을 할 수 없었어

account for는 '…을 설명하다, 책임지다,' account for+숫자는 '…을 차지하다.'

💡 **Example**

- Pat couldn't account for his late arrival.
  팻은 늦게 온 것에 대한 설명을 할 수 없었어.
- I'll give a brief account for the meeting.
  내가 그 회의의 간략한 내용을 설명해 줄게.

 Dialog

A: You need to account for the money you spent.
B: I can show you every bill I paid.

A: 넌 네가 쓴 돈에 대해 책임을 져야 해.
B: 내가 지불한 모든 청구서를 네게 보여줄 수 있어.

Let me make myself clear

내가 분명히 말할게

make clear는 '…을 분명히 (설명)하다,' Do I make myself clear?는 "내 말을 알아들었어?"

💡 Example

- He tried to make his opinion clear.
  걔는 자기 의견을 분명히 하려고 했어.

- Let me make myself clear. This is a mistake.
  분명히 말하는데 이것은 실수야.

 Dialog

A: My parents want to know which university I'll attend.
B: You should make clear the one you prefer.

A: 부모님은 내가 어떤 대학을 다닐 건지 알고 싶어하셔.
B: 네가 좋아하는 대학을 분명히 해야 돼.

I think I got it across to her

내가 걔한테 이해시켰다고 생각해

get across (to sb)는 '…에게 이해되다' = come across.

💡 Example

- I'm just trying to get across my points.
  난 단지 내 논점을 이해시키려고 노력하고 있어.

- He saw the project through until it was finished.
  걘 프로젝트가 끝날 때까지 지켜봤어.

 Dialog

A: Did you explain everything to Lucy?
B: Yeah, I think I got it across to her.

A: 넌 모든 것을 루시에게 설명했니?
B: 응, 내가 걔한테 이해시켰다고 생각해.

208

Can you **make yourself understood**?

나에게 네 뜻을 이해시킬 수 있니?

make oneself understood는 '…의 생각을 이해시키다.'

💡 **Example**

- Sarah **made herself understood** when I met her.
  새라는 만났을 때 자기 생각을 분명히 이해시켰어.
- Can you **make yourself understood**?
  나에게 네 뜻을 이해시킬 수 있니?

 Dialog

A: Can you **make yourself understood** in Japanese?
B: No, not yet.

A: 일본어는 좀 할 수 있나요?
B: 아뇨, 아직요.

209

How should I **put it**?

내가 어떻게 표현해야 되지?

put it은 '표현하다' = express. put it simply는 '간단히 표현하자면.'

💡 **Example**

- To **put it simply,** I'm moving away.
  간단히 말하자면 난 이사 가버릴거야.
- I decided to **put it very honestly**.
  난 매우 정직하게 말하기로 결정했어.

 Dialog

A: How would you **put it**?
B: Just tell them you need a bigger salary.

A: 어떻게 표현하겠니?
B: 단지 봉급이 더 필요하다고 걔들한테 말해.

My kids always come first

내 아이들이 가장 중요해

come first는 '가장 중요하다'로 come 앞에 가장 중요하다고 생각되는 사람[사물]을 말한다.

Example

- Work comes first for the older generation.
  옛 세대들에게는 일이 가장 중요한 가치야.

- I stayed home because my children always come first.
  내 애들이 항상 나한테는 가장 중요하기 때문에 집에 남았어.

 Dialog

A: When you work at this company, punctuality comes first.
B: That's pretty much the same for all companies.

A: 이 회사에서 일할 땐 시간을 잘 지켜야 돼.
B: 그건 다른 모든 회사들도 거의 같을거야.

Guess What?

Let's hit the road
잘 출발하자

출발하다, 떠나다. 이는 슬랭으로 현재 있는 장소에서 단순히 나가는 것을 말하기도 하고 문맥에 따라서는 여행을 시작하다(to leave a place, and sometimes it means to begin a trip)라는 뜻으로도 쓰인다.

You can make a big difference

네가 큰 차이를 만들 수 있어

make a difference는 '…가 중요하다, 영향을 미치다' <=> make no difference.

💡 **Example**

- You can make a big difference.
  네가 큰 차이를 만들 수 있어.

- She tried to make a difference by doing something for you.
  걘 너를 위해 뭔가를 함으로써 영향을 미치려고 했어.

A: You are always kind to poor people.
B: I want to make a difference in their lives.

A: 넌 항상 가난한 사람들에게 친절해.
B: 난 그들의 생활에 영향을 미치고 싶어.

He doesn't make much of money

걘 돈을 그다지 중요하게 여기지 않아

make much of는 '…을 중요시하다' <=> make little of(얕보다, 등한시하다).

💡 **Example**

- My boss made much of the fact that I left early.
  보스는 내가 일찍 나간걸 중시했어.

- The teacher made much of the fact that he cheated.
  선생님은 걔 부정행위를 중시했어.

A: Larry looks so handsome today.
B: People are making much of his new haircut.

A: 래리가 오늘 아주 잘 생겨 보이네.
B: 사람들은 걔가 새로 머리 자른 것을 중시하고 있어.

I always put honesty before benefit

난 항상 이익보다 정직을 우선시해

put A before B는 'B보다 A를 중요시하다,' '우선시하다.'

💡 Example

- Lisa puts others before herself most of the time.
  리사는 대부분 자신보다 남을 우선시해.
- I had to put studying before relaxing.
  난 쉬는 것보다 공부하는 것을 중요시해야만 해.

A: What is the philosophy of your company?
B: I always tell my employees to put honesty before benefit.

A: 네 회사의 철학이 뭐니?
B: 난 항상 직원들에게 이윤보다는 정직을 우선시하라고 말해.

I think you made your point

네가 충분히 논점을 설명했다고 생각해

make one's point는 '…의 주장을 밝히다,' '…주장이 정당함을 보여주다.'

💡 Example

- It took a long time for Tina to make her point.
  티나가 자기 주장을 밝히는데 오랜 시간이 걸렸어.
- Nick made the case that he should skip school.
  닉은 자신이 결석해야 한다고 주장했어.

A: Do you need me to explain more?
B: No, I think you made your point.

A: 내가 좀 더 설명해야 되니?
B: 아니야, 네가 충분히 논점을 설명했다고 생각해.

I **put forward** my ideas

난 내 아이디어들을 제안했어

put forward sth은 '…을 제안하다,' '제출하다.' sth의 자리에는 idea나 proposal.

Example
- The proposals were put forward by our staff.
  그 제안들은 우리 직원들이 내놓았어.
- He put forward a plan for the future.
  걘 미래 계획을 제안했어.

 Dialog

A: Renee **put forward** her ideas.
B: Did you think they were worthwhile?

A: 르네는 자신의 아이디어들을 제안했어.
B: 그 아이디어들이 가치가 있다고 생각되었니?

If my memory serves, we've met before

내 기억이 맞는다면 우린 전에 만났었어

if my memory serves는 '내 기억이 맞다면.' 뭔가 확실하지 않을 때 조심스럽게 말하는 방법.

Example
- If my memory serves, we've met before.
  내 기억이 맞는다면 우린 전에 만났었어.
- If my memory serves, it's almost your birthday.
  내 기억이 맞는다면 거의 네 생일이 되어가.

 Dialog

A: Where do you keep the bottle opener?
B: **If my memory serves,** it's in that drawer.

A: 병 따개를 어느 곳에 두었니?
B: 내 기억이 맞는다면 저 서랍 안에 있어.

Does that name ring a bell?

그 이름 기억나니?

ring a bell은 '기억이 나다'로 들어보거나 본 적이 있다는 의미의 구어체 표현.

💡 Example

- Jeffery Tabor's name rings a bell.
  제프리 테이버의 이름이 기억나.

- I grew up in Friendsville. Does that place ring a bell?
  난 프렌즈빌에서 자랐어. 그곳 기억이 나니?

 Dialog

A: Does that name ring a bell?
B: I'm sure I went to school with her brother years ago.

A: 그 이름 기억나니?
B: 몇 년 전 걔 남동생과 함께 학교를 다닌 것이 확실해.

Let it go. It's all in the past

잊어라. 모두 과거지사야

let it go는 '잊다,' '잊어버리다.'

💡 Example

- Let it go. It's all in the past.
  잊어라. 모두 과거지사야.

- At some point, you just got to let it go, right?
  언젠가는 그냥 잊어야 하는 거야, 알겠니?

 Dialog

A: Nicole had a terrible divorce last year.
B: Well, I hope she's been able to let it go.

A: 니콜은 작년에 끔찍한 이혼을 했어.
B: 글쎄, 걔가 잊어버릴 수 있기를 바래.

It completely slipped my mind
그걸 정말 깜박했어

slip one's mind는 '깜박하다.' mind 대신에 memory를 써서 사용하기도 한다.

 Example

- Her birthday party completely slipped my mind.
  걔 생일파티를 완전히 깜박했어요.
- The dentist appointment slipped Joan's memory.
  조안은 치과 예약을 깜박 잊었어.

 Dialog

A: Did you clean up the break room?
B: Oh my gosh, that slipped my mind.
  A: 휴게실을 청소했니?
  B: 어머나, 깜박했어요.

Just give it some thought
그냥 생각 좀 해봐

give sth some thought는 '…을 생각해보다,' give it some thought의 형태로 많이 쓰인다.

 Example

- He gave no thought to the topic of his report.
  걘 보고서 주제에 대해 신경을 안 써.
- You should give it some thought.
  넌 그걸 좀 생각해봐야 해.

Dialog

A: I don't know if I can do that.
B: Well, just give it some thought.
  A: 내가 그걸 할 수 있을 지 모르겠어.
  B: 글쎄, 그냥 생각 좀 해봐.

221

I have a nice restaurant in mind

좋은 식당을 생각하고 있어

have sth in mind는 '…을 마음속에 생각하고 있다.' 이미 뭔가 결정하였거나 의견을 정한 상태.

💡 Example

- Sit down, I have something serious in mind to discuss.
  앉아. 의논할 심각한 일이 있어.

- Fiona had the trip in mind.
  피오나는 그 여행을 떠나려고 생각하고 있었어.

A: Where will the wedding take place?
B: I have a nice restaurant in mind.

　A: 결혼식 어디에서 할거야?
　B: 좋은 식당을 생각하고 있어.

222

If you ask me, he's a loser

내 생각으로는 걘 멍청이야

if you ask me는 '내 생각으로는.' 자기 의견을 조심스럽게 말하기 앞서 꺼내는 표현.

💡 Example

- If you ask me, I'd move in with him.
  내 의견을 말하자면 걔 집에 이사하고 싶어.

- If you ask me, she is dying to get people's attention.
  내 의견을 말하자면 걘 사람들의 관심을 끌려고 안달이야.

A: Brett says he can't work any more.
B: If you ask me, he's just being lazy.

　A: 브레트는 더 이상 일할 수 없다고 말해.
　B: 내 개인 의견을 말하자면 걘 너무 게을러.

The way I see it, we have time

내 생각에 시간은 충분해

the way I see it는 '내가 보기엔.' 어떤 판단을 함에 있어 자기 생각임을 한정지어 말할 때.

💡 Example

- **From what I've seen,** there are many problems.
  내가 본 바로는 너무 문제가 많아.

- **The way I see it,** you've got no choice on that.
  내가 보기엔 넌 그 문제에 대해 선택의 여지가 없어.

A: George just got a visa for England.
B: **The way I see it,** he plans to move there.

A: 조지는 방금 영국 입국 비자를 받았어.
B: 내가 보기엔 걘 영국으로 이주할 계획이야

On second thought, I fell for her

다시 생각해보니 난 그녀에게 반했어

on second thought는 '다시 생각해보니.'

💡 Example

- **On second thought,** she decided to move.
  다시 생각한 끝에 걘 이사하기로 결정했어.

- **On second thought,** we should call Brad.
  다시 생각해보니 우린 브래드를 불러야만 해.

A: Let's go out to eat at a restaurant tonight.
B: **On second thought,** we should stay home and save money.

A: 오늘 밤 외식하자.
B: 다시 생각해보니 집에 남아 돈을 절약해야 해.

I need you to sleep on it

곰곰히 생각해야 돼

sleep on it은 '…깊이 생각하다' = need more time to think.

💡 **Example**

- Let me sleep on it and give you an answer tomorrow.
  깊이 생각해보고 낼 답줄게.

- Jill needs more time to think your proposal.
  질은 네 제안을 생각할 시간이 더 필요해.

A: So, did you decide to rent the apartment?
B: I need to sleep on it before making a decision.
  A: 그래서 그 아파트를 임대하기로 결정했니?
  B: 결정하기 전에 깊이 생각해볼 필요가 있지.

He came across as very unkind

걔가 아주 불친절하게 여겨졌어

come across as~는 '…로 간주되다.' come across as+형용사[~ing].

💡 **Example**

- Taylor came across as being very self-confident.
  테일러는 아주 자신만만한 것으로 보였지.

- Aaron was deemed as being the best student.
  아론은 최고 학생으로 간주되었어.

A: Why did you get angry at Rachel?
B: She came across as very unkind.
  A: 왜 레이첼에게 화가 났니?
  B: 걔가 아주 불친절하게 여겨졌어.

Does any solution come to mind?

어떤 해결책이 떠올라?

Sth come to mind는 '…라는 생각이 들다.' come to think of는 '그러고 보니.'

💡 **Example**

- You can say the first thing that comes to mind.
  제일 먼저 떠오르는 생각 말해봐.

- Come to think of it, you should take a day off.
  생각해보니 너 하루를 쉬어야 해.

 Dialog

A: That law firm is full of nothing but ambulance chasers.
B: Come to think of it, they do have a bad reputation.

A: 그 법률 사무소에는 질 낮은 변호사밖에 없어.
B: 그러고 보니 걔네들 평판이 나빠.

It makes me think of the boss

그걸보니 상사가 떠올라

make sb think of~는 '…에게 …을 생각이 들게 하다.'

💡 **Example**

- It got me thinking that he could become a doctor.
  걘 의사가 될거라는 생각이 들었어.

- You made me think that you still loved me.
  네가 여전히 날 사랑한다는 생각이 들게 했어.

 Dialog

A: It is so beautiful outside today.
B: It makes me think of last summer.

A: 오늘 밖이 무지 아름다워.
B: 지난 여름을 생각나게 하네.

229

It's cheaper than I bargained for
그건 생각했던 것보다 저렴했어
~than sb bargained for는 '…가 예상하는 것 이상으로.'

💡 **Example**
- The trip was longer than we bargained for.
  여행은 우리가 예상한 것 이상으로 길었어.
- The movie was funnier than she bargained for.
  영화는 걔가 예상한 것보다 더 재미있었어.

A: Did you buy a new notebook computer?
B: Yes, it was **more expensive than I bargained for**.

A: 새로운 노트북 컴퓨터를 구입했니?
B: 그래, 내가 예상한 것보다 더 비쌌어.

230

Don't hold your breath
기대하지마
not hold one's breath는 '기대하지 않다.' 원래 숨죽이고 기대하는데 그러지 말라는 이야기.

💡 **Example**
- Don't hold your breath for the economy to improve.
  경제가 증진될 걸로 기대하지 마라.
- If you are waiting for him to apologize, don't hold your breath.
  그가 사과하기를 기다린다면, 기대하지 마라.

A: I'm going to be very rich someday.
B: Yeah, **don't hold your breath for** that to happen.

A: 난 언젠가 아주 부자가 될 거야.
B: 그래, 다만 꼭 그렇게 기대하지는마.

231

I can't take on any extra work
어떤 추가적인 일도 맡을 수가 없어
take on은 '(일, 책임 등을) 맡다.' 목적어로는 work나 responsibility가 주로 온다.

💡 **Example**
- We took on a few new students in class.
  우린 수업에 새로운 학생 몇 명을 받았어.
- She's all set to take on more responsibility in the office.
  걘 사무실에서 더 많은 책임을 맡을 준비가 되어 있어.

A: Can you help me with decorating?
B: Sorry, I can't take on any extra work.
  A: 내가 장식하는데 도와줄 수 있니?
  B: 미안, 난 어떤 추가적인 일도 맡을 수가 없어.

232

Who's going to take over the company?
누가 회사를 인수할거니?
take over는 '떠맡다,' '양도받다.' 뭔가를 책임진다는 의미로 take control of와 같은 뜻.

💡 **Example**
- Who is going to take over the company?
  누가 회사를 인수할거니?
- You can take over the meeting.
  네가 회의를 맡을 수 있어.

A: I'm going to take over as class president.
B: Did you win a student election?
  A: 난 학급 반장 직을 떠맡을 거야.
  B: 학생 선거에서 승리했니?

I got cold feet before my wedding

난 결혼식전에 겁이 났어

get[have] cold feet는 '…겁을 먹다,' '주눅이 들다' = lose courage.

💡 **Example**
- Donna got cold feet before her job interview.
  도나는 입사면접에 앞서 겁먹었어.
- Many people get cold feet before a big decision.
  많은 사람들이 큰 결정에 앞서 겁먹어.

A: So they didn't get married?
B: No, the bride got cold feet.

A: 그래서 걔들이 결혼을 안 했니?
B: 아니, 신부가 겁을 먹었어.

I had the nerve to hit him

난 용기내 걔를 때렸어

get up[have] the nerve (to~)는 '…을 할 용기가 있다,' 혹은 '뻔뻔스럽게도 …을 하다.'

💡 **Example**
- Tim had the nerve to talk back to his teacher.
  팀은 용기내 선생님한테 말대꾸했어.
- You need to get up the nerve to quit your job.
  넌 직장을 그만둘 용기를 낼 필요가 있어.

A: Why haven't they gotten married yet?
B: They haven't gotten up the nerve to talk to their parents.

A: 왜 걔들은 아직 결혼을 하지 않은 거야?
B: 걔들은 부모님에게 말할 용기를 내지 못한 거야.

Blue jeans are always in

청바지는 항상 유행이지

be in[be in fashion]은 '유행하다' <=> be out[be out of fashion].

💡 **Example**

- Long skirts are out this spring.
  긴 스커트는 금년 봄에 유행이 지났어.

- Blue jeans are always in.
  청바지는 항상 유행이지.

 Dialog

A: Louis Vuitton bags are in this year.
B: I hope my boyfriend buys me one.

A: 루이비통 가방이 금년에 유행이야.
B: 난 내 남친이 하나 사주기를 바래.

Short hairstyles are catching on

짧은 머리가 유행하고 있어

catch on은 '유행하다,' '널리 퍼지다.' catch on to하면 '알아채다', '이해하다'라는 의미.

💡 **Example**

- New fashions catch on every year.
  새로운 패션이 매년 유행하고 있어.

- Short hairstyles for women are catching on.
  여성들에게 짧은 머리가 유행하고 있어.

 Dialog

A: I see many people wearing NBA hats.
B: That style has really caught on.

A: 많은 사람들이 NBA 모자를 쓰고 있는 것을 볼 수 있어.
B: 그 스타일은 진짜 유행이야.

This dress will set a new trend
이 드레스가 새로운 유행을 선도할거야
set a trend는 '새로운 트렌드를 만들다,' set the trend는 '특정분야의 트렌드를 주도하다.'

💡 **Example**
- I think this jewelry will set a new trend.
  이 보석이 새로운 유행을 선도하는 것 같아.
- Madonna has been a trend setter for many years.
  마돈나는 오랫동안 유행을 선도했어.

A: Many people like that pop singer.
B: She sets fashion trends for young women.
  A: 많은 사람들이 저 팝가수를 좋아해.
  B: 걘 젊은 여자애들의 유행을 선도해.

He was left out in the cold
걘 배제당했어
leave sb out in the cold는 '무시하다,' '배제당하다,' '냉대하다.'

💡 **Example**
- He was left out in the cold when the plan changed.
  계획이 바뀔 때 걘 고립되었어.
- They decided to leave Cathy out in the cold.
  걔들은 캐시를 무시하기로 했어.

A: Has anyone from NY called you yet?
B: No, they have left me out in the cold.
  A: 뉴욕에서 누구도 너한테 연락을 하지 않았니?
  B: 아니, 걔들은 날 무시했어.

He won't take it lying down

갠 그걸 참고있지 않을거야

take sth lying down은 불평없이 불합리한 처사를 '감수하다,' '참다.'

💡 **Example**

- I don't plan to take the insult lying down.
  난 모욕 받은 것에 대해 참지 않을거야.

- Ginger can't take the bad news lying down.
  진저는 그 나쁜 소식을 참을 수가 없었어.

 **Dialog**

A: Was Eric fired from his job?
B: Yes, but he won't take the firing lying down.

A: 에릭은 해고되었니?
B: 응, 갠 잘린 것에 대해 참지 못했어.

It's the other way around

그건 반대야

the other way around는 '반대로,' '다른 방향으로.' on the contrary는 '반대로,' '한편.'

💡 **Example**

- On the contrary, you are wrong.
  반대로 네가 틀렸어.

- I didn't fail. It's the other way around.
  내가 실패하지 않았어. 그 반대야.

 **Dialog**

A: I heard that you lied to Peter.
B: It's the other way around. Peter lied to me.

A: 네가 피터에게 거짓말을 했다고 들었어.
B: 반대야. 피터가 나한테 거짓말을 했지.

241

I'll take her side
난 걔 편을 들거야

take one's side는 '…의 편을 들다,' '동의하다' = be on one's side. Which side are you on?(누구편야?).

- My husband told me he is on my side.
  내 남편은 내 편이라고 했어.
- We all get old. Time is on no one's side.
  우린 모두가 늙어. 시간은 누구 편도 아니야.

Dialog

A: Do you agree with what Helen said?
B: Yes, I'll take her side in the argument.

A: 헬렌이 말한 것에 대해 동의하니?
B: 그럼, 난 토론할 때 걔 편을 들거야.

242

I'm not into it
난 그런거 안해

'be into sb[sth]은 '관심이 있다,' '흥미가 있다,' '…에 열중하다.' I'm so into you(난 너한테 빠졌어).

- Frank is into collecting postcards.
  프랭크는 우편엽서를 모으는데 열심이야.
- I am into riding motorcycles.
  난 오토바이를 타는데 흥미를 가지고 있지.

Dialog

A: Do you want to go to that hip new bar after work?
B: I'm into it.

A: 퇴근 후에 새로 문 연 끝내주는 술집에 갈래?
B: 거, 끌리는데.

243

My girlfriend goes in for shopping
내 여친은 쇼핑에 몰두해 있어
go in for는 '…에 흥미를 갖기 시작하다,' '몰두하다.'

💡 **Example**

- My girlfriend goes in for shopping.
  내 여친은 쇼핑에 몰두해 있어.
- Carl goes in for watching sports on TV.
  칼은 TV로 스포츠를 시청하는데 빠져있어.

 **Dialog**

A: Would you like to come to the club?
B: No, I don't go in for drinking alcohol.
  A: 클럽에 오고 싶니?
  B: 아니, 술 마시는데 흥미가 없어.

244

We can't wait to meet her
몹시 보고 싶네
can't wait to+V는 '몹시 …하고 싶다.' can't wait until~는 '…을 몹시하고 싶다.'

💡 **Example**

- I can't wait for vacation.
  난 휴가가 몹시 기다려져.
- I can't wait for the new computer game.
  난 새로운 컴퓨터 게임이 몹시 기다려져.

 **Dialog**

A: I'll bring my girlfriend to dinner tonight.
B: We can't wait to meet her.
  A: 오늘 밤 저녁에 내 여친을 데려올게.
  B: 몹시 보고 싶네.

I'd rather take the subway

난 차라리 지하철을 타겠어

would rather+V는 '차라리 …하겠다.' would rather not+V는 '차라리 …하지 않겠다.'

Example
- I'd rather not meet you for dinner.
  차라리 너랑 저녁식사를 하지 않는게 좋겠어.
- I'd rather take the subway.
  난 차라리 지하철을 타겠어.

Dialog

A: Let's go to a movie tonight.
B: I would rather stay home and watch TV.
  A: 오늘 밤 영화를 보러 가자.
  B: 차라리 집에 남아서 TV를 보고 싶어.

Guess What?

It's a hard nut to crack
그건 어려운 문제야

"깨기 어려운 호두"라는 뜻으로 난제, 즉 이해하거나 극복하기 어려운 문제(a problem is hard to overcome or to understand)라는 뜻이다. 또한 사람에게 쓰이면 상대하기 만만치 않은 사람을 뜻한다.

246

It's not my cup of tea
내 타입이 아냐
be not one's cup of tea는 '…의 타입이 아냐.'

💡 Example
- Blind dates are not my cup of tea.
  블라인드 데이트는 내 스타일이 아냐.
- This Russian food is not my cup of tea.
  이 러시아 음식은 내 타입이 아냐.

 Dialog

A: Did you enjoy salsa dancing?
B: I hated it. It's not my cup of tea.
  A: 넌 살사 춤을 즐겼니?
  B: 난 아주 싫어해. 내 타입이 아냐.

247

That's my thing
내 취향이야
be one's thing (to+V)는 '…의 취향이다' = be one's style.

💡 Example
- It's my style to come late to parties.
  파티에 늦게 오는게 내 스타일이야.
- This shirt is your style.
  이 셔츠는 네 스타일이다.

 Dialog

A: Cheryl always wears black clothes.
B: She told me that's her style.
  A: 셰릴은 항상 검은 옷을 입어.
  B: 걘 그게 자기 스타일이래.

It figures that Karl is German
짐이 독일인인 것 같아

it figures that S+V는 '…인 것 같다.' That figures는 '그것은 당연하다,' '생각한 대로이다.'

💡 **Example**

- It figures that Karl is German.
  칼이 독일인인 것 같아.

- He never called you? That figures.
  걔가 너한테 결코 전화하지 않았지? 그럴 줄 알았어.

 Dialog

A: Julia stole all of the money we had.
B: It figures that she took everything.

A: 줄리아는 우리가 가진 모든 돈을 훔쳤어.
B: 걔가 모든 것을 가져간 것 같아.

I came up with a good idea
난 좋은 아이디어를 생각해냈어

come up with+제안[아이디어]는 '…을 내어놓다,' '생각해내다,' '제안하다.'

💡 **Example**

- You'd better come up with something better than that.
  그것보다 나은 뭔가를 제안하는 게 좋겠어.

- We'd better come up with a good plan soon!
  빨리 좋은 계획을 생각해내야겠어!

 Dialog

A: Let me see what you've come up with.
B: It's not much, but it's a start.

A: 네가 어떤 안을 내놓았는지 한번 보자.
B: 대단하진 않아. 하지만 이건 시작이니까.

250

Does she make up a story?
걔가 이야기를 꾸며내는거야?
make up (a story)는 '(이야기 등) 꾸며내다.' 화장하면 딴 사람이 되듯이.

💡 **Example**
- I need to make up an excuse for dad.
  난 아빠한테 변명을 꾸며내야 해.
- Don't make up a lie. Tell me the truth.
  거짓말을 꾸며내지마. 사실을 말해라.

 Dialog

A: I think Kelly has been lying to us.
B: But why would she make up a story?

A: 켈리가 우리한테 거짓말하는 것으로 생각돼.
B: 왜 걔가 이야기를 꾸며낼까?

251

Let's try to think up something new
새로운 뭔가를 생각해내보자
think up은 '생각해내다,' '고안하다.' 특정한 생각이나 아이디어 혹은 변명 등을 만들어낼 때.

💡 **Example**
- Let's try to think up something new.
  새로운 뭔가를 생각해내보자.
- Tina couldn't think up an idea for the class project.
  티나는 학급 프로젝트를 위해 아이디어를 생각해낼 수가 없었어.

 Dialog

A: The story you wrote is very interesting.
B: It took a long time to think it up.

A: 네가 쓴 스토리는 정말 재미있어.
B: 생각해내는데 오랜 시간이 걸렸어.

252

I feel so left out

나 소외감 느껴져

be[feel] left out (of~)는 '(…로부터) 소외감을 느끼다.'

Example
- I was left out of the card game.
  난 카드게임에서 왕따 당했어.
- Nobody calls me these days. I feel so left out.
  요즘 아무도 날 부르지 않아. 소외감 느껴.

A: Karen's brother seems upset about something.
B: He was left out of Karen's wedding.

A: 카렌의 오빠는 뭔가 화난 것 같아
B: 카렌의 결혼식에 소외감을 느꼈어.

253

I was under the weather

난 기분이 안 좋았어

(be[feel]) under the weather는 '기분이 좀 안 좋은,' '몸이 안좋은.'

Example
- I couldn't go to Taegu because I was under the weather.
  몸이 안 좋아서 대구에 갈 수 없었어.
- Terry is under the weather and is lying in bed.
  테리는 몸이 안 좋아 침대에 누워있어.

A: Why is our boss so late today?
B: He's at home because he's under the weather.

A: 왜 우리 사장이 오늘 늦는 거야?
B: 기분이 안 좋아서 집에 계셔.

He is really pissed off

걘 정말 열받았어

be pissed off (at/with~)는 '화나다.' ~off 다음에 with[at]+사람[사물] 혹은 ~ing.

💡 Example

- I heard that Sam is really pissed off at you.
  샘이 정말 너한테 화났다며.
- I just got fired today and I'm really pissed off.
  오늘 짤렸어. 왕짜증난다.

 Dialog

A: I heard that Bob was fired today.
B: It's true. He is really pissed off.

A: 밥이 오늘 해고되었다며.
B: 맞아. 정말 열받았어.

Cockroaches got on my nerves

바퀴벌레 때문에 신경이 거슬려

get on one's nerves는 '…의 신경을 거슬리게 하다.'

💡 Example

- The slow Internet connection got on my nerves.
  인터넷 접속속도가 넘 늦어 짜증나.
- Does Sharon ever get on your nerves?
  샤론이 네 신경을 거슬리게 한 적 있어?

 Dialog

A: What is the most difficult thing about being married?
B: Husbands and wives can get on each other's nerves.

A: 결혼생활에 가장 어려운 점이 뭐야?
B: 부부가 서로 신경을 거슬리게 할 때.

256

Don't get worked up over her

걔 때문에 화내지마

get worked up (about/over~)는 '(…에) 열받다,' '흥분하다,' '화내다.'

💡 **Example**

- Don't get worked up over your argument with him.
  걔와의 논쟁에 넘 열 받지마.

- My parents got worked up over my poor grades.
  내 부모님은 내 형편없는 학점에 열 받으셨어.

 Dialog

A: My son went to a pop music concert last night.
B: Many kids were worked up about the singers.

A: 아들이 지난 밤에 팝 뮤직 콘서트에 갔어.
B: 많은 애들이 가수들에 열광적이었어.

257

You've got to apologize to me

넌 내게 사과해야 돼

apologize to sb for+N[~ing]는 'sb에게 …을 사과하다.'

💡 **Example**

- I must apologize for my colleague's behavior.
  제 동료가 한 행동을 사과드립니다.

- You've got to apologize to me.
  넌 내게 사과해야 돼

 Dialog

A: Ray is very angry at Jenny.
B: It seems to me that she should apologize.

A: 레이는 제니에게 무척 화가 나있어.
B: 걔가 사과해야 할 것으로 보여.

258

Don't fret about it

너무 초초해하지마

fret about~는 '…을 초조해하다.'

 Example

- Older people fret about small things.
  노인들은 작은 일들로 속을 태우셔.
- The students fret about paying for school.
  학생들이 학비로 가슴 조아리고 있어

 Dialog

A: Do you think the students will like me?
B: Don't fret about it. They'll love you.

A: 학생들이 나를 좋아할까?
B: 너무 초초해하지마. 걔들이 널 좋아할거야.

259

What a shame!

그거 참 안됐네!

be a shame to~는 '정말 실망이다,' '안됐다.'

 Example

- It's a shame to waste all of that food.
  이 음식들을 다 버린다는 게 안타까운 일이에요.
- What a shame you got here too late.
  네가 여기 이렇게 늦게 오다니 너무하네.

Dialog

A: Tony crashed her car and is in the hospital.
B: What a shame!

A: 토니가 차사고 나서 병원에 입원했어.
B: 그거 참 안됐네!

You let me down
넌 난 실망시켰어

let[get] sb down은 '…을 실망시키다,' be let down는 '실망했어,' be a little down은 '좀 낙담하다.'

💡 **Example**

- She **let** the group **down** when she was absent.
  걔 불참으로 그 그룹이 실망했어.

- You have to work hard. **Don't let me down.**
  열심히 일 해야 돼. 날 실망시키지마.

 Dialog

A: Why are you so angry?
B: **You let me down.** I thought I could trust you.

A: 왜 내게 화나 있는 거야?
B: 실망했어. 널 믿을 수 있다고 생각했는데.

Our heart goes out to you
당신께 깊이 애도를 표합니다

one's heart goes out to sb는 '…에게 위로의 맘을 전하다,' '…을 가엾게 여기다.'

💡 **Example**

- **Our heart goes out to** you in this difficult time.
  이 어려운 때 네게 위로의 맘을 전한다.

- **My heart went out to** my aunt after her accident.
  사고후 이모를 위로했어.

 Dialog

A: There were many people killed in the flood.
B: **My heart goes out to** the people that survived.

A: 홍수로 사망한 많은 사람들이 있다.
B: 생존한 사람들에게 위로의 마음을 전한다.

I have had it with this job

이 직업이 지긋지긋해

have had it with = have had enough는 '더 이상 못참다,' '질색이다.'

Example

- They have had enough of the high rent here.
  걔들은 이 동네 높은 월세에 지쳤어.
- We have had enough of this old computer.
  더 이상 이 낡은 컴퓨터를 못 쓰겠어.

Dialog

A: I have had enough of that dog barking.
B: Can someone make it be quiet?

A: 그 강아지 짖는 것에 질렸어.
B: 누군가 개를 조용히 해줄 수는 없니?

Everyone thinks highly of him

모두가 걜 높게 평가하고 있어

think highly of~는 '존경하다,' '존중하다.' highly 앞에 so, very 등의 부사로 강조.

Example

- The chef thinks highly of chocolate cake.
  주방장이 초코렛 케익을 중요시해.
- I think highly of BMW motorcycles.
  난 BMW 오토바이를 높게 평가해.

Dialog

A: Richard seems to be very popular here.
B: Everyone thinks highly of him.

A: 리차드는 여기서 인기가 매우 높아.
B: 모두가 그를 높게 평가하고 있어.

I'm not myself

내가 제 정신이 아냐

be not oneself는 '제정신이 아니다' = be not all there(정신나가다).

💡 **Example**

- Jim is not himself since coming back from the hospital.
  짐은 퇴원후 제 정신아냐.
- I was drinking all night, and I'm not myself today.
  밤새 마셔 오늘 난 제 정신아냐

 Dialog

A: You have been very quiet this morning.
B: I don't feel good. I'm not myself.

A: 오늘 아침 좀 조용하네.
B: 기분이 좋지 않아. 제 정신이 아냐.

He must be out of his mind

걔 미쳤나 봐

be out of one's mind는 '정신나가다,' '제정신이 아니다' = lose one's mind.

💡 **Example**

- You are out of your mind to date her.
  걔와 데이트를 하다니 너 정신이 나갔구나.
- The customer was out of her mind to pay such a high price.
  그렇게 고가를 지불하다니 그 고객은 제 정신이 아니었나 봐.

 Dialog

A: John is wearing a t-shirt in the snowstorm.
B: I can't believe it. He must be out of his mind.

A: 존은 눈 폭풍 속에서 티셔츠를 입고 있어.
B: 믿을 수가 없네. 미쳤나 봐.

That makes two of us

나도 마찬가지야

that makes two of us~는 '(상대방 말에 동의하며) 나도 마찬가지야,' '나도 같은 생각야.'

💡 **Example**

- You like this music? So do I.
  이 음악 좋아해? 나도 그래.
- I heard he collects stamps. Me too.
  걔가 우표수집한다며. 나도 그래.

 **Dialog**

A: I'm tired and I want to go home.
B: Yeah, that makes two of us.

A: 피곤해서 집에 가고 싶어.
B: 그래, 나도 마찬가지야.

It suits me just fine

나한테 딱 맞아

suit sb fine는 '좋다,' '괜찮다.'

💡 **Example**

- Eating out every night suits Tara fine.
  타라는 매일 저녁 외식하는 것이 괜찮대.
- The artwork suits the new owner fine.
  그 작품은 새 소장가에게 잘 어울려.

 **Dialog**

A: Do you like working at the post office?
B: Sure. It suits me just fine.

A: 우체국에서 일하는 것 좋으니?
B: 그럼. 나한테 딱 맞아.

A cup of tea will do for me

차 한 잔이면 돼요

~will do for sb는 '…는 …에게 괜찮다,' '족하다.'

💡 **Example**

- This old car will do as a means of transportation.
  이 낡은 차도 이동수단으로 충분해.

- A small cake will do for the party.
  케익 작은 거면 파티에 충분할거야.

A: Hi honey. Are you hungry tonight?
B: No. Just a small meal will do for me.

A: 여보. 오늘 밤 배고파?
B: 아뇨. 소식해도 좋아.

My old car is going to fall apart

내 낡은 차는 부서실거야

fall apart는 '산산조각나다,' '상황이 악화되다.'

💡 **Example**

- Christian fell apart after losing his job.
  크리스찬은 실직 후 완전 쓰러져버렸어.

- Some people fall apart during difficult times.
  일부 사람들은 어려운 시기에 무너져 버린다.

A: I think I need to buy a new car.
B: Why? Is your old car going to fall apart?

A: 난 새 차를 살 필요가 있다고 생각해.
B: 왜? 네 옛날 차가 부서졌니?

That depends on the weather

그건 날씨에 달려 있어

that depends on~은 '…에 달려 있다.'

 Example

- That depends on which person you talk to.
  네가 누구와 이야기하느냐에 달려있어.
- That depends on the route you take on the subway.
  네가 지하철에서 어떤 노선을 타느냐에 달려있지.

 Dialog

A: Are you coming on the class trip?
B: That depends on whether my parents allow it.
  A: 너 학급 견학에 올 거니?
  B: 부모님이 허락하는지 여부에 달려있어.

If worst comes to worst,

최악의 경우에,

if worst comes to worst는 '최악의 경우에.' 상황이 최악으로 치달을 경우에 쓴다.

 Example

- If worst comes to worst, we won't have enough food.
  최악의 경우에는 우린 음식이 충분치 않게 될거야.
- If worst comes to worst, the nations will go to war.
  최악의 경우에는 그 국가들이 전쟁을 하게 될거야.

Dialog

A: Our computer is broken and can't be fixed.
B: If worst comes to worst, we'll borrow another one.
  A: 우리 컴퓨터는 고장이 나서 고칠 수가 없어.
  B: 최악의 경우에는 우린 하나 더 빌려야 돼.

Don't push your luck
괜한 욕심 부리지마

push one's luck은 '운을 믿고 밀어부치다.' 의역하면 '너무 무리하다,' '괜한 욕심부리지마.'

💡 **Example**

- She pushed her luck when she invested too much.
  걘 운을 믿고 과잉투자를 밀어 부쳤어.

- I'll stop because I don't want to push my luck.
  난 운을 믿지 않기 때문에 여기서 그만둘게.

 Dialog

A: Someday I'm going to go skydiving.
B: That's very dangerous. Don't push your luck.

A: 언젠가 난 스카이다이빙을 하려고 해.
B: 매우 위험해. 운을 테스트하지마.

I missed out on a great opportunity
난 정말 좋은 기회를 놓쳤어

miss out on+기회는 '(좋은 기회를) 놓치다' = pass up one's chance = lose a chance.

💡 **Example**

- Brian missed out on the class party.
  브라이언은 학급 파티 기회를 놓쳤어.

- She won't miss out on the award ceremony.
  걘 시상식 기회를 놓치지 않을 거야.

 Dialog

A: Are you going shopping tomorrow?
B: Yes. I don't want to miss out on some bargains.

A: 내일 쇼핑하러 갈 거니?
B: 응. 일부 할인 품목들을 놓치고 싶지 않아.

It makes no difference to me

아무 거라도 좋아

make no difference (to sb)는 '(…에게) 차이가 없다,' '중요하지 않다.'

💡 **Example**

- The type of music makes no difference to us.
  음악의 종류는 우리에겐 중요치 않아.
- My girlfriend's friends make no difference to me.
  여친의 친구들은 내겐 중요치 않아.

 Dialog

A: What kind of ice cream do you want?
B: Oh, it makes no difference to me.

A: 넌 어떤 종류의 아이스크림을 원하니?
B: 오, 아무거라도 좋아.

It must run in the family

집안 내력임에 틀림없어

run in the family는 '(병, 특징 등) 집안 내력이다.'

💡 **Example**

- Being short runs in Melissa's family.
  키 작은 것은 멜리사 집안의 내력이죠.
- Does intelligence run in your family?
  네 집안은 대대로 머리가 좋으니?

 Dialog

A: Fred's mom and two of her brothers had cancer.
B: That's too bad. It must run in the family.

A: 프레드의 엄마와 남동생 2명이 암이래.
B: 안됐군. 집안 내력임에 틀림없어.

I got the hang of it

난 요령을 익혔어

get the hang of~는 '…의 요령을 익히다' = get the knack of~.

💡 **Example**

- Sam couldn't get the hang of using chopsticks.
  샘은 젓가락 사용법을 배울 수가 없었어.
- You'll get the hang of using your new cell phone.
  새로운 휴대폰 사용법을 터득하게 될 거야.

A: Have you learned how to salsa dance yet?
B: Well, I'm starting to get the hang of it.

A: 살사 댄스를 아직 배우지 못했니?
B: 저, 요령을 익히기 시작했어.

I can't complain

아주 좋지

can't complain은 '아주 좋아'라는 의미. 더 이상 불평을 할 수 없을 정도로 괜찮다.

💡 **Example**

- Harriet can't complain about her new boots.
  해리엇은 새로 산 부츠에 대해 불만이 없을 정도로 좋아해.
- I can't complain about the food here.
  여기 음식은 불평할 수 없을 정도로 좋아요.

A: Are you enjoying being married to Ben?
B: I can't complain. He's a good man.

A: 벤과의 결혼을 즐기고 있니?
B: 아주 좋지. 벤은 좋은 사람이야.

Your test scores could be better
네 성적이 별로야

could be better는 '그냥 그래.' 더 좋을 수도 있었는데 그렇지 않다 <=> could be worse(그나마 다행).

💡 **Example**

- Your test scores could be better.
  네 성적이 별로야.

- This vacation tour could be better.
  이 방학여행은 별로야.

 **Dialog**

A: How have you been feeling lately?
B: I could be better. I'm still sick.

A: 요즘 느낌이 어때?
B: 별로야. 여전히 아파.

I'm going to go with it
나 이걸로 할게

go with sth은 '선택하다,' '그냥 해보다' = choose.

💡 **Example**

- You should go with the newest computer.
  넌 가장 최신의 컴퓨터를 선택해야 돼.

- I decided not to go with the LG phone.
  난 LG 전화기를 택하지 않기로 했어.

 **Dialog**

A: Which ring do you prefer?
B: I'm going to go with the silver one.

A: 어느 반지를 더 원하니?
B: 난 은 반지로 갈거야.

280

I'll call the shots
내가 결정할게

call the shots은 결정을 할 위치나 자리에서 '결정을 내린다'는 의미.

💡 **Example**
- Ken calls the shots on the football team.
  켄은 축구팀에서 최종 결정권을 가지고 있어.
- My boss calls the shots at work.
  내 보스는 직장에서 결정권을 갖고 있지.

A: Are you in charge today?
B: That's right. I'll call the shots.

A: 너 오늘 당번이지?
B: 맞아. 내가 모든 걸 결정하지.

281

I have my heart set on marrying her
난 걔랑 결혼하기로 마음을 먹었어

have one's heart[mind] set on sth은 '…으로 마음을 먹다,' '작심하다.'

💡 **Example**
- I have my heart set on marrying her.
  난 걔랑 결혼하기로 마음을 먹었어.
- They had their heart set on a big party.
  걔들은 큰 파티를 하려고 마음을 먹었대.

A: My son has his heart set on going to Africa.
B: That will be an expensive trip to make.

A: 내 아들은 아프리카에 가려고 작심을 했어.
B: 여행비가 비쌀거야.

282

He has things his way
걘 자기 맘대로 해

have things own[one's] way = get one's own way는 '자기 멋대로 하다.'

💡 **Example**

- Lucy demands to have everything her way.
  루시는 모든 걸 자기 식대로 하자고 요구해.

- It's nice to have things my way here.
  여기서는 내 맘대로 할 수 있어서 좋아.

A: Why do you act so selfish all the time?
B: I need to have things my way.

A: 넌 왜 항상 이기적으로 행동하니?
B: 난 내 식대로 해야 돼.

283

You can suit yourself
네가 좋을 대로 해

suit oneself는 '…의 좋을대로 하다.' 주로 명령문형태.

💡 **Example**

- I decorated the apartment to suit myself.
  난 아파트를 나 좋을 대로 장식했어.

- I don't agree, but you can suit yourself.
  난 동의하지 않지만 네가 좋을 대로 해.

A: I'm tired and going home.
B: Suit yourself, but you'll be sorry later.

A: 난 피곤해서 집에 갈 거야.
B: 네 좋을 대로 해 그런데 나중에 후회할 걸.

He's really hung up on Jill
걘은 정말이지 질에게 집착해
be hung up on sb[sth]는 '…에 집착하다.'

 **Example**
- The committee got hung up on an issue.
  위원회가 한 문제에 몰두했어.
- Don't get hung up on that report.
  그 보고서에 집착하지마.

Dialog

A: **Jack is really hung up on that actress.**
B: **Well, she is quite beautiful.**
  A: 잭은 진짜 그 여배우에게 집착하고 있어.
  B: 그래, 그녀는 정말 예뻐.

I'll follow my father's suit
난 아버지를 본받을거야
follow suit는 카드 게임에서 방금 나온 패와 같은 패를 낸다는 의미에서 '선례를 따르다.'

 **Example**
- I'm confused, so don't follow my example.
  난 혼동되었어. 나의 선례를 따라 하지마.
- The students followed their teacher's example.
  학생들이 선생님의 모범을 따랐어.

Dialog

A: **I will follow my father's example.**
B: **He seems to know the secret of success.**
  A: 난 아버지의 모범을 따라갈 거야.
  B: 네 아버지께서는 성공의 비결을 알고 계신 것 같아.

Jane held on to the belief

제인은 그 신념을 끝까지 지켰어

hold on to~는 '…을 지키다,' '고수하다' = hold fast to.

💡 Example

- Jane held on to the belief that he was innocent.
  제인은 걔가 무죄라는 믿음을 고수했어.

- You should hold on to that jewelry.
  넌 그 보석을 지키고 있어야 해.

 Dialog

A: Wow, it is so windy outside today.
B: Yeah, it's difficult to hold on to my umbrella.
   A: 와, 오늘 밖이 무지 바람이 부네.
   B: 그래, 우산을 잡고 있기가 어렵네.

You have to stick to your diet

넌 다이어트를 계속해야 돼

stick to sth은 어려움이 있음에도 '계속하다,' '고수하다.'

💡 Example

- We decided to stick to our schedule.
  우리 일정을 고수하기로 결정했어.

- You have to stick to your diet.
  넌 다이어트를 계속해야 돼.

 Dialog

A: Do you think I'll be successful?
B: Stick to your plans and you'll be OK.
   A: 내가 성공할 것 같아요?
   B: 네 계획대로 계속하면 괜찮을거야.

It brought about a change in the law

그로 인해 법이 개정되었어

bring about sth은 '…의 결과를 초래하다.'

Example

- The crime brought about a change in the law.
  그 범죄로 인해 법이 개정되었지.

- The party brought about some new friendships.
  그 파티로 새로운 친구들이 생겼어.

A: The economy has been terrible this year.
B: It should bring about some new government programs.

A: 금년에 경제가 끔찍했어.
B: 이에 따라 정부로부터 새로운 프로그램이 나오게 될거야.

I ended up missing the bus

난 결국 버스를 놓치게 됐어

end up sth[~ing]은 '…의 결과를 초래하다.'

Example

- We ended up spending the night in the Paris airport.
  우리는 결국 파리공항에서 밤을 지새게 되었어.

- Michelle ended up missing the bus.
  미셸은 결국 버스를 놓치게 되었어.

A: What happened to Bob at his workplace.
B: He ended up getting fired by his boss.

A: 직장에서 밥에게 무슨 일이 생겼니?
B: 걘 결국 보스한테 잘리고 말았어.

You had it coming

네가 자초한거야

had it coming은 사역동사용법으로 '…자연스러운 결과이다,' '자업자득이다.'

💡 **Example**

- You failed the test, but you had it coming.
  넌 시험에 떨어졌지만 자업자득이야.

- You had it coming after you made her angry.
  넌 걔를 화나게 했으니까 자업자득인 거야.

 Dialog

A: Brooke broke up with Jack today.
B: Jack had it coming. He's no good.

 A: 브룩은 오늘 잭하고 헤어졌어.
 B: 잭의 자업자득이지. 걘 별로야.

I stood up for my little kid

난 남동생을 옹호했어

stand up for sb[sth]은 '…을 옹호하다,' '지지하다.'

💡 **Example**

- You need to stand up for what you believe in.
  넌 네가 믿는 것을 지킬 필요가 있어.

- She stood by her husband even when he was in prison.
  걘 남편이 감옥에 있을 때에도 남편 옆을 지켜주었어

 Dialog

A: I stood up for my little brother.
B: Good. Some other kids were bothering him.

 A: 난 남동생을 옹호했어.
 B: 좋아. 다른 애들 몇 명이 걜 괴롭히고 있었어.

I'm flattered you remember me
날 기억해주다니 으쓱해지네
be honored for~는 '…에 대해 칭찬받다,' '표창받다,' be flattered 역시 칭찬받다.

💡 **Example**

- I **am flattered** that you remember me.
  날 기억해주다니 으쓱해지네.

- All mothers **are recognized for** their hard work.
  모든 어머니들은 고생한 걸로 인정 받아.

 **Dialog**

A: Is your father going to be retiring soon?
B: Yes, he'll **be honored for** the years he worked.

   A: 네 아버지께서 조만간 은퇴하시니?
   B: 응, 장기간 일한 걸로 표창을 받을 거야.

Guess What?

Stop hiding your head in the sand!
현실을 직시하라고!

그림에서 보듯 모래에 머리만 파묻고 있다는 것은 자기에게만 안보이면 마치 실제 없는 것처럼 생각하는 어리석음을 비꼬는 표현이다. 비유적으로 현실을 직시하지 않다, 현실을 회피하다(the person is ignoring or not facing an obvious problem or issue)라는 의미로 쓰인다. 동사는 have 외에도 bury, hide 등이 쓰인다.

293

I gave him credit for getting it done

난 걔에게 일을 해낸 것을 인정해줬어

credit A with B는 'B에 대한 공을 A에게 돌리다' = give sb credit <=> take credit for.

💡 **Example**

- I give Bart credit for finishing dental school.
  난 바트가 치대를 마친 걸 장하다고 했어.
- Tanya took credit for our group's success.
  타냐는 우리 그룹성공의 공을 인정받았어.

 Dialog

A: You look really healthy these days.
B: I credit my doctor with making me better.

A: 넌 요즘 정말 건강해 보여.
B: 날 그렇게 만들어 준 공은 바로 내 의사에 있어.

294

I convinced Sam of his honesty

난 샘에게 걔의 정직함을 납득시켰어

convince A of B는 'A에게 B를 납득시키다.' be convinced that은 '…을 확신하다.'

💡 **Example**

- She convinced Jay to help with the homework.
  걘 제이에게 숙제도와달라고 설득했어.
- The family remained convinced of her innocence.
  그 가족은 걔의 결백을 계속 확신했어.

 Dialog

A: Jeff convinced everyone of his honesty.
B: We all believe in him.

A: 제프는 모두에게 자신의 정직함을 납득시켰어.
B: 우리 모두는 걜 신뢰해.

295

I encouraged him to give it a try

걔한테 한번 해보라고 격려해줬어

encourage sb to+V는 '…가 …을 하도록 격려하다.'

💡 **Example**

- James was encouraged to cook her some dinner.
  제임스는 걔한테 저녁을 요리해달라는 권유를 받았어.
- I encouraged him to go and take the exam.
  걔한테 가서 시험보라고 격려해줬어.

A: Your daughter is a talented piano player.
B: We've encouraged her to take more piano lessons.

A: 네 딸은 재능 있는 피아노 연주자야.
B: 우린 좀 더 피아노 레슨을 받도록 걜 격려했어.

296

I talked her into going home

걜 설득해서 집으로 가게 했어

talk sb into ~ing는 '…가 …을 하도록 납득시키다' <=> take sb out of ~ing.

💡 **Example**

- There's no way you're going to talk me into this.
  날 설득해 그걸 하게 할 수는 없어.
- My mom talked me in coming with her.
  엄마가 같이 가자고 날 설득했어.

A: I want to play a computer game.
B: I'll try to talk Sarah into bringing some over.

A: 난 컴퓨터 게임을 하고 싶어.
B: 내가 새라한테 몇 개 가져오라고 설득해볼게.

297

He cautioned her to slow down
걔 속도를 줄이라고 주의줬어

caution sb to+V는 '…에게 …하라고 주의주다,' '경고하다.'

💡 **Example**
- The teacher cautioned the students against drug abuse.
  선생님이 학생들에게 마약을 남용하지 말라고 주의를 줬어.
- The policeman cautioned her to slow down.
  경찰은 걔한테 속도줄이라고 주의줬어.

 Dialog

A: Did you hear that Brady had an accident?
B: I cautioned him against driving home.

A: 브래디가 사고 난 것 들었니?
B: 내가 걔한테 집에 갈 때 운전하지 말라고 주의를 줬는데.

298

I was required to stay at home
집에 머물도록 요청받았어

be required to+V는 '…하는 것이 요구되다,' '요청받다.'

💡 **Example**
- The party requires a cake and drinks.
  파티에는 케익과 음료수가 필수지.
- They required us to arrive early.
  걔들은 우리에게 일찍 도착하라고 요청했어.

 Dialog

A: Did you go jogging this afternoon?
B: No, I was required to stay at home.

A: 너 오늘 오후 조깅을 하러 갔었니?
B: 아니, 집에 머물도록 요청 받았어.

I'd appreciate it if you kept it secret

네가 그걸 비밀로 해주면 고맙겠어

I would appreciate it if you could+V[과거동사]~는 '…해주면 감사하겠다.' 부탁의 표현.

Example

- I'd appreciate it if you kept it secret.
  네가 그걸 비밀로 해주면 고맙겠어.

- I'd appreciate it if you would let me know.
  알려주시면 고맙겠어요.

A: I'd appreciate it if you could bring an appetizer.
B: Is there anything else you need?

A: 전채요리를 가져다 주시면 감사하겠습니다.
B: 다른 것 또 필요한 게 있으세요?

I'll be there for you

내가 너의 힘이 되어줄게

be there for~는 '…의 힘이 되어주다,' '…로 거기에 가다.'

Example

- They'll be there for your race.
  너 경기를 위해 걔들이 가있을 거야.

- She'll be there for Josh's graduation.
  조쉬의 졸업식을 위해 걔가 거기에 갈 거야.

A: I'll be there for you if you have problems.
B: Thanks. I appreciate your friendship.

A: 너한테 문제가 생기면 내가 힘이 되어줄게.
B: 고마워. 우정에 감사해.

301

I always keep my word

난 항상 약속을 지켜

keep one's word는 자기가 한 '약속을 지키다' = keep one's promise.

💡 **Example**
- You'd better honor your promise to our kids.
  넌 우리 애들에게 약속을 지키는 게 좋을 거야.
- She had to go to her hometown to fulfill a promise.
  걘 약속을 지키기 위해 고향으로 가야만 했어.

A: Are you still coming to my party?
B: Sure. I always keep my word.

A: 내 파티에 올 거니?
B: 그럼, 난 항상 약속을 지키잖아.

302

Are you all set for your trip?

여행준비는 다 되었니?

be (all) set to+V는 '…에 대한 준비가 되다.' 준비됐다고 할 때는 All set.

💡 **Example**
- I'm packed and all set to go on vacation.
  나 짐 다 쌌고 이제 휴가떠날 준비가 됐어.
- Are you all set for your vacation?
  휴가 떠날 준비는 다 된거야?

A: Are you all set for your trip?
B: I have a few more things to get and then I'll be ready.

A: 여행준비는 다 되었니?
B: 몇 가지 더 사야 할 것이 있는데 그러면 준비가 끝나.

303

It dates back to Roman times
이건 로마시대로 거슬러 올라가

date back to+N은 주로 과거의 특정시간으로 '거슬러 올라가다.'

💡 **Example**

- The Chinese furniture dates back to the last century.
  이 중국가구는 지난 세기 것이야.
- This mummy dates back to ancient Egypt.
  이 미라는 고대 이집트로 거슬러 올라가.

A: **This is a very old coin.**
B: **It dates back to Roman times.**

  A: 이건 아주 오래된 동전이야.
  B: 이건 로마시대로 거슬러 올라가.

304

I contributed food to charity
난 자선단체에 음식을 기부했어

contribute sth to+N은 '…에 …을 기부하다' = make a contribution.

💡 **Example**

- Can you contribute some money to our school?
  우리 학교에 돈 좀 기부할 수 있어?
- Mom contributed food to the party.
  엄마는 그 파티에 음식을 기부했어.

A: **The flood really created a mess.**
B: **I will contribute money to the clean up.**

  A: 홍수로 정말 난리가 났어.
  B: 난 정화사업에 돈을 기부할거야.

305

It'll take time to sort it out
정리하는데 시간이 걸릴거야

sort sth out (from sth)은 '…을 …로부터 가려내다,' '분류하다.'

💡 **Example**

- The factory had to sort out its faulty goods.
  공장은 흠 있는 물품을 골라내야 했어.

- Let's sort the report out together.
  같이 보고서를 분류하자.

 Dialog

A: This bedroom is a real mess.
B: It will take time to sort it out.

A: 이 침실은 진짜 엉망이야.
B: 정리하는데 시간이 걸릴거야.

306

I've been there myself
나 자신도 그래 봤거든

have been there은 '…을 경험한 적이 있다,' '거기 가본 적이 있다.'

💡 **Example**

- Don't drink too much. Been there, done that.
  과음하지마. 다 해봤어.

- You're right. We have all been there.
  맞아. 우린 다 경험해봤어.

 Dialog

A: I'm having trouble finding a job.
B: I understand. I've been there myself.

A: 난 구직하는데 고생을 하고 있어.
B: 알아. 나 자신도 그래 봤거든.

307

I got the most out of things I own

내가 가진 것을 최대한 잘 활용했어

get the most out of~는 '…을 최대한 이용하다.'

Example
- My wife and I get the most out of life.
  아내와 함께 난 인생을 최대한 즐길거야.
- Who got the most out of that class?
  누가 그 수업을 최대한 잘 이용했니?

Dialog

A: You've worn that old coat for years.
B: I like to get the most out of things I own.
   A: 넌 수년간 그 오래된 코트를 낡도록 입었어.
   B: 난 내 것들을 최대한 활용하고 싶어.

308

She put the old car to use

걘 중고차를 잘 사용했어

make use of~는 '…을 이용하다,' put sth to use 역시 '…을 이용하다.'

Example
- The diners made good use of the extra food.
  식당들은 남은 음식들을 잘 이용했어.
- Cathy put the old car to use.
  캐시는 중고차를 잘 사용했어.

Dialog

A: Can you make use of these clothes?
B: Sure, I'll give them to my brother.
   A: 이 옷들을 잘 이용할 수 있나요?
   B: 그럼, 난 남동생한테 줄거야.

309

It took time to resolve the conflict
갈등을 해결하는데 시간이 걸렸어
resolve a conflict은 '갈등을 해결하다' = get sth resolved.

💡 **Example**

- It took an hour to resolve the argument.
  논쟁을 해결하는데 한 시간이 걸렸어.

- Let's try to get this resolved.
  이것을 해결하기 위해 노력하자.

 Dialog

A: I want to punch Frank in the nose.
B: Fighting is the wrong way to resolve a conflict.
  A: 난 프랭크 코에 주먹을 날리고 싶어.
  B: 싸움은 갈등을 해소하는데 좋지않은 방식이야.

310

Everything will work itself out
모든게 저절로 해결될거야
sth work itself out은 어려운 상황이 '잘 해결되다.'

💡 **Example**

- The problem between them worked itself out.
  걔들 간 문제는 스스로 해결되었어.

- Your trouble will work itself out soon.
  네 고민은 조만간 스스로 해결될거야.

 Dialog

A: My washing machine is very loud.
B: Maybe the noise will work itself out.
  A: 내 세탁기가 너무 시끄러워.
  B: 아마도 그 소음은 저절로 없어질거야.

311

Don't bother me with that
그걸로 날 괴롭히지 마라

bother A with B는 'A를 B로 괴롭히다' = harass sb = nag sb.

Example
- Sorry to bother you, but your mom is calling.
  폐를 끼쳐 미안한데 네 엄마가 전화했어.
- John harassed the girl until she left.
  존은 그 여자애가 떠날 때까지 괴롭혔어.

Dialog

A: Would you like to buy a vacuum cleaner?
B: Don't bother me with that right now.

A: 진공청소기를 사고 싶니?
B: 지금은 그걸로 날 괴롭히지 마라.

312

He cheated her out of her money
걘 그녀를 속여서 돈을 빼앗었어

cheat sb out of~는 '…를 속여서 …를 빼앗다.' cheat은 '부정하다,' '컨닝하다'로도 쓰인다.

Example
- Harry cheated her out of the rent money.
  해리는 걜 속여서 임대료를 빼앗았어.
- They cheated me out of a prize!
  걔들이 날 속여서 상을 갈취해갔어!

Dialog

A: The lawyer cheated Terry out of her money.
B: I hope she can get some back.

A: 변호사는 테리를 속여서 돈을 빼앗았어.
B: 걔가 조금이라도 돌려받기를 바래.

313

We were deprived of food

우리는 음식을 빼앗겼어

be deprived of~는 '…을 빼앗기다.' deprive sb of sth는 '…에게서 …을 빼앗다.'

💡 **Example**

- Linda was deprived of freedom after being arrested.
  린다는 체포된 이후 자유를 빼앗겼어.

- The people were deprived of sunlight during the rainy days.
  사람들은 우기 동안 햇볕을 쬐지 못했어.

 Dialog

A: Was it difficult to stay in jail?
B: We were deprived of food and water for a while.

A: 감옥에 있는 게 힘들었지?
B: 우린 한 동안 음식과 물을 빼앗겼어.

314

We can handle it. Bring it on

우리가 다룰 수 있어. 덤벼

bring it on은 '덤비다.' 주로 명령문 형태로 '덤벼봐'라는 뜻으로 쓰인다.

💡 **Example**

- If you're tough enough, bring it on!
  네가 터프하다면 덤벼봐.

- We can handle it. Bring it on.
  우리가 다룰 수 있어. 덤벼라.

 Dialog

A: I can beat you up any time.
B: When you're ready to fight, bring it on.

A: 난 널 아무 때나 두들겨 팰 수 있어.
B: 싸울 준비가 되어 있으면 덤벼.

Come on, don't call him names

왜 그래. 걔한테 욕하지마

call sb names는 '…의 욕을 하다,' call sb's name은 '…의 이름을 부르다.'

💡 **Example**

- The fight started after he insulted my girlfriend.
  걔가 내 여친을 모욕해 싸움이 시작됐어.

- She got so angry she began to shout at everyone.
  걘 넘 화나 모두에게 소리치기 시작했어.

A: Jethro is just a dummy.
B: Come on, don't call him names.

A: 제스로는 그냥 바보야.
B: 왜 그래. 걔한테 욕하지마.

They had words about something

걔네들은 무슨 문제로 말다툼했어

have words with sb[about sth]는 '…와 …에 대해 말다툼하다,' have a word은 '얘기하다.'

💡 **Example**

- I need to have a few words with you right now.
  난 지금 너하고 이야기 좀 나눠야겠어.

- Some of the students were at odds with the teacher.
  일부 학생들이 선생님과 의견이 달랐어.

A: Were Jimmy and Bill really fighting?
B: No, but they had words about something.

A: 지미와 빌은 정말로 싸우고 있었던 거니?
B: 아니, 단지 무슨 문제에 대해 말다툼을 했어.

317

Don't try to get back at him
걔한테 앙갚음하려고 하지마

get back at sb (for ~ing)는 '…에게 앙갚음하다.'

💡 **Example**

- I'll get back at Carol for saying bad things about me.
  캐롤이 나에 대해 나쁘게 말한 데 대해 앙갚음 할 거야.
- Don't try to get back at him.
  걔한테 앙갚음 하려고 노력하지마.

 Dialog

A: Why did Mark break your window?
B: He was trying to get back at me.

A: 왜 마크가 네 창문을 부쉈니?
B: 나한테 복수하려고 한 것 같아.

318

I'll get even with my boss
사장에게 보복할거야

get even with sb (for ~ing)는 '…에게 (…한 것에 대해) 보복하다.'

💡 **Example**

- I'll get even with my enemies some day.
  난 언젠가 적들에게 복수할 거야.
- I will get even with my boss for firing me.
  날 해고한 데 대해 사장에게 보복할거야.

 Dialog

A: Brad decided to get even with his ex-girlfriend.
B: What is he going to do?

A: 브래드는 옛날 여친에 대해 복수하기로 했어.
B: 그래서 뭘 할 건대?

319

Try to patch things up with Chris
크리스와 화해하도록 해

patch things up with sb는 '…와 화해하다' = patch things[it] up.

💡 **Example**

- Try to patch things up with your family.
  네 가족과 화해하도록 해.
- We'll patch things up when we get together.
  만날 때 서로 이견을 조정할 거야.

 Dialog

A: Why did you meet with Ron?
B: I wanted to patch things up after our argument.

A: 왜 론과 만났니?
B: 다툰 끝에 난 서로 화해하기를 원했어.

320

Don't go behind my back
내게 배신 때리지마

go behind one's back은 '…을 배신하다.'

💡 **Example**

- She went behind my back to the boss.
  걘 내 뒤에서 사장에게 날 비난했어.
- I went behind my wife's back to buy the computer.
  아내 모르게 컴퓨터를 샀어.

 Dialog

A: Should I tell someone about the problem?
B: Don't go behind your teacher's back.

A: 그 문제에 대해 누군가에게 얘기해도 되니?
B: 네 선생님을 배신하지는마.

321

She got away with murder
걘 잘못하고도 벌을 받지 않았어

get away with~는 '(나쁜 짓을 하고도) 벌을 받지 않다.' murder는 관용어로 '잘못된 행동.'

 Example

- I think Helen got away with murder.
  헬렌은 잘못하고도 벌받지 않았다고 생각해.
- She got away with stealing something from the store.
  걘 가게에서 뭔가를 훔치고도 벌을 모면했어.

 Dialog

A: Did you watch the trial?
B: Yes. The man got away with robbing the bank.
  A: 그 재판을 잘 보았니?
  B: 그럼. 그 사람은 은행을 털고서도 처벌을 받지 않았지.

322

I hope it teaches him a lesson
걔가 교훈을 얻기를 바래

teach sb a lesson은 '…에게 교훈을 주다,' '혼내주다.' 이렇게 교훈을 받는 것은 learn a lesson.

 Example

- These problems really taught me a lesson.
  이 문제들로 난 진짜 교훈을 얻었어.
- I'll teach you a lesson about disrespecting me!
  날 무시한 데 대해 널 혼낼거야!

Dialog

A: Did Harry get sent to jail?
B: Yes. I hope it teaches him a lesson.
  A: 해리가 투옥되었니?
  B: 그래. 걔가 교훈을 얻기를 바래.

I'll have to break off right now

지금 당장 그만 둬야겠어

break off는 '(말이나 행동을) 중단하다' = leave off.

💡 **Example**

- The speaker broke off in mid-sentence.
  발표자는 말도중에 중단했어.

- We left off on page number eighty one.
  우리는 81페이지에서 그만뒀어.

 Dialog

A: I will have to break off right now.
B: Do you have other plans?

　A: 지금 당장 그만 둬야겠어.
　B: 다른 계획이 있어?

Knock it off

그만둬

knock it off는 다른 사람이 하던 일을 그만두라고 할 때 '그만두다' = cut it out = come it off.

💡 **Example**

- Let's knock off early and grab a beer.
  빨리 끝내고 맥주 마시러 가자.

- Come off it! You don't have that many problems.
  집어쳐! 넌 그렇게 많은 문제를 가지고 있지는 않아.

 Dialog

A: It's too cold. Turn up the heat!
B: Knock it off. The temperature is fine.

　A: 너무 추워. 난방을 세게 해라.
　B: 그만둬. 온도가 적당해.

325

I can't keep him from drinking

난 걔가 술 마시는 것을 막을 수가 없어

keep sb from+N[~ing]는 '…가 …하는 것을 막아주다, 보호하다.'

💡 **Example**

- Keep the TV from playing too loud.
  TV를 너무 크게 틀어놓지마.

- I can't keep him from drinking.
  난 걔가 술 마시는 것을 막을 수가 없어.

 Dialog

A: Do these vitamins really work?
B: They kept me from getting sick.

A: 이 비타민이 진짜로 효과가 있니?
B: 내가 병드는 것을 방지해줬어.

326

Keep away from the boss

보스 옆에 가지마

keep away from sb[sth]는 '…을 멀리하다,' '가까이 가지 못하다.'

💡 **Example**

- Keep away from that old house.
  저기 고가를 멀리해라.

- Keep away from the sharp knives.
  날카로운 칼들은 멀리해라.

 Dialog

A: Keep away from the boss. He's in a bad mood.
B: I saw that he looked upset.

A: 보스로부터 떨어져 있어라. 아주 기분이 안 좋아.
B: 보스가 화가 나 있는 것 같아.

Don't sneak out of work on Friday

금요일에 사무실에서 빠져 나오지마

sneak out of~는 '…로부터 조용히 빠져 나오다.'

Example

- Don't sneak out of work on Friday.
  금요일에 사무실에서 빠져 나오지마.
- Three students sneaked out of school.
  학생 3명이 학교에서 조용히 빠져 나왔어.

A: Are you sure you can meet me today?
B: Sure. I'll sneak out of our office meeting.

A: 오늘 확실히 나하고 만날 수 있니?
B: 그럼. 사무실 회의에서 빠져 나올게.

Guess What?

She drinks like a fish

걘 술고래처럼 술을 마셔

"물고기처럼 마시다"라는 말은 술을 자주 그리고 많이 마시는(a person consumes a lot of alcohol, and is probably an alcoholic) 사람으로 알코올중독자일 수도 있다. 우리말로는 "술고래다"라고 옮기면 된다.

I ran a risk of failing the exam

시험낙제할 위험을 감수했어

run a risk of ~ing는 '위험을 무릅쓰다' = take[run] the risk of ~ing.

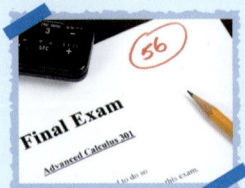

💡 **Example**

- Every soldier runs a risk of being shot.
  모든 병사들은 총에 맞을 위험을 감수하고 있어.
- I didn't study and run a risk of failing the exam.
  난 공부를 하지 않아서 시험에 떨어질 위험이 있어.

 Dialog

A: We are going to break into the school tonight.
B: You run a risk of being caught by the police.

   A: 우린 오늘 밤 학교에 침입할 계획이야.
   B: 경찰에 잡힐 위험을 무릅써야 할 거야.

Did you enroll in my English class?

넌 내 영어 수업에 신청을 했니?

enroll in~은 '등록하다,' enroll sb on the list of는 '…을 …의 명부에 올리다'라는 표현이다.

💡 **Example**

- Laura wants to enroll in Princeton University.
  로라는 프린스톤 대학에 등록하고 싶어해.
- Did you enroll in my English class?
  넌 내 영어 수업에 신청을 했니?

 Dialog

A: I hope to enroll in a course this summer.
B: Any course in particular?

   A: 올 여름에 한 과목 등록하고 싶어.
   B: 특별히 생각하고 있는 과목이라도 있니?

I was discharged from the army

난 육군제대했어

be discharged from the arm는 '육군 제대하다' <=> be in the service(복무중이다)

💡 **Example**

- Mark left the army after being injured.
  마크는 부상당한 후 제대했어.

- The older students are finished with their military service.
  나이 든 학생들은 군 복무를 마쳤어.

 Dialog

A: What is the happiest day you can remember?
B: It was when I was discharged from the army.

A: 네가 기억하는 가장 행복한 순간은?
B: 내가 제대했던 날이었어.

I was insured for traffic accidents

난 교통사고관련 보험에 들어있어

be insured for+돈은 '…짜리 보험에 가입되다.'

💡 **Example**

- The large diamond was insured for a million dollars.
  그 큰 다이아는 백만 불짜리 보험에 들어있어.

- Our home is insured for floods and fires.
  집은 홍수와 화재에 대비해 보험에 들어있어.

 Dialog

A: Your car was damaged in the accident.
B: Yeah, but I was insured for traffic accidents.

A: 네 차는 사고로 손상되었어.
B: 그런데 난 교통사고관련 보험에 들어있어.

332

I bought insurance for my house

난 우리 집에 보험을 들어놨어

buy insurance는 '보험에 가입하다.' sell insurance to sb하면 '…에게 보험을 판매하다.'

 Example

- I must buy insurance for my house.
  난 우리 집을 보험에 들어야 해.

- I'm not interested in purchasing life insurance.
  생명보험 드는데 관심 없어.

Dialog

A: I was wondering if you sold travel insurance.
B: I'm sorry we don't, but our sister company does.

A: 여행자 보험을 판매하시는지요.
B: 죄송하지만 저흰 안팔지만 저희 자회사에선 판매하죠.

333

I filed an insurance claim to rebuild it

다시 짓기 위해 보험을 청구했어

file an insurance claim (to+V)은 '(…하기 위해) 보험을 청구하다.'

 Example

- Jim was arrested after committing insurance fraud.
  짐은 보험 사기후 체포됐어.

- They filed an insurance claim to replace their car.
  걔들은 차바꾸려 보험을 청구했어.

Dialog

A: Wow, the flood destroyed your house.
B: I have to file an insurance claim to rebuild it.

A: 와, 홍수로 네 집이 부서졌네.
B: 집을 다시 짓기 위해 보험을 청구해야 돼.

My insurance covers that damage

그 피해는 내 보험으로 처리 돼

(insurance) covers that~은 '(보험이) …에 적용이 되다.'

💡 **Example**

- Jackie's operation was covered by her insurance.
  재키 수술은 보험처리됐어.

- His insurance covers that property.
  그 부동산은 걔 보험대상으로 처리되었어.

 Dialog

A: The tree fell right on my house.
B: I hope my insurance covers that damage.
  A: 나무가 바로 내 집에 넘어졌어.
  B: 보험이 적용되기를 바래.

It did damage to the car

그것으로 차량에 피해를 봤어

do damage to+N는 '…에 손해를 입히다.' damage is done'은 손해가 이미 이루어졌음을 의미.

💡 **Example**

- This software can cause damage to your computer.
  이 소프트웨어는 네 컴퓨터에 피해를 줄 수 있어.

- It could do some serious damage to our firm's image.
  그건 우리 회사의 이미지에 꽤 심각한 피해를 줄 수 있어.

 Dialog

A: Was anyone hurt in the accident?
B: No, but it did damage to the car.
  A: 그 사고로 누가 다쳤니?
  B: 아니, 그냥 차만 피해를 보았어.

His long vacation did him good

걘 휴가를 오래 갔다 와서 좋아졌어

do sb good은 '…에게 이익을 주다' <=> do sb harm(손해를 끼치다).

Example
- The economic problems have done us harm.
  경제문제가 우리에게 피해를 주었어.
- Your uncle is doing good in his business.
  네 삼촌이 사업에서 이익을 내고 있어.

Dialog

A: Harold looks much healthier now.
B: His long vacation did him good.

A: 해롤드는 이제 훨씬 더 건강해 보여.
B: 휴가를 오래 갔다 와서 좋아진 거야.

No harm done

피해준 것 없어

No harm done은 '어떤 피해도 받지 않다' = No damage done.

Example
- No damage. It's an easy problem to fix.
  피해는 없어. 고치기 쉬운 문제야.
- Don't worry about it. No harm done.
  걱정하지마. 피해는 없어.

Dialog

A: I'm sorry I spilled juice on your sofa.
B: No harm done. I'll have it cleaned.

A: 소파에 주스를 흘려서 미안합니다.
B: 피해준 것 없어요. 세탁을 할 거에요.

I'll make it up to you later

내가 나중에 보상해줄게

make it up to sb는 '…에게 보상하다' = make up for.

💡 **Example**

- I'll make it up to you later.
  내가 나중에 보상해줄게.
- There is no way to make it up to me.
  나한테 보상해줄 방법이 없어.

A: He'll have to make up for the time he's been away.
B: He said he'll make it up this weekend.

A: 걔는 자기가 비운 시간을 보충해야 할거야.
B: 걔 이번 주에 자기가 못한 시간만큼 일하겠대.

You should pay for all the damage

넌 모든 피해에 대해 배상해야 돼

pay for all the damage는 '모든 손해에 대해 배상을 하다.'

💡 **Example**

- I'll pay for all the damage to your house.
  네 집에 입힌 모든 피해에 대해 배상해줄게.
- She paid for all the damage she caused.
  걘 자신이 초래한 모든 피해에 대해 배상했어.

A: The item inside the package was broken.
B: Well, the shipper should pay for all the damage.

A: 그 꾸러미 안에 있는 물품이 부서졌어.
B: 글쎄, 운송업체가 모든 피해에 대해 배상해야 돼.

340

They were on the baseball team
걔네들은 야구팀 소속야
be on sth은 '…에 소속되어 있다.'

💡 **Example**

- They were on the baseball team.
  걔네들은 야구팀 소속야.

- Is Frank on our chess team?
  프랭크가 우리 체스팀에 소속되어 있니?

 Dialog

A: Christy is on the student council.
B: Good, she's a very smart girl.
　A: 크리스티가 학생회소속이야.
　B: 좋아, 걘 정말 영리한 아이야.

341

I'm cut out for being a lawyer
나는 변호사가 될 자질이 있어
be cut out for~는 '…에 제격이다,' '…할 자질이 있다.'

💡 **Example**

- Most people aren't cut out for being politicians.
  대부분 사람들은 정치인이 되기에 적합하지 않아.

- He was cut out for working as an actor.
  그는 배우로서 적격이었어.

 Dialog

A: You can't run very fast, John.
B: I'm not cut out for being in a race.
　A: 존, 넌 아주 빨리 뛸 수 없어.
　B: 난 경주에 참여하는 게 적합하지 않아.

342

Older people are eligible for discounts

어르신들은 할인을 받을 수 있어

be eligible for+N[to+V]는 '…에 적당하다,' '알맞다.'

💡 **Example**

- The soldiers are eligible for a vacation.
  병사들은 휴가를 받을 권한이 있어.

- Older people are eligible for discounts.
  나이 드신 분들은 할인을 받을 수 있어.

A: Mark has worked the hardest of anyone.
B: He is eligible for a bonus at work.

A: 마크는 누구보다 더 열심히 일했어.
B: 걘 직장에서 보너스를 받을 만해.

343

It serves her right

걔한테는 당연하지

serve (sb) right는 '…에게 당연한 대우를 하다.' It serves you right는 '고소하다.'

💡 **Example**

- It serves criminals right to be sent to jail.
  범법자들을 감옥에 보내는 것은 당연한 일이야.

- It serves him right to fail the class.
  그가 낙제를 한 것을 보니 고소하네.

A: Aurora got thrown out of her apartment.
B: It serves her right. She never paid her rent.

A: 오로라는 자기 아파트로부터 쫓겨 났어.
B: 당연하지. 걘 집세를 한번도 내지 않았거든.

Stress can make you turn grey faster
스트레스는 머리가 더 빨리 세게 할 수 있다
turn grey는 '흰머리가 나다,' '하늘 등이 회색으로 변하다.'

 Example
- This letter turned out to be very important.
  이 편지는 아주 중요한 것으로 판명되었어.
- I thought you said the weather turned cold.
  날씨가 추워졌다고 네가 말했던 것으로 생각되는데.

 Dialog

A: The skies often turn grey in January.
B: It's the most gloomy time of the year.
 A: 1월에는 하늘이 종종 회색으로 변해.
 B: 1년 중 가장 우울한 때야.

He'll do anything for me
걘 날 위해서라면 뭐든 하거든
do anything for+N[to+V]은 '…을 위해 뭐든지 하다.'

 Example
- I would do anything to avoid studying.
  난 공부를 피할 수 있다면 뭐든지 할 거야.
- She is willing to do anything for money.
  걘 돈을 위해서라면 뭐든지 할 용의가 있어.

Dialog

A: So, it looks like you have a pretty good friend there.
B: Yeah. He'll do anything for me.
 A: 넌 정말 좋은 친구를 가진 것 같아.
 B: 맞아. 걘 날 위해서라면 뭐든 하려고 하거든.

346

He didn't wave, let alone say hello

걘 인사하기는 커녕 손짓조차 안했어

let alone~은 '…은 커녕.' 부정문 뒤에 이어지는 표현으로 비교대상에 따라 다양한 품사가 온다.

Example

- We couldn't pay the interest, let alone the full amount.
  우린 원금은 고사하고 이자도 낼 수가 없어.

- They didn't fly overseas, let alone to Europe.
  걔들은 유럽은 커녕 해외에 나갈 수가 없어.

Dialog

A: Did you pay Brian the money you owe him?
B: I can't pay my bills, let alone Brian's money.

A: 넌 브라이언에게 빚진 돈을 갚았니?
B: 브라이언 돈은 커녕 내 청구서도 못 갚고 있어.

347

No wonder they're so tanned

그들이 그렇게 그을릴 만도 하군

No wonder (S+V)는 '…은 놀랍지 않다, 그도 그럴 것이.'

Example

- No wonder that movie is so popular.
  그 영화가 그렇게 인기 있는 것은 놀랍지 않아.

- It's natural for girls to like you.
  여자애들이 널 좋아하는 것은 당연해.

Dialog

A: The Smiths just got back from vacation.
B: No wonder they're so tanned.

A: 스미스 가족이 휴가를 끝내고 막 돌아왔어요.
B: 그들이 그렇게 그을릴 만도 하군요.

348

Is this the way you clean the house?
너는 집을 이렇게 청소해?
be the way that S+V는 '…하는 방식이다.'

🔆 **Example**

- Is this the way your mom cleans the house?
  너희 어머니는 집을 이렇게 청소하시니?

- This is the way that the system works.
  이게 바로 그 시스템이 돌아가는 방식이야.

 **Dialog**

A: Why are you eating with your hands?
B: **This is the way that** everyone eats food here.
  A: 왜 네 손으로 먹고 있니?
  B: 여기서는 모든 사람들이 이렇게 먹어.

349

Sally is nothing like that
샐리는 그렇지가 않아
be nothing like that~은 '그렇지 않다,' '최고이다' = be nothing like ~ing.

🔆 **Example**

- There's nothing like that in the world.
  그건 천하 일품이야.

- There's nothing like sleeping in on a Sunday.
  일요일 늦잠 자는 느낌은 최고지.

 **Dialog**

A: Is it true that Sally is unkind to her family?
B: No, Sally **is nothing like that**.
  A: 샐리가 가족들을 잘 대하지 않다는 게 사실이니?
  B: 아니야, 샐리는 그렇지가 않아.

350

This wine is second to none

이 포도주는 일류야

second to none은 '그 어느 것에도 뒤지지 않는' = second next to none.

Example

- Sandra is second to none in her science class.
  산드라는 과학 수업에서 최고야.
- The wine at this restaurant is second to none.
  이 식당의 포도주는 일류야.

 Dialog

A: This is a very nice jacket.
B: The company that made it is second to none.

A: 이건 아주 좋은 윗도리야.
B: 그걸 만든 회사는 제일가는 회사야.

351

The best part is it pays a lot of money

최고로 좋은 점은 돈을 많이 준다는거야

The best part is~는 '가장 좋은 부분은 …이다.' <=> The hard part is~.

Example

- The hard part is to stay awake at night.
  애로사항은 밤늦게까지 깨어 있다는거야.
- The best part is the ending of the movie.
  가장 좋은 부분은 영화의 맨 끝이야.

 Dialog

A: So you got a new job?
B: Yes, and the best part is it pays a lot of money.

A: 그래 넌 새 직장을 잡았니?
B: 그래, 최고로 좋은 점은 돈을 많이 준다는거야.

352

He's the best poet I've ever seen
걘 내가 본 최고의 시인이야
the best~ I've ever seen은 '내가 본 것 중 최고의 …이다.'

💡 **Example**
- The concert had the best music I've ever heard.
  그 연주회는 들은 것 중에 최고의 음악을 선사했어.
- That was the best zoo I've ever visited.
  그 동물원은 내가 방문했던 것중에 최고였어.

 Dialog

A: Dan is the best athlete I have ever seen.
B: He prefers exercising rather than staying at home.
  A: 댄은 내가 본 최고의 운동선수야.
  B: 걘 집에 머무는 것보다 운동하는 것을 선호해.

353

She is just shy of turning 70
막 70세가 되기 직전이셔
be shy of ~ing는 '…하기를 꺼리다,' '…하지 않다.'

💡 **Example**
- He was too shy to ask Melissa to dance.
  걘 멜리사에게 춤추자고 말하기를 두려워해.
- Her daughter is very shy around strangers.
  걔 딸은 모르는 사람에겐 낯을 가려.

 Dialog

A: How old is your grandmother?
B: She is just shy of turning 70.
  A: 할머니가 몇 세시니?
  B: 막 70세가 되기 직전이셔.

354

He came close to death in the battle

갠 전투중에 거의 죽을 뻔했어

come close to sth[~ing]는 '거의 …할 뻔하다' = come near ~ing.

💡 Example

- The soldiers came close to death in the battle.
  병사들이 전투에서 거의 죽을 뻔했어.
- The couple came close to meeting a movie star.
  그 커플은 무비 스타를 거의 만날 뻔했어.

A: Did you visit the Hawaiian Islands?
B: No, but we came close to sailing there.

A: 하와이 섬들을 방문했었니?
B: 아니, 그래도 그곳을 항해할 뻔 했어.

355

I stopped short of drinking it

난 그걸 마시려다 참았어

stop short of sth[~ing]는 '…까지는 하지 않다.'

💡 Example

- Too many people stop short of their desires.
  너무 많은 사람들이 욕망을 이루지 못해.
- I had some wine but stopped short of drinking it.
  와인이 좀 있는데 마시지 않았어.

A: Did Ray ask his girlfriend to marry him?
B: No, he stopped short of popping the question.

A: 레이가 여친에게 결혼하자고 요청했니?
B: 아니, 갠 그 문제를 꺼내려다가 말았어.

356

Make spaghetti, or something like that

스파게티나 그런 것들을 만들어봐

~ or something like that은 '비슷한거야.'

💡 Example
- You can wash the dishes, and things like that.
  넌 설거지나 그 비슷한 일을 해봐.
- Paris was romantic, like in the movies.
  파리는 영화에서처럼 낭만적이야.

 Dialog

A: What should I cook for dinner?
B: Make spaghetti, or something like that.

A: 저녁에 뭘 요리할까?
B: 스파게티나 그런 것들을 만들어봐.

357

I can't remember the last time we met

우리가 마지막으로 만난 때를 기억할 수가 없어

can't remember the last time S+V는 '…한 마지막 때를 기억하지 못하다.'

💡 Example
- We can't remember the last time it snowed.
  마지막으로 눈온 때를 기억할 수 없어.
- I can't remember the last time I had a good meal.
  이렇게 맛난 음식은 생전 처음야.

 Dialog

A: I can't remember the last time we met.
B: It was at least ten years ago.

A: 우리가 마지막으로 만난 때를 기억할 수가 없어.
B: 적어도 10년 전은 되겠지.

It never happened to me before

한번도 그런 적이 없었어

never happened to sb before는 '처음으로 일어난 일이다.'

💡 **Example**
- This feeling has never happened to me before.
  이런 감정은 정말 처음이야.
- A car accident has never happened to me before.
  자동차 사고는 이번이 처음야.

Dialog

A: Have you won any money gambling?
B: No, that never happened to me before.

A: 도박을 해서 돈을 딴 적이 있니?
B: 아니, 한번도 그런 적이 없었어.

I never heard of such a thing

그런 걸 들어본 적이 없어

never heard of such a thing은 '그런 것을 처음 들어보다.'

💡 **Example**
- He'd never heard of such a thing as a TV in a car.
  걘 카TV란 걸 들어본 적이 없어.
- Tim has never heard of my favorite singer.
  팀은 내가 좋아하는 가수를 들어본 적이 없대.

Dialog

A: A monkey was climbing the side of my apartment building.
B: No way! I never heard of such a thing.

A: 원숭이가 내 아파트 빌딩을 타고 올라갔어.
B: 절대 아냐! 그런 걸 들어본 적이 없어.

360

I've never seen anything like it
이런 건 처음 본다

never seen anything like it은 '···같은 것은 처음으로 본다.'

💡 **Example**

- I've never seen anything like that before in my life.
  내 일생 동안 그런 것 첨 봐.

- Have you ever seen anything like that before?
  과거에 그런 걸 본 적이 있니?

 Dialog

A: Look at the high score of this game.
B: Wow! I've never seen anything like it.

　A: 이 경기의 높은 점수를 봐라.
　B: 와! 이런 건 처음 본다.

361

Jason has gone too far
제이슨은 너무 지나쳤어

have gone too far는 '···가 지나치다,' '무리였다' = go[went] too far.

💡 **Example**

- Jason has gone too far and angered everyone.
  제이슨은 지나쳐서 모두를 화나게 했어.

- The fighting couple went too far and upset their parents.
  그 싸우던 커플은 선을 넘어서 부모들을 당황시켰어.

 Dialog

A: Look at all the ads in this newspaper.
B: I think the advertisers have gone too far.

　A: 이 신문에 난 모든 광고를 봐라.
　B: 광고주들이 지나친 것으로 생각해.

The store closed without notice

그 가게가 갑자기 문닫았어

on such short notice는 '갑작스럽게,' without notice는 '갑자기.'

Example

- There was short notice before the meeting was held.
  회의개최 통보가 너무 갑작스러웠어.
- My favorite store closed without notice.
  내가 좋아하는 가게가 갑자기 문닫았어.

A: Can we have a party tonight?
B: It will be difficult on such short notice.

A: 오늘 밤에 파티할까?
B: 그렇게 갑자기는 어려울걸.

MEMO